Amazon Virtual Private Cloud User Guide

A catalogue record for this book is available from the Hong Kong Public Libraries.

Published in Hong Kong by Samurai Media Limited.

Email: info@samuraimedia.org

ISBN 9789888408184

Contents

What Is Amazon VPC?

Amazon Virtual Private Cloud (Amazon VPC) enables you to launch AWS resources into a virtual network that you've defined. This virtual network closely resembles a traditional network that you'd operate in your own data center, with the benefits of using the scalable infrastructure of AWS.

Amazon VPC Concepts

As you get started with Amazon VPC, you should understand the key concepts of this virtual network, and how it is similar to or different from your own networks. This section provides a brief description of the key concepts for Amazon VPC.

Amazon VPC is the networking layer for Amazon EC2. If you're new to Amazon EC2, see What is Amazon EC2? in the *Amazon EC2 User Guide for Linux Instances* to get a brief overview.

Topics

- VPCs and Subnets
- Supported Platforms
- Default and Nondefault VPCs
- Accessing the Internet
- Accessing a Corporate or Home Network
- Accessing Services Through AWS PrivateLink

VPCs and Subnets

A *virtual private cloud* (VPC) is a virtual network dedicated to your AWS account. It is logically isolated from other virtual networks in the AWS Cloud. You can launch your AWS resources, such as Amazon EC2 instances, into your VPC. You can configure your VPC by modifying its IP address range; create subnets; and configure route tables, network gateways, and security settings.

A *subnet* is a range of IP addresses in your VPC. You can launch AWS resources into a specified subnet. Use a public subnet for resources that must be connected to the internet, and a private subnet for resources that won't be connected to the internet. For more information about public and private subnets, see VPC and Subnet Basics.

To protect the AWS resources in each subnet, you can use multiple layers of security, including security groups and network access control lists (ACL). For more information, see Security.

Supported Platforms

The original release of Amazon EC2 supported a single, flat network that's shared with other customers called the *EC2-Classic* platform. Earlier AWS accounts still support this platform, and can launch instances into either EC2-Classic or a VPC. Accounts created after 2013-12-04 support EC2-VPC only. For more information, see Detecting Your Supported Platforms and Whether You Have a Default VPC.

By launching your instances into a VPC instead of EC2-Classic, you gain the ability to:

- Assign static private IPv4 addresses to your instances that persist across starts and stops
- Optionally associate an IPv6 CIDR block to your VPC and assign IPv6 addresses to your instances
- Assign multiple IP addresses to your instances
- Define network interfaces, and attach one or more network interfaces to your instances
- Change security group membership for your instances while they're running
- Control the outbound traffic from your instances (egress filtering) in addition to controlling the inbound traffic to them (ingress filtering)

- Add an additional layer of access control to your instances in the form of network access control lists (ACL)
- Run your instances on single-tenant hardware

Default and Nondefault VPCs

If your account supports the EC2-VPC platform only, it comes with a *default VPC* that has a *default subnet* in each Availability Zone. A default VPC has the benefits of the advanced features provided by EC2-VPC, and is ready for you to use. If you have a default VPC and don't specify a subnet when you launch an instance, the instance is launched into your default VPC. You can launch instances into your default VPC without needing to know anything about Amazon VPC.

Regardless of which platforms your account supports, you can create your own VPC, and configure it as you need. This is known as a *nondefault VPC*. Subnets that you create in your nondefault VPC and additional subnets that you create in your default VPC are called *nondefault subnets*.

Accessing the Internet

You control how the instances that you launch into a VPC access resources outside the VPC.

Your default VPC includes an internet gateway, and each default subnet is a public subnet. Each instance that you launch into a default subnet has a private IPv4 address and a public IPv4 address. These instances can communicate with the internet through the internet gateway. An internet gateway enables your instances to connect to the internet through the Amazon EC2 network edge.

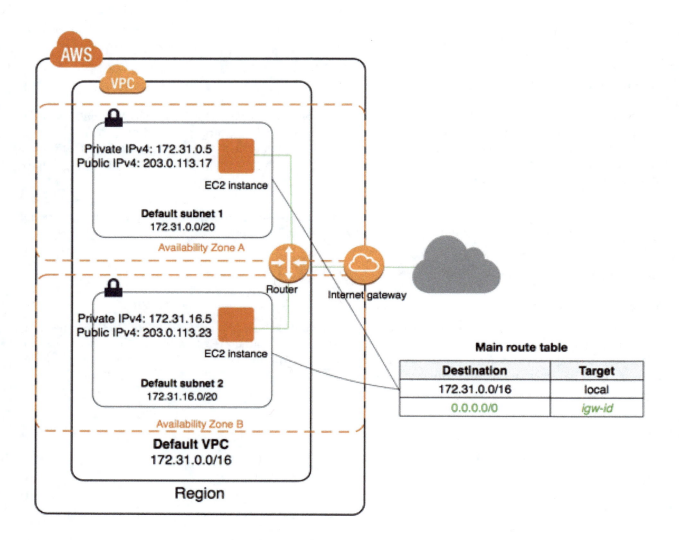

By default, each instance that you launch into a nondefault subnet has a private IPv4 address, but no public IPv4 address, unless you specifically assign one at launch, or you modify the subnet's public IP address attribute. These instances can communicate with each other, but can't access the internet.

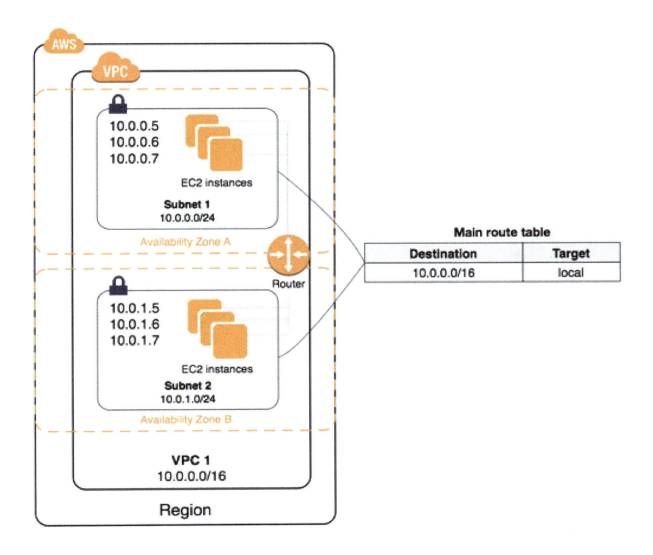

You can enable internet access for an instance launched into a nondefault subnet by attaching an internet gateway to its VPC (if its VPC is not a default VPC) and associating an Elastic IP address with the instance.

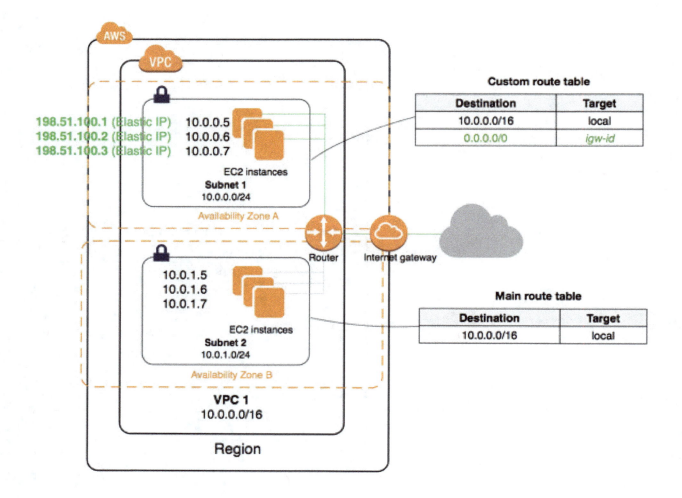

Alternatively, to allow an instance in your VPC to initiate outbound connections to the internet but prevent unsolicited inbound connections from the internet, you can use a network address translation (NAT) device for IPv4 traffic. NAT maps multiple private IPv4 addresses to a single public IPv4 address. A NAT device has an Elastic IP address and is connected to the internet through an internet gateway. You can connect an instance in a private subnet to the internet through the NAT device, which routes traffic from the instance to the internet gateway, and routes any responses to the instance.

For more information, see NAT.

You can optionally associate an Amazon-provided IPv6 CIDR block with your VPC and assign IPv6 addresses to your instances. Instances can connect to the internet over IPv6 through an internet gateway. Alternatively, instances can initiate outbound connections to the internet over IPv6 using an egress-only internet gateway. For more information, see Egress-Only Internet Gateways. IPv6 traffic is separate from IPv4 traffic; your route tables must include separate routes for IPv6 traffic.

Accessing a Corporate or Home Network

You can optionally connect your VPC to your own corporate data center using an IPsec AWS managed VPN connection, making the AWS Cloud an extension of your data center.

A VPN connection consists of a virtual private gateway attached to your VPC and a customer gateway located in your data center. A virtual private gateway is the VPN concentrator on the Amazon side of the VPN connection. A customer gateway is a physical device or software appliance on your side of the VPN connection.

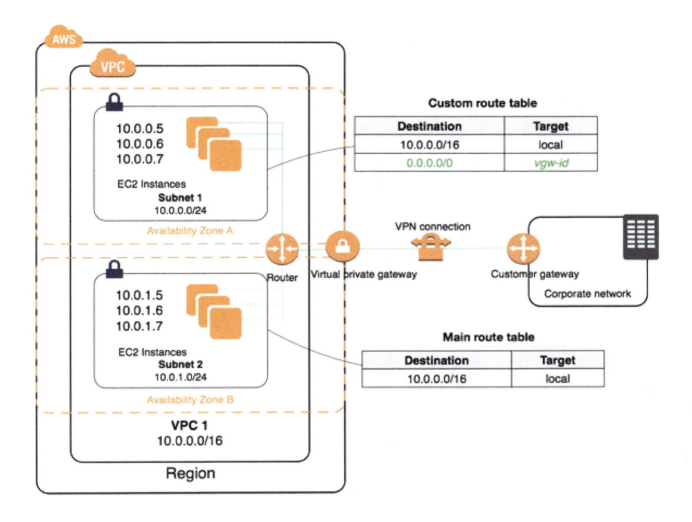

For more information, see AWS Managed VPN Connections.

Accessing Services Through AWS PrivateLink

AWS PrivateLink is a highly available, scalable technology that enables you to privately connect your VPC to supported AWS services, services hosted by other AWS accounts (VPC endpoint services), and supported AWS Marketplace partner services. You do not require an internet gateway, NAT device, public IP address, AWS Direct Connect connection, or VPN connection to communicate with the service. Traffic between your VPC and the service does not leave the Amazon network.

To use AWS PrivateLink, create an interface VPC endpoint for a service in your VPC. This creates an elastic network interface in your subnet with a private IP address that serves as an entry point for traffic destined to the service. For more information, see VPC Endpoints.

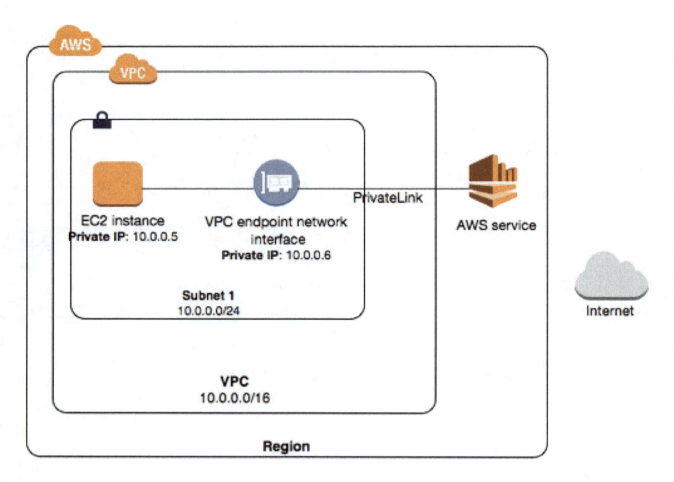

You can create your own AWS PrivateLink-powered service (endpoint service) and enable other AWS customers to access your service. For more information, see VPC Endpoint Services (AWS PrivateLink).

How to Get Started with Amazon VPC

To get a hands-on introduction to Amazon VPC, complete the exercise Getting Started. The exercise guides you through the steps to create a nondefault VPC with a public subnet, and to launch an instance into your subnet.

If you have a default VPC, and you want to get started launching instances into your VPC without performing any additional configuration on your VPC, see Launching an EC2 Instance into Your Default VPC.

To learn about the basic scenarios for Amazon VPC, see Scenarios and Examples. You can configure your VPC and subnets in other ways to suit your needs.

The following table lists related resources that you might find useful as you work with this service.

Resource	Description
Amazon Virtual Private Cloud Connectivity Options	A whitepaper that provides an overview of the options for network connectivity.
Amazon VPC forum	A community-based forum for discussing technical questions related to Amazon VPC.
AWS Developer Resources	A central starting point to find documentation, code samples, release notes, and other information to help you create innovative applications with AWS.

Resource	Description
AWS Support Center	The home page for AWS Support.
Contact Us	A central contact point for inquiries concerning AWS billing, accounts, and events.

Using Amazon VPC with Other AWS Services

Amazon VPC integrates with many other AWS services; furthermore, some services require a VPC in your account to carry out certain functions. Below are examples of services that use Amazon VPC.

Service	Relevant Topic
AWS Data Pipeline	Launching Resources for Your Pipeline into a VPC
Amazon EC2	Amazon EC2 and Amazon VPC
Auto Scaling	Auto Scaling and Amazon VPC
Elastic Beanstalk	Using AWS Elastic Beanstalk with Amazon VPC
Elastic Load Balancing	Setting Up Elastic Load Balancing
Amazon ElastiCache	Using ElastiCache with Amazon VPC
Amazon EMR	Select a Subnet for the Cluster
AWS OpsWorks	Running a Stack in a VPC
Amazon RDS	Amazon RDS and Amazon VPC
Amazon Redshift	Managing Clusters in a VPC
Route 53	Working with Private Hosted Zones
Amazon WorkSpaces	Create and Configure Your VPC

To get a detailed view of the VPCs, subnets, and other VPC resources in your account and their relation to each other, you can use the AWS Config service. For more information, see the *AWS Config Developer Guide*.

Accessing Amazon VPC

Amazon VPC provides a web-based user interface, the Amazon VPC console. If you've signed up for an AWS account, you can access the Amazon VPC console by signing into the AWS Management Console and choosing **VPC**.

If you prefer to use a command line interface, you have the following options:

AWS Command Line Interface (AWS CLI)
Provides commands for a broad set of AWS services, and is supported on Windows, macOS, and Linux/Unix. To get started, see AWS Command Line Interface User Guide. For more information about the commands for Amazon VPC, see ec2.

AWS Tools for Windows PowerShell
Provides commands for a broad set of AWS services for those who script in the PowerShell environment. To get started, see AWS Tools for Windows PowerShell User Guide.

Amazon VPC provides a Query API. These requests are HTTP or HTTPS requests that use the HTTP verbs GET or POST and a Query parameter named `Action`. For more information, see Actions in the *Amazon EC2 API Reference*.

To build applications using language-specific APIs instead of submitting a request over HTTP or HTTPS, AWS provides libraries, sample code, tutorials, and other resources for software developers. These libraries provide basic functions that automatically take care of tasks such as cryptographically signing your requests, retrying requests, and handling error responses. For more information, see AWS SDKs and Tools.

Pricing for Amazon VPC

There's no additional charge for using Amazon VPC. You pay the standard rates for the instances and other Amazon EC2 features that you use. There are charges for using an AWS managed VPN connection and using a NAT gateway. For more information, see Amazon VPC Pricing and Amazon EC2 Pricing.

Amazon VPC Limits

There are limits to the number of Amazon VPC components that you can provision. You can request an increase for some of these limits. For more information, see Amazon VPC Limits.

PCI DSS Compliance

Amazon VPC supports the processing, storage, and transmission of credit card data by a merchant or service provider, and has been validated as being compliant with Payment Card Industry (PCI) Data Security Standard (DSS). For more information about PCI DSS, including how to request a copy of the AWS PCI Compliance Package, see PCI DSS Level 1.

Getting Started

The following topics will help you set up a nondefault VPC quickly. If you already have a default VPC and you want to get started launching instances into it (and not creating or configuring a new VPC), see Launching an EC2 Instance into Your Default VPC.

If you want resources in your VPC to communicate over IPv6, you can set up a VPC with an associated IPv6 CIDR block.

Topics

- Getting Started With Amazon VPC
- Getting Started with IPv6 for Amazon VPC

Getting Started With Amazon VPC

In this exercise, you'll create a VPC with IPv4 CIDR block, a subnet with an IPv4 CIDR block, and launch a public-facing instance into your subnet. Your instance will be able to communicate with the Internet, and you'll be able to access your instance from your local computer using SSH (if it's a Linux instance) or Remote Desktop (if it's a Windows instance). In your real world environment, you can use this scenario to create a public-facing web server; for example, to host a blog.

Note
This exercise is intended to help you set up your own nondefault VPC quickly. If you already have a default VPC and you want to get started launching instances into it (and not creating or configuring a new VPC), see Launching an EC2 Instance into Your Default VPC. If you want to get started setting up a nondefault VPC that supports IPv6, see Getting Started with IPv6 for Amazon VPC.

To complete this exercise, you'll do the following:

- Create a nondefault VPC with a single public subnet. Subnets enable you to group instances based on your security and operational needs. A public subnet is a subnet that has access to the Internet through an Internet gateway.
- Create a security group for your instance that allows traffic only through specific ports.
- Launch an Amazon EC2 instance into your subnet.
- Associate an Elastic IP address with your instance. This allows your instance to access the Internet.

Before you can use Amazon VPC for the first time, you must sign up for Amazon Web Services (AWS). When you sign up, your AWS account is automatically signed up for all services in AWS, including Amazon VPC. If you haven't created an AWS account already, go to http://aws.amazon.com, and then choose **Create a Free Account**.

Note
This exercise assumes that your account supports the EC2-VPC platform only. If your account also supports the older EC2-Classic platform, you can still follow the steps in this exercise; however, you will not have a default VPC in your account to compare against your nondefault VPC. For more information, see Supported Platforms.

Topics
- Step 1: Create the VPC
- Step 2: Create a Security Group
- Step 3: Launch an Instance into Your VPC
- Step 4: Assign an Elastic IP Address to Your Instance
- Step 5: Clean Up

Step 1: Create the VPC

In this step, you'll use the Amazon VPC wizard in the Amazon VPC console to create a VPC. The wizard performs the following steps for you:

- Creates a VPC with a /16 IPv4 CIDR block (a network with 65,536 private IP addresses). For more information about CIDR notation and the sizing of a VPC, see Your VPC.
- Attaches an Internet gateway to the VPC. For more information about Internet gateways, see Internet Gateways.
- Creates a size /24 IPv4 subnet (a range of 256 private IP addresses) in the VPC.
- Creates a custom route table, and associates it with your subnet, so that traffic can flow between the subnet and the Internet gateway. For more information about route tables, see Route Tables.

The following diagram represents the architecture of your VPC after you've completed this step.

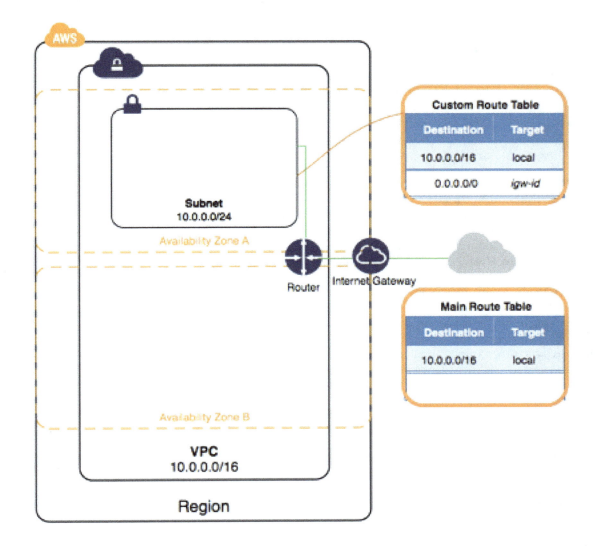

Note

This exercise covers the first scenario in the VPC wizard. For more information about the other scenarios, see Scenarios for Amazon VPC.

To create a VPC using the Amazon VPC Wizard

1. Open the Amazon VPC console at https://console.aws.amazon.com/vpc/.

2. In the navigation bar, on the top-right, take note of the region in which you'll be creating the VPC. Ensure that you continue working in the same region for the rest of this exercise, as you cannot launch an instance into your VPC from a different region. For more information about regions, see Regions and Availability Zones.

3. In the navigation pane, choose **VPC dashboard**, and then choose **Start VPC Wizard**.

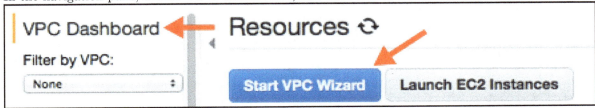

Note

Do not choose **Your VPCs** in the navigation pane; you cannot access the VPC wizard from this page.

4. Choose the first option, **VPC with a Single Public Subnet**, and then choose **Select**.

5. On the configuration page, enter a name for your VPC in the **VPC name** field; for example, `my-vpc`, and enter a name for your subnet in the **Subnet name** field. This helps you to identify the VPC and subnet in the Amazon VPC console after you've created them. For this exercise, you can leave the rest of the configuration settings on the page, and choose **Create VPC**.

(Optional) If you prefer, you can modify the configuration settings as follows, and then choose **Create VPC**.

- The **IPv4 CIDR block** displays the IPv4 address range that you'll use for your VPC (`10.0.0.0/16`), and the **Public subnet's IPv4 CIDR** field displays the IPv4 address range you'll use for the subnet (`10.0.0.0/24`). If you don't want to use the default CIDR ranges, you can specify your own. For more information, see VPC and Subnet Sizing.
- The **Availability Zone** list enables you to select the Availability Zone in which to create the subnet. You can leave **No Preference** to let AWS choose an Availability Zone for you. For more information, see Regions and Availability Zones.
- In the **Service endpoints** section, you can select a subnet in which to create a VPC endpoint to Amazon S3 in the same region. For more information, see VPC Endpoints.
- The **Enable DNS hostnames** option, when set to **Yes**, ensures that instances that are launched into your VPC receive a DNS hostname. For more information, see Using DNS with Your VPC.
- The **Hardware tenancy** option enables you to select whether instances launched into your VPC are run on shared or dedicated hardware. Selecting a dedicated tenancy incurs additional costs. For more information about hardware tenancy, see Dedicated Instances in the *Amazon EC2 User Guide for Linux Instances*.

6. A status window shows the work in progress. When the work completes, choose **OK** to close the status window.

7. The **Your VPCs** page displays your default VPC and the VPC that you just created. The VPC that you created is a nondefault VPC, therefore the **Default VPC** column displays **No**.

Viewing Information About Your VPC

After you've created the VPC, you can view information about the subnet, the Internet gateway, and the route tables. The VPC that you created has two route tables — a main route table that all VPCs have by default, and a custom route table that was created by the wizard. The custom route table is associated with your subnet, which means that the routes in that table determine how the traffic for the subnet flows. If you add a new subnet to your VPC, it uses the main route table by default.

To view information about your VPC

1. Open the Amazon VPC console at https://console.aws.amazon.com/vpc/.

2. In the navigation pane, choose **Your VPCs**. Take note of the name and the ID of the VPC that you created (look in the **Name** and **VPC ID** columns). You will use this information to identify the components that are associated with your VPC.

3. In the navigation pane, choose **Subnets**. The console displays the subnet that was created when you created your VPC. You can identify the subnet by its name in **Name** column, or you can use the VPC information that you obtained in the previous step and look in the **VPC** column.

4. In the navigation pane, choose **Internet Gateways**. You can find the Internet gateway that's attached to your VPC by looking at the **VPC** column, which displays the ID and the name (if applicable) of the VPC.

5. In the navigation pane, choose **Route Tables**. There are two route tables associated with the VPC. Select the custom route table (the **Main** column displays **No**), and then choose the **Routes** tab to display the route information in the details pane:

   - The first row in the table is the local route, which enables instances within the VPC to communicate. This route is present in every route table by default, and you can't remove it.
   - The second row shows the route that the Amazon VPC wizard added to enable traffic destined for an IPv4 address outside the VPC (0.0.0.0/0) to flow from the subnet to the Internet gateway.

6. Select the main route table. The main route table has a local route, but no other routes.

Step 2: Create a Security Group

A security group acts as a virtual firewall to control the traffic for its associated instances. To use a security group, you add the inbound rules to control incoming traffic to the instance, and outbound rules to control the outgoing traffic from your instance. To associate a security group with an instance, you specify the security group when you launch the instance. If you add and remove rules from the security group, we apply those changes to the instances associated with the security group automatically.

Your VPC comes with a *default security group*. Any instance not associated with another security group during launch is associated with the default security group. In this exercise, you'll create a new security group, WebServerSG, and specify this security group when you launch an instance into your VPC.

Topics

- Rules for the WebServerSG Security Group
- Creating Your WebServerSG Security Group

Rules for the WebServerSG Security Group

The following table describes the inbound and outbound rules for the WebServerSG security group. You'll add the inbound rules yourself. The outbound rule is a default rule that allows all outbound communication to anywhere — you do not need to add this rule yourself.

Inbound
Source IP
0.0.0.0/0
0.0.0.0/0
Public IPv4 address range of your home network
Public IPv4 address range of your home network
Outbound
Destination IP
0.0.0.0/0

Creating Your WebServerSG Security Group

You can create your security group using the Amazon VPC console.

To create the WebServerSG security group and add rules

25

1. Open the Amazon VPC console at https://console.aws.amazon.com/vpc/.

2. In the navigation pane, choose **Security Groups**.

3. Choose **Create Security Group**.

4. In the **Group name** field, enter `WebServerSG` as the name of the security group, and provide a description. You can optionally use the **Name tag** field to create a tag for the security group with a key of `Name` and a value that you specify.

5. Select the ID of your VPC from the **VPC** menu, and then choose **Yes, Create**.

6. Select the `WebServerSG` security group that you just created (you can view its name in the **Group Name** column).

7. On the **Inbound Rules** tab, choose **Edit** and add rules for inbound traffic as follows, and then choose **Save** when you're done:

    1. Select **HTTP** from the **Type** list, and enter `0.0.0.0/0` in the **Source** field.

    2. Choose **Add another rule**, then select **HTTPS** from the **Type** list, and enter `0.0.0.0/0` in the **Source** field.

    3. Choose **Add another rule**. If you're launching a Linux instance, select **SSH** from the **Type** list, or if you're launching a Windows instance, select **RDP** from the **Type** list. Enter your network's public IP address range in the **Source** field. If you don't know this address range, you can use `0.0.0.0/0` for this exercise. **Important**
    If you use `0.0.0.0/0`, you enable all IP addresses to access your instance using SSH or RDP. This is acceptable for the short exercise, but it's unsafe for production environments. In production, you'll authorize only a specific IP address or range of addresses to access your instance.

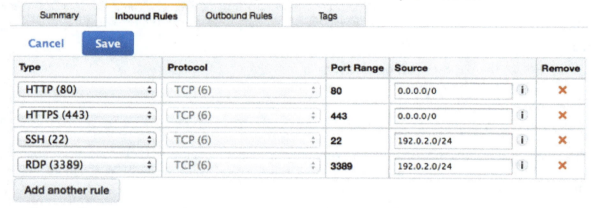

Step 3: Launch an Instance into Your VPC

When you launch an EC2 instance into a VPC, you must specify the subnet in which to launch the instance. In this case, you'll launch an instance into the public subnet of the VPC you created. You'll use the Amazon EC2 launch wizard in the Amazon EC2 console to launch your instance.

The following diagram represents the architecture of your VPC after you've completed this step.

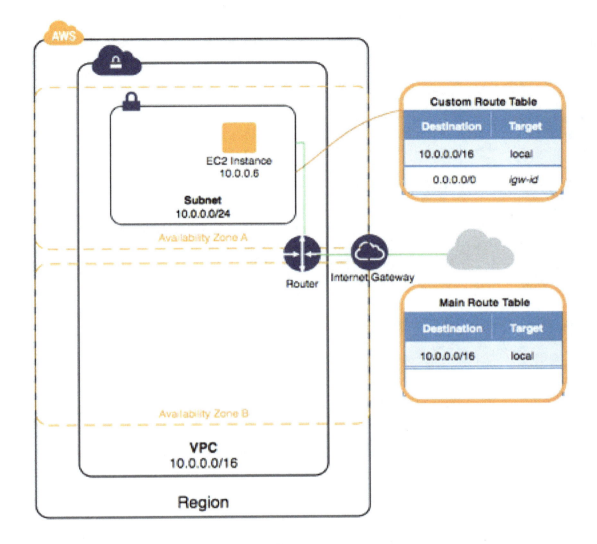

To launch an EC2 instance into a VPC

1. Open the Amazon EC2 console at https://console.aws.amazon.com/ec2/.

2. In the navigation bar, on the top-right, ensure that you select the same region in which you created your VPC and security group.

3. From the dashboard, choose **Launch Instance**.

4. On the first page of the wizard, choose the AMI that you want to use. For this exercise, we recommend that you choose an Amazon Linux AMI or a Windows AMI.

5. On the **Choose an Instance Type** page, you can select the hardware configuration and size of the instance to launch. By default, the wizard selects the first available instance type based on the AMI you selected. You can leave the default selection, and then choose **Next: Configure Instance Details**.

6. On the **Configure Instance Details** page, select the VPC that you created from the **Network** list, and the subnet from the **Subnet** list. Leave the rest of the default settings, and go through the next pages of the wizard until you get to the **Add Tags** page.

7. On the **Add Tags** page, you can tag your instance with a Name tag; for example Name=MyWebServer. This helps you to identify your instance in the Amazon EC2 console after you've launched it. Choose **Next: Configure Security Group** when you are done.

8. On the **Configure Security Group** page, the wizard automatically defines the launch-wizard-x security group to allow you to connect to your instance. Instead, choose the **Select an existing security group** option, select the **WebServerSG** group that you created previously, and then choose **Review and Launch**.

9. On the **Review Instance Launch** page, check the details of your instance, and then choose **Launch**.

10. In the **Select an existing key pair or create a new key pair** dialog box, you can choose an existing key pair, or create a new one. If you create a new key pair, ensure that you download the file and store it in a secure location. You'll need the contents of the private key to connect to your instance after it's launched.

    To launch your instance, select the acknowledgment check box, and then choose **Launch Instances**.

11. On the confirmation page, choose **View Instances** to view your instance on the **Instances** page. Select your instance, and view its details in the **Description** tab. The **Private IPs** field displays the private IP address that's assigned to your instance from the range of IP addresses in your subnet.

For more information about the options available in the Amazon EC2 launch wizard, see Launching an Instance in the *Amazon EC2 User Guide for Linux Instances*.

Step 4: Assign an Elastic IP Address to Your Instance

In the previous step, you launched your instance into a public subnet — a subnet that has a route to an Internet gateway. However, the instance in your subnet also needs a public IPv4 address to be able to communicate with the Internet. By default, an instance in a nondefault VPC is not assigned a public IPv4 address. In this step, you'll allocate an Elastic IP address to your account, and then associate it with your instance. For more information about Elastic IP addresses, see Elastic IP Addresses.

The following diagram represents the architecture of your VPC after you've completed this step.

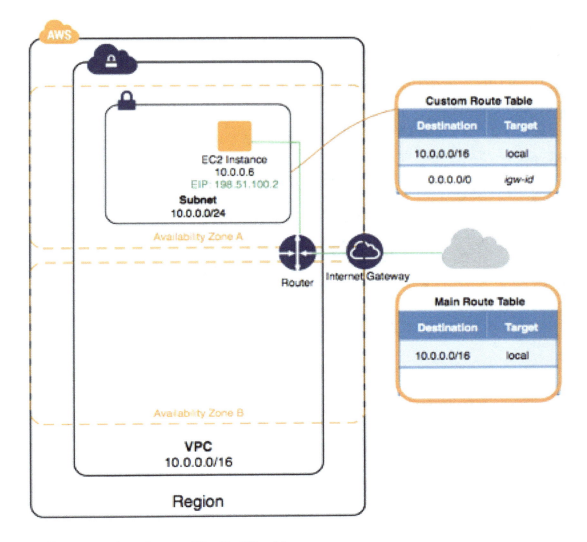

Custom Route Table

Destination	Target
10.0.0.0/16	local
0.0.0.0/0	igw-id

Main Route Table

Destination	Target
10.0.0.0/16	local

To allocate and assign an Elastic IP address

1. Open the Amazon VPC console at https://console.aws.amazon.com/vpc/.

2. In the navigation pane, choose **Elastic IPs**.

3. Choose **Allocate new address**, and then **Allocate**. **Note**
   If your account supports EC2-Classic, first choose **VPC**.

4. Select the Elastic IP address from the list, choose **Actions**, and then choose **Associate Address**.

5. For **Resource type**, ensure that **Instance** is selected. Choose your instance from the **Instance** list. Choose **Associate** when you're done.

Your instance is now accessible from the Internet. You can connect to your instance through its Elastic IP address using SSH or Remote Desktop from your home network. For more information about how to connect to a Linux instance, see Connecting to Your Linux Instance in the *Amazon EC2 User Guide for Linux Instances*. For more information about how to connect to a Windows instance, see Connect to Your Windows Instance Using RDP in the *Amazon EC2 User Guide for Windows Instances*.

This completes the exercise; you can choose to continue using your instance in your VPC, or if you do not need the instance, you can terminate it and release its Elastic IP address to avoid incurring charges for them. You can also delete your VPC — note that you are not charged for the VPC and VPC components created in this exercise (such as the subnets and route tables).

Step 5: Clean Up

Before you can delete a VPC, you must terminate any instances that are running in the VPC. If you delete a VPC using the VPC console, it also deletes resources that are associated with the VPC, such as subnets, security groups, network ACLs, DHCP options sets, route tables, and Internet gateways.

To terminate your instance, release your Elastic IP address, and delete your VPC

1. Open the Amazon EC2 console at https://console.aws.amazon.com/ec2/.

2. In the navigation pane, choose **Instances**.

3. Select your instance, choose **Actions**, then **Instance State**, and then select **Terminate**.

4. In the dialog box, expand the **Release attached Elastic IPs** section, and select the check box next to the Elastic IP address. Choose **Yes, Terminate**.

5. Open the Amazon VPC console at https://console.aws.amazon.com/vpc/.

6. In the navigation pane, choose **Your VPCs**.

7. Select the VPC, choose **Actions**, and then choose **Delete VPC**.

8. When prompted for confirmation, choose **Yes, Delete**.

Getting Started with IPv6 for Amazon VPC

In this exercise, you create a VPC with an IPv6 CIDR block, a subnet with an IPv6 CIDR block, and launch a public-facing instance into your subnet. Your instance will be able to communicate with the Internet over IPv6, and you'll be able to access your instance over IPv6 from your local computer using SSH (if it's a Linux instance) or Remote Desktop (if it's a Windows instance). In your real world environment, you can use this scenario to create a public-facing web server, for example, to host a blog.

To complete this exercise, do the following:

- Create a nondefault VPC with an IPv6 CIDR block and a single public subnet. Subnets enable you to group instances based on your security and operational needs. A public subnet is a subnet that has access to the Internet through an Internet gateway.
- Create a security group for your instance that allows traffic only through specific ports.
- Launch an Amazon EC2 instance into your subnet, and associate an IPv6 address with your instance during launch. An IPv6 address is globally unique, and allows your instance to communicate with the Internet.

For more information about IPv4 and IPv6 addressing, see IP Addressing in Your VPC.

Before you can use Amazon VPC for the first time, you must sign up for Amazon Web Services (AWS). When you sign up, your AWS account is automatically signed up for all services in AWS, including Amazon VPC. If you haven't created an AWS account already, go to http://aws.amazon.com and choose **Create a Free Account**.

Topics

- Step 1: Create the VPC
- Step 2: Create a Security Group
- Step 3: Launch an Instance

Step 1: Create the VPC

In this step, you use the Amazon VPC wizard in the Amazon VPC console to create a VPC. The wizard performs the following steps for you:

- Creates a VPC with a /16 IPv4 CIDR block and associates a /56 IPv6 CIDR block with the VPC. For more information, see Your VPC. The size of the IPv6 CIDR block is fixed (/56) and the range of IPv6 addresses is automatically allocated from Amazon's pool of IPv6 addresses (you cannot select the range yourself).
- Attaches an Internet gateway to the VPC. For more information about Internet gateways, see Internet Gateways.
- Creates a subnet with an /24 IPv4 CIDR block and a /64 IPv6 CIDR block in the VPC. The size of the IPv6 CIDR block is fixed (/64).
- Creates a custom route table, and associates it with your subnet, so that traffic can flow between the subnet and the Internet gateway. For more information about route tables, see Route Tables.

The following diagram represents the architecture of your VPC after you've completed this step.

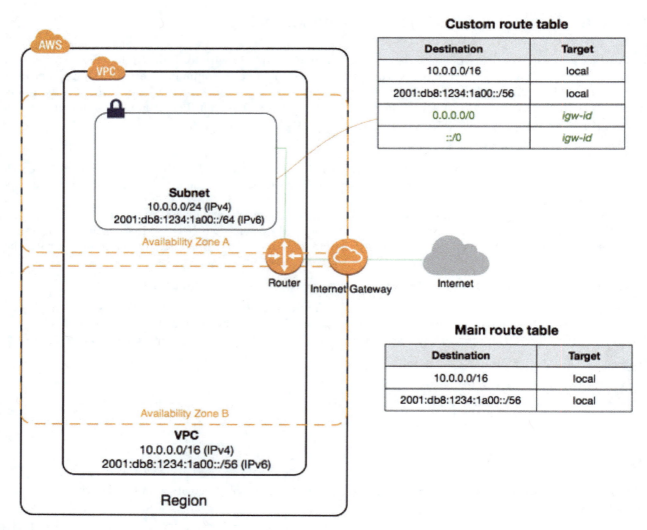

Custom route table

Destination	Target
10.0.0.0/16	local
2001:db8:1234:1a00::/56	local
0.0.0.0/0	*igw-id*
::/0	*igw-id*

Main route table

Destination	Target
10.0.0.0/16	local
2001:db8:1234:1a00::/56	local

Note

This exercise covers the first scenario in the VPC wizard. For more information about the other scenarios, see Scenarios for Amazon VPC.

To create a VPC using the Amazon VPC wizard

1. Open the Amazon VPC console at https://console.aws.amazon.com/vpc/.

2. In the navigation bar, on the top-right, take note of the region in which you are creating the VPC. Ensure that you continue working in the same region for the rest of this exercise, as you cannot launch an instance into your VPC from a different region. For more information about regions, see Regions and Availability Zones.

3. In the navigation pane, choose **VPC dashboard** and choose **Start VPC Wizard**.

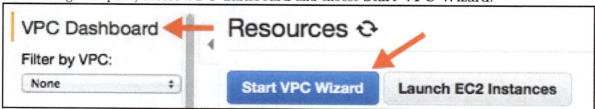

Note

Do not choose **Your VPCs** in the navigation pane; you cannot access the VPC wizard from this page.

4. Choose the first option, **VPC with a Single Public Subnet**, and choose **Select**.

5. On the configuration page, enter a name for your VPC for **VPC name**; for example, my-vpc, and enter a name for your subnet for **Subnet name**. This helps you to identify the VPC and subnet in the Amazon VPC console after you've created them.

6. For **IPv4 CIDR block**, you can leave the default setting (10.0.0.0/16), or specify your own. For more information, see VPC Sizing.

   For **IPv6 CIDR block**, choose **Amazon-provided IPv6 CIDR block**.

7. For **Public subnet's IPv4 CIDR**, leave the default setting, or specify your own. For **Public subnet's IPv6 CIDR**, choose **Specify a custom IPv6 CIDR**. You can leave the default hexadecimal pair value for the IPv6 subnet (00).

8. Leave the rest of the default configurations on the page, and choose **Create VPC**.

9. A status window shows the work in progress. When the work completes, choose **OK** to close the status window.

10. The **Your VPCs** page displays your default VPC and the VPC that you just created.

Viewing Information About Your VPC

After you've created the VPC, you can view information about the subnet, Internet gateway, and route tables. The VPC that you created has two route tables — a main route table that all VPCs have by default, and a custom route table that was created by the wizard. The custom route table is associated with your subnet, which means that the routes in that table determine how the traffic for the subnet flows. If you add a new subnet to your VPC, it uses the main route table by default.

To view information about your VPC

1. Open the Amazon VPC console at https://console.aws.amazon.com/vpc/.

2. In the navigation pane, choose **Your VPCs**. Take note of the name and the ID of the VPC that you created (look in the **Name** and **VPC ID** columns). You use this information to identify the components that are associated with your VPC.

3. In the navigation pane, choose **Subnets**. The console displays the subnet that was created when you created your VPC. You can identify the subnet by its name in **Name** column, or you can use the VPC information that you obtained in the previous step and look in the **VPC** column.

4. In the navigation pane, choose **Internet Gateways**. You can find the Internet gateway that's attached to your VPC by looking at the **VPC** column, which displays the ID and the name (if applicable) of the VPC.

5. In the navigation pane, choose **Route Tables**. There are two route tables associated with the VPC. Select the custom route table (the **Main** column displays **No**), and then choose the **Routes** tab to display the route information in the details pane:

   - The first two rows in the table are the local routes, which enable instances within the VPC to communicate over IPv4 and IPv6. You can't remove these routes.
   - The next row shows the route that the Amazon VPC wizard added to enable traffic destined for an IPv4 address outside the VPC (0.0.0.0/0) to flow from the subnet to the Internet gateway.
   - The next row shows the route that enables traffic destined for an IPv6 address outside the VPC (::/0) to flow from the subnet to the Internet gateway.

6. Select the main route table. The main route table has a local route, but no other routes.

Step 2: Create a Security Group

A security group acts as a virtual firewall to control the traffic for its associated instances. To use a security group, add the inbound rules to control incoming traffic to the instance, and outbound rules to control the outgoing traffic from your instance. To associate a security group with an instance, specify the security group when you launch the instance.

Your VPC comes with a *default security group*. Any instance not associated with another security group during launch is associated with the default security group. In this exercise, you create a new security group, `WebServerSG`, and specify this security group when you launch an instance into your VPC.

Topics

- Rules for the WebServerSG Security Group
- Creating Your WebServerSG Security Group

Rules for the WebServerSG Security Group

The following table describes the inbound and outbound rules for the `WebServerSG` security group. You add the inbound rules yourself. The outbound rule is a default rule that allows all outbound communication to anywhere — you do not need to add this rule yourself.

Inbound
Source IP
::/0
::/0
IPv6 address range of your home network
Outbound
Destination IP
0.0.0.0/0
::/0

Note

If you want to use your web server instance for IPv4 traffic too, you must add rules that enable access over IPv4; in this case, HTTP and HTTPS traffic from all IPv4 addresses (0.0.0.0/0) and SSH/RDP access from the IPv4 address range of your home network.

Creating Your WebServerSG Security Group

You can create your security group using the Amazon VPC console.

To create the WebServerSG security group and add rules

1. Open the Amazon VPC console at https://console.aws.amazon.com/vpc/.

2. In the navigation pane, choose **Security Groups, Create Security Group**.

3. For **Group name**, enter `WebServerSG` as the name of the security group and provide a description. You can optionally use the **Name tag** field to create a tag for the security group with a key of `Name` and a value that you specify.

4. Select the ID of your VPC from the **VPC** menu and choose **Yes, Create**.

5. Select the `WebServerSG` security group that you just created (you can view its name in the **Group Name** column).

6. On the **Inbound Rules** tab, choose **Edit**, add rules for inbound traffic as follows, and then choose **Save** when you're done:

   1. For **Type**, choose **HTTP** and enter ::/0 in the **Source** field.

   2. Choose **Add another rule**, For **Type**, choose **HTTPS**, and then enter ::/0 in the **Source** field.

   3. Choose **Add another rule**. If you're launching a Linux instance, choose **SSH** for **Type**, or if you're launching a Windows instance, choose **RDP**. Enter your network's public IPv6 address range in the **Source** field. If you don't know this address range, you can use ::/0 for this exercise. **Important** If you use ::/0, you enable all IPv6 addresses to access your instance using SSH or RDP. This is acceptable for the short exercise, but it's unsafe for production environments. In production, authorize only a specific IP address or range of addresses to access your instance.

Step 3: Launch an Instance

When you launch an EC2 instance into a VPC, you must specify the subnet in which to launch the instance. In this case, you'll launch an instance into the public subnet of the VPC you created. Use the Amazon EC2 launch wizard in the Amazon EC2 console to launch your instance.

To ensure that your instance is accessible from the Internet, assign an IPv6 address from the subnet range to the instance during launch. This ensures that your instance can communicate with the Internet over IPv6.

The following diagram represents the architecture of your VPC after you've completed this step.

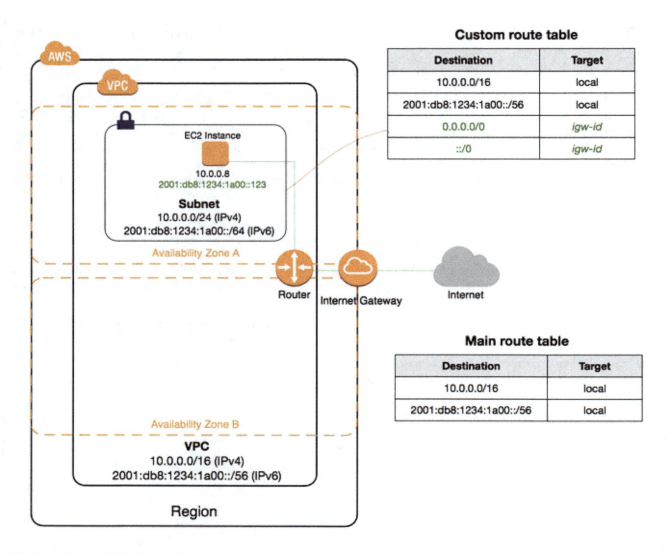

Custom route table

Destination	Target
10.0.0.0/16	local
2001:db8:1234:1a00::/56	local
0.0.0.0/0	*igw-id*
::/0	*igw-id*

Main route table

Destination	Target
10.0.0.0/16	local
2001:db8:1234:1a00::/56	local

To launch an EC2 instance into a VPC

1. Open the Amazon EC2 console at https://console.aws.amazon.com/ec2/.

2. In the navigation bar, on the top-right, ensure that you select the same region in which you created your VPC and security group.

3. From the dashboard, choose **Launch Instance**.

4. On the first page of the wizard, choose the AMI to use. For this exercise, we recommend that you choose an Amazon Linux AMI or a Windows AMI.

5. On the **Choose an Instance Type** page, you can select the hardware configuration and size of the instance to launch. By default, the wizard selects the first available instance type based on the AMI that you selected. You can leave the default selection and choose **Next: Configure Instance Details**.

6. On the **Configure Instance Details** page, select the VPC that you created from the **Network** list and the subnet from the **Subnet** list.

7. For **Auto-assign IPv6 IP**, choose **Enable**.

8. Leave the rest of the default settings, and go through the next pages of the wizard until you get to the **Add Tags** page.

9. On the **Add Tags** page, you can tag your instance with a `Name` tag; for example `Name=MyWebServer`. This helps you to identify your instance in the Amazon EC2 console after you've launched it. Choose **Next: Configure Security Group** when you are done.

10. On the **Configure Security Group** page, the wizard automatically defines the launch-wizard-x security group to allow you to connect to your instance. Instead, choose the **Select an existing security group** option, select the **WebServerSG** group that you created previously, and then choose **Review and Launch**.

11. On the **Review Instance Launch** page, check the details of your instance and choose **Launch**.

12. In the **Select an existing key pair or create a new key pair** dialog box, you can choose an existing key pair, or create a new one. If you create a new key pair, ensure that you download the file and store it in a secure location. You need the contents of the private key to connect to your instance after it's launched.

    To launch your instance, select the acknowledgment check box and choose **Launch Instances**.

13. On the confirmation page, choose **View Instances** to view your instance on the **Instances** page. Select your instance, and view its details in the **Description** tab. The **Private IPs** field displays the private IPv4 address that's assigned to your instance from the range of IPv4 addresses in your subnet. The **IPv6 IPs** field displays the IPv6 address that's assigned to your instance from the range of IPv6 addresses in your subnet.

For more information about the options available in the Amazon EC2 launch wizard, see Launching an Instance in the *Amazon EC2 User Guide for Linux Instances*.

You can connect to your instance through its IPv6 address using SSH or Remote Desktop from your home network. For more information about how to connect to a Linux instance, see Connecting to Your Linux Instance in the *Amazon EC2 User Guide for Linux Instances*. For more information about how to connect to a Windows instance, see Connect to Your Windows Instance Using RDP in the *Amazon EC2 User Guide for Windows Instances*.

Note
If you also want your instance to be accessible via an IPv4 address over the Internet, SSH, or RDP, you must associate an Elastic IP address (a static public IPv4 address) to your instance, and you must adjust your security group rules to allow access over IPv4. To do this, see the steps in Getting Started.

Scenarios and Examples

This section has examples for creating and configuring a VPC, including scenarios for how to use the VPC wizard in the Amazon VPC console.

Scenario	Usage
Scenario 1: VPC with a Single Public Subnet	Use the VPC wizard to create a VPC for running a single-tier, public-facing web application such as a blog or simple web site.
Scenario 2: VPC with Public and Private Subnets (NAT)	Use the VPC wizard to create a VPC for running a public-facing web application, while still maintaining non-publicly accessible back-end servers in a second subnet.
Scenario 3: VPC with Public and Private Subnets and AWS Managed VPN Access	Use the VPC wizard to create a VPC for extending your data center into the cloud, and also directly access the Internet from your VPC.
Scenario 4: VPC with a Private Subnet Only and AWS Managed VPN Access	Use the VPC wizard to create a VPC for extending your data center into the cloud, and leverage Amazon's infrastructure without exposing your network to the Internet.
Example: Create an IPv4 VPC and Subnets Using the AWS CLI	Use the AWS CLI to create a VPC and and a public and private subnet.
Example: Create an IPv6 VPC and Subnets Using the AWS CLI	Use the AWS CLI to create a VPC with an associated IPv6 CIDR block, and a public and private subnet each with an associated IPv6 CIDR block.

Scenario 1: VPC with a Single Public Subnet

The configuration for this scenario includes a virtual private cloud (VPC) with a single public subnet, and an Internet gateway to enable communication over the Internet. We recommend this configuration if you need to run a single-tier, public-facing web application, such as a blog or a simple website.

This topic assumes that you'll use the VPC wizard in the Amazon VPC console to create the VPC.

This scenario can also be optionally configured for IPv6—you can use the VPC wizard to create a VPC and subnet with associated IPv6 CIDR blocks. Instances launched into the public subnet can receive IPv6 addresses, and communicate using IPv6. For more information about IPv4 and IPv6 addressing, see IP Addressing in Your VPC.

Topics

- Overview
- Routing
- Security
- Implementing Scenario 1

Overview

The following diagram shows the key components of the configuration for this scenario.

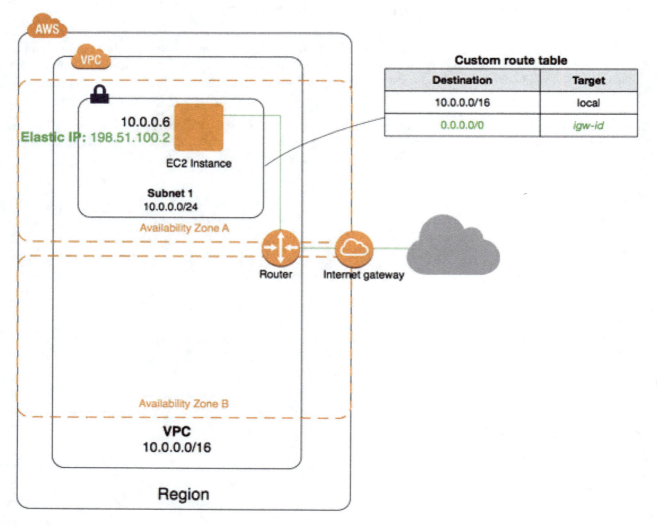

Custom route table	
Destination	**Target**
10.0.0.0/16	local
0.0.0.0/0	*igw-id*

Note

If you completed the exercise Getting Started, then you've already implemented this scenario using the VPC wizard in the Amazon VPC console.

The configuration for this scenario includes the following:

- A virtual private cloud (VPC) with a size /16 IPv4 CIDR block (example: 10.0.0.0/16). This provides 65,536 private IPv4 addresses.
- A subnet with a size /24 IPv4 CIDR block (example: 10.0.0.0/24). This provides 256 private IPv4 addresses.
- An Internet gateway. This connects the VPC to the Internet and to other AWS services.
- An instance with a private IPv4 address in the subnet range (example: 10.0.0.6), which enables the instance to communicate with other instances in the VPC, and an Elastic IPv4 address (example: 198.51.100.2), which is a public IPv4 address that enables the instance to be reached from the Internet.
- A custom route table associated with the subnet. The route table entries enable instances in the subnet to use IPv4 to communicate with other instances in the VPC, and to communicate directly over the Internet. A subnet that's associated with a route table that has a route to an Internet gateway is known as a *public subnet*.

For more information about subnets, see VPCs and Subnets. For more information about Internet gateways, see Internet Gateways.

Overview for IPv6

You can optionally enable IPv6 for this scenario. In addition to the components listed above, the configuration includes the following:

- A size /56 IPv6 CIDR block associated with the VPC (example: 2001:db81a00::/56). Amazon automatically assigns the CIDR; you cannot choose the range yourself.
- A size /64 IPv6 CIDR block associated with the public subnet (example: 2001:db81a00::/64). You can choose the range for your subnet from the range allocated to the VPC. You cannot choose the size of the subnet IPv6 CIDR block.
- An IPv6 address assigned to the instance from the subnet range (example: 2001:db81a00::123).
- Route table entries in the custom route table that enable instances in the VPC to use IPv6 to communicate with each other, and directly over the Internet.

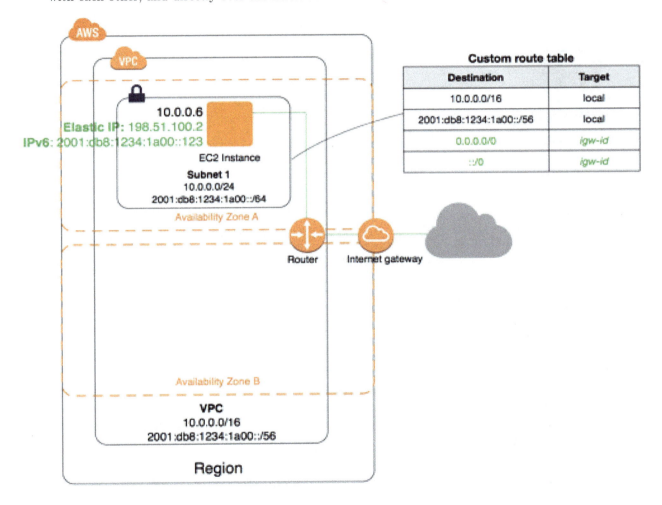

Routing

Your VPC has an implied router (shown in the configuration diagram above). In this scenario, the VPC wizard creates a custom route table that routes all traffic destined for an address outside the VPC to the Internet gateway, and associates this route table with the subnet.

The following table shows the route table for the example in the configuration diagram above. The first entry is the default entry for local IPv4 routing in the VPC; this entry enables the instances in this VPC to communicate

41

with each other. The second entry routes all other IPv4 subnet traffic to the Internet gateway (for example, `igw-1a2b3c4d`).

Destination	Target
10.0.0.0/16	local
0.0.0.0/0	*igw-id*

Routing for IPv6

If you associate an IPv6 CIDR block with your VPC and subnet, your route table must include separate routes for IPv6 traffic. The following table shows the custom route table for this scenario if you choose to enable IPv6 communication in your VPC. The second entry is the default route that's automatically added for local routing in the VPC over IPv6. The fourth entry routes all other IPv6 subnet traffic to the Internet gateway.

Destination	Target
10.0.0.0/16	local
2001:db81a00::/56	local
0.0.0.0/0	*igw-id*
::/0	igw-id

Security

AWS provides two features that you can use to increase security in your VPC: *security groups* and *network ACLs*. Security groups control inbound and outbound traffic for your instances, and network ACLs control inbound and outbound traffic for your subnets. In most cases, security groups can meet your needs; however, you can also use network ACLs if you want an additional layer of security for your VPC. For more information, see Security.

For this scenario, you use a security group but not a network ACL. If you'd like to use a network ACL, see Recommended Rules for Scenario 1.

Your VPC comes with a default security group. An instance that's launched into the VPC is automatically associated with the default security group if you don't specify a different security group during launch. You can add rules to the default security group, but the rules may not be suitable for other instances that you launch into the VPC. Instead, we recommend that you create a custom security group for your web server.

For this scenario, create a security group named `WebServerSG`. When you create a security group, it has a single outbound rule that allows all traffic to leave the instances. You must modify the rules to enable inbound traffic and restrict the outbound traffic as needed. You specify this security group when you launch instances into the VPC.

The following are the inbound and outbound rules for IPv4 traffic for the WebServerSG security group.

Inbound
Source
0.0.0.0/0
0.0.0.0/0
Public IPv4 address range of your network
Public IPv4 address range of your network
The security group ID (sg-xxxxxxxx)
Outbound (Optional)
Destination
0.0.0.0/0

Security for IPv6

If you associate an IPv6 CIDR block with your VPC and subnet, you must add separate rules to your security group to control inbound and outbound IPv6 traffic for your web server instance. In this scenario, the web server will be able to receive all Internet traffic over IPv6, and SSH or RDP traffic from your local network over IPv6.

The following are the IPv6-specific rules for the WebServerSG security group (which are in addition to the rules listed above).

Inbound
Source
::/0
::/0
IPv6 address range of your network
IPv6 address range of your network
Outbound (Optional)
Destination
::/0

Implementing Scenario 1

To implement scenario 1, create a VPC using the VPC wizard, create and configure the WebServerSG security group, and then launch an instance into your VPC.

These procedures include optional steps for enabling and configuring IPv6 communication for your VPC. You do not have to perform these steps if you do not want to use IPv6 in your VPC.

To create a VPC

1. Open the Amazon VPC console at https://console.aws.amazon.com/vpc/.

2. In the dashboard, choose **Start VPC Wizard**.

3. Select the first option, **VPC with a Single Public Subnet**, and then choose **Select**.

4. For **VPC name** and **Subnet name**, you can name your VPC and subnet to help you to identify them later in the console. You can specify your own IPv4 CIDR block range for the VPC and subnet, or you can leave the default values (10.0.0.0/16 and 10.0.0.0/24 respectively).

5. (Optional, IPv6-only) For **IPv6 CIDR block**, choose **Amazon-provided IPv6 CIDR block**. For **Public subnet's IPv6 CIDR**, choose **Specify a custom IPv6 CIDR** and specify the hexadecimal pair value for your subnet, or leave the default value (00).

6. You can leave the rest of the default settings, and choose **Create VPC**.

To create the WebServerSG security group

1. Open the Amazon VPC console at https://console.aws.amazon.com/vpc/.

2. In the navigation pane, choose **Security Groups**.

3. Choose **Create Security Group**.

4. Provide a name and description for the security group. In this topic, the name `WebServerSG` is used as an example. Select the ID of your VPC from the **VPC** menu, and then choose **Yes, Create**.

5. Select the WebServerSG security group that you just created. The details pane include a tab for information about the security group, plus tabs for working with its inbound rules and outbound rules.

6. On the **Inbound Rules** tab, choose **Edit**, and then do the following:

- Select **HTTP** from the **Type** list, and enter `0.0.0.0/0` in the **Source** field.
- Choose **Add another rule**, then select **HTTPS** from the **Type** list, and enter `0.0.0.0/0` in the **Source** field.
- Choose **Add another rule**, then select **SSH** (for Linux) or **RDP** (for Windows) from the **Type** list. Enter your network's public IP address range in the **Source** field. (If you don't know this address range, you can use `0.0.0.0/0` for testing purposes; in production, you authorize only a specific IP address or range of addresses to access your instance.)
- (Optional) Choose **Add another rule**, then select **ALL traffic** from the **Type** list. In the **Source** field, enter the ID of the WebServerSG security group.
- (Optional, IPv6-only) Choose **Add another rule**, select **HTTP** from the **Type** list, and enter `::/0` in the **Source** field.
- (Optional, IPv6-only) Choose **Add another rule**, select **HTTPS** from the **Type** list, and enter `::/0` in the **Source** field.
- (Optional, IPv6-only) Choose **Add another rule**, select **SSH** (for Linux) or **RDP** (for Windows) from the **Type** list. Enter your network's IPv6 address range in the **Source** field. (If you don't know this address range, you can use `::/0` for testing purposes; in production, you authorize only a specific IPv6 address or range of addresses to access your instance.)

7. Choose **Save**.

8. (Optional) On the **Outbound Rules** tab, choose **Edit**. Locate the default rule that enables all outbound traffic, choose **Remove**, and then choose **Save**.

To launch an instance into the VPC

1. Open the Amazon EC2 console at https://console.aws.amazon.com/ec2/.

2. From the dashboard, choose **Launch Instance**.

3. Follow the directions in the wizard. Choose an AMI, choose an instance type, and then choose **Next: Configure Instance Details**. **Note**
   If you intend to use your instance for IPv6 communication, you must choose a supported instance type; for example, T2. For more information, see Amazon EC2 Instance Types.

4. On the **Configure Instance Details** page, select the VPC that you created in step 1 from the **Network** list, and then specify a subnet.

5. (Optional) By default, instances launched into a nondefault VPC are not assigned a public IPv4 address. To be able to connect to your instance, you can assign a public IPv4 address now, or allocate an Elastic IP address and assign it to your instance after it's launched. To assign a public IPv4 address now, ensure that you select **Enable** from the **Auto-assign Public IP** list. **Note**
   You can only use the auto-assign public IP feature for a single, new network interface with the device index of eth0. For more information, see Assigning a Public IPv4 Address During Instance Launch.

6. (Optional, IPv6-only) You can auto-assign an IPv6 address to your instance from the subnet range. For **Auto-assign IPv6 IP**, choose **Enable**.

7. On the next two pages of the wizard, you can configure storage for your instance, and add tags. On the **Configure Security Group** page, select the **Select an existing security group** option, and select the **WebServerSG** security group that you created in step 2. Choose **Review and Launch**.

8. Review the settings that you've chosen. Make any changes that you need, and then choose **Launch** to choose a key pair and launch your instance.

9. If you did not assign a public IPv4 address to your instance in step 5, you will not be able to connect to it over IPv4. Assign an Elastic IP address to the instance:

   1. Open the Amazon VPC console at https://console.aws.amazon.com/vpc/.

   2. In the navigation pane, choose **Elastic IPs**.

   3. Choose **Allocate new address**.

4. Choose **Allocate**. **Note**
   If your account supports EC2-Classic, first choose **VPC**.

5. Select the Elastic IP address from the list, choose **Actions**, and then choose **Associate address**.

6. Select the instance to associate the address with, and then choose **Associate**.

You can now connect to your instances in the VPC. For information about how to connect to a Linux instance, see Connect to Your Linux Instance in the *Amazon EC2 User Guide for Linux Instances*. For information about how to connect to a Windows instance, see Connect to Your Windows Instance in the *Amazon EC2 User Guide for Windows Instances*.

Scenario 2: VPC with Public and Private Subnets (NAT)

The configuration for this scenario includes a virtual private cloud (VPC) with a public subnet and a private subnet. We recommend this scenario if you want to run a public-facing web application, while maintaining back-end servers that aren't publicly accessible. A common example is a multi-tier website, with the web servers in a public subnet and the database servers in a private subnet. You can set up security and routing so that the web servers can communicate with the database servers.

The instances in the public subnet can send outbound traffic directly to the Internet, whereas the instances in the private subnet can't. Instead, the instances in the private subnet can access the Internet by using a network address translation (NAT) gateway that resides in the public subnet. The database servers can connect to the Internet for software updates using the NAT gateway, but the Internet cannot establish connections to the database servers.

Note
You can also use the VPC wizard to configure a VPC with a NAT instance; however, we recommend that you use a NAT gateway. For more information, see NAT Gateways.

This topic assumes that you'll use the VPC wizard in the Amazon VPC console to create the VPC and NAT gateway.

This scenario can also be optionally configured for IPv6—you can use the VPC wizard to create a VPC and subnets with associated IPv6 CIDR blocks. Instances launched into the subnets can receive IPv6 addresses, and communicate using IPv6. Instances in the private subnet can use an egress-only Internet gateway to connect to the Internet over IPv6, but the Internet cannot establish connections to the private instances over IPv6. For more information about IPv4 and IPv6 addressing, see IP Addressing in Your VPC.

Topics

- Overview
- Routing
- Security
- Implementing Scenario 2
- Implementing Scenario 2 with a NAT Instance

Overview

The following diagram shows the key components of the configuration for this scenario.

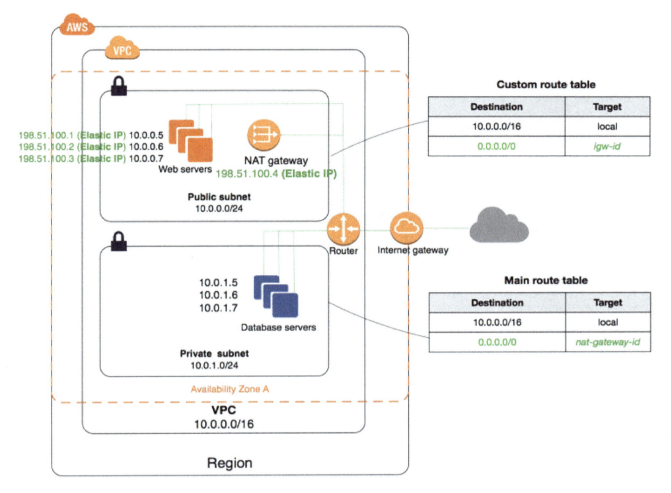

The configuration for this scenario includes the following:

- A VPC with a size /16 IPv4 CIDR block (example: 10.0.0.0/16). This provides 65,536 private IPv4 addresses.
- A public subnet with a size /24 IPv4 CIDR block (example: 10.0.0.0/24). This provides 256 private IPv4 addresses. A public subnet is a subnet that's associated with a route table that has a route to an Internet gateway.
- A private subnet with a size /24 IPv4 CIDR block (example: 10.0.1.0/24). This provides 256 private IPv4 addresses.
- An Internet gateway. This connects the VPC to the Internet and to other AWS services.
- Instances with private IPv4 addresses in the subnet range (examples: 10.0.0.5, 10.0.1.5). This enables them to communicate with each other and other instances in the VPC.
- Instances in the public subnet with Elastic IPv4 addresses (example: 198.51.100.1), which are public IPv4 addresses that enable them to be reached from the Internet. The instances can have public IP addresses assigned at launch instead of Elastic IP addresses. Instances in the private subnet are back-end servers that don't need to accept incoming traffic from the Internet and therefore do not have public IP addresses; however, they can send requests to the Internet using the NAT gateway (see the next bullet).
- A NAT gateway with its own Elastic IPv4 address. Instances in the private subnet can send requests to the Internet through the NAT gateway over IPv4 (for example, for software updates).
- A custom route table associated with the public subnet. This route table contains an entry that enables instances in the subnet to communicate with other instances in the VPC over IPv4, and an entry that enables instances in the subnet to communicate directly with the Internet over IPv4.
- The main route table associated with the private subnet. The route table contains an entry that enables instances in the subnet to communicate with other instances in the VPC over IPv4, and an entry that

47

enables instances in the subnet to communicate with the Internet through the NAT gateway over IPv4.

For more information about subnets, see VPCs and Subnets. For more information about Internet gateways, see Internet Gateways. For more information about NAT gateways, see NAT Gateways.

Overview for IPv6

You can optionally enable IPv6 for this scenario. In addition to the components listed above, the configuration includes the following:

- A size /56 IPv6 CIDR block associated with the VPC (example: 2001:db81a00::/56). Amazon automatically assigns the CIDR; you cannot choose the range yourself.
- A size /64 IPv6 CIDR block associated with the public subnet (example: 2001:db81a00::/64). You can choose the range for your subnet from the range allocated to the VPC. You cannot choose the size of the VPC IPv6 CIDR block.
- A size /64 IPv6 CIDR block associated with the private subnet (example: 2001:db81a01::/64). You can choose the range for your subnet from the range allocated to the VPC. You cannot choose the size of the subnet IPv6 CIDR block.
- IPv6 addresses assigned to the instances from the subnet range (example: 2001:db81a00::1a).
- An egress-only Internet gateway. This enables instances in the private subnet to send requests to the Internet over IPv6 (for example, for software updates). An egress-only Internet gateway is necessary if you want instances in the private subnet to be able to initiate communication with the Internet over IPv6. For more information, see Egress-Only Internet Gateways.
- Route table entries in the custom route table that enable instances in the public subnet to use IPv6 to communicate with each other, and directly over the Internet.
- Route table entries in the main route table that enable instances in the private subnet to use IPv6 to communicate with each other, and to communicate with the Internet through an egress-only Internet gateway.

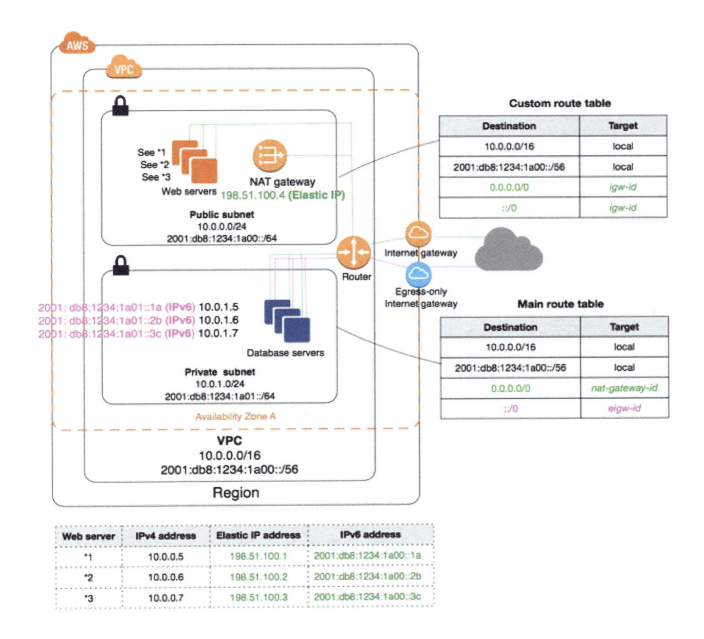

Web server	IPv4 address	Elastic IP address	IPv6 address
*1	10.0.0.5	198.51.100.1	2001:db8:1234:1a00::1a
*2	10.0.0.6	198.51.100.2	2001:db8:1234:1a00::2b
*3	10.0.0.7	198.51.100.3	2001:db8:1234:1a00::3c

Routing

In this scenario, the VPC wizard updates the main route table used with the private subnet, and creates a custom route table and associates it with the public subnet.

In this scenario, all traffic from each subnet that is bound for AWS (for example, to the Amazon EC2 or Amazon S3 endpoints) goes over the Internet gateway. The database servers in the private subnet can't receive traffic from the Internet directly because they don't have Elastic IP addresses. However, the database servers can send and receive Internet traffic through the NAT device in the public subnet.

Any additional subnets that you create use the main route table by default, which means that they are private subnets by default. If you want to make a subnet public, you can always change the route table that it's associated with.

The following tables describe the route tables for this scenario.

Main Route Table

The first entry is the default entry for local routing in the VPC; this entry enables the instances in the VPC to communicate with each other. The second entry sends all other subnet traffic to the NAT gateway (for example, `nat-12345678901234567`).

Destination	Target
10.0.0.0/16	local
0.0.0.0/0	*nat-gateway-id*

Custom Route Table

The first entry is the default entry for local routing in the VPC; this entry enables the instances in this VPC to communicate with each other. The second entry routes all other subnet traffic to the Internet over the Internet gateway (for example, `igw-1a2b3d4d`).

Destination	Target
10.0.0.0/16	local
0.0.0.0/0	*igw-id*

Routing for IPv6

If you associate an IPv6 CIDR block with your VPC and subnets, your route tables must include separate routes for IPv6 traffic. The following tables show the route tables for this scenario if you choose to enable IPv6 communication in your VPC.

Main Route Table

The second entry is the default route that's automatically added for local routing in the VPC over IPv6. The fourth entry routes all other IPv6 subnet traffic to the egress-only Internet gateway.

Destination	Target
10.0.0.0/16	local
2001:db81a00::/56	local
0.0.0.0/0	*nat-gateway-id*
::/0	egress-only-igw-id

Custom Route Table

The second entry is the default route that's automatically added for local routing in the VPC over IPv6. The fourth entry routes all other IPv6 subnet traffic to the Internet gateway.

Destination	Target
10.0.0.0/16	local
2001:db81a00::/56	local
0.0.0.0/0	*igw-id*
::/0	igw-id

Security

AWS provides two features that you can use to increase security in your VPC: *security groups* and *network ACLs*. Security groups control inbound and outbound traffic for your instances, and network ACLs control inbound and outbound traffic for your subnets. In most cases, security groups can meet your needs; however, you can also use network ACLs if you want an additional layer of security for your VPC. For more information, see Security.

For scenario 2, you'll use security groups but not network ACLs. If you'd like to use a network ACL, see Recommended Rules for Scenario 2.

Your VPC comes with a default security group. An instance that's launched into the VPC is automatically associated with the default security group if you don't specify a different security group during launch. For this scenario, we recommend that you create the following security groups instead of using the default security group:

- **WebServerSG**: Specify this security group when you launch the web servers in the public subnet.
- **DBServerSG**: Specify this security group when you launch the database servers in the private subnet.

The instances assigned to a security group can be in different subnets. However, in this scenario, each security group corresponds to the type of role an instance plays, and each role requires the instance to be in a particular subnet. Therefore, in this scenario, all instances assigned to a security group are in the same subnet.

The following table describes the recommended rules for the WebServerSG security group, which allow the web servers to receive Internet traffic, as well as SSH and RDP traffic from your network. The web servers can also initiate read and write requests to the database servers in the private subnet, and send traffic to the Internet; for example, to get software updates. Because the web server doesn't initiate any other outbound communication, the default outbound rule is removed.

Note
These recommendations include both SSH and RDP access, and both Microsoft SQL Server and MySQL access. For your situation, you might only need rules for Linux (SSH and MySQL) or Windows (RDP and Microsoft SQL Server).

WebServerSG: Recommended Rules

Inbound
Source
0.0.0.0/0
0.0.0.0/0
Your home network's public IPv4 address range
Your home network's public IPv4 address range
Outbound
Destination
The ID of your DBServerSG security group
The ID of your DBServerSG security group
0.0.0.0/0
0.0.0.0/0

The following table describes the recommended rules for the DBServerSG security group, which allow read or write database requests from the web servers. The database servers can also initiate traffic bound for the Internet (the route table sends that traffic to the NAT gateway, which then forwards it to the Internet over the Internet gateway).

DBServerSG: Recommended Rules

Inbound
Source
The ID of your WebServerSG security group
The ID of your WebServerSG security group

Outbound
Destination
0.0.0.0/0
0.0.0.0/0

(Optional) The default security group for a VPC has rules that automatically allow assigned instances to communicate with each other. To allow that type of communication for a custom security group, you must add the following rules:

Inbound
Source
The ID of the security group
Outbound
Destination
The ID of the security group

(Optional) If you launch a bastion host in your public subnet to use as a proxy for SSH or RDP traffic from your home network to your private subnet, add a rule to the DBServerSG security group that allows inbound SSH or RDP traffic from the bastion instance or its associated security group.

Security for IPv6

If you associate an IPv6 CIDR block with your VPC and subnets, you must add separate rules to your WebServerSG and DBServerSG security groups to control inbound and outbound IPv6 traffic for your instances. In this scenario, the web servers will be able to receive all Internet traffic over IPv6, and SSH or RDP traffic from your local network over IPv6. They can also initiate outbound IPv6 traffic to the Internet. The database servers can initiate outbound IPv6 traffic to the Internet.

The following are the IPv6-specific rules for the WebServerSG security group (which are in addition to the rules listed above).

Inbound
Source
::/0
::/0
IPv6 address range of your network
IPv6 address range of your network
Outbound
Destination
::/0
::/0

The following are the IPv6-specific rules for the DBServerSG security group (which are in addition to the rules listed above).

Outbound
Destination
::/0
::/0

Implementing Scenario 2

You can use the VPC wizard to create the VPC, subnets, NAT gateway, and optionally, an egress-only Internet gateway. You must specify an Elastic IP address for your NAT gateway; if you don't have one, you must first allocate one to your account. If you want to use an existing Elastic IP address, ensure that it's not currently associated with another instance or network interface. The NAT gateway is automatically created in the public subnet of your VPC.

These procedures include optional steps for enabling and configuring IPv6 communication for your VPC. You do not have to perform these steps if you do not want to use IPv6 in your VPC.

(Optional) To allocate an Elastic IP address for the NAT gateway (IPv4)

1. Open the Amazon VPC console at https://console.aws.amazon.com/vpc/.

2. In the navigation pane, choose **Elastic IPs**.

3. Choose **Allocate new address**.

4. Choose **Allocate. Note**
   If your account supports EC2-Classic, first choose **VPC**.

To create a VPC

1. Open the Amazon VPC console at https://console.aws.amazon.com/vpc/.

2. On the VPC dashboard, choose **Start VPC Wizard**.

3. Choose the second option, **VPC with Public and Private Subnets**, and **Select**.

4. For **VPC name, Public subnet name** and **Private subnet name**, you can name your VPC and subnets to help you identify them later in the console. You can specify your own IPv4 CIDR block range for the VPC and subnets, or you can leave the default values.

5. (Optional, IPv6-only) For **IPv6 CIDR block**, choose **Amazon-provided IPv6 CIDR block**. For **Public subnet's IPv6 CIDR**, choose **Specify a custom IPv6 CIDR** and specify the hexadecimal pair value for your subnet, or leave the default value. For **Private subnet's IPv6 CIDR**, choose **Specify a custom IPv6 CIDR**. Specify the hexadecimal pair value for the IPv6 subnet or leave the default value.

6. In the **Specify the details of your NAT gateway** section, specify the allocation ID for an Elastic IP address in your account.

7. You can leave the rest of the default values on the page, and choose **Create VPC**.

Because the WebServerSG and DBServerSG security groups reference each other, create all the security groups required for this scenario before you add rules to them.

To create the WebServerSG and DBServerSG security groups

1. Open the Amazon VPC console at https://console.aws.amazon.com/vpc/.

2. In the navigation pane, choose **Security Groups, Create Security Group**.

3. Provide a name and description for the security group. In this topic, the name `WebServerSG` is used as an example. For **VPC**, select the ID of the VPC you created and choose **Yes, Create**.

4. Choose **Create Security Group** again.

5. Provide a name and description for the security group. In this topic, the name `DBServerSG` is used as an example. For **VPC**, select the ID of your VPC and choose **Yes, Create**.

To add rules to the WebServerSG security group

1. Select the WebServerSG security group that you created. The details pane displays the details for the security group, plus tabs for working with its inbound and outbound rules.

2. On the **Inbound Rules** tab, choose **Edit** and add rules for inbound traffic as follows:

   1. Choose **Type, HTTP**. For **Source**, enter 0.0.0.0/0.

   2. Choose **Add another rule, Type, HTTPS**. For **Source**, enter 0.0.0.0/0.

   3. Choose **Add another rule, Type, SSH**. For **Source**, enter your network's public IPv4 address range.

   4. Choose **Add another rule, Type, RDP**. For **Source**, enter your network's public IPv4 address range.

   5. (Optional, IPv6-only) Choose **Add another rule, Type, HTTP**. For **Source**, enter ::/0.

   6. (Optional, IPv6-only) Choose **Add another rule, Type, HTTPS**. For **Source**, enter ::/0.

   7. (Optional, IPv6-only) Choose **Add another rule, Type, SSH** (for Linux) or **RDP** (for Windows). For **Source**, enter your network's IPv6 address range.

   8. Choose **Save**.

3. On the **Outbound Rules** tab, choose **Edit** and add rules for outbound traffic as follows:

   1. Locate the default rule that enables all outbound traffic and choose **Remove**.

   2. Choose **Type, MS SQL**. For **Destination**, specify the ID of the DBServerSG security group.

   3. Choose **Add another rule, Type, MySQL**. For **Destination**, specify the ID of the DBServerSG security group.

   4. Choose **Add another rule, Type, HTTPS**. For **Destination**, enter 0.0.0.0/0.

   5. Choose **Add another rule, Type, HTTP**. For **Destination**, enter 0.0.0.0/0.

   6. (Optional, IPv6-only) Choose **Add another rule, Type, HTTPS**. For **Destination**, enter ::/0.

   7. (Optional, IPv6-only) Choose **Add another rule, Type, HTTP**. For **Destination**, enter ::/0.

   8. Choose **Save**.

To add the recommended rules to the DBServerSG security group

1. Select the DBServerSG security group that you created. The details pane displays the details for the security group, plus tabs for working with its inbound and outbound rules.

2. On the **Inbound Rules** tab, choose **Edit** and add rules for inbound traffic as follows:

   1. Choose **Type, MS SQL**. For **Source**, specify the ID of your WebServerSG security group.

   2. Choose **Add another rule, Type, MYSQL**. For **Source**, specify the ID of your WebServerSG security group.

   3. Choose **Save**.

3. On the **Outbound Rules** tab, choose **Edit** and add rules for outbound traffic as follows:

   1. Locate the default rule that enables all outbound traffic and choose **Remove**.

   2. Choose **Type, HTTP**. For **Destination**, enter 0.0.0.0/0.

   3. Choose **Add another rule, Type, HTTPS**. For **Destination**, enter 0.0.0.0/0.

   4. (Optional, IPv6-only) Choose **Add another rule, Type, HTTP**. For **Destination**, enter ::/0.

   5. (Optional, IPv6-only) Choose **Add another rule, Type, HTTPS**. For **Destination**, enter ::/0.

   6. Choose **Save**.

You can now launch instances into your VPC.

To launch an instance (web server or database server)

1. Open the Amazon EC2 console at https://console.aws.amazon.com/ec2/.

2. From the dashboard, choose **Launch Instance**.

3. Select an AMI and an instance type and choose **Next: Configure Instance Details. Note**
   If you intend to use your instance for IPv6 communication, you must choose a supported instance type; for example, T2. For more information, see Amazon EC2 Instance Types.

4. On the **Configure Instance Details** page, for **Network**, select the VPC that you created earlier and then select a subnet. For example, launch a web server into the public subnet and the database server into the private subnet.

5. (Optional) By default, instances launched into a nondefault VPC are not assigned a public IPv4 address. To be able to connect to your instance in the public subnet, you can assign a public IPv4 address now, or allocate an Elastic IP address and assign it to your instance after it's launched. To assign a public IPv4 address now, ensure that you choose **Enable** from the **Auto-assign Public IP** list. You do not need to assign a public IP address to an instance in the private subnet. **Note**
   You can only use the auto-assign public IPv4 feature for a single, new network interface with the device index of eth0. For more information, see Assigning a Public IPv4 Address During Instance Launch.

6. (Optional, IPv6-only) You can auto-assign an IPv6 address to your instance from the subnet range. For **Auto-assign IPv6 IP**, choose **Enable**.

7. On the next two pages of the wizard, you can configure storage for your instance, and add tags. On the **Configure Security Group** page, choose the **Select an existing security group** option, and select one of the security groups you created earlier (**WebServerSG** for a web server or **DBServerSG** for a database server). Choose **Review and Launch**.

8. Review the settings that you've chosen. Make any changes that you need and choose **Launch** to choose a key pair and launch your instance.

If you did not assign a public IPv4 address to your instance in the public subnet in step 5, you will not be able to connect to it. Before you can access an instance in your public subnet, you must assign it an Elastic IP address.

To allocate an Elastic IP address and assign it to an instance (IPv4)

1. Open the Amazon VPC console at https://console.aws.amazon.com/vpc/.

2. In the navigation pane, choose **Elastic IPs**.

3. Choose **Allocate new address**.

4. Choose **Allocate. Note**
   If your account supports EC2-Classic, first choose **VPC**.

5. Select the Elastic IP address from the list and choose **Actions, Associate address**.

6. Select the network interface or instance. For **Private IP**, select the corresponding address to associate the Elastic IP address with and choose **Associate**.

You can now connect to your instances in the VPC. For information about how to connect to a Linux instance, see Connect to Your Linux Instance in the *Amazon EC2 User Guide for Linux Instances*. For information about how to connect to a Windows instance, see Connect to Your Windows Instance in the *Amazon EC2 User Guide for Windows Instances*.

Implementing Scenario 2 with a NAT Instance

You can implement scenario 2 using a NAT instance instead of a NAT gateway. For more information about NAT instances, see NAT Instances.

You can follow the same procedures as above; however, in the NAT section of the VPC wizard, choose **Use a NAT instance instead** and specify the details for your NAT instance. You will also require a security group for your NAT instance (`NATSG`), which allows the NAT instance to receive Internet-bound traffic from instances in the private subnet, as well as SSH traffic from your network. The NAT instance can also send traffic to the Internet, so that instances in the private subnet can get software updates.

After you've created the VPC with the NAT instance, you must change the security group associated with the NAT instance to the new `NATSG` security group (by default, the NAT instance is launched using the default security group).

NATSG: Recommended Rules

Inbound
Source
10.0.1.0/24
10.0.1.0/24
Your network's public IP address range
Outbound
Destination
0.0.0.0/0
0.0.0.0/0

To create the NATSG security group

1. Open the Amazon VPC console at https://console.aws.amazon.com/vpc/.

2. In the navigation pane, choose **Security Groups**, and the choose **Create Security Group**.

3. Specify a name and description for the security group. In this topic, the name `NATSG` is used as an example. For **VPC**, select the ID of your VPC and choose **Yes, Create**.

4. Select the NATSG security group that you created. The details pane displays the details for the security group, plus tabs for working with its inbound and outbound rules.

5. On the **Inbound Rules** tab, choose **Edit** and add rules for inbound traffic as follows:

    1. Choose **Type, HTTP** . For **Source**, enter the IP address range of your private subnet.

    2. Choose **Add another rule, Type, HTTPS**. For **Source**, enter the IP address range of your private subnet.

    3. Choose **Add another rule, Type, SSH**. For **Source**, enter your network's public IP address range.

    4. Choose **Save**.

6. On the **Outbound Rules** tab, choose **Edit** and add rules for outbound traffic as follows:

    1. Locate the default rule that enables all outbound traffic and choose **Remove**.

    2. Choose **Type, HTTP**. For **Destination**, enter 0.0.0.0/0.

    3. Choose **Add another rule, Type, HTTPS**. For **Destination**, enter 0.0.0.0/0.

    4. Choose **Save**.

When the VPC wizard launched the NAT instance, it used the default security group for the VPC. You need to associate the NAT instance with the NATSG security group instead.

To change the security group of the NAT instance

1. Open the Amazon EC2 console at https://console.aws.amazon.com/ec2/.

2. In the navigation pane, choose **Network Interfaces**.

3. Select the network interface for the NAT instance from the list and choose **Actions, Change Security Groups**.

4. In the **Change Security Groups** dialog box, for **Security groups**, select the NATSG security group that you created (see Security) and choose **Save**.

Scenario 3: VPC with Public and Private Subnets and AWS Managed VPN Access

The configuration for this scenario includes a virtual private cloud (VPC) with a public subnet and a private subnet, and a virtual private gateway to enable communication with your own network over an IPsec VPN tunnel. We recommend this scenario if you want to extend your network into the cloud and also directly access the Internet from your VPC. This scenario enables you to run a multi-tiered application with a scalable web front end in a public subnet, and to house your data in a private subnet that is connected to your network by an IPsec VPN connection.

This topic assumes that you'll use the VPC wizard in the Amazon VPC console to create the VPC and the VPN connection.

This scenario can also be optionally configured for IPv6—you can use the VPC wizard to create a VPC and subnets with associated IPv6 CIDR blocks. Instances launched into the subnets can receive IPv6 addresses. Currently, we do not support IPv6 communication over a VPN connection; however, instances in the VPC can communicate with each other via IPv6, and instances in the public subnet can communicate over the Internet via IPv6. For more information about IPv4 and IPv6 addressing, see IP Addressing in Your VPC.

Topics

- Overview
- Routing
- Security
- Implementing Scenario 3

Overview

The following diagram shows the key components of the configuration for this scenario.

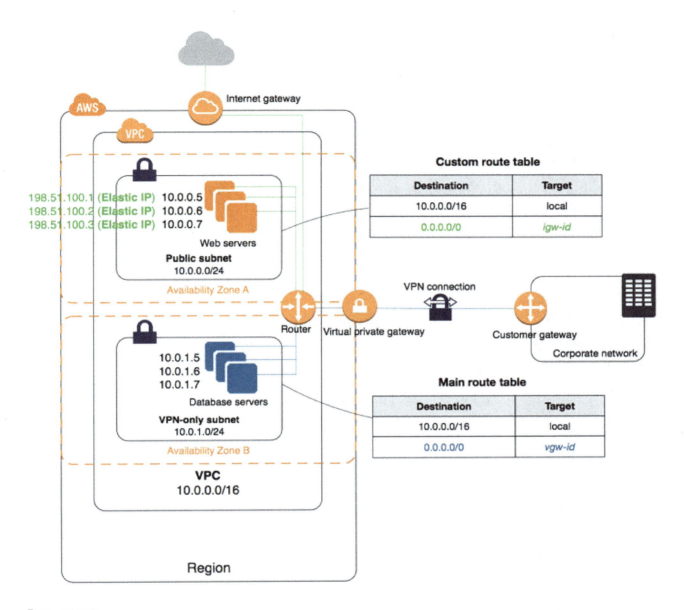

Important

For this scenario, the* Amazon VPC Network Administrator Guide* describes what your network administrator needs to do to configure the Amazon VPC customer gateway on your side of the VPN connection.

The configuration for this scenario includes the following:

- A virtual private cloud (VPC) with a size /16 IPv4 CIDR (example: 10.0.0.0/16). This provides 65,536 private IPv4 addresses.
- A public subnet with a size /24 IPv4 CIDR (example: 10.0.0.0/24). This provides 256 private IPv4 addresses. A public subnet is a subnet that's associated with a route table that has a route to an Internet gateway.
- A VPN-only subnet with a size /24 IPv4 CIDR (example: 10.0.1.0/24). This provides 256 private IPv4 addresses.
- An Internet gateway. This connects the VPC to the Internet and to other AWS products.
- A VPN connection between your VPC and your network. The VPN connection consists of a virtual private gateway located on the Amazon side of the VPN connection and a customer gateway located on your side of the VPN connection.
- Instances with private IPv4 addresses in the subnet range (examples: 10.0.0.5 and 10.0.1.5), which enables

the instances to communicate with each other and other instances in the VPC.

- Instances in the public subnet with Elastic IP addresses (example: 198.51.100.1), which are public IPv4 addresses that enable them to be reached from the Internet. The instances can have public IPv4 addresses assigned at launch instead of Elastic IP addresses. Instances in the VPN-only subnet are back-end servers that don't need to accept incoming traffic from the Internet, but can send and receive traffic from your network.
- A custom route table associated with the public subnet. This route table contains an entry that enables instances in the subnet to communicate with other instances in the VPC, and an entry that enables instances in the subnet to communicate directly with the Internet.
- The main route table associated with the VPN-only subnet. The route table contains an entry that enables instances in the subnet to communicate with other instances in the VPC, and an entry that enables instances in the subnet to communicate directly with your network.

For more information about subnets, see VPCs and Subnets and IP Addressing in Your VPC. For more information about Internet gateways, see Internet Gateways. For more information about your VPN connection, see AWS Managed VPN Connections. For more information about configuring a customer gateway, see the *Amazon VPC Network Administrator Guide*.

Overview for IPv6

You can optionally enable IPv6 for this scenario. In addition to the components listed above, the configuration includes the following:

- A size /56 IPv6 CIDR block associated with the VPC (example: 2001:db81a00::/56). AWS automatically assigns the CIDR; you cannot choose the range yourself.
- A size /64 IPv6 CIDR block associated with the public subnet (example: 2001:db81a00::/64). You can choose the range for your subnet from the range allocated to the VPC. You cannot choose the size of the IPv6 CIDR.
- A size /64 IPv6 CIDR block associated with the VPN-only subnet (example: 2001:db81a01::/64). You can choose the range for your subnet from the range allocated to the VPC. You cannot choose the size of the IPv6 CIDR.
- IPv6 addresses assigned to the instances from the subnet range (example: 2001:db81a00::1a).
- Route table entries in the custom route table that enable instances in the public subnet to use IPv6 to communicate with each other, and directly over the Internet.
- A route table entry in the main route table that enable instances in the VPN-only subnet to use IPv6 to communicate with each other.

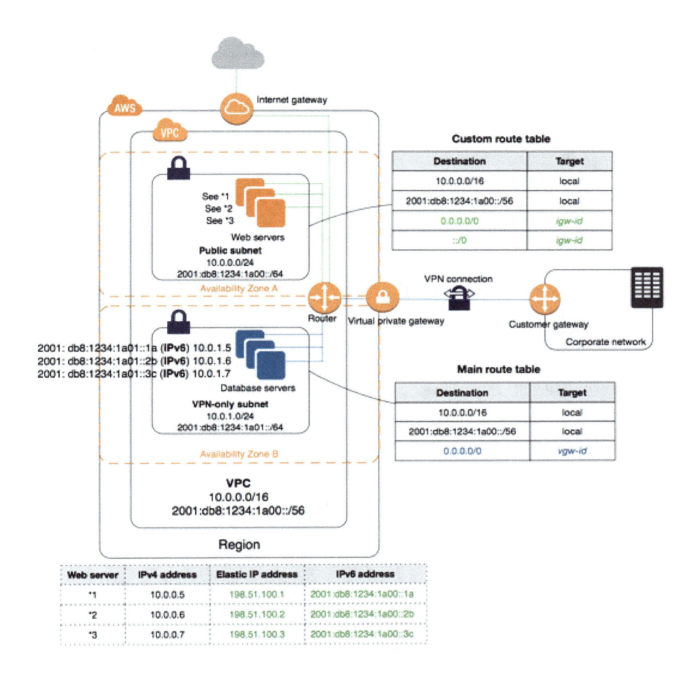

Custom route table	
Destination	Target
10.0.0.0/16	local
2001:db8:1234:1a00::/56	local
0.0.0.0/0	igw-id
::/0	igw-id

Main route table	
Destination	Target
10.0.0.0/16	local
2001:db8:1234:1a00::/56	local
0.0.0.0/0	vgw-id

Web server	IPv4 address	Elastic IP address	IPv6 address
*1	10.0.0.5	198.51.100.1	2001:db8:1234:1a00::1a
*2	10.0.0.6	198.51.100.2	2001:db8:1234:1a00::2b
*3	10.0.0.7	198.51.100.3	2001:db8:1234:1a00::3c

Routing

Your VPC has an implied router (shown in the configuration diagram for this scenario). In this scenario, the VPC wizard updates the main route table used with the VPN-only subnet, and creates a custom route table and associates it with the public subnet.

The instances in the VPN-only subnet can't reach the Internet directly; any Internet-bound traffic must first traverse the virtual private gateway to your network, where the traffic is then subject to your firewall and corporate security policies. If the instances send any AWS-bound traffic (for example, requests to the Amazon S3 or Amazon EC2 APIs), the requests must go over the virtual private gateway to your network and then egress to the Internet before reaching AWS. Currently, we do not support IPv6 for VPN connections.

Tip

Any traffic from your network going to an Elastic IP address for an instance in the public subnet goes over the Internet, and not over the virtual private gateway. You could instead set up a route and security group rules that enable the traffic to come from your network over the virtual private gateway to the public subnet.

The VPN connection is configured either as a statically-routed VPN connection or as a dynamically-routed VPN connection (using BGP). If you select static routing, you'll be prompted to manually enter the IP prefix for your network when you create the VPN connection. If you select dynamic routing, the IP prefix is advertised automatically to the virtual private gateway for your VPC using BGP.

The following tables describe the route tables for this scenario.

Main Route Table

The first entry is the default entry for local routing in the VPC; this entry enables the instances in the VPC to communicate with each other over IPv4. The second entry routes all other IPv4 subnet traffic from the private subnet to your network over the virtual private gateway (for example, `vgw-1a2b3c4d`).

Destination	Target
10.0.0.0/16	local
0.0.0.0/0	*vgw-id*

Custom Route Table

The first entry is the default entry for local routing in the VPC; this entry enables the instances in the VPC to communicate with each other. The second entry routes all other IPv4 subnet traffic from the public subnet to the Internet over the Internet gateway (for example, `igw-1a2b3c4d`).

Destination	Target
10.0.0.0/16	local
0.0.0.0/0	*igw-id*

Alternate Routing

Alternatively, if you want instances in the private subnet to access the Internet, you can create a network address translation (NAT) gateway or instance in the public subnet, and set up the routing so that the Internet-bound traffic for the subnet goes to the NAT device. This enables the instances in the VPN-only subnet to send requests over the Internet gateway (for example, for software updates).

For more information about setting up a NAT device manually, see NAT. For information about using the VPC wizard to set up a NAT device, see Scenario 2: VPC with Public and Private Subnets (NAT).

To enable the private subnet's Internet-bound traffic to go to the NAT device, you must update the main route table as follows.

The first entry is the default entry for local routing in the VPC. The second row entry for routes the subnet traffic bound for your customer network (in this case, assume your local network's IP address is `172.16.0.0/12`) to the virtual private gateway. The third entry sends all other subnet traffic to a NAT gateway.

Destination	Target
10.0.0.0/16	local
172.16.0.0/12	*vgw-id*
0.0.0.0/0	*nat-gateway-id*

Routing for IPv6

If you associate an IPv6 CIDR block with your VPC and subnets, your route tables must include separate routes for IPv6 traffic. The following tables show the route tables for this scenario if you choose to enable IPv6 communication in your VPC.

Main Route Table

The second entry is the default route that's automatically added for local routing in the VPC over IPv6.

Destination	Target
10.0.0.0/16	local
2001:db81a00::/56	local
0.0.0.0/0	*vgw-id*

Custom Route Table

The second entry is the default route that's automatically added for local routing in the VPC over IPv6. The fourth entry routes all other IPv6 subnet traffic to the Internet gateway.

Destination	Target
10.0.0.0/16	local
2001:db81a00::/56	local
0.0.0.0/0	*igw-id*
::/0	igw-id

Security

AWS provides two features that you can use to increase security in your VPC: *security groups* and *network ACLs*. Security groups control inbound and outbound traffic for your instances, and network ACLs control inbound and outbound traffic for your subnets. In most cases, security groups can meet your needs; however, you can also use network ACLs if you want an additional layer of security for your VPC. For more information, see Security.

For scenario 3, you'll use security groups but not network ACLs. If you'd like to use a network ACL, see Recommended Rules for Scenario 3.

Your VPC comes with a default security group. An instance that's launched into the VPC is automatically associated with the default security group if you don't specify a different security group during launch. For this scenario, we recommend that you create the following security groups instead of using the default security group:

- **WebServerSG**: Specify this security group when you launch web servers in the public subnet.
- **DBServerSG**: Specify this security group when you launch database servers in the VPN-only subnet.

The instances assigned to a security group can be in different subnets. However, in this scenario, each security group corresponds to the type of role an instance plays, and each role requires the instance to be in a particular subnet. Therefore, in this scenario, all instances assigned to a security group are in the same subnet.

The following table describes the recommended rules for the WebServerSG security group, which allow the web servers to receive Internet traffic, as well as SSH and RDP traffic from your network. The web servers can also initiate read and write requests to the database servers in the VPN-only subnet, and send traffic to the Internet; for example, to get software updates. Because the web server doesn't initiate any other outbound communication, the default outbound rule is removed.

Note
The group includes both SSH and RDP access, and both Microsoft SQL Server and MySQL access. For your

situation, you might only need rules for Linux (SSH and MySQL) or Windows (RDP and Microsoft SQL Server).

WebServerSG: Recommended Rules

Inbound
Source
0.0.0.0/0
0.0.0.0/0
Your network's public IP address range
Your network's public IP address range
Outbound
The ID of your DBServerSG security group
The ID of your DBServerSG security group
0.0.0.0/0
0.0.0.0/0

The following table describes the recommended rules for the DBServerSG security group, which allow Microsoft SQL Server and MySQL read and write requests from the web servers and SSH and RDP traffic from your network. The database servers can also initiate traffic bound for the Internet (your route table sends that traffic over the virtual private gateway).

DBServerSG: Recommended Rules

Inbound
Source
The ID of your WebServerSG security group
The ID of your WebServerSG security group
Your network's IPv4 address range
Your network's IPv4 address range
Outbound
Destination
0.0.0.0/0
0.0.0.0/0

(Optional) The default security group for a VPC has rules that automatically allow assigned instances to communicate with each other. To allow that type of communication for a custom security group, you must add the following rules:

Inbound
Source
The ID of the security group
Outbound
Destination
The ID of the security group

Security for IPv6

If you associate an IPv6 CIDR block with your VPC and subnets, you must add separate rules to your WebServerSG and DBServerSG security groups to control inbound and outbound IPv6 traffic for your instances. In this scenario, the web servers will be able to receive all Internet traffic over IPv6, and SSH or RDP traffic from your local network over IPv6. They can also initiate outbound IPv6 traffic to the Internet. The database servers cannot initiate outbound IPv6 traffic to the Internet, so they do not require any additional security group rules.

The following are the IPv6-specific rules for the WebServerSG security group (which are in addition to the rules listed above).

Inbound			
Source			
::/0			
::/0			
IPv6 address range of your network			
IPv6 address range of your network			
Outbound			
Destination			
::/0			
::/0			

Implementing Scenario 3

To implement scenario 3, get information about your customer gateway, and create the VPC using the VPC wizard. The VPC wizard creates a VPN connection for you with a customer gateway and virtual private gateway.

These procedures include optional steps for enabling and configuring IPv6 communication for your VPC. You do not have to perform these steps if you do not want to use IPv6 in your VPC.

To prepare your customer gateway

1. Determine the device you'll use as your customer gateway. For more information about the devices that we've tested, see Amazon Virtual Private Cloud FAQs. For more information about the requirements for your customer gateway, see the Amazon VPC Network Administrator Guide.

2. Obtain the Internet-routable IP address for the customer gateway's external interface. The address must be static and may be behind a device performing network address translation (NAT).

3. If you want to create a statically-routed VPN connection, get the list of internal IP ranges (in CIDR notation) that should be advertised across the VPN connection to the virtual private gateway. For more information, see VPN Routing Options.

To create a VPC using the VPC wizard

1. Open the Amazon VPC console at https://console.aws.amazon.com/vpc/.

2. On the dashboard, choose **Start VPC Wizard**.

3. Select the third option, **VPC with Public and Private Subnets and Hardware VPN Access**, and then choose **Select**.

4. For **VPC name**, **Public subnet name** and **Private subnet name**, you can name your VPC and subnets to help you identify them later in the console. You can specify your own IPv4 CIDR block range for the VPC and subnets, or you can leave the default values.

5. (Optional, IPv6-only) For **IPv6 CIDR block**, choose **Amazon-provided IPv6 CIDR block**. For **Public subnet's IPv6 CIDR**, choose **Specify a custom IPv6 CIDR** and specify the hexadecimal pair value for your subnet, or leave the default value. For **Private subnet's IPv6 CIDR**, choose **Specify a custom IPv6 CIDR**. Specify the hexadecimal pair value for the IPv6 subnet or leave the default value.

6. Choose **Next**.

7. On the **Configure your VPN** page, do the following, and then choose **Create VPC**:

   - In **Customer Gateway IP**, specify the public IP address of your VPN router.

   - Optionally specify a name for your customer gateway and VPN connection.

- In **Routing Type**, select one of the routing options as follows:
  - If your VPN router supports Border Gateway Protocol (BGP), select **Dynamic (requires BGP)**.
  - If your VPN router does not support BGP, choose **Static**. In **IP Prefix**, add each IP range for your network in CIDR notation.

  For more information, see VPN Routing Options.

8. When the wizard is done, choose **VPN Connections** in the navigation pane. Select the VPN connection that the wizard created, and choose **Download Configuration**. In the dialog box, select the vendor for your customer gateway, the platform, and the software version, and then choose **Yes, Download**.

9. Save the text file containing the VPN configuration and give it to the network administrator along with this guide: Amazon VPC Network Administrator Guide. The VPN won't work until the network administrator configures the customer gateway.

Create the WebServerSG and DBServerSG security groups. These security groups will reference each other, therefore you must create them before you add rules to them.

To create the WebServerSG and DBServerSG security groups

1. Open the Amazon VPC console at https://console.aws.amazon.com/vpc/.

2. In the navigation pane, choose **Security Groups**.

3. Choose **Create Security Group**.

4. Provide a name and description for the security group. In this topic, the name `WebServerSG` is used as an example. Select the ID of your VPC from the **VPC** list, and then choose **Yes, Create**.

5. Choose **Create Security Group** again.

6. Provide a name and description for the security group. In this topic, the name `DBServerSG` is used as an example. Select the ID of your VPC from the **VPC** list, and then choose **Yes, Create**.

To add rules to the WebServerSG security group

1. Select the WebServerSG security group that you created. The details pane displays the details for the security group, plus tabs for working with its inbound and outbound rules.

2. On the **Inbound Rules** tab, choose **Edit** and add rules for inbound traffic as follows:

   1. Select **HTTP** from the **Type** list, and enter 0.0.0.0/0 in the **Source** field.

   2. Choose **Add another rule**, then select **HTTPS** from the **Type** list, and enter 0.0.0.0/0 in the **Source** field.

   3. Choose **Add another rule**, then select **SSH** from the **Type** list. Enter your network's public IP address range in the **Source** field.

   4. Choose **Add another rule**, then select **RDP** from the **Type** list. Enter your network's public IP address range in the **Source** field.

   5. (Optional, IPv6-only) Choose **Add another rule**, **Type**, **HTTP**. For **Source**, enter ::/0.

   6. (Optional, IPv6-only) Choose **Add another rule**, **Type**, **HTTPS**. For **Source**, enter ::/0.

   7. (Optional, IPv6-only) Choose **Add another rule**, **Type**, **SSH** (for Linux) or **RDP** (for Windows). For **Source**, enter your network's IPv6 address range.

   8. Choose **Save**.

3. On the **Outbound Rules** tab, choose **Edit** and add rules for outbound traffic as follows:

   1. Locate the default rule that enables all outbound traffic, and then choose **Remove**.

2. Select **MS SQL** from the **Type** list. In the **Destination** field, specify the ID of the DBServerSG security group.

3. Choose **Add another rule**, then select **MySQL** from the **Type** list. In the **Destination** field, specify the ID of the DBServerSG security group.

4. Choose **Add another rule**, then select **HTTPS** from the **Type** list. In the **Destination** field, enter 0.0.0.0/0.

5. Choose **Add another rule**, then select **HTTP** from the **Type** list. In the **Destination** field, enter 0.0.0.0/0.

6. Choose **Save**.

To add the recommended rules to the DBServerSG security group

1. Select the DBServerSG security group that you created. The details pane displays the details for the security group, plus tabs for working with its inbound and outbound rules.

2. On the **Inbound Rules** tab, choose **Edit** and add rules for inbound traffic as follows:

    1. Select **SSH** from the **Type** list, and enter the IP address range of your network in the **Source** field.

    2. Choose **Add another rule**, then select **RDP** from the **Type** list, and enter the IP address range of your network in the **Source** field.

    3. Choose **Add another rule**, then select **MS SQL** from the **Type** list. Specify the ID of your WebServerSG security group in the **Source** field.

    4. Choose **Add another rule**, then select **MYSQL** from the **Type** list. Specify the ID of your WebServerSG security group in the **Source** field.

    5. Choose **Save**.

3. On the **Outbound Rules** tab, choose **Edit** and add rules for outbound traffic as follows:

    1. Locate the default rule that enables all outbound traffic, and then choose **Remove**.

    2. Select **HTTP** from the **Type** list. In the **Destination** field, enter 0.0.0.0/0.

    3. Choose **Add another rule**, then select **HTTPS** from the **Type** list. In the **Destination** field, enter 0.0.0.0/0.

    4. Choose **Save**.

After your network administrator configures your customer gateway, you can launch instances into your VPC.

To launch an instance (web server or database server)

1. Open the Amazon EC2 console at https://console.aws.amazon.com/ec2/.

2. Choose **Launch Instance** on the dashboard.

3. Follow the directions in the wizard. Choose an AMI, choose an instance type, and then choose **Next: Configure Instance Details**. **Note**
   If you intend to use your instance for IPv6 communication, you must choose a supported instance type; for example, T2. For more information, see Amazon EC2 Instance Types.

4. On the **Configure Instance Details** page, select the VPC that you created earlier from the **Network** list, and then select a subnet. For example, launch a web server into the public subnet and the database server into the private subnet.

5. (Optional) By default, instances launched into a nondefault VPC are not assigned a public IPv4 address. To be able to connect to your instance in the public subnet, you can assign a public IPv4 address now, or allocate an Elastic IP address and assign it to your instance after it's launched. To assign a public IP address now, ensure that you select **Enable** from the **Auto-assign Public IP** list. You do not need to

assign a public IP address to an instance in the private subnet. **Note**
You can only use the auto-assign public IP address feature with a single, new network interface with the device index of eth0. For more information, see Assigning a Public IPv4 Address During Instance Launch.

6. (Optional, IPv6-only) You can auto-assign an IPv6 address to your instance from the subnet range. For **Auto-assign IPv6 IP**, choose **Enable**.

7. On the next two pages of the wizard, you can configure storage for your instance, and add tags. On the **Configure Security Group** page, select the **Select an existing security group** option, and select one of the security groups that you created (**WebServerSG** for a web server instance or **DBServerSG** for a database server instance). Choose **Review and Launch**.

8. Review the settings that you've chosen. Make any changes that you need, and then choose **Launch** to choose a key pair and launch your instance.

For the instances running in the VPN-only subnet, you can test their connectivity by pinging them from your network. For more information, see Testing the VPN Connection.

If you did not assign a public IPv4 address to your instance in the public subnet in step 5, you will not be able to connect to it. Before you can access an instance in your public subnet, you must assign it an Elastic IP address.

To allocate an Elastic IP address and assign it to an instance using the console

1. Open the Amazon VPC console at https://console.aws.amazon.com/vpc/.

2. In the navigation pane, choose **Elastic IPs**.

3. Choose **Allocate new address**.

4. Choose **Allocate**. **Note**
If your account supports EC2-Classic, first choose **VPC**.

5. Select the Elastic IP address from the list, and choose **Actions**, **Associate address**.

6. Select the network interface or instance. Select the address to associate the Elastic IP address with from the corresponding **Private IP** list, and then choose **Associate**.

In scenario 3, you need a DNS server that enables your public subnet to communicate with servers on the Internet, and you need another DNS server that enables your VPN-only subnet to communicate with servers in your network.

Your VPC automatically has a set of DHCP options with domain-name-servers=AmazonProvidedDNS. This is a DNS server that Amazon provides to enable any public subnets in your VPC to communicate with the Internet over an Internet gateway. You must provide your own DNS server and add it to the list of DNS servers your VPC uses. Sets of DHCP options aren't modifiable, so you must create a set of DHCP options that includes both your DNS server and the Amazon DNS server, and update the VPC to use the new set of DHCP options.

To update the DHCP options

1. Open the Amazon VPC console at https://console.aws.amazon.com/vpc/.

2. In the navigation pane, choose **DHCP Options Sets**.

3. Choose **Create DHCP options set**.

4. In the **Create DHCP options set** dialog box, in the **Domain name servers** box, specify the address of the Amazon DNS server (AmazonProvidedDNS) and the address of your DNS server (for example,`192.0.2.1`), separated by a comma, and then choose **Yes, Create**.

5. In the navigation pane, choose **Your VPCs**.

6. Select the VPC, and then choose **Actions**, **Edit DHCP Options Set**.

7. Select the ID of the new set of options from the **DHCP options set** list and then choose **Save**.

8. (Optional) The VPC now uses this new set of DHCP options and therefore has access to both DNS servers. If you want, you can delete the original set of options that the VPC used.

You can now connect to your instances in the VPC. For information about how to connect to a Linux instance, see Connect to Your Linux Instance in the *Amazon EC2 User Guide for Linux Instances*. For information about how to connect to a Windows instance, see Connect to Your Windows Instance in the *Amazon EC2 User Guide for Windows Instances*.

Scenario 4: VPC with a Private Subnet Only and AWS Managed VPN Access

The configuration for this scenario includes a virtual private cloud (VPC) with a single private subnet, and a virtual private gateway to enable communication with your own network over an IPsec VPN tunnel. There is no Internet gateway to enable communication over the Internet. We recommend this scenario if you want to extend your network into the cloud using Amazon's infrastructure without exposing your network to the Internet.

This topic assumes that you'll use the VPC wizard in the Amazon VPC console to create the VPC and the VPN connection.

This scenario can also be optionally configured for IPv6—you can use the VPC wizard to create a VPC and subnet with associated IPv6 CIDR blocks. Instances launched into the subnet can receive IPv6 addresses. Currently, we do not support IPv6 communication over a VPN connection; however, instances in the VPC can communicate with each other via IPv6. For more information about IPv4 and IPv6 addressing, see IP Addressing in Your VPC.

Topics

- Overview
- Routing
- Security
- Implementing Scenario 4

Overview

The following diagram shows the key components of the configuration for this scenario.

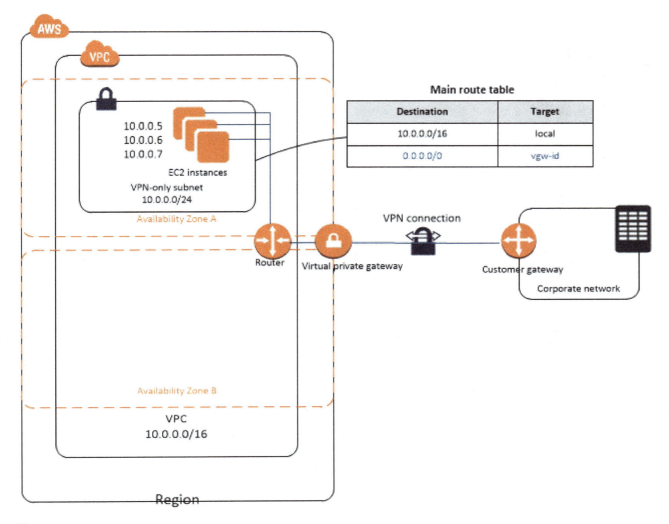

Main route table

Destination	Target
10.0.0.0/16	local
0.0.0.0/0	vgw-id

Important

For this scenario, the *Amazon VPC Network Administrator Guide* describes what your network administrator needs to do to configure the Amazon VPC customer gateway on your side of the VPN connection.

The configuration for this scenario includes the following:

- A virtual private cloud (VPC) with a size /16 CIDR (example: 10.0.0.0/16). This provides 65,536 private IP addresses.
- A VPN-only subnet with a size /24 CIDR (example: 10.0.0.0/24). This provides 256 private IP addresses.
- A VPN connection between your VPC and your network. The VPN connection consists of a virtual private gateway located on the Amazon side of the VPN connection and a customer gateway located on your side of the VPN connection.
- Instances with private IP addresses in the subnet range (examples: 10.0.0.5, 10.0.0.6, and 10.0.0.7), which enables the instances to communicate with each other and other instances in the VPC.
- A custom route table associated with the subnet. The route table contains a route that enables instances in the subnet to communicate with other instances in the VPC, and a route that enables instances in the subnet to communicate directly with your network.

For more information about subnets, see VPCs and Subnets and IP Addressing in Your VPC. For more information about your VPN connection, see AWS Managed VPN Connections. For more information about configuring a customer gateway, see the * Amazon VPC Network Administrator Guide*.

71

Overview for IPv6

You can optionally enable IPv6 for this scenario. In addition to the components listed above, the configuration includes the following:

- A size /56 IPv6 CIDR block associated with the VPC (example: 2001:db81a00::/56). AWS automatically assigns the CIDR; you cannot choose the range yourself.
- A size /64 IPv6 CIDR block associated with the VPN-only subnet (example: 2001:db81a00::/64). You can choose the range for your subnet from the range allocated to the VPC. You cannot choose the size of the IPv6 CIDR.
- IPv6 addresses assigned to the instances from the subnet range (example: 2001:db81a00::1a).
- A route table entry in the custom route table that enable instances in the private subnet to use IPv6 to communicate with each other.

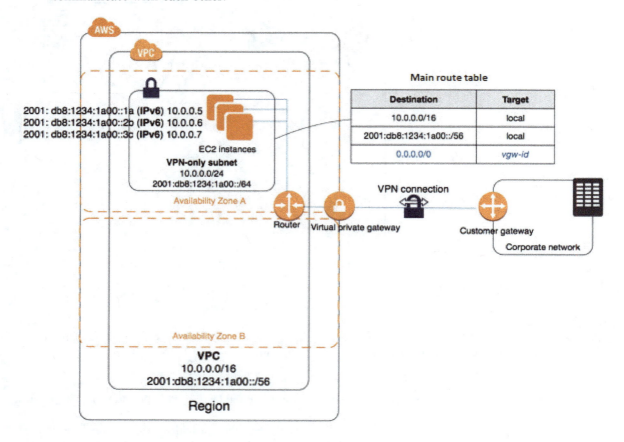

Routing

Your VPC has an implied router (shown in the configuration diagram for this scenario). In this scenario, the VPC wizard creates a route table that routes all traffic destined for an address outside the VPC to the VPN connection, and associates the route table with the subnet.

The following describes the route table for this scenario. The first entry is the default entry for local routing in the VPC; this entry enables the instances in this VPC to communicate with each other. The second entry routes all other subnet traffic to the virtual private gateway (for example, vgw-1a2b3c4d).

Destination	Target
10.0.0.0/16	local

Destination	Target
0.0.0.0/0	*vgw-id*

The VPN connection is configured either as a statically-routed VPN connection or as a dynamically routed VPN connection (using BGP). If you select static routing, you'll be prompted to manually enter the IP prefix for your network when you create the VPN connection. If you select dynamic routing, the IP prefix is advertised automatically to your VPC through BGP.

The instances in your VPC can't reach the Internet directly; any Internet-bound traffic must first traverse the virtual private gateway to your network, where the traffic is then subject to your firewall and corporate security policies. If the instances send any AWS-bound traffic (for example, requests to Amazon S3 or Amazon EC2), the requests must go over the virtual private gateway to your network and then to the Internet before reaching AWS. Currently, we do not support IPv6 for VPN connections.

Routing for IPv6

If you associate an IPv6 CIDR block with your VPC and subnets, your route table includes separate routes for IPv6 traffic. The following describes the custom route table for this scenario. The second entry is the default route that's automatically added for local routing in the VPC over IPv6.

Destination	Target
10.0.0.0/16	local
2001:db81a00::/56	local
0.0.0.0/0	*vgw-id*

Security

AWS provides two features that you can use to increase security in your VPC: *security groups* and *network ACLs*. Security groups control inbound and outbound traffic for your instances, and network ACLs control inbound and outbound traffic for your subnets. In most cases, security groups can meet your needs; however, you can also use network ACLs if you want an additional layer of security for your VPC. For more information, see Security.

For scenario 4, you'll use the default security group for your VPC but not a network ACL. If you'd like to use a network ACL, see Recommended Rules for Scenario 4.

Your VPC comes with a default security group whose initial settings deny all inbound traffic, allow all outbound traffic, and allow all traffic between the instances assigned to the security group. For this scenario, we recommend that you add inbound rules to the default security group to allow SSH traffic (Linux) and Remote Desktop traffic (Windows) from your network.

Important
The default security group automatically allows assigned instances to communicate with each other, so you don't have to add a rule to allow this. If you use a different security group, you must add a rule to allow this.

The following table describes the inbound rules that you should add to the default security group for your VPC.

Default Security Group: Recommended Rules

Inbound
Source
Private IPv4 address range of your network
Private IPv4 address range of your network

Security for IPv6

If you associate an IPv6 CIDR block with your VPC and subnets, you must add separate rules to your security group to control inbound and outbound IPv6 traffic for your instances. In this scenario, the database servers cannot be reached over the VPN connection using IPv6; therefore, no additional security group rules are required.

Implementing Scenario 4

To implement scenario 4, get information about your customer gateway, and create the VPC using the VPC wizard, The VPC wizard creates a VPN connection for you with a customer gateway and virtual private gateway.

To prepare your customer gateway

1. Determine the device you'll use as your customer gateway. For information about the devices that we've tested, see Amazon Virtual Private Cloud FAQs. For more information about the requirements for your customer gateway, see the *Amazon VPC Network Administrator Guide.*

2. Obtain the Internet-routable IP address for the customer gateway's external interface. The address must be static and may be behind a device performing network address translation (NAT).

3. If you want to create a statically-routed VPN connection, get the list of internal IP ranges (in CIDR notation) that should be advertised across the VPN connection to the virtual private gateway. For more information, see VPN Routing Options.

Use the VPC wizard to create your VPC and a VPN connection.

To create a VPC using the VPC wizard

1. Open the Amazon VPC console at https://console.aws.amazon.com/vpc/.

2. On the dashboard, choose **Start VPC Wizard**.

3. Select the fourth option, **VPC with a Private Subnet Only and Hardware VPN Access**, and then choose **Select**.

4. On the first page of the wizard, confirm the details for your VPC and private subnet. Naming your VPC and subnet helps you identify them later in the console.

5. (Optional, IPv6-only) For **IPv6 CIDR block**, choose **Amazon-provided IPv6 CIDR block**. For **Private subnet's IPv6 CIDR**, choose **Specify a custom IPv6 CIDR**. Specify the hexadecimal pair value for the IPv6 subnet or leave the default value (00).

6. Choose **Next**.

7. On the **Configure your VPN** page, do the following, and then choose **Create VPC**:

   - In **Customer Gateway IP**, specify the public IP address of your VPN router.

   - Optionally specify a name for your customer gateway and VPN connection.

   - In **Routing Type**, select one of the routing options as follows:

     - If your VPN router supports Border Gateway Protocol (BGP), select **Dynamic (requires BGP)**.
     - If your VPN router does not support BGP, choose **Static**. In **IP Prefix**, add each IP range for your network in CIDR notation.

   For more information, see VPN Routing Options.

8. When the wizard is done, choose **VPN Connections** in the navigation pane. Select the VPN connection that the wizard created, and choose **Download Configuration**. In the dialog box, select the vendor for the customer gateway, the platform, and the software version, and then choose **Yes, Download**.

9. Save the text file containing the VPN configuration and give it to the network administrator along with this guide: Amazon VPC Network Administrator Guide. The VPN won't work until the network administrator configures the customer gateway.

For this scenario, you need to update the default security group with new inbound rules that allow SSH and Remote Desktop (RDP) access from your network. If you don't want instances to initiate outbound communication, you can also remove the default outbound rule.

To update the rules for the default security group

1. Open the Amazon VPC console at https://console.aws.amazon.com/vpc/.

2. Choose **Security Groups** in the navigation pane, and then select the default security group for the VPC. The details pane displays the details for the security group, plus tabs for working with its inbound and outbound rules.

3. On the **Inbound Rules** tab, choose **Edit** and add rules for inbound traffic as follows:

   1. Select **SSH** from the **Type** list, and enter your network's private IP address range in the **Source** field; for example, `172.0.0.0/8`.

   2. Choose **Add another rule**, then select **RDP** from the **Type** list, and enter your network's private IP address range in the **Source** field.

   3. Choose **Save**.

4. (Optional) On the **Outbound Rules** tab, choose **Edit**, locate the default rule that enables all outbound traffic, choose **Remove**, and then choose **Save**.

After your network administrator configures your customer gateway, you can launch instances into your VPC. If you're already familiar with launching instances outside a VPC, then you already know most of what you need to know to launch an instance into a VPC.

To launch an instance

1. Open the Amazon EC2 console at https://console.aws.amazon.com/ec2/.

2. Choose **Launch Instance** on the dashboard.

3. Follow the directions in the wizard. Choose an AMI, choose an instance type, and then choose **Next: Configure Instance Details**. **Note**
   If you intend to use your instance for IPv6 communication, you must choose a supported instance type; for example, T2. For more information, see Amazon EC2 Instance Types.

4. On the **Configure Instance Details** page, select the VPC that you created earlier from the **Network** list, and then select the subnet. Choose **Next: Add Storage**.

5. On the next two pages of the wizard, you can configure storage for your instance, and add tags. On the **Configure Security Group** page, select the **Select an existing security group** option, and select the default security group. Choose **Review and Launch**.

6. Review the settings that you've chosen. Make any changes that you need, and then choose **Launch** to choose a keypair and launch your instance.

In scenario 4, you need a DNS server that enables your VPN-only subnet to communicate with servers in your network. You must create a new set of DHCP options that includes your DNS server and then configure the VPC to use that set of options.

Note
Your VPC automatically has a set of DHCP options with domain-name-servers=AmazonProvidedDNS. This is a DNS server that Amazon provides to enable any public subnets in your VPC to communicate with the Internet over an Internet gateway. Scenario 4 doesn't have any public subnets, so you don't need this set of DHCP options.

To update the DHCP options

1. Open the Amazon VPC console at https://console.aws.amazon.com/vpc/.

2. In the navigation pane, choose **DHCP Options Sets**.

3. Choose **Create DHCP Options Set**.

4. In the **Create DHCP Options Set** dialog box, in the **Domain name servers** box, enter the address of your DNS server, and then choose **Yes, Create**. In this example, your DNS server is 192.0.2.1.

5. In the navigation pane, choose **Your VPCs**.

6. Select the VPC, and then choose **Edit** in the **Summary** tab.

7. Select the ID of the new set of options from the **DHCP options set** list and then choose **Save**.

8. (Optional) The VPC now uses this new set of DHCP options and therefore uses your DNS server. If you want, you can delete the original set of options that the VPC used.

You can now use SSH or RDP to connect to your instance in the VPC. For information about how to connect to a Linux instance, see Connect to Your Linux Instance in the *Amazon EC2 User Guide for Linux Instances*. For information about how to connect to a Windows instance, see Connect to Your Windows Instance in the *Amazon EC2 User Guide for Windows Instances*.

Example: Create an IPv4 VPC and Subnets Using the AWS CLI

The following example uses AWS CLI commands to create a nondefault VPC with an IPv4 CIDR block, and a public and private subnet in the VPC. After you've created the VPC and subnets, you can launch an instance in the public subnet and connect to it. To begin, you must first install and configure the AWS CLI. For more information, see Getting Set Up with the AWS Command Line Interface.

Topics

- Step 1: Create a VPC and Subnets
- Step 2: Make Your Subnet Public
- Step 3: Launch an Instance into Your Subnet
- Step 4: Clean Up

Step 1: Create a VPC and Subnets

The first step is to create a VPC and two subnets. This example uses the CIDR block 10.0.0.0/16 for the VPC, but you can choose a different CIDR block. For more information, see VPC and Subnet Sizing.

To create a VPC and subnets using the AWS CLI

1. Create a VPC with a 10.0.0.0/16 CIDR block.

```
1 aws ec2 create-vpc --cidr-block 10.0.0.0/16
```

In the output that's returned, take note of the VPC ID.

```
1 {
2    "Vpc": {
3        "VpcId": "vpc-2f09a348",
4        ...
5    }
6 }
```

2. Using the VPC ID from the previous step, create a subnet with a 10.0.1.0/24 CIDR block.

```
1 aws ec2 create-subnet --vpc-id vpc-2f09a348 --cidr-block 10.0.1.0/24
```

3. Create a second subnet in your VPC with a 10.0.0.0/24 CIDR block.

```
1 aws ec2 create-subnet --vpc-id vpc-2f09a348 --cidr-block 10.0.0.0/24
```

Step 2: Make Your Subnet Public

After you've created the VPC and subnets, you can make one of the subnets a public subnet by attaching an Internet gateway to your VPC, creating a custom route table, and configuring routing for the subnet to the Internet gateway.

To make your subnet a public subnet

1. Create an Internet gateway.

```
1 aws ec2 create-internet-gateway
```

In the output that's returned, take note of the Internet gateway ID.

```
1  {
2      "InternetGateway": {
3          ...
4          "InternetGatewayId": "igw-1ff7a07b",
5          ...
6      }
7  }
```

2. Using the ID from the previous step, attach the Internet gateway to your VPC.

```
1  aws ec2 attach-internet-gateway --vpc-id vpc-2f09a348 --internet-gateway-id igw-1ff7a07b
```

3. Create a custom route table for your VPC.

```
1  aws ec2 create-route-table --vpc-id vpc-2f09a348
```

In the output that's returned, take note of the route table ID.

```
1  {
2      "RouteTable": {
3          ...
4          "RouteTableId": "rtb-c1c8faa6",
5          ...
6      }
7  }
```

4. Create a route in the route table that points all traffic (0.0.0.0/0) to the Internet gateway.

```
1  aws ec2 create-route --route-table-id rtb-c1c8faa6 --destination-cidr-block 0.0.0.0/0 --
       gateway-id igw-1ff7a07b
```

5. To confirm that your route has been created and is active, you can describe the route table and view the
   results.

```
1  aws ec2 describe-route-tables --route-table-id rtb-c1c8faa6
```

```
1  {
2      "RouteTables": [
3          {
4              "Associations": [],
5              "RouteTableId": "rtb-c1c8faa6",
6              "VpcId": "vpc-2f09a348",
7              "PropagatingVgws": [],
8              "Tags": [],
9              "Routes": [
10                 {
11                     "GatewayId": "local",
12                     "DestinationCidrBlock": "10.0.0.0/16",
13                     "State": "active",
14                     "Origin": "CreateRouteTable"
15                 },
16                 {
17                     "GatewayId": "igw-1ff7a07b",
18                     "DestinationCidrBlock": "0.0.0.0/0",
19                     "State": "active",
20                     "Origin": "CreateRoute"
21                 }
```

```
22            ]
23         }
24      ]
25 }
```

6. The route table is currently not associated with any subnet. You need to associate it with a subnet in your VPC so that traffic from that subnet is routed to the Internet gateway. First, use the `describe-subnets` command to get your subnet IDs. You can use the `--filter` option to return the subnets for your new VPC only, and the `--query` option to return only the subnet IDs and their CIDR blocks.

```
1 aws ec2 describe-subnets --filters "Name=vpc-id,Values=vpc-2f09a348" --query 'Subnets[*].{
     ID:SubnetId,CIDR:CidrBlock}'
```

```
1 [
2    {
3        "CIDR": "10.0.1.0/24",
4        "ID": "subnet-b46032ec"
5    },
6    {
7        "CIDR": "10.0.0.0/24",
8        "ID": "subnet-a46032fc"
9    }
10 ]
```

7. You can choose which subnet to associate with the custom route table, for example, `subnet-b46032ec`. This subnet will be your public subnet.

```
1 aws ec2 associate-route-table  --subnet-id subnet-b46032ec --route-table-id rtb-c1c8faa6
```

8. You can optionally modify the public IP addressing behavior of your subnet so that an instance launched into the subnet automatically receives a public IP address. Otherwise, you should associate an Elastic IP address with your instance after launch so that it's reachable from the Internet.

```
1 aws ec2 modify-subnet-attribute --subnet-id subnet-b46032ec --map-public-ip-on-launch
```

Step 3: Launch an Instance into Your Subnet

To test that your subnet is public and that instances in the subnet are accessible via the Internet, launch an instance into your public subnet and connect to it. First, you must create a security group to associate with your instance, and a key pair with which you'll connect to your instance. For more information about security groups, see Security Groups for Your VPC. For more information about key pairs, see Amazon EC2 Key Pairs in the *Amazon EC2 User Guide for Linux Instances*.

To launch and connect to an instance in your public subnet

1. Create a key pair and use the `--query` option and the `--output` text option to pipe your private key directly into a file with the `.pem` extension.

```
1 aws ec2 create-key-pair --key-name MyKeyPair --query 'KeyMaterial' --output text >
     MyKeyPair.pem
```

In this example, you launch an Amazon Linux instance. If you use an SSH client on a Linux or Mac OS X operating system to connect to your instance, use the following command to set the permissions of your private key file so that only you can read it.

```
1 chmod 400 MyKeyPair.pem
```

2. Create a security group in your VPC, and add a rule that allows SSH access from anywhere.

```
1 aws ec2 create-security-group --group-name SSHAccess --description "Security group for SSH
    access" --vpc-id vpc-2f09a348
```

```
1 {
2     "GroupId": "sg-e1fb8c9a"
3 }
```

```
1 aws ec2 authorize-security-group-ingress --group-id sg-e1fb8c9a --protocol tcp --port 22 --
    cidr 0.0.0.0/0
```

Note

If you use 0.0.0.0/0, you enable all IPv4 addresses to access your instance using SSH. This is acceptable for this short exercise, but in production, authorize only a specific IP address or range of addresses.

1. Launch an instance into your public subnet, using the security group and key pair you've created. In the output, take note of the instance ID for your instance.

```
1 aws ec2 run-instances --image-id ami-a4827dc9 --count 1 --instance-type t2.micro --key-name
    MyKeyPair --security-group-ids sg-e1fb8c9a --subnet-id subnet-b46032ec
```

Note

In this example, the AMI is an Amazon Linux AMI in the US East (N. Virginia) region. If you're in a different region, you'll need the AMI ID for a suitable AMI in your region. For more information, see Finding a Linux AMI in the *Amazon EC2 User Guide for Linux Instances*.

1. Your instance must be in the **running** state in order to connect to it. Describe your instance and confirm its state, and take note of its public IP address.

```
1 aws ec2 describe-instances --instance-id i-0146854b7443af453
```

```
1  {
2      "Reservations": [
3          {
4              ...
5              "Instances": [
6                  {
7                      ...
8                      "State": {
9                          "Code": 16,
10                         "Name": "running"
11                     },
12                     ...
13                     "PublicIpAddress": "52.87.168.235",
14                     ...
15                 }
16             ]
17         }
18     ]
19 }
```

2. When your instance is in the running state, you can connect to it using an SSH client on a Linux or Mac OS X computer by using the following command:

```
1 ssh -i "MyKeyPair.pem" ec2-user@52.87.168.235
```

If you're connecting from a Windows computer, use the following instructions: Connecting to Your Linux Instance from Windows Using PuTTY.

Step 4: Clean Up

After you've verified that you can connect to your instance, you can terminate it if you no longer need it. To do this, use the terminate-instances command. To delete the other resources you've created in this example, use the following commands in their listed order:

1. Delete your security group:

```
1 aws ec2 delete-security-group --group-id sg-e1fb8c9a
```

2. Delete your subnets:

```
1 aws ec2 delete-subnet --subnet-id subnet-b46032ec
```

```
1 aws ec2 delete-subnet --subnet-id subnet-a46032fc
```

3. Delete your custom route table:

```
1 aws ec2 delete-route-table --route-table-id rtb-c1c8faa6
```

4. Detach your Internet gateway from your VPC:

```
1 aws ec2 detach-internet-gateway --internet-gateway-id igw-1ff7a07b --vpc-id vpc-2f09a348
```

5. Delete your Internet gateway:

```
1 aws ec2 delete-internet-gateway --internet-gateway-id igw-1ff7a07b
```

6. Delete your VPC:

```
1 aws ec2 delete-vpc --vpc-id vpc-2f09a348
```

Example: Create an IPv6 VPC and Subnets Using the AWS CLI

The following example uses AWS CLI commands to create a nondefault VPC with an IPv6 CIDR block, a public subnet, and a private subnet with outbound Internet access only. After you've created the VPC and subnets, you can launch an instance in the public subnet and connect to it. You can launch an instance in your private subnet and verify that it can connect to the Internet. To begin, you must first install and configure the AWS CLI. For more information, see Getting Set Up with the AWS Command Line Interface.

Topics

- Step 1: Create a VPC and Subnets
- Step 2: Configure a Public Subnet
- Step 3: Configure an Egress-Only Private Subnet
- Step 4: Modify the IPv6 Addressing Behavior of the Subnets
- Step 5: Launch an Instance into Your Public Subnet
- Step 6: Launch an Instance into Your Private Subnet
- Step 7: Clean Up

Step 1: Create a VPC and Subnets

The first step is to create a VPC and two subnets. This example uses the IPv4 CIDR block 10.0.0.0/16 for the VPC, but you can choose a different CIDR block. For more information, see VPC and Subnet Sizing.

To create a VPC and subnets using the AWS CLI

1. Create a VPC with a 10.0.0.0/16 CIDR block and associate an IPv6 CIDR block with the VPC.

```
1 aws ec2 create-vpc --cidr-block 10.0.0.0/16 --amazon-provided-ipv6-cidr-block
```

In the output that's returned, take note of the VPC ID.

```
1 {
2     "Vpc": {
3         "VpcId": "vpc-2f09a348",
4         ...
5 }
```

2. Describe your VPC to get the IPv6 CIDR block that's associated with the VPC.

```
1 aws ec2 describe-vpcs --vpc-id vpc-2f09a348
```

```
1 {
2     "Vpcs": [
3         {
4             ...
5             "Ipv6CidrBlockAssociationSet": [
6                 {
7                     "Ipv6CidrBlock": "2001:db8:1234:1a00::/56",
8                     "AssociationId": "vpc-cidr-assoc-17a5407e",
9                     "Ipv6CidrBlockState": {
10                         "State": "ASSOCIATED"
11                     }
12                 }
13             ],
14             ...
15 }
```

3. Create a subnet with a `10.0.0.0/24` IPv4 CIDR block and a `2001:db8:1234:1a00::/64` IPv6 CIDR block (from the ranges that were returned in the previous step).

```
1 aws ec2 create-subnet --vpc-id vpc-2f09a348 --cidr-block 10.0.0.0/24 --ipv6-cidr-block
    2001:db8:1234:1a00::/64
```

4. Create a second subnet in your VPC with a `10.0.1.0/24` IPv4 CIDR block and a `2001:db8:1234:1a01::/64` IPv6 CIDR block.

```
1 aws ec2 create-subnet --vpc-id vpc-2f09a348 --cidr-block 10.0.1.0/24 --ipv6-cidr-block
    2001:db8:1234:1a01::/64
```

Step 2: Configure a Public Subnet

After you've created the VPC and subnets, you can make one of the subnets a public subnet by attaching an Internet gateway to your VPC, creating a custom route table, and configuring routing for the subnet to the Internet gateway. In this example, a route table is created that routes all IPv4 traffic and IPv6 traffic to an Internet gateway.

To make your subnet a public subnet

1. Create an Internet gateway.

```
1 aws ec2 create-internet-gateway
```

In the output that's returned, take note of the Internet gateway ID.

```
1 {
2     "InternetGateway": {
3         ...
4         "InternetGatewayId": "igw-1ff7a07b",
5         ...
6     }
7 }
```

2. Using the ID from the previous step, attach the Internet gateway to your VPC.

```
1 aws ec2 attach-internet-gateway --vpc-id vpc-2f09a348 --internet-gateway-id igw-1ff7a07b
```

3. Create a custom route table for your VPC.

```
1 aws ec2 create-route-table --vpc-id vpc-2f09a348
```

In the output that's returned, take note of the route table ID.

```
1 {
2     "RouteTable": {
3         ...
4         "RouteTableId": "rtb-c1c8faa6",
5         ...
6     }
7 }
```

4. Create a route in the route table that points all IPv6 traffic (`::/0`) to the Internet gateway.

```
1 aws ec2 create-route --route-table-id rtb-c1c8faa6 --destination-ipv6-cidr-block ::/0 --
    gateway-id igw-1ff7a07b
```

Note

If you intend to use your public subnet for IPv4 traffic too, you need to add another route for 0.0.0.0/0 traffic that points to the Internet gateway.

1. To confirm that your route has been created and is active, you can describe the route table and view the results.

```
aws ec2 describe-route-tables --route-table-id rtb-c1c8faa6
```

```
{
    "RouteTables": [
        {
            "Associations": [],
            "RouteTableId": "rtb-c1c8faa6",
            "VpcId": "vpc-2f09a348",
            "PropagatingVgws": [],
            "Tags": [],
            "Routes": [
                {
                    "GatewayId": "local",
                    "DestinationCidrBlock": "10.0.0.0/16",
                    "State": "active",
                    "Origin": "CreateRouteTable"
                },
                {
                    "GatewayId": "local",
                    "Origin": "CreateRouteTable",
                    "State": "active",
                    "DestinationIpv6CidrBlock": "2001:db8:1234:1a00::/56"
                },
                {
                    "GatewayId": "igw-1ff7a07b",
                    "Origin": "CreateRoute",
                    "State": "active",
                    "DestinationIpv6CidrBlock": "::/0"
                }
            ]
        }
    ]
}
```

2. The route table is not currently associated with any subnet. Associate it with a subnet in your VPC so that traffic from that subnet is routed to the Internet gateway. First, describe your subnets to get their IDs. You can use the --filter option to return the subnets for your new VPC only, and the --query option to return only the subnet IDs and their IPv4 and IPv6 CIDR blocks.

```
aws ec2 describe-subnets --filters "Name=vpc-id,Values=vpc-2f09a348" --query 'Subnets[*].{
    ID:SubnetId,IPv4CIDR:CidrBlock,IPv6CIDR:Ipv6CidrBlockAssociationSet[*].Ipv6CidrBlock}'
```

```
[
    {
        "IPv6CIDR": [
            "2001:db8:1234:1a00::/64"
        ],
        "ID": "subnet-b46032ec",
        "IPv4CIDR": "10.0.0.0/24"
```

```
 8        },
 9        {
10            "IPv6CIDR": [
11                "2001:db8:1234:1a01::/64"
12            ],
13            "ID": "subnet-a46032fc",
14            "IPv4CIDR": "10.0.1.0/24"
15        }
16 ]
```

3. You can choose which subnet to associate with the custom route table, for example, subnet-b46032ec. This subnet will be your public subnet.

```
1 aws ec2 associate-route-table  --subnet-id subnet-b46032ec --route-table-id rtb-c1c8faa6
```

Step 3: Configure an Egress-Only Private Subnet

You can configure the second subnet in your VPC to be an IPv6 egress-only private subnet. Instances that are launched in this subnet are able to access the Internet over IPv6 (for example, to get software updates) through an egress-only Internet gateway, but hosts on the Internet cannot reach your instances.

To make your subnet an egress-only private subnet

1. Create an egress-only Internet gateway for your VPC. In the output that's returned, take note of the gateway ID.

```
1 aws ec2 create-egress-only-internet-gateway --vpc-id vpc-2f09a348
```

```
 1 {
 2     "EgressOnlyInternetGateway": {
 3         "EgressOnlyInternetGatewayId": "eigw-015e0e244e24dfe8a",
 4         "Attachments": [
 5             {
 6                 "State": "attached",
 7                 "VpcId": "vpc-2f09a348"
 8             }
 9         ]
10     }
11 }
```

2. Create a custom route table for your VPC. In the output that's returned, take note of the route table ID.

```
1 aws ec2 create-route-table --vpc-id vpc-2f09a348
```

3. Create a route in the route table that points all IPv6 traffic (::/0) to the egress-only Internet gateway.

```
1 aws ec2 create-route --route-table-id rtb-abc123ab --destination-ipv6-cidr-block ::/0 --
    egress-only-internet-gateway-id eigw-015e0e244e24dfe8a
```

4. Associate the route table with the second subnet in your VPC (you described the subnets in the previous section). This subnet will be your private subnet with egress-only IPv6 Internet access.

```
1 aws ec2 associate-route-table --subnet-id subnet-a46032fc --route-table-id rtb-abc123ab
```

Step 4: Modify the IPv6 Addressing Behavior of the Subnets

You can modify the IP addressing behavior of your subnets so that instances launched into the subnets automatically receive IPv6 addresses. When you launch an instance into the subnet, a single IPv6 address is assigned from the range of the subnet to the primary network interface (eth0) of the instance.

```
1 aws ec2 modify-subnet-attribute --subnet-id subnet-b46032ec --assign-ipv6-address-on-creation
```

```
1 aws ec2 modify-subnet-attribute --subnet-id subnet-a46032fc --assign-ipv6-address-on-creation
```

Step 5: Launch an Instance into Your Public Subnet

To test that your public subnet is public and that instances in the subnet are accessible from the Internet, launch an instance into your public subnet and connect to it. First, you must create a security group to associate with your instance, and a key pair with which you'll connect to your instance. For more information about security groups, see Security Groups for Your VPC. For more information about key pairs, see Amazon EC2 Key Pairs in the *Amazon EC2 User Guide for Linux Instances*.

To launch and connect to an instance in your public subnet

1. Create a key pair and use the --query option and the --output text option to pipe your private key directly into a file with the .pem extension.

```
1 aws ec2 create-key-pair --key-name MyKeyPair --query 'KeyMaterial' --output text >
  MyKeyPair.pem
```

In this example, launch an Amazon Linux instance. If you use an SSH client on a Linux or OS X operating system to connect to your instance, use the following command to set the permissions of your private key file so that only you can read it.

```
1 chmod 400 MyKeyPair.pem
```

2. Create a security group for your VPC, and add a rule that allows SSH access from any IPv6 address.

```
1 aws ec2 create-security-group --group-name SSHAccess --description "Security group for SSH
  access" --vpc-id vpc-2f09a348
```

```
1 {
2     "GroupId": "sg-e1fb8c9a"
3 }
```

```
1 aws ec2 authorize-security-group-ingress --group-id sg-e1fb8c9a --ip-permissions '[{"
  IpProtocol": "tcp", "FromPort": 22, "ToPort": 22, "Ipv6Ranges": [{"CidrIpv6":
  "::/0"}]}]'
```

Note
If you use ::/0, you enable all IPv6 addresses to access your instance using SSH. This is acceptable for this short exercise, but in production, authorize only a specific IP address or range of addresses to access your instance.

1. Launch an instance into your public subnet, using the security group and key pair that you've created. In the output, take note of the instance ID for your instance.

```
1 aws ec2 run-instances --image-id ami-a4827dc9 --count 1 --instance-type t2.micro --key-name
  MyKeyPair --security-group-ids sg-e1fb8c9a --subnet-id subnet-b46032ec
```

Note
In this example, the AMI is an Amazon Linux AMI in the US East (N. Virginia) region. If you're in a different region, you need the AMI ID for a suitable AMI in your region. For more information, see Finding a Linux AMI in the *Amazon EC2 User Guide for Linux Instances*.

86

1. Your instance must be in the **running** state in order to connect to it. Describe your instance and confirm its state, and take note of its IPv6 address.

```
1 aws ec2 describe-instances --instance-id i-0146854b7443af453
```

```
1  {
2      "Reservations": [
3          {
4              ...
5              "Instances": [
6                  {
7                      ...
8                      "State": {
9                          "Code": 16,
10                         "Name": "running"
11                     },
12                     ...
13                     "NetworkInterfaces": {
14                         "Ipv6Addresses": {
15                             "Ipv6Address": "2001:db8:1234:1a00::123"
16                         }
17                     ...
18                 }
19             ]
20         }
21     ]
22 }
```

2. When your instance is in the running state, you can connect to it using an SSH client on a Linux or OS X computer by using the following command. Your local computer must have an IPv6 address configured.

```
1 ssh -i "MyKeyPair.pem" ec2-user@2001:db8:1234:1a00::123
```

If you're connecting from a Windows computer, use the following instructions: Connecting to Your Linux Instance from Windows Using PuTTY.

Step 6: Launch an Instance into Your Private Subnet

To test that instances in your egress-only private subnet can access the Internet, launch an instance in your private subnet and connect to it using a bastion instance in your public subnet (you can use the instance you launched in the previous section). First, you must create a security group for the instance. The security group must have a rule that allows your bastion instance to connect using SSH, and a rule that allows the **ping6** command (ICMPv6 traffic) to verify that the instance is not accessible from the Internet.

1. Create a security group in your VPC, and add a rule that allows inbound SSH access from the IPv6 address of the instance in your public subnet, and a rule that allows all ICMPv6 traffic:

```
1 aws ec2 create-security-group --group-name SSHAccessRestricted --description "Security
    group for SSH access from bastion" --vpc-id vpc-2f09a348
```

```
1 {
2     "GroupId": "sg-aabb1122"
3 }
```

```
1 aws ec2 authorize-security-group-ingress --group-id sg-aabb1122 --ip-permissions '[{"
    IpProtocol": "tcp", "FromPort": 22, "ToPort": 22, "Ipv6Ranges": [{"CidrIpv6": "2001:db8
    :1234:1a00::123/128"}]}]'
```

```
1  aws ec2 authorize-security-group-ingress --group-id sg-aabb1122 --ip-permissions '[{"
       IpProtocol": "58", "FromPort": -1, "ToPort": -1, "Ipv6Ranges": [{"CidrIpv6":
       "::/0"}]}]'
```

2. Launch an instance into your private subnet, using the security group you've created and the same key pair you used to launch the instance in the public subnet.

```
1  aws ec2 run-instances --image-id ami-a4827dc9 --count 1 --instance-type t2.micro --key-name
       MyKeyPair --security-group-ids sg-aabb1122 --subnet-id subnet-a46032fc
```

Use the describe-instances command to verify that your instance is running, and to get its IPv6 address.

3. Configure SSH agent forwarding on your local machine, and then connect to your instance in the public subnet. For Linux, use the following commands:

```
1  ssh-add MyKeyPair.pem
```

```
1  ssh -A ec2-user@2001:db8:1234:1a00::123
```

For OS X, use the following commands:

```
1  ssh-add -K MyKeyPair.pem
```

```
1  ssh -A ec2-user@2001:db8:1234:1a00::123
```

For Windows, use the following instructions: To configure SSH agent forwarding for Windows (PuTTY). Connect to the instance in the public subnet by using its IPv6 address.

4. From your instance in the public subnet (the bastion instance), connect to your instance in the private subnet by using its IPv6 address:

```
1  ssh ec2-user@2001:db8:1234:1a01::456
```

5. From your private instance, test that you can connect to the Internet by running the ping6 command for a website that has ICMP enabled, for example:

```
1  ping6 -n ietf.org
```

```
1  PING ietf.org(2001:1900:3001:11::2c) 56 data bytes
2  64 bytes from 2001:1900:3001:11::2c: icmp_seq=1 ttl=46 time=73.9 ms
3  64 bytes from 2001:1900:3001:11::2c: icmp_seq=2 ttl=46 time=73.8 ms
4  64 bytes from 2001:1900:3001:11::2c: icmp_seq=3 ttl=46 time=73.9 ms
5  ...
```

6. To test that hosts on the Internet cannot reach your instance in the private subnet, use the ping6 command from a computer that's enabled for IPv6. You should get a timeout response. If you get a valid response, then your instance is accessible from the Internet—check the route table that's associated with your private subnet and verify that it does not have a route for IPv6 traffic to an Internet gateway.

```
1  ping6 2001:db8:1234:1a01::456
```

Step 7: Clean Up

After you've verified that you can connect to your instance in the public subnet and that your instance in the private subnet can access the Internet, you can terminate the instances if you no longer need them. To do this, use the terminate-instances command. To delete the other resources you've created in this example, use the following commands in their listed order:

1. Delete your security groups:

```
1 aws ec2 delete-security-group --group-id sg-e1fb8c9a
```

```
1 aws ec2 delete-security-group --group-id sg-aabb1122
```

2. Delete your subnets:

```
1 aws ec2 delete-subnet --subnet-id subnet-b46032ec
```

```
1 aws ec2 delete-subnet --subnet-id subnet-a46032fc
```

3. Delete your custom route tables:

```
1 aws ec2 delete-route-table --route-table-id rtb-c1c8faa6
```

```
1 aws ec2 delete-route-table --route-table-id rtb-abc123ab
```

4. Detach your Internet gateway from your VPC:

```
1 aws ec2 detach-internet-gateway --internet-gateway-id igw-1ff7a07b --vpc-id vpc-2f09a348
```

5. Delete your Internet gateway:

```
1 aws ec2 delete-internet-gateway --internet-gateway-id igw-1ff7a07b
```

6. Delete your egress-only Internet gateway:

```
1 aws ec2 delete-egress-only-internet-gateway  --egress-only-internet-gateway-id eigw-015
    e0e244e24dfe8a
```

7. Delete your VPC:

```
1 aws ec2 delete-vpc --vpc-id vpc-2f09a348
```

VPCs and Subnets

To get started with Amazon Virtual Private Cloud (Amazon VPC), you create a VPC and subnets. For a general overview of Amazon VPC, see What Is Amazon VPC?.

Topics

- VPC and Subnet Basics
- VPC and Subnet Sizing
- Subnet Routing
- Subnet Security
- Connections with Your Local Network and Other VPCs
- Working with VPCs and Subnets

VPC and Subnet Basics

A virtual private cloud (VPC) is a virtual network dedicated to your AWS account. It is logically isolated from other virtual networks in the AWS Cloud. You can launch your AWS resources, such as Amazon EC2 instances, into your VPC.

When you create a VPC, you must specify a range of IPv4 addresses for the VPC in the form of a Classless Inter-Domain Routing (CIDR) block; for example, 10.0.0.0/16. This is the primary CIDR block for your VPC. For more information about CIDR notation, see RFC 4632.

The following diagram shows a new VPC with an IPv4 CIDR block, and the main route table.

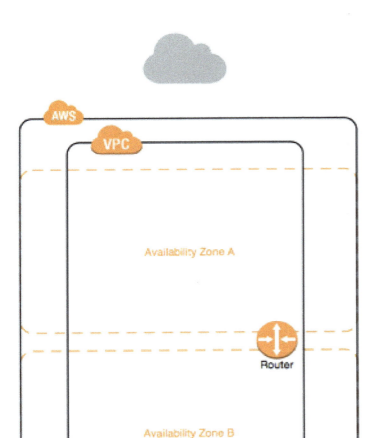

Main route table

Destination	Target
10.0.0.0/16	local

A VPC spans all the Availability Zones in the region. After creating a VPC, you can add one or more subnets in each Availability Zone. When you create a subnet, you specify the CIDR block for the subnet, which is a subset of the VPC CIDR block. Each subnet must reside entirely within one Availability Zone and cannot span zones. Availability Zones are distinct locations that are engineered to be isolated from failures in other Availability

Zones. By launching instances in separate Availability Zones, you can protect your applications from the failure of a single location. We assign a unique ID to each subnet.

You can also optionally assign an IPv6 CIDR block to your VPC, and assign IPv6 CIDR blocks to your subnets.

The following diagram shows a VPC that has been configured with subnets in multiple Availability Zones. 1A, 1B, 2A, and 3A are instances in your VPC. An IPv6 CIDR block is associated with the VPC, and an IPv6 CIDR block is associated with subnet 1. An internet gateway enables communication over the internet, and a virtual private network (VPN) connection enables communication with your corporate network.

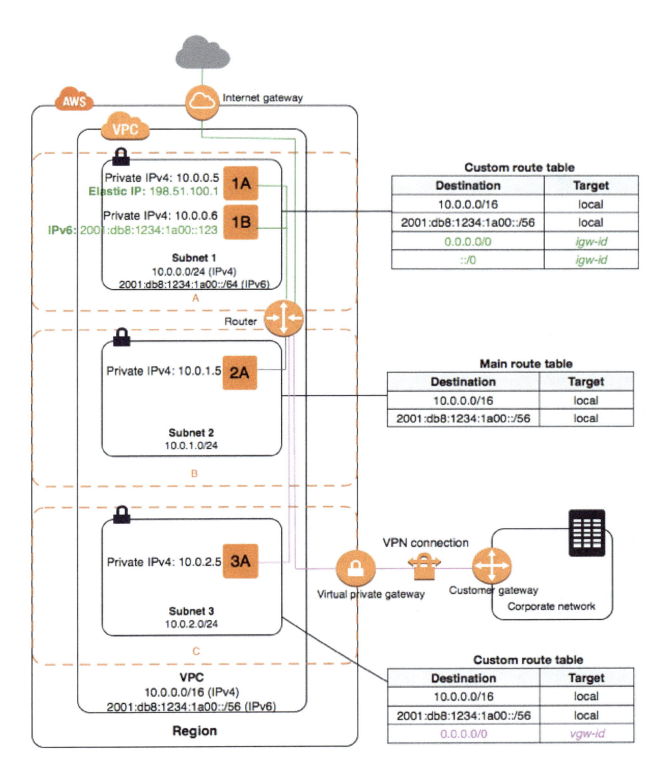

Custom route table

Destination	Target
10.0.0.0/16	local
2001:db8:1234:1a00::/56	local
0.0.0.0/0	*igw-id*
::/0	*igw-id*

Main route table

Destination	Target
10.0.0.0/16	local
2001:db8:1234:1a00::/56	local

Custom route table

Destination	Target
10.0.0.0/16	local
2001:db8:1234:1a00::/56	local
0.0.0.0/0	*vgw-id*

If a subnet's traffic is routed to an internet gateway, the subnet is known as a *public subnet*. In this diagram, subnet 1 is a public subnet. If you want your instance in a public subnet to communicate with the internet over IPv4, it must have a public IPv4 address or an Elastic IP address (IPv4). For more information about public IPv4 addresses, see Public IPv4 Addresses. If you want your instance in the public subnet to communicate with the internet over IPv6, it must have an IPv6 address.

If a subnet doesn't have a route to the internet gateway, the subnet is known as a *private subnet*. In this diagram, subnet 2 is a private subnet.

If a subnet doesn't have a route to the internet gateway, but has its traffic routed to a virtual private gateway for a VPN connection, the subnet is known as a *VPN-only subnet*. In this diagram, subnet 3 is a VPN-only subnet. Currently, we do not support IPv6 traffic over a VPN connection.

For more information, see Scenarios and Examples, Internet Gateways, or AWS Managed VPN Connections.

Note

Regardless of the type of subnet, the internal IPv4 address range of the subnet is always private—we do not announce the address block to the internet.

You have a limit on the number of VPCs and subnets you can create in your account. For more information, see Amazon VPC Limits.

VPC and Subnet Sizing

Amazon VPC supports IPv4 and IPv6 addressing, and has different CIDR block size limits for each. By default, all VPCs and subnets must have IPv4 CIDR blocks—you can't change this behavior. You can optionally associate an IPv6 CIDR block with your VPC.

For more information about IP addressing, see IP Addressing in Your VPC.

Topics

- VPC and Subnet Sizing for IPv4
- Adding IPv4 CIDR Blocks to a VPC
- VPC and Subnet Sizing for IPv6

VPC and Subnet Sizing for IPv4

When you create a VPC, you must specify an IPv4 CIDR block for the VPC. The allowed block size is between a /16 netmask (65,536 IP addresses) and /28 netmask (16 IP addresses). After you've created your VPC, you can associate secondary CIDR blocks with the VPC. For more information, see Adding IPv4 CIDR Blocks to a VPC.

When you create a VPC, we recommend that you specify a CIDR block (of /16 or smaller) from the private IPv4 address ranges as specified in RFC 1918:

- 10.0.0.0 - 10.255.255.255 (10/8 prefix)
- 172.16.0.0 - 172.31.255.255 (172.16/12 prefix)
- 192.168.0.0 - 192.168.255.255 (192.168/16 prefix)

You can create a VPC with a publicly routable CIDR block that falls outside of the private IPv4 address ranges specified in RFC 1918; however, for the purposes of this documentation, we refer to *private IP addresses* as the IPv4 addresses that are within the CIDR range of your VPC.

Note

If you're creating a VPC for use with another AWS service, check the service documentation to verify if there are specific requirements for the IP address range or networking components.

The CIDR block of a subnet can be the same as the CIDR block for the VPC (for a single subnet in the VPC), or a subset of the CIDR block for the VPC (for multiple subnets). The allowed block size is between a /28 netmask and /16 netmask. If you create more than one subnet in a VPC, the CIDR blocks of the subnets cannot overlap.

For example, if you create a VPC with CIDR block 10.0.0.0/24, it supports 256 IP addresses. You can break this CIDR block into two subnets, each supporting 128 IP addresses. One subnet uses CIDR block 10.0.0.0/25 (for addresses 10.0.0.0 - 10.0.0.127) and the other uses CIDR block 10.0.0.128/25 (for addresses 10.0.0.128 - 10.0.0.255).

There are many tools available to help you calculate subnet CIDR blocks; for example, see http://www.subnet-calculator.com/cidr.php. Also, your network engineering group can help you determine the CIDR blocks to specify for your subnets.

The first four IP addresses and the last IP address in each subnet CIDR block are not available for you to use, and cannot be assigned to an instance. For example, in a subnet with CIDR block 10.0.0.0/24, the following five IP addresses are reserved:

- 10.0.0.0: Network address.
- 10.0.0.1: Reserved by AWS for the VPC router.
- 10.0.0.2: Reserved by AWS. The IP address of the DNS server is always the base of the VPC network range plus two; however, we also reserve the base of each subnet range plus two. For VPCs with multiple CIDR blocks, the IP address of the DNS server is located in the primary CIDR. For more information, see Amazon DNS Server.
- 10.0.0.3: Reserved by AWS for future use.
- 10.0.0.255: Network broadcast address. We do not support broadcast in a VPC, therefore we reserve this address.

Adding IPv4 CIDR Blocks to a VPC

You can associate secondary IPv4 CIDR blocks with your VPC. When you associate a CIDR block with your VPC, a route is automatically added to your VPC route tables to enable routing within the VPC (the destination is the CIDR block and the target is local).

In the following example, the VPC on the left has a single CIDR block (10.0.0.0/16) and two subnets. The VPC on the right represents the architecture of the same VPC after you've added a second CIDR block (10.2.0.0/16) and created a new subnet from the range of the second CIDR.

VPC with 1 CIDR block

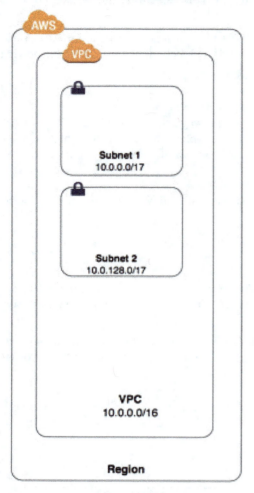

VPC with 2 CIDR blocks

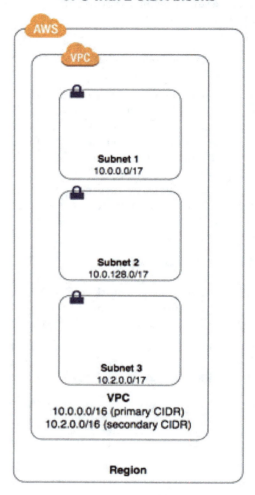

Main route table

Destination	Target
10.0.0.0/16	local

Main route table

Destination	Target
10.0.0.0/16	local
10.2.0.0/16	local

To add a CIDR block to your VPC, the following rules apply:

- The allowed block size is between a /28 netmask and /16 netmask.
- The CIDR block must not overlap with any existing CIDR block that's associated with the VPC.
- There are restrictions on the ranges of IPv4 addresses you can use. For more information, see IPv4 CIDR Block Association Restrictions.
- You cannot increase or decrease the size of an existing CIDR block.
- You have a limit on the number of CIDR blocks you can associate with a VPC and the number of routes you can add to a route table. You cannot associate a CIDR block if this results in you exceeding your limits. For more information, see Amazon VPC Limits.
- The CIDR block must not be the same or larger than the CIDR range of a route in any of the VPC route tables. For example, if you have a route with a destination of 10.0.0.0/24 to a virtual private gateway, you cannot associate a CIDR block of the same range or larger. However, you can associate a CIDR block of 10.0.0.0/25 or smaller.
- If you've enabled your VPC for ClassicLink, you can associate CIDR blocks from the 10.0.0.0/16 and 10.1.0.0/16 ranges, but you cannot associate any other CIDR block from the 10.0.0.0/8 range.

- The following rules apply when you add IPv4 CIDR blocks to a VPC that's part of a VPC peering connection:
  - If the VPC peering connection is `active`, you can add CIDR blocks to a VPC provided they do not overlap with a CIDR block of the peer VPC.
  - If the VPC peering connection is `pending-acceptance`, the owner of the requester VPC cannot add any CIDR block to the VPC, regardless of whether it overlaps with the CIDR block of the accepter VPC. Either the owner of the accepter VPC must accept the peering connection, or the owner of the requester VPC must delete the VPC peering connection request, add the CIDR block, and then request a new VPC peering connection.
  - If the VPC peering connection is `pending-acceptance`, the owner of the accepter VPC can add CIDR blocks to the VPC. If a secondary CIDR block overlaps with a CIDR block of the requester VPC, the VPC peering connection request fails and cannot be accepted.
- If you're using AWS Direct Connect to connect to multiple VPCs through a direct connect gateway, the VPCs that are associated with the direct connect gateway must not have overlapping CIDR blocks. If you add a CIDR block to one of the VPCs that's associated with the direct connect gateway, ensure that the new CIDR block does not overlap with an existing CIDR block of any other associated VPC. For more information, see Direct Connect Gateways in the *AWS Direct Connect User Guide*.
- When you add or remove a CIDR block, it can go through various states: `associating` | `associated` | `disassociating` | `disassociated` | `failing` | `failed`. The CIDR block is ready for you to use when it's in the `associated` state.

The following table provides an overview of permitted and restricted CIDR block associations, which depend on the IPv4 address range in which your VPC's primary CIDR block resides.

IPv4 CIDR Block Association Restrictions

IP address range in which your primary VPC CIDR block resides	Restricted CIDR block associations	Permitted CIDR block associations
10.0.0.0/8	CIDR blocks from other RFC 1918***** ranges (172.16.0.0/12 and 192.168.0.0/16). If your primary CIDR falls within the 10.0.0.0/15 range, you cannot add a CIDR block from the 10.0.0.0/16 range. A CIDR block from the 198.19.0.0/16 range.	Any other CIDR from the 10.0.0.0/8 range that's not restricted. Any publicly routable IPv4 CIDR block (non-RFC 1918), or a CIDR block from the 100.64.0.0/10 range.
172.16.0.0/12	CIDR blocks from other RFC 1918***** ranges (10.0.0.0/8 and 192.168.0.0/16). A CIDR block from the 172.31.0.0/16 range. A CIDR block from the 198.19.0.0/16 range.	Any other CIDR from the 172.16.0.0/12 range that's not restricted. Any publicly routable IPv4 CIDR block (non-RFC 1918), or a CIDR block from the 100.64.0.0/10 range.
192.168.0.0/16	CIDR blocks from other RFC 1918***** ranges (172.16.0.0/12 and 10.0.0.0/8). A CIDR block from the 198.19.0.0/16 range.	Any other CIDR from the 192.168.0.0/16 range. Any publicly routable IPv4 CIDR block (non-RFC 1918), or a CIDR block from the 100.64.0.0/10 range.

IP address range in which your primary VPC CIDR block resides	Restricted CIDR block associations	Permitted CIDR block associations
198.19.0.0/16	CIDR blocks from RFC 1918***** ranges.	Any publicly routable IPv4 CIDR block (non-RFC 1918), or a CIDR block from the 100.64.0.0/10 range.
Publicly routable CIDR block (non-RFC 1918), or a CIDR block from the 100.64.0.0/10 range.	CIDR blocks from the RFC 1918***** ranges. A CIDR block from the 198.19.0.0/16 range.	Any other publicly routable IPv4 CIDR block (non-RFC 1918), or a CIDR block from the 100.64.0.0/10 range.

*****RFC 1918 ranges are the private IPv4 address ranges specified in RFC 1918.

You can disassociate a CIDR block that you've associated with your VPC; however, you cannot disassociate the CIDR block with which you originally created the VPC (the primary CIDR block). To view the primary CIDR for your VPC in the Amazon VPC console, choose **Your VPCs**, select your VPC, and take note of the first entry under **CIDR blocks**. Alternatively, you can use the describe-vpcs command:

```
aws ec2 describe-vpcs --vpc-id vpc-1a2b3c4d
```

In the output that's returned, the primary CIDR is returned in the top-level `CidrBlock` element (the second-last element in the example output below).

```
{
    "Vpcs": [
        {
            "VpcId": "vpc-1a2b3c4d",
            "InstanceTenancy": "default",
            "Tags": [
                {
                    "Value": "MyVPC",
                    "Key": "Name"
                }
            ],
            "CidrBlockAssociations": [
                {
                    "AssociationId": "vpc-cidr-assoc-3781aa5e",
                    "CidrBlock": "10.0.0.0/16",
                    "CidrBlockState": {
                        "State": "associated"
                    }
                },
                {
                    "AssociationId": "vpc-cidr-assoc-0280ab6b",
                    "CidrBlock": "10.2.0.0/16",
                    "CidrBlockState": {
                        "State": "associated"
                    }
                }
            ],
            "State": "available",
            "DhcpOptionsId": "dopt-e0fe0e88",
            "CidrBlock": "10.0.0.0/16",
            "IsDefault": false
```

```
32          }
33      ]
34  }
```

VPC and Subnet Sizing for IPv6

You can associate a single IPv6 CIDR block with an existing VPC in your account, or when you create a new VPC. The CIDR block uses a fixed prefix length of /56. You cannot choose the range of addresses or the IPv6 CIDR block size; we assign the block to your VPC from Amazon's pool of IPv6 addresses.

If you've associated an IPv6 CIDR block with your VPC, you can associate an IPv6 CIDR block with an existing subnet in your VPC, or when you create a new subnet. A subnet's IPv6 CIDR block uses a fixed prefix length of /64.

For example, you create a VPC and specify that you want to associate an IPv6 CIDR block with the VPC. Amazon assigns the following IPv6 CIDR block to your VPC: 2001:db8:1234:1a00::/56. You can create a subnet and associate an IPv6 CIDR block from this range; for example, 2001:db8:1234:1a00::/64.

You can disassociate an IPv6 CIDR block from a subnet, and you can disassociate an IPv6 CIDR block from a VPC. After you've disassociated an IPv6 CIDR block from a VPC, you cannot expect to receive the same CIDR if you associate an IPv6 CIDR block with your VPC again later.

The first four IPv6 addresses and the last IPv6 address in each subnet CIDR block are not available for you to use, and cannot be assigned to an instance. For example, in a subnet with CIDR block 2001:db8:1234:1a00/64, the following five IP addresses are reserved:

- 2001:db8:1234:1a00::
- 2001:db8:1234:1a00::1
- 2001:db8:1234:1a00::2
- 2001:db8:1234:1a00::3
- 2001:db8:1234:1a00:ffff:ffff:ffff:ffff

Subnet Routing

Each subnet must be associated with a route table, which specifies the allowed routes for outbound traffic leaving the subnet. Every subnet that you create is automatically associated with the main route table for the VPC. You can change the association, and you can change the contents of the main route table. For more information, see Route Tables.

In the previous diagram, the route table associated with subnet 1 routes all IPv4 traffic (0.0.0.0/0) and IPv6 traffic (::/0) to an internet gateway (for example, igw-1a2b3c4d). Because instance 1A has an IPv4 Elastic IP address and instance 1B has an IPv6 address, they can be reached from the internet over IPv4 and IPv6 respectively.

Note
(IPv4 only) The Elastic IPv4 address or public IPv4 address that's associated with your instance is accessed through the internet gateway of your VPC. Traffic that goes through a VPN connection between your instance and another network traverses a virtual private gateway, not the internet gateway, and therefore does not access the Elastic IPv4 address or public IPv4 address.

The instance 2A can't reach the internet, but can reach other instances in the VPC. You can allow an instance in your VPC to initiate outbound connections to the internet over IPv4 but prevent unsolicited inbound connections from the internet using a network address translation (NAT) gateway or instance. Because you can allocate a limited number of Elastic IP addresses, we recommend that you use a NAT device if you have more instances that require a static public IP address. For more information, see NAT. To initiate outbound-only communication to the internet over IPv6, you can use an egress-only internet gateway. For more information, see Egress-Only Internet Gateways.

The route table associated with subnet 3 routes all IPv4 traffic (0.0.0.0/0) to a virtual private gateway (for example, `vgw-1a2b3c4d`). Instance 3A can reach computers in the corporate network over the VPN connection.

Subnet Security

AWS provides two features that you can use to increase security in your VPC: *security groups* and *network ACLs*. Security groups control inbound and outbound traffic for your instances, and network ACLs control inbound and outbound traffic for your subnets. In most cases, security groups can meet your needs; however, you can also use network ACLs if you want an additional layer of security for your VPC. For more information, see Security.

By design, each subnet must be associated with a network ACL. Every subnet that you create is automatically associated with the VPC's default network ACL. You can change the association, and you can change the contents of the default network ACL. For more information, see Network ACLs.

You can create a flow log on your VPC or subnet to capture the traffic that flows to and from the network interfaces in your VPC or subnet. You can also create a flow log on an individual network interface. Flow logs are published to CloudWatch Logs. For more information, see VPC Flow Logs.

Connections with Your Local Network and Other VPCs

You can optionally set up a connection between your VPC and your corporate or home network. If you have an IPv4 address prefix in your VPC that overlaps with one of your networks' prefixes, any traffic to the network's prefix is dropped. For example, let's say that you have the following:

- A VPC with CIDR block `10.0.0.0/16`
- A subnet in that VPC with CIDR block `10.0.1.0/24`
- Instances running in that subnet with IP addresses `10.0.1.4` and `10.0.1.5`
- On-premises host networks using CIDR blocks `10.0.37.0/24` and `10.1.38.0/24`

When those instances in the VPC try to talk to hosts in the `10.0.37.0/24` address space, the traffic is dropped because `10.0.37.0/24` is part of the larger prefix assigned to the VPC (`10.0.0.0/16`). The instances can talk to hosts in the `10.1.38.0/24` space because that block isn't part of `10.0.0.0/16`.

You can also create a VPC peering connection between your VPCs, or with a VPC in another AWS account. A VPC peering connection enables you to route traffic between the VPCs using private IP addresses; however, you cannot create a VPC peering connection between VPCs that have overlapping CIDR blocks. For more information, see Amazon VPC Peering Guide.

We therefore recommend that you create a VPC with a CIDR range large enough for expected future growth, but not one that overlaps with current or expected future subnets anywhere in your corporate or home network, or that overlaps with current or future VPCs.

We currently do not support VPN connections over IPv6.

Working with VPCs and Subnets

The following procedures are for manually creating a VPC and subnets. You also have to manually add gateways and routing tables. Alternatively, you can use the Amazon VPC wizard to create a VPC plus its subnets, gateways, and routing tables in one step. For more information, see Scenarios and Examples.

Topics

- Creating a VPC
- Creating a Subnet in Your VPC
- Associating a Secondary IPv4 CIDR Block with Your VPC
- Associating an IPv6 CIDR Block with Your VPC
- Associating an IPv6 CIDR Block with Your Subnet
- Launching an Instance into Your Subnet
- Deleting Your Subnet
- Disassociating an IPv4 CIDR Block from Your VPC
- Disassociating an IPv6 CIDR Block from Your VPC or Subnet
- Deleting Your VPC

Creating a VPC

You can create an empty VPC using the Amazon VPC console.

To create a VPC using the console

1. Open the Amazon VPC console at https://console.aws.amazon.com/vpc/.

2. In the navigation pane, choose **Your VPCs, Create VPC**.

3. Specify the following VPC details as necessary and choose **Create VPC**.

   - **Name tag**: Optionally provide a name for your VPC. Doing so creates a tag with a key of `Name` and the value that you specify.
   - **IPv4 CIDR block**: Specify an IPv4 CIDR block for the VPC. We recommend that you specify a CIDR block from the private (non-publicly routable) IP address ranges as specified in RFC 1918; for example, `10.0.0.0/16`, or `192.168.0.0/16`. **Note**
     You can specify a range of publicly routable IPv4 addresses; however, we currently do not support direct access to the internet from publicly routable CIDR blocks in a VPC. Windows instances cannot boot correctly if launched into a VPC with ranges from `224.0.0.0` to `255.255.255.255` (Class D and Class E IP address ranges).
   - **IPv6 CIDR block**: Optionally associate an IPv6 CIDR block with your VPC by choosing **Amazon-provided IPv6 CIDR block**.
   - **Tenancy**: Select a tenancy option. Dedicated tenancy ensures that your instances run on single-tenant hardware. For more information, see Dedicated Instances in the *Amazon EC2 User Guide for Linux Instances*.

Alternatively, you can use a command line tool.

To create a VPC using a command line tool

- create-vpc (AWS CLI)
- New-EC2Vpc (AWS Tools for Windows PowerShell)

To describe a VPC using a command line tool

- describe-vpcs (AWS CLI)
- Get-EC2Vpc (AWS Tools for Windows PowerShell)

For more information about IP addresses, see IP Addressing in Your VPC.

After you've created a VPC, you can create subnets. For more information, see Creating a Subnet in Your VPC.

Creating a Subnet in Your VPC

To add a new subnet to your VPC, you must specify an IPv4 CIDR block for the subnet from the range of your VPC. You can specify the Availability Zone in which you want the subnet to reside. You can have multiple subnets in the same Availability Zone.

You can optionally specify an IPv6 CIDR block for your subnet if an IPv6 CIDR block is associated with your VPC.

To add a subnet to your VPC using the console

1. Open the Amazon VPC console at https://console.aws.amazon.com/vpc/.

2. In the navigation pane, choose **Subnets**, **Create Subnet**.

3. Specify the subnet details as necessary and choose **Create Subnet**.

   - **Name tag**: Optionally provide a name for your subnet. Doing so creates a tag with a key of `Name` and the value that you specify.
   - **VPC**: Choose the VPC for which you're creating the subnet.
   - **Availability Zone**: Optionally choose an Availability Zone in which your subnet will reside, or leave the default **No Preference** to let AWS choose an Availability Zone for you.
   - **IPv4 CIDR block**: Specify an IPv4 CIDR block for your subnet, for example, `10.0.1.0/24`. For more information, see VPC and Subnet Sizing for IPv4.
   - **IPv6 CIDR block**: (Optional) If you've associated an IPv6 CIDR block with your VPC, choose **Specify a custom IPv6 CIDR**. Specify the hexadecimal pair value for the subnet, or leave the default value.

4. (Optional) If required, repeat the steps above to create more subnets in your VPC.

Alternatively, you can use a command line tool.

To add a subnet using a command line tool

- create-subnet (AWS CLI)
- New-EC2Subnet (AWS Tools for Windows PowerShell)

To describe a subnet using a command line tool

- describe-subnets (AWS CLI)
- Get-EC2Subnet (AWS Tools for Windows PowerShell)

After you've created a subnet, you can do the following:

- Configure your routing. To make your subnet a public subnet, you must attach an internet gateway to your VPC. For more information, see Creating and Attaching an Internet Gateway. You can then create a custom route table, and add route to the internet gateway. For more information, see Creating a Custom Route Table. For other routing options, see Route Tables.
- Modify the subnet settings to specify that all instances launched in that subnet receive a public IPv4 address, or an IPv6 address, or both. For more information, see IP Addressing Behavior for Your Subnet.
- Create or modify your security groups as needed. For more information, see Security Groups for Your VPC.
- Create or modify your network ACLs as needed. For more information about network ACLs, see Network ACLs.

Associating a Secondary IPv4 CIDR Block with Your VPC

You can add another IPv4 CIDR block to your VPC. Ensure that you have read the applicable restrictions.

After you've associated a CIDR block, the status goes to `associating`. The CIDR block is ready to use when it's in the `associated` state.

To add a CIDR block to your VPC using the console

1. Open the Amazon VPC console at https://console.aws.amazon.com/vpc/.

2. In the navigation pane, choose **Your VPCs**.

3. Select the VPC, and choose **Actions**, **Edit CIDRs**.

4. Choose **Add IPv4 CIDR**, and enter the CIDR block to add; for example, `10.2.0.0/16`. Choose the tick icon.

5. Choose **Close**.

Alternatively, you can use a command line tool.

To add a CIDR block using a command line tool

- associate-vpc-cidr-block (AWS CLI)
- Register-EC2VpcCidrBlock (AWS Tools for Windows PowerShell)

After you've added the IPv4 CIDR blocks that you need, you can create subnets. For more information, see Creating a Subnet in Your VPC.

Associating an IPv6 CIDR Block with Your VPC

You can associate an IPv6 CIDR block with any existing VPC. The VPC must not have an existing IPv6 CIDR block associated with it.

To associate an IPv6 CIDR block with a VPC using the console

1. Open the Amazon VPC console at https://console.aws.amazon.com/vpc/.

2. In the navigation pane, choose **Your VPCs**.

3. Select your VPC, choose **Actions**, **Edit CIDRs**.

4. Choose **Add IPv6 CIDR**. After the IPv6 CIDR block is added, choose **Close**.

Alternatively, you can use a command line tool.

To associate an IPv6 CIDR block with a VPC using a command line tool

- associate-vpc-cidr-block (AWS CLI)
- Register-EC2VpcCidrBlock (AWS Tools for Windows PowerShell)

Associating an IPv6 CIDR Block with Your Subnet

You can associate an IPv6 CIDR block with an existing subnet in your VPC. The subnet must not have an existing IPv6 CIDR block associated with it.

To associate an IPv6 CIDR block with a subnet using the console

1. Open the Amazon VPC console at https://console.aws.amazon.com/vpc/.

2. In the navigation pane, choose **Subnets**.

3. Select your subnet, choose **Subnet Actions**, **Edit IPv6 CIDRs**.

4. Choose **Add IPv6 CIDR**. Specify the hexadecimal pair for the subnet (for example, 00) and confirm the entry by choosing the tick icon.

5. Choose **Close**.

Alternatively, you can use a command line tool.

To associate an IPv6 CIDR block with a subnet using a command line tool

- associate-subnet-cidr-block (AWS CLI)
- Register-EC2SubnetCidrBlock (AWS Tools for Windows PowerShell)

Launching an Instance into Your Subnet

After you've created your subnet and configured your routing, you can launch an instance into your subnet using the Amazon EC2 console.

To launch an instance into your subnet using the console

1. Open the Amazon EC2 console at https://console.aws.amazon.com/ec2/.

2. On the dashboard, choose **Launch Instance**.

3. Follow the directions in the wizard. Select an AMI and an instance type and choose **Next: Configure Instance Details. Note**
If you want your instance to communicate over IPv6, you must select a supported instance type. All current generation instance types support IPv6 addresses.

4. On the **Configure Instance Details** page, ensure that you have selected the required VPC in the **Network** list, then select the subnet in to which to launch the instance. Keep the other default settings on this page and choose **Next: Add Storage**.

5. On the next pages of the wizard, you can configure storage for your instance, and add tags. On the **Configure Security Group** page, choose from any existing security group that you own, or follow the wizard directions to create a new security group. Choose **Review and Launch** when you're done.

6. Review your settings and choose **Launch**.

7. Select an existing key pair that you own or create a new one, and then choose **Launch Instances** when you're done.

Alternatively, you can use a command line tool.

To launch an instance into your subnet using a command line tool

- run-instances (AWS CLI)
- New-EC2Instance (AWS Tools for Windows PowerShell)

Deleting Your Subnet

If you no longer need your subnet, you can delete it. You must terminate any instances in the subnet first.

To delete your subnet using the console

1. Open the Amazon EC2 console at https://console.aws.amazon.com/ec2/.

2. Terminate all instances in the subnet. For more information, see Terminate Your Instance in the *EC2 User Guide*.

3. Open the Amazon VPC console at https://console.aws.amazon.com/vpc/.

4. In the navigation pane, choose **Subnets**.

5. Select the subnet to delete and choose **Subnet Actions, Delete Subnet**.

6. In the **Delete Subnet** dialog box, choose **Yes, Delete**.

Alternatively, you can use a command line tool.

To delete a subnet using a command line tool

- delete-subnet (AWS CLI)
- Remove-EC2Subnet (AWS Tools for Windows PowerShell)

Disassociating an IPv4 CIDR Block from Your VPC

If your VPC has more than one IPv4 CIDR block associated with it, you can disassociate an IPv4 CIDR block from the VPC. You cannot disassociate the primary IPv4 CIDR block. You can only disassociate an entire CIDR block; you cannot disassociate a subset of a CIDR block or a merged range of CIDR blocks. You must first delete all subnets in the CIDR block.

To remove a CIDR block from a VPC using the console

1. Open the Amazon VPC console at https://console.aws.amazon.com/vpc/.

2. In the navigation pane, choose **Your VPCs**.

3. Select the VPC, and choose **Actions, Edit CIDRs**.

4. Under **VPC IPv4 CIDRs**, choose the delete button (a cross) for the CIDR block to remove.

5. Choose **Close**.

Alternatively, you can use a command line tool.

To remove an IPv4 CIDR block from a VPC using a command line tool

- disassociate-vpc-cidr-block (AWS CLI)
- Unregister-EC2VpcCidrBlock (AWS Tools for Windows PowerShell)

Disassociating an IPv6 CIDR Block from Your VPC or Subnet

If you no longer want IPv6 support in your VPC or subnet, but you want to continue using your VPC or subnet for creating and communicating with IPv4 resources, you can disassociate the IPv6 CIDR block.

To disassociate an IPv6 CIDR block, you must first unassign any IPv6 addresses that are assigned to any instances in your subnet. For more information, see Unassigning an IPv6 Address From an Instance.

To disassociate an IPv6 CIDR block from a subnet using the console

1. Open the Amazon VPC console at https://console.aws.amazon.com/vpc/.

2. In the navigation pane, choose **Subnets**.

3. Select your subnet, choose **Subnet Actions, Edit IPv6 CIDRs**.

4. Remove the IPv6 CIDR block for the subnet by choosing the cross icon.

5. Choose **Close**.

To disassociate an IPv6 CIDR block from a VPC using the console

1. Open the Amazon VPC console at https://console.aws.amazon.com/vpc/.

2. In the navigation pane, choose **Your VPCs**.

3. Select your VPC, choose **Actions, Edit CIDRs**.

4. Remove the IPv6 CIDR block by choosing the cross icon.

5. Choose **Close**.

Note

Disassociating an IPv6 CIDR block does not automatically delete any security group rules, network ACL rules, or route table routes that you've configured for IPv6 networking. You must manually modify or delete these rules or routes.

Alternatively, you can use a command line tool.

To disassociate an IPv6 CIDR block from a subnet using a command line tool

- disassociate-subnet-cidr-block (AWS CLI)
- Unregister-EC2SubnetCidrBlock (AWS Tools for Windows PowerShell)

To disassociate an IPv6 CIDR block from a VPC using a command line tool

- disassociate-vpc-cidr-block (AWS CLI)
- Unregister-EC2VpcCidrBlock (AWS Tools for Windows PowerShell)

Deleting Your VPC

You can delete your VPC at any time. However, you must terminate all instances in the VPC first. When you delete a VPC using the VPC console, we delete all its components, such as subnets, security groups, network ACLs, route tables, internet gateways, VPC peering connections, and DHCP options.

If you have a VPN connection, you don't have to delete it or the other components related to the VPN (such as the customer gateway and virtual private gateway). If you plan to use the customer gateway with another VPC, we recommend that you keep the VPN connection and the gateways. Otherwise, your network administrator must configure the customer gateway again after you create a new VPN connection.

To delete your VPC using the console

1. Open the Amazon EC2 console at https://console.aws.amazon.com/ec2/.

2. Terminate all instances in the VPC. For more information, see Terminate Your Instance in the *Amazon EC2 User Guide for Linux Instances*.

3. Open the Amazon VPC console at https://console.aws.amazon.com/vpc/.

4. In the navigation pane, choose **Your VPCs**.

5. Select the VPC to delete and choose **Actions**, **Delete VPC**.

6. To delete the VPN connection, select the option to do so; otherwise, leave it unselected. Choose **Yes, Delete**.

Alternatively, you can use a command line tool. When you delete a VPC using the command line, you must first terminate all instances, delete all subnets, custom security groups, and custom route tables, and detach any internet gateway in the VPC.

To delete a VPC using a command line tool

- delete-vpc (AWS CLI)
- Remove-EC2Vpc (AWS Tools for Windows PowerShell)

Default VPC and Default Subnets

If you created your AWS account after 2013-12-04, it supports only EC2-VPC. In this case, you have a *default VPC* in each AWS Region. A default VPC is ready for you to use so that you don't have to create and configure your own VPC. You can immediately start launching Amazon EC2 instances into your default VPC. You can also use services such as Elastic Load Balancing, Amazon RDS, and Amazon EMR in your default VPC.

A default VPC is suitable for getting started quickly, and for launching public instances such as a blog or simple website. You can modify the components of your default VPC as needed. If you prefer to create a nondefault VPC that suits your specific requirements; for example, using your preferred CIDR block range and subnet sizes, see the example scenarios.

Topics

- Default VPC Components
- Availability and Supported Platforms
- Viewing Your Default VPC and Default Subnets
- Launching an EC2 Instance into Your Default VPC
- Deleting Your Default Subnets and Default VPC
- Creating a Default VPC
- Creating a Default Subnet

Default VPC Components

When we create a default VPC, we do the following to set it up for you:

- Create a VPC with a size /16 IPv4 CIDR block (172.31.0.0/16). This provides up to 65,536 private IPv4 addresses.
- Create a size /20 default subnet in each Availability Zone. This provides up to 4,096 addresses per subnet, a few of which are reserved for our use.
- Create an internet gateway and connect it to your default VPC.
- Create a main route table for your default VPC with a rule that sends all IPv4 traffic destined for the internet to the internet gateway.
- Create a default security group and associate it with your default VPC.
- Create a default network access control list (ACL) and associate it with your default VPC.
- Associate the default DHCP options set for your AWS account with your default VPC.

The following figure illustrates the key components that we set up for a default VPC.

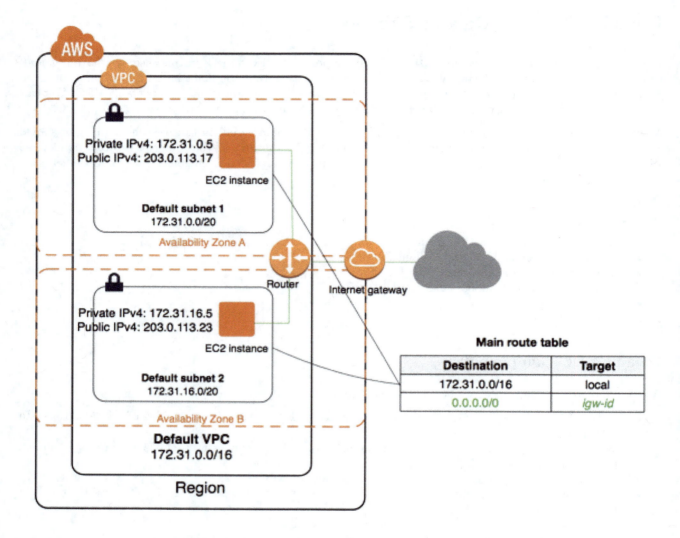

Main route table	
Destination	**Target**
172.31.0.0/16	local
0.0.0.0/0	*igw-id*

You can use a default VPC as you would use any other VPC:

- Add additional nondefault subnets.
- Modify the main route table.
- Add additional route tables.
- Associate additional security groups.
- Update the rules of the default security group.
- Add VPN connections.
- Add more IPv4 CIDR blocks.

You can use a default subnet as you would use any other subnet; add custom route tables and set network ACLs. You can also specify a specific default subnet when you launch an EC2 instance.

You can optionally associate an IPv6 CIDR block with your default VPC. For more information, Working with VPCs and Subnets.

Default Subnets

By default, a default subnet is a public subnet, because the main route table sends the subnet's traffic that is destined for the internet to the internet gateway. You can make a default subnet into a private subnet by removing the route from the destination 0.0.0.0/0 to the internet gateway. However, if you do this, any EC2 instance running in that subnet can't access the internet.

Instances that you launch into a default subnet receive both a public IPv4 address and a private IPv4 address, and both public and private DNS hostnames. Instances that you launch into a nondefault subnet in a default VPC don't receive a public IPv4 address or a DNS hostname. You can change your subnet's default public IP addressing behavior. For more information, see Modifying the Public IPv4 Addressing Attribute for Your Subnet.

From time to time, AWS may add a new Availability Zone to a region. In most cases, we automatically create a new default subnet in this Availability Zone for your default VPC within a few days. However, if you made any modifications to your default VPC, we do not add a new default subnet. If you want a default subnet for the new Availability Zone, you can create one yourself. For more information, see Creating a Default Subnet.

Availability and Supported Platforms

If you created your AWS account after 2013-12-04, it supports only EC2-VPC. In this case, we create a default VPC for you in each AWS Region. Therefore, unless you create a nondefault VPC and specify it when you launch an instance, we launch your instances into your default VPC.

If you created your AWS account before 2013-03-18, it supports both EC2-Classic and EC2-VPC in regions that you've used before, and only EC2-VPC in regions that you haven't used. In this case, we create a default VPC in each region in which you haven't created any AWS resources. Unless you create a nondefault VPC and specify it when you launch an instance in a new region, we launch the instance into your default VPC for that region. However, if you launch an instance in a region that you've used before, we launch the instance into EC2-Classic.

If you created your AWS account between 2013-03-18 and 2013-12-04, it may support only EC2-VPC. Alternatively, it may support both EC2-Classic and EC2-VPC in some of the regions that you've used. For information about detecting the platform support in each region for your AWS account, see Detecting Your Supported Platforms and Whether You Have a Default VPC. For information about when each region was enabled for default VPCs, see Announcement: Enabling regions for the default VPC feature set in the AWS forum for Amazon VPC.

If an AWS account supports only EC2-VPC, any IAM accounts associated with this AWS account also support only EC2-VPC, and use the same default VPC as the AWS account.

If your AWS account supports both EC2-Classic and EC2-VPC, you can either create a new AWS account or launch your instances into a region that you haven't used before. You might do this to get the benefits of using EC2-VPC with the simplicity of launching instances into EC2-Classic. If you'd still prefer to add a default VPC to a region that doesn't have one and supports EC2-Classic, see "I really want a default VPC for my existing EC2 account. Is that possible?" in the Default VPCs FAQ.

For more information about the EC2-Classic and EC2-VPC platforms, see Supported Platforms.

Detecting Your Supported Platforms and Whether You Have a Default VPC

You can use the Amazon EC2 console or the command line to determine whether your AWS account supports both platforms, or if you have a default VPC.

To detect platform support using the Amazon EC2 console

1. Open the Amazon EC2 console at https://console.aws.amazon.com/ec2/.

2. In the navigation bar, use the region selector on the top right to select your region.

3. On the Amazon EC2 console dashboard, look for **Supported Platforms** under **Account Attributes**. If there are two values, EC2 and VPC, you can launch instances into either platform. If there is one value, VPC, you can launch instances only into EC2-VPC.

For example, the following indicates that the account supports the EC2-VPC platform only, and has a default VPC with the identifier vpc-1a2b3c4d.

Supported Platforms

VPC

Default VPC

vpc-1a2b3c4d

If you delete your default VPC, the **Default VPC** value displayed is None. For more information, see Deleting Your Default Subnets and Default VPC.

To detect platform support using the command line

- describe-account-attributes (AWS CLI)
- Get-EC2AccountAttributes (AWS Tools for Windows PowerShell)

The supported-platforms attribute in the output indicates which platforms you can launch EC2 instances into.

Viewing Your Default VPC and Default Subnets

You can view your default VPC and subnets using the Amazon VPC console or the command line.

To view your default VPC and subnets using the Amazon VPC console

1. Open the Amazon VPC console at https://console.aws.amazon.com/vpc/.

2. In the navigation pane, choose **Your VPCs**.

3. In the **Default VPC** column, look for a value of **Yes**. Take note of the ID of the default VPC.

4. In the navigation pane, choose **Subnets**.

5. In the search bar, type the ID of the default VPC. The returned subnets are subnets in your default VPC.

6. To verify which subnets are default subnets, look for a value of **Yes** in the **Default Subnet **column.

To describe your default VPC using the command line

- Use the describe-vpcs (AWS CLI)
- Use the Get-EC2Vpc (AWS Tools for Windows PowerShell)

Use the commands with the isDefault filter and set the filter value to true.

To describe your default subnets using the command line

- Use the describe-subnets (AWS CLI)
- Use the Get-EC2Subnet (AWS Tools for Windows PowerShell)

Use the commands with the vpc-id filter and set the filter value to the ID of the default VPC. In the output, the DefaultForAz field is set to true for default subnets.

Launching an EC2 Instance into Your Default VPC

When you launch an EC2 instance without specifying a subnet, it's automatically launched into a default subnet in your default VPC. By default, we select an Availability Zone for you and launch the instance into the corresponding subnet for that Availability Zone. Alternatively, you can select the Availability Zone for your instance by selecting its corresponding default subnet in the console, or by specifying the subnet or the Availability Zone in the AWS CLI.

Launching an EC2 Instance Using the Console

To launch an EC2 instance into your default VPC

1. Open the Amazon EC2 console at https://console.aws.amazon.com/ec2/.

2. From the EC2 dashboard, choose **Launch Instance**.

3. Follow the directions in the wizard. Select an AMI, and choose an instance type. You can accept the default settings for the rest of the wizard by choosing **Review and Launch**. This takes you directly to the **Review Instance Launch** page.

4. Review your settings. In the **Instance Details** section, the default for **Subnet** is **No preference (default subnet in any Availability Zone)**. This means that the instance is launched into the default subnet of the Availability Zone that we select. Alternatively, choose **Edit instance details** and select the default subnet for a particular Availability Zone.

5. Choose **Launch** to choose a key pair and launch the instance.

Launching an EC2 Instance Using the Command Line

You can use one of the following commands to launch an EC2 instance:

- run-instances (AWS CLI)
- New-EC2Instance (AWS Tools for Windows PowerShell)

To launch an EC2 instance into your default VPC, use these commands without specifying a subnet or an Availability Zone.

To launch an EC2 instance into a specific default subnet in your default VPC, specify its subnet ID or Availability Zone.

Deleting Your Default Subnets and Default VPC

You can delete a default subnet or default VPC just as you can delete any other subnet or VPC. However, if you delete your default subnets or default VPC, you must explicitly specify a subnet in another VPC in which to launch your instance, because you can't launch instances into EC2-Classic. If you do not have another VPC, you must create a nondefault VPC and nondefault subnet. For more information, see Creating a VPC.

If you delete your default VPC, you can create a new one. For more information, see Creating a Default VPC.

If you delete a default subnet, you can create a new one. For more information, see Creating a Default Subnet. Alternatively, you can create a nondefault subnet in your default VPC and contact AWS Support to mark the subnet as a default subnet. You must provide the following details: your AWS account ID, the region, and the subnet ID. To ensure that your new default subnet behaves as expected, modify the subnet attribute to assign public IP addresses to instances that are launched in that subnet. For more information, see Modifying the Public IPv4 Addressing Attribute for Your Subnet. You can only have one default subnet per Availability Zone. You cannot create a default subnet in a nondefault VPC.

Creating a Default VPC

If you delete your default VPC, you can create a new one. You cannot restore a previous default VPC that you deleted, and you cannot mark an existing nondefault VPC as a default VPC. If your account supports EC2-Classic, you cannot use these procedures to create a default VPC in a region that supports EC2-Classic.

When you create a default VPC, it is created with the standard components of a default VPC, including a default subnet in each Availability Zone. You cannot specify your own components. The subnet CIDR blocks of your new default VPC may not map to the same Availability Zones as your previous default VPC. For example, if the subnet with CIDR block 172.31.0.0/20 was created in **us-east-2a** in your previous default VPC, it may be created in **us-east-2b** in your new default VPC.

If you already have a default VPC in the region, you cannot create another one.

To create a default VPC using the Amazon VPC console

1. Open the Amazon VPC console at https://console.aws.amazon.com/vpc/.
2. In the navigation pane, choose **Your VPCs**.
3. Choose **Actions, Create Default VPC**.
4. Choose **Create**. Close the confirmation screen.

To create a default VPC using the command line

- You can use the create-default-vpc AWS CLI command. This command does not have any input parameters.

```
1 aws ec2 create-default-vpc
```

```
 1 {
 2     "Vpc": {
 3         "VpcId": "vpc-3f139646",
 4         "InstanceTenancy": "default",
 5         "Tags": [],
 6         "Ipv6CidrBlockAssociationSet": [],
 7         "State": "pending",
 8         "DhcpOptionsId": "dopt-61079b07",
 9         "CidrBlock": "172.31.0.0/16",
10         "IsDefault": true
11     }
12 }
```

Alternatively, you can use the New-EC2DefaultVpc Tools for Windows PowerShell command or the CreateDefaultVpc Amazon EC2 API action.

Creating a Default Subnet

You can create a default subnet in an Availability Zone that does not have one. For example, you might want to create a default subnet if you have deleted a default subnet, or if AWS has added a new Availability Zone and did not automatically create a default subnet for that zone in your default VPC.

When you create a default subnet, it is created with a size /20 IPv4 CIDR block in the next available contiguous space in your default VPC. The following rules apply:

- You cannot specify the CIDR block yourself.
- You cannot restore a previous default subnet that you deleted.
- You can have only one default subnet per Availability Zone.
- You cannot create a default subnet in a nondefault VPC.

If there is not enough address space in your default VPC to create a size /20 CIDR block, the request fails. If you need more address space, you can add an IPv4 CIDR block to your VPC.

If you've associated an IPv6 CIDR block with your default VPC, the new default subnet does not automatically receive an IPv6 CIDR block. Instead, you can associate an IPv6 CIDR block with the default subnet after you create it. For more information, see Associating an IPv6 CIDR Block with Your Subnet.

Currently, you can create a default subnet using the AWS CLI, an AWS SDK, or the Amazon EC2 API only.

To create a default subnet using the command line

- Use the create-default-subnet AWS CLI command and specify the Availability Zone in which to create the subnet.

```
1 aws ec2 create-default-subnet --availability-zone us-east-2a
```

```
1  {
2      "Subnet": {
3          "AvailabilityZone": "us-east-2a",
4          "Tags": [],
5          "AvailableIpAddressCount": 4091,
6          "DefaultForAz": true,
7          "Ipv6CidrBlockAssociationSet": [],
8          "VpcId": "vpc-1a2b3c4d",
9          "State": "available",
10         "MapPublicIpOnLaunch": true,
11         "SubnetId": "subnet-1122aabb",
12         "CidrBlock": "172.31.32.0/20",
13         "AssignIpv6AddressOnCreation": false
14     }
15 }
```

Alternatively, you can use the CreateDefaultSubnet Amazon EC2 API action.

IP Addressing in Your VPC

IP addresses enable resources in your VPC to communicate with each other, and with resources over the Internet. Amazon EC2 and Amazon VPC support the IPv4 and IPv6 addressing protocols.

By default, Amazon EC2 and Amazon VPC use the IPv4 addressing protocol. When you create a VPC, you must assign it an IPv4 CIDR block (a range of private IPv4 addresses). Private IPv4 addresses are not reachable over the Internet. To connect to your instance over the Internet, or to enable communication between your instances and other AWS services that have public endpoints, you can assign a globally-unique public IPv4 address to your instance.

You can optionally associate an IPv6 CIDR block with your VPC and subnets, and assign IPv6 addresses from that block to the resources in your VPC. IPv6 addresses are public and reachable over the Internet.

Note
To ensure that your instances can communicate with the Internet, you must also attach an Internet gateway to your VPC. For more information, see Internet Gateways.

Your VPC can operate in dual-stack mode: your resources can communicate over IPv4, or IPv6, or both. IPv4 and IPv6 addresses are independent of each other; you must configure routing and security in your VPC separately for IPv4 and IPv6.

The following table summarizes the differences between IPv4 and IPv6 in Amazon EC2 and Amazon VPC.

IPv4 and IPv6 Characteristics and Restrictions

IPv4	IPv6
The format is 32-bit, 4 groups of up to 3 numerical digits.	The format is 128-bit, 8 groups of 4 hexadecimal digits.
Default and required for all VPCs; cannot be removed.	Opt-in only.
The VPC CIDR block size can be from /16 to /28.	The VPC CIDR block size is fixed at /56.
The subnet CIDR block size can be from /16 to /28.	The subnet CIDR block size is fixed at /64.
You can choose the private IPv4 CIDR block for your VPC.	We choose the IPv6 CIDR block for your VPC from Amazon's pool of IPv6 addresses. You cannot select your own range.
There is a distinction between private and public IP addresses. To enable communication with the Internet, a public IPv4 address is mapped to the primary private IPv4 address through network address translation (NAT).	No distinction between public and private IP addresses. IPv6 addresses are public.
Supported on all instance types.	Supported on all current generation instance types and the C3, R3, and I2 previous generation instance types. For more information, see Instance Types.
Supported in EC2-Classic, and EC2-Classic connections with a VPC via ClassicLink.	Not supported in EC2-Classic, and not supported for EC2-Classic connections with a VPC via ClassicLink.

IPv4	IPv6
Supported on all AMIs.	Automatically supported on AMIs that are configured for DHCPv6. Amazon Linux versions 2016.09.0 and later and Windows Server 2008 R2 and later are configured for DHCPv6. For other AMIs, you must manually configure your instance to recognize any assigned IPv6 addresses.
An instance receives an Amazon-provided private DNS hostname that corresponds to its private IPv4 address, and if applicable, a public DNS hostname that corresponds to its public IPv4 or Elastic IP address.	Amazon-provided DNS hostnames are not supported.
Elastic IPv4 addresses are supported.	Elastic IPv6 addresses are not supported.
Supported for VPC VPN connections and customer gateways, NAT devices, and VPC endpoints.	Not supported for VPC VPN connections and customer gateways, NAT devices, and VPC endpoints.

We support IPv6 traffic over a virtual private gateway to an AWS Direct Connect connection. For more information, see the AWS Direct Connect User Guide.

Topics

- Private IPv4 Addresses
- Public IPv4 Addresses
- IPv6 Addresses
- IP Addressing Behavior for Your Subnet
- Working with IP Addresses
- Migrating to IPv6

Private IPv4 Addresses

Private IPv4 addresses (also referred to as *private IP addresses* in this topic) are not reachable over the Internet, and can be used for communication between the instances in your VPC. When you launch an instance into a VPC, a primary private IP address from the IPv4 address range of the subnet is assigned to the default network interface (eth0) of the instance. Each instance is also given a private (internal) DNS hostname that resolves to the private IP address of the instance. If you don't specify a primary private IP address, we select an available IP address in the subnet range for you. For more information about network interfaces, see Elastic Network Interfaces in the *Amazon EC2 User Guide for Linux Instances*.

You can assign additional private IP addresses, known as secondary private IP addresses, to instances that are running in a VPC. Unlike a primary private IP address, you can reassign a secondary private IP address from one network interface to another. A private IP address remains associated with the network interface when the instance is stopped and restarted, and is released when the instance is terminated. For more information about primary and secondary IP addresses, see Multiple IP Addresses in the *Amazon EC2 User Guide for Linux Instances*.

Note
We refer to private IP addresses as the IP addresses that are within the IPv4 CIDR range of the VPC. Most VPC IP address ranges fall within the private (non-publicly routable) IP address ranges specified in RFC 1918; however, you can use publicly routable CIDR blocks for your VPC. Regardless of the IP address range of your VPC, we do not support direct access to the Internet from your VPC's CIDR block, including a publicly-routable CIDR block. You must set up Internet access through a gateway; for example, an Internet gateway, virtual private gateway, a VPN connection, or AWS Direct Connect.

Public IPv4 Addresses

All subnets have an attribute that determines whether a network interface created in the subnet automatically receives a public IPv4 address (also referred to as a *public IP address* in this topic). Therefore, when you launch an instance into a subnet that has this attribute enabled, a public IP address is assigned to the primary network interface (eth0) that's created for the instance. A public IP address is mapped to the primary private IP address through network address translation (NAT).

You can control whether your instance receives a public IP address by doing the following:

- Modifying the public IP addressing attribute of your subnet. For more information, see Modifying the Public IPv4 Addressing Attribute for Your Subnet.
- Enabling or disabling the public IP addressing feature during instance launch, which overrides the subnet's public IP addressing attribute. For more information, see Assigning a Public IPv4 Address During Instance Launch.

A public IP address is assigned from Amazon's pool of public IP addresses; it's not associated with your account. When a public IP address is disassociated from your instance, it's released back into the pool, and is no longer available for you to use. You cannot manually associate or disassociate a public IP address. Instead, in certain cases, we release the public IP address from your instance, or assign it a new one. For more information, see Public IP Addresses in the *Amazon EC2 User Guide for Linux Instances*.

If you require a persistent public IP address allocated to your account that can be assigned to and removed from instances as you require, use an Elastic IP address instead. For more information, see Elastic IP Addresses.

If your VPC is enabled to support DNS hostnames, each instance that receives a public IP address or an Elastic IP address is also given a public DNS hostname. We resolve a public DNS hostname to the public IP address of the instance outside the instance network, and to the private IP address of the instance from within the instance network. For more information, see Using DNS with Your VPC.

IPv6 Addresses

You can optionally associate an IPv6 CIDR block with your VPC and subnets. For more information, see the following topics:

- Associating an IPv6 CIDR Block with Your VPC
- Associating an IPv6 CIDR Block with Your Subnet

Your instance in a VPC receives an IPv6 address if an IPv6 CIDR block is associated with your VPC and your subnet, and if one of the following is true:

- Your subnet is configured to automatically assign an IPv6 address to the primary network interface of an instance during launch.
- You manually assign an IPv6 address to your instance during launch.
- You assign an IPv6 address to your instance after launch.
- You assign an IPv6 address to a network interface in the same subnet, and attach the network interface to your instance after launch.

When your instance receives an IPv6 address during launch, the address is associated with the primary network interface (eth0) of the instance. You can disassociate the IPv6 address from the primary network interface. We do not support IPv6 DNS hostnames for your instance.

An IPv6 address persists when you stop and start your instance, and is released when you terminate your instance. You cannot reassign an IPv6 address while it's assigned to another network interface—you must first unassign it.

You can assign additional IPv6 addresses to your instance by assigning them to a network interface attached to your instance. The number of IPv6 addresses you can assign to a network interface, and the number of network interfaces you can attach to an instance varies per instance type. For more information, see IP Addresses Per Network Interface Per Instance Type in the *Amazon EC2 User Guide*.

IPv6 addresses are globally unique, and therefore reachable over the Internet. You can control whether instances are reachable via their IPv6 addresses by controlling the routing for your subnet, or by using security group and network ACL rules. For more information, see Security.

For more information about reserved IPv6 address ranges, see IANA IPv6 Special-Purpose Address Registry and RFC4291.

IP Addressing Behavior for Your Subnet

All subnets have a modifiable attribute that determines whether a network interface created in that subnet is assigned a public IPv4 address and, if applicable, an IPv6 address. This includes the primary network interface (eth0) that's created for an instance when you launch an instance in that subnet.

Regardless of the subnet attribute, you can still override this setting for a specific instance during launch. For more information, see Assigning a Public IPv4 Address During Instance Launch and Assigning an IPv6 Address During Instance Launch.

Working with IP Addresses

You can modify the IP addressing behavior of your subnet, assign a public IPv4 address to your instance during launch, and assign or unassign IPv6 addresses to and from your instance.

Topics

- Modifying the Public IPv4 Addressing Attribute for Your Subnet
- Modifying the IPv6 Addressing Attribute for Your Subnet
- Assigning a Public IPv4 Address During Instance Launch
- Assigning an IPv6 Address During Instance Launch
- Assigning an IPv6 Address to an Instance
- Unassigning an IPv6 Address From an Instance
- API and Command Overview

Modifying the Public IPv4 Addressing Attribute for Your Subnet

By default, nondefault subnets have the IPv4 public addressing attribute set to `false`, and default subnets have this attribute set to `true`. An exception is a nondefault subnet created by the Amazon EC2 launch instance wizard — the wizard sets the attribute to `true`. You can modify this attribute using the Amazon VPC console.

To modify your subnet's public IPv4 addressing behavior

1. Open the Amazon VPC console at https://console.aws.amazon.com/vpc/.

2. In the navigation pane, choose **Subnets**.

3. Select your subnet and choose **Subnet Actions, Modify auto-assign IP settings**.

4. The **Enable auto-assign public IPv4 address** check box, if selected, requests a public IPv4 address for all instances launched into the selected subnet. Select or clear the check box as required, and then choose **Save**.

Modifying the IPv6 Addressing Attribute for Your Subnet

By default, all subnets have the IPv6 addressing attribute set to `false`. You can modify this attribute using the Amazon VPC console. If you enable the IPv6 addressing attribute for your subnet, network interfaces created in the subnet receive an IPv6 address from the range of the subnet. Instances launched into the subnet receive an IPv6 address on the primary network interface.

Your subnet must have an associated IPv6 CIDR block.

Note
If you enable the IPv6 addressing feature for your subnet, your network interface or instance only receives an IPv6 address if it's created using version 2016-11-15 or later of the Amazon EC2 API. The Amazon EC2 console uses the latest API version.

To modify your subnet's IPv6 addressing behavior

1. Open the Amazon VPC console at https://console.aws.amazon.com/vpc/.

2. In the navigation pane, choose **Subnets**.

3. Select your subnet and choose **Subnet Actions**, **Modify auto-assign IP settings**.

4. The **Enable auto-assign IPv6 address** check box, if selected, requests an IPv6 address for all network interfaces created in the selected subnet. Select or clear the check box as required, and then choose **Save**.

Assigning a Public IPv4 Address During Instance Launch

You can control whether your instance in a default or nondefault subnet is assigned a public IPv4 address during launch.

Important
You can't manually disassociate the public IPv4 address from your instance after launch. Instead, it's automatically released in certain cases, after which you cannot reuse it. If you require a persistent public IP address that you can associate or disassociate at will, associate an Elastic IP address with the instance after launch instead. For more information, see Elastic IP Addresses.

To assign a public IPv4 address to an instance during launch

1. Open the Amazon EC2 console at https://console.aws.amazon.com/ec2/.

2. Choose **Launch Instance**.

3. Choose an AMI and an instance type and choose **Next: Configure Instance Details**.

4. On the **Configure Instance Details** page, select a VPC from the **Network** list. The **Auto-assign Public IP** list is displayed. Select **Enable** or **Disable** to override the default setting for the subnet. **Important**
A public IPv4 address cannot be assigned if you specify more than one network interface. Additionally, you cannot override the subnet setting using the auto-assign public IPv4 feature if you specify an existing network interface for eth0.

5. Follow the remaining steps in the wizard to launch your instance.

6. On the **Instances** screen, select your instance. On the **Description** tab, in the **IPv4 Public IP** field, you can view your instance's public IP address. Alternatively, in the navigation pane, choose **Network Interfaces** and select the eth0 network interface for your instance. You can view the public IP address in the **IPv4 Public IP** field. **Note**
The public IPv4 address is displayed as a property of the network interface in the console, but it's mapped to the primary private IPv4 address through NAT. Therefore, if you inspect the properties of your network interface on your instance, for example, through `ipconfig` on a Windows instance, or `ifconfig` on a Linux instance, the public IP address is not displayed. To determine your instance's public IP address from

within the instance, you can use instance metadata. For more information, see Instance Metadata and User Data.

This feature is only available during launch. However, whether or not you assign a public IPv4 address to your instance during launch, you can associate an Elastic IP address with your instance after it's launched. For more information, see Elastic IP Addresses.

Assigning an IPv6 Address During Instance Launch

You can auto-assign an IPv6 address to your instance during launch. To do this, you must launch your instance into a VPC and subnet that has an associated IPv6 CIDR block. The IPv6 address is assigned from the range of the subnet, and is assigned to the primary network interface (eth0).

To auto-assign an IPv6 address to an instance during launch

1. Open the Amazon EC2 console at https://console.aws.amazon.com/ec2/.

2. Choose **Launch Instance**.

3. Select an AMI and an instance type and choose **Next: Configure Instance Details**. **Note** Select an instance type that supports IPv6 addresses.

4. On the **Configure Instance Details** page, select a VPC from **Network** and a subnet from **Subnet**. For **Auto-assign IPv6 IP**, choose **Enable**.

5. Follow the remaining steps in the wizard to launch your instance.

Alternatively, if you want to assign a specific IPv6 address from the subnet range to your instance during launch, you can assign the address to the primary network interface for your instance.

To assign a specific IPv6 address to an instance during launch

1. Open the Amazon EC2 console at https://console.aws.amazon.com/ec2/.

2. Choose **Launch Instance**.

3. Select an AMI and an instance type and choose **Next: Configure Instance Details**. **Note** Select an instance type that supports IPv6 addresses.

4. On the **Configure Instance Details** page, select a VPC from **Network** and a subnet from **Subnet**.

5. Go to the **Network interfaces** section. For the eth0 network interface, under **IPv6 IPs**, choose **Add IP**.

6. Enter an IPv6 address from the range of the subnet.

7. Follow the remaining steps in the wizard to launch your instance.

For more information about assigning multiple IPv6 addresses to your instance during launch, see Working with Multiple IPv6 Addresses in the *Amazon EC2 User Guide for Linux Instances*

Assigning an IPv6 Address to an Instance

If your instance is in a VPC and subnet with an associated IPv6 CIDR block, you can use the Amazon EC2 console to assign an IPv6 address to your instance from the range of the subnet.

To associate an IPv6 address with your instance

1. Open the Amazon EC2 console at https://console.aws.amazon.com/ec2/.

2. In the navigation pane, choose **Instances** and select your instance.

3. Choose **Actions, Networking, Manage IP Addresses**.

4. Under **IPv6 Addresses**, choose **Assign new IP**. You can specify an IPv6 address from the range of the subnet, or leave the **Auto-assign** value to let Amazon choose an IPv6 address for you.

5. Choose **Save**.

Alternatively, you can assign an IPv6 address to a network interface. For more information, see Assigning an IPv6 Address in the *Elastic Network Interfaces* topic in the *Amazon EC2 User Guide for Linux Instances*.

Unassigning an IPv6 Address From an Instance

If you no longer need an IPv6 address for your instance, you can disassociate it from the instance using the Amazon EC2 console.

To disassociate an IPv6 address from your instance

1. Open the Amazon EC2 console at https://console.aws.amazon.com/ec2/.

2. In the navigation pane, choose **Instances** and select your instance.

3. Choose **Actions**, **Networking**, **Manage IP Addresses**.

4. Under **IPv6 Addresses**, choose **Unassign** for the IPv6 address.

5. Choose **Save**.

Alternatively, you can disassociate an IPv6 address from a network interface. For more information, see Unassigning an IPv6 Address in the *Elastic Network Interfaces* topic in the *Amazon EC2 User Guide for Linux Instances*.

API and Command Overview

You can perform the tasks described on this page using the command line or an API. For more information about the command line interfaces and a list of available APIs, see Accessing Amazon VPC.

Assign a public IPv4 address during launch

- Use the `--associate-public-ip-address` or the `--no-associate-public-ip-address` option with the run-instances command. (AWS CLI)
- Use the `-AssociatePublicIp` parameter with the New-EC2Instance command. (AWS Tools for Windows PowerShell)

Assign an IPv6 address during launch

- Use the `--ipv6-addresses` option with the run-instances command. (AWS CLI)
- Use the `-Ipv6Addresses` parameter with the New-EC2Instance command. (AWS Tools for Windows PowerShell)

Modify a subnet's IP addressing behavior

- modify-subnet-attribute (AWS CLI)
- Edit-EC2SubnetAttribute (AWS Tools for Windows PowerShell)

Assign an IPv6 address to a network interface

- assign-ipv6-addresses (AWS CLI)
- Register-EC2Ipv6AddressList (AWS Tools for Windows PowerShell)

Unassign an IPv6 address from a network interface

- unassign-ipv6-addresses (AWS CLI)
- Unregister-EC2Ipv6AddressList (AWS Tools for Windows PowerShell)

Migrating to IPv6

If you have an existing VPC that supports IPv4 only, and resources in your subnet that are configured to use IPv4 only, you can enable IPv6 support for your VPC and resources. Your VPC can operate in dual-stack mode — your resources can communicate over IPv4, or IPv6, or both. IPv4 and IPv6 communication are independent of each other.

You cannot disable IPv4 support for your VPC and subnets; this is the default IP addressing system for Amazon VPC and Amazon EC2.

Note
This topic assumes that you have an existing VPC with public and private subnets. If you're looking for information about setting up a new VPC for use with IPv6, see Getting Started with IPv6 for Amazon VPC.

The following table provides an overview of the steps to enable your VPC and subnets to use IPv6.

Step	Notes
Step 1: Associate an IPv6 CIDR Block with Your VPC and Subnets	Associate an Amazon-provided IPv6 CIDR block with your VPC and with your subnets.
Step 2: Create and Configure an Egress-Only Internet Gateway for a Private Subnet	If you're using a NAT device in your private subnet, it does not support IPv6 traffic. Instead, create an egress-only internet gateway for your private subnet to enable outbound communication to the internet over IPv6 and prevent inbound communication. An egress-only internet gateway supports IPv6 traffic only.
Step 3: Update Your Route Tables	Update your route tables to route your IPv6 traffic. For a public subnet, create a route that routes all IPv6 traffic from the subnet to the internet gateway. For a private subnet, create a route that routes all internet-bound IPv6 traffic from the subnet to the egress-only internet gateway.
Step 4: Update Your Security Group Rules	Update your security group rules to include rules for IPv6 addresses. This enables IPv6 traffic to flow to and from your instances. If you've created custom network ACL rules to control the flow of traffic to and from your subnet, you must include rules for IPv6 traffic.
Step 5: Change Your Instance Type	If your instance type does not support IPv6, change the instance type.
Step 6: Assign IPv6 Addresses to Your Instances	Assign IPv6 addresses to your instances from the IPv6 address range of your subnet.
Step 7: (Optional) Configure IPv6 on Your Instances	If your instance was launched from an AMI that is not configured to use DHCPv6, you must manually configure your instance to recognize an IPv6 address assigned to the instance.

Before you migrate to using IPv6, ensure that you have read the features of IPv6 addressing for Amazon VPC: IPv4 and IPv6 Characteristics and Restrictions.

Topics

- Example: Enabling IPv6 in a VPC With a Public and Private Subnet
- Step 1: Associate an IPv6 CIDR Block with Your VPC and Subnets
- Step 2: Create and Configure an Egress-Only Internet Gateway for a Private Subnet
- Step 3: Update Your Route Tables
- Step 4: Update Your Security Group Rules
- Step 5: Change Your Instance Type
- Step 6: Assign IPv6 Addresses to Your Instances
- Step 7: (Optional) Configure IPv6 on Your Instances

Example: Enabling IPv6 in a VPC With a Public and Private Subnet

In this example, your VPC has a public and a private subnet. You have a database instance in your private subnet that has outbound communication with the internet through a NAT gateway in your VPC. You have a public-facing web server in your public subnet that has internet access through an internet gateway. The following diagram represents the architecture of your VPC.

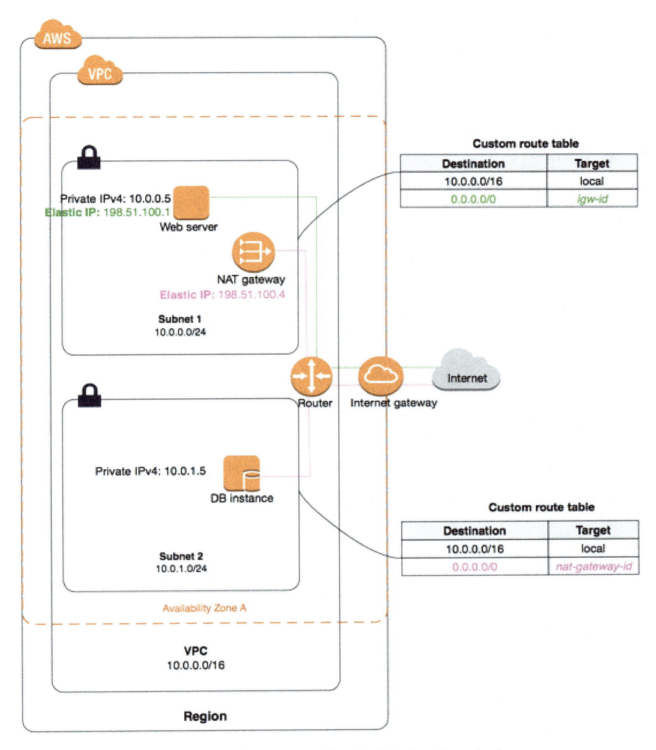

Custom route table

Destination	Target
10.0.0.0/16	local
0.0.0.0/0	igw-id

Custom route table

Destination	Target
10.0.0.0/16	local
0.0.0.0/0	nat-gateway-id

The security group for your web server (`sg-11aa22bb`) has the following inbound rules:

Type	Protocol	Port range	Source	Comment
All traffic	All	All	sg-33cc44dd	Allows inbound access for all traffic from instances associated with sg-33cc44dd (the database instance).
HTTP	TCP	80	0.0.0.0/0	Allows inbound traffic from the internet over HTTP.
HTTPS	TCP	443	0.0.0.0/0	Allows inbound traffic from the internet over HTTPS.
SSH	TCP	22	203.0.113.123/32	Allows inbound SSH access from your local computer; for example, when you need to connect to your instance to perform administration tasks.

The security group for your database instance (`sg-33cc44dd`) has the following inbound rule:

Type	Protocol	Port range	Source	Comment
MySQL	TCP	3306	sg-11aa22bb	Allows inbound access for MySQL traffic from instances associated with sg-11aa22bb (the web server instance).

Both security groups have the default outbound rule that allows all outbound IPv4 traffic, and no other outbound rules.

Your web server is `t2.medium` instance type. Your database server is an `m3.large`.

You want your VPC and resources to be enabled for IPv6, and you want them to operate in dual-stack mode; in other words, you want to use both IPv6 and IPv4 addressing between resources in your VPC and resources over the internet.

After you've completed the steps, your VPC will have the following configuration.

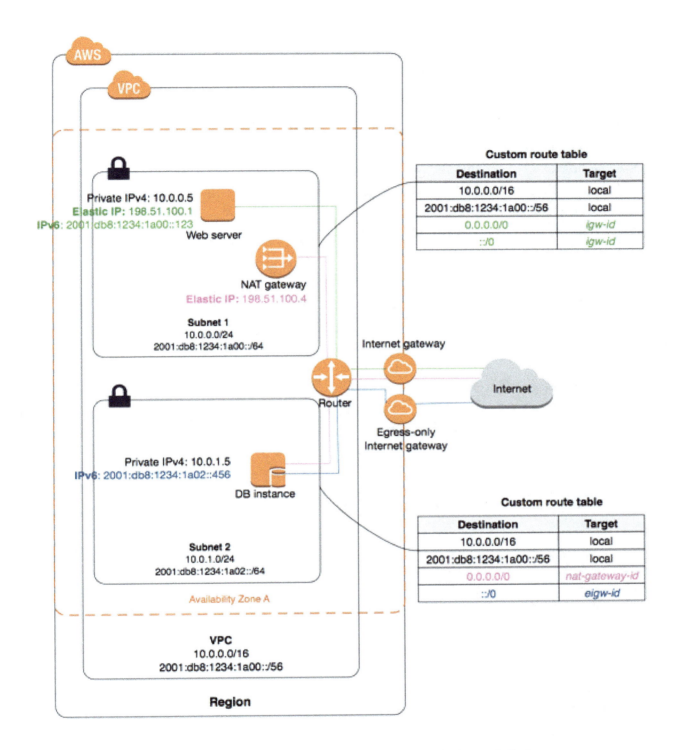

Custom route table

Destination	Target
10.0.0.0/16	local
2001:db8:1234:1a00::/56	local
0.0.0.0/0	*igw-id*
::/0	*igw-id*

Custom route table

Destination	Target
10.0.0.0/16	local
2001:db8:1234:1a00::/56	local
0.0.0.0/0	*nat-gateway-id*
::/0	*eigw-id*

Step 1: Associate an IPv6 CIDR Block with Your VPC and Subnets

You can associate an IPv6 CIDR block with your VPC, and then associate a **/64** CIDR block from that range with each subnet.

To associate an IPv6 CIDR block with a VPC

1. Open the Amazon VPC console at https://console.aws.amazon.com/vpc/.

2. In the navigation pane, choose **Your VPCs**.

3. Select your VPC, choose **Actions**, **Edit CIDRs**.

4. Choose **Add IPv6 CIDR**. After the IPv6 CIDR block has been added, choose **Close**.

To associate an IPv6 CIDR block with a subnet

1. Open the Amazon VPC console at https://console.aws.amazon.com/vpc/.

2. In the navigation pane, choose **Subnets**.

3. Select your subnet, choose **Subnet Actions**, **Edit IPv6 CIDRs**.

4. Choose **Add IPv6 CIDR**. Specify the hexadecimal pair for the subnet (for example, 00) and confirm the entry by choosing the tick icon.

5. Choose **Close**. Repeat the steps for the other subnets in your VPC.

For more information, see VPC and Subnet Sizing for IPv6.

Step 2: Create and Configure an Egress-Only Internet Gateway for a Private Subnet

An egress-only internet gateway enables outbound communication to the internet over IPv6 and prevents inbound communication.

To create an egress-only Internet Gateway

1. Open the Amazon VPC console at https://console.aws.amazon.com/vpc/.

2. In the navigation pane, choose **Egress Only Internet Gateways**, **Create Egress Only Internet Gateway**.

3. Select the VPC in which to create the egress-only internet gateway. Choose **Create**.

For more information, see Egress-Only Internet Gateways.

Step 3: Update Your Route Tables

For a public subnet, you must update the route table to enable instances (such as web servers) to use the internet gateway for IPv6 traffic. If you do not have internet gateway, see Creating and Attaching an Internet Gateway.

For a private subnet, you must update the route table to enable instances (such as database instances) to use the egress-only internet gateway for IPv6 traffic.

To update your route table for a public subnet

1. Open the Amazon VPC console at https://console.aws.amazon.com/vpc/.

2. In the navigation pane, choose **Route Tables** and select the route table that's associated with the public subnet.

3. On the **Routes** tab, choose **Edit**.

4. Choose **Add another route**. Specify ::/0 for **Destination**, select the internet gateway ID for **Target**, and then choose **Save**.

To update your route table for a private subnet

1. Open the Amazon VPC console at https://console.aws.amazon.com/vpc/.

2. In the navigation pane, choose **Route Tables** and select the route table that's associated with the private subnet.

3. On the **Routes** tab, choose **Edit**.

4. Choose **Add another route**. For **Destination**, specify ::/0. For **Target**, select the egress-only internet gateway ID you created in the previous step, and then choose **Save**.

For more information, see Routing Options.

Step 4: Update Your Security Group Rules

To enable your instances to send and receive traffic over IPv6, you must update your security group rules to include rules for IPv6 addresses.

For example, in the example above, you can update the web server security group (**sg-11aa22bb**) to add rules that allow inbound HTTP, HTTPS, and SSH access from IPv6 addresses. You do not need to make any changes to the inbound rules for your database security group; the rule that allows all communication from **sg-11aa22bb** includes IPv6 communication by default.

To update your security group rules

1. Open the Amazon VPC console at https://console.aws.amazon.com/vpc/.

2. In the navigation pane, choose **Security Groups** and select your web server security group.

3. In the **Inbound Rules** tab, choose **Edit**.

4. For each rule, choose **Add another rule**, and choose **Save** when you're done. For example, to add a rule that allows all HTTP traffic over IPv6, for **Type**, select **HTTP** and for **Source**, enter ::/0.

By default, an outbound rule that allows all IPv6 traffic is automatically added your security groups when you associate an IPv6 CIDR block with your VPC. However, if you modified the original outbound rules for your security group, this rule is not automatically added, and you must add equivalent outbound rules for IPv6 traffic. For more information, see Security Groups for Your VPC.

Update Your Network ACL Rules

If you associate an IPv6 CIDR block with your VPC, we automatically add rules to the default network ACL to allow IPv6 traffic, provided you haven't modified its default rules. If you've modified your default network ACL or if you've created a custom network ACL with rules to control the flow of traffic to and from your subnet, you must manually add rules for IPv6 traffic. For more information about recommended network ACL rules, see Recommended Network ACL Rules for Your VPC.

Step 5: Change Your Instance Type

All current generation instance types support IPv6. For more information, see Instance Types.

If your instance type does not support IPv6, you must resize the instance to a supported instance type. In the example above, the database instance is an m3.large instance type, which does not support IPv6. You must resize the instance to a supported instance type, for example, m4.large.

To resize your instance, be aware of the compatibility limitations. For more information, see Compatibility for Resizing Instances in the *Amazon EC2 User Guide for Linux Instances*. In this scenario, if your database instance was launched from an AMI that uses HVM virtualization, you can resize it to an m4.large instance type by using the following procedure.

Important
To resize your instance, you must stop it. Stopping and starting an instance changes the public IPv4 address for the instance, if it has one. If you have any data stored on instance store volumes, the data is erased.

To resize your instance

1. Open the Amazon EC2 console at https://console.aws.amazon.com/ec2/.

2. In the navigation pane, choose **Instances**, and select the database instance.

3. Choose **Actions, Instance State, Stop**.

4. In the confirmation dialog box, choose **Yes, Stop**.

5. With the instance still selected, choose **Actions, Instance Settings, Change Instance Type**.

6. For **Instance Type**, choose the new instance type, and then choose **Apply**.

7. To restart the stopped instance, select the instance and choose **Actions, Instance State, Start**. In the confirmation dialog box, choose **Yes, Start**.

If your instance is an instance store-backed AMI, you can't resize your instance using the earlier procedure. Instead, you can create an instance store-backed AMI from your instance, and launch a new instance from your AMI using a new instance type. For more information, see Creating an Instance Store-Backed Linux AMI in the *Amazon EC2 User Guide for Linux Instances*, and Creating an Instance Store-Backed Windows AMI in the *Amazon EC2 User Guide for Windows Instances*.

You may not be able to migrate to a new instance type if there are compatibility limitations. For example, if your instance was launched from an AMI that uses PV virtualization, the only instance type that supports both PV virtualization and IPv6 is C3. This instance type may not be suitable for your needs. In this case, you may have to reinstall your software on a base HVM AMI, and launch a new instance.

If you launch an instance from a new AMI, you can assign an IPv6 address to your instance during launch.

Step 6: Assign IPv6 Addresses to Your Instances

After you've verified that your instance type supports IPv6, you can assign an IPv6 address to your instance using the Amazon EC2 console. The IPv6 address is assigned to the primary network interface (eth0) for the instance.

To assign an IPv6 address to your instance

1. Open the Amazon EC2 console at https://console.aws.amazon.com/ec2/.

2. In the navigation pane, choose **Instances**.

3. Select your instance, and choose **Actions, Networking, Manage IP Addresses**.

4. Under **IPv6 Addresses**, choose **Assign new IP**. You can enter a specific IPv6 address from the range of your subnet, or you can leave the default `Auto-Assign` value to let Amazon choose one for you.

5. Choose **Yes, Update**.

Alternatively, if you launch a new instance (for example, if you were unable to resize your instance and you created a new AMI instead), you can assign an IPv6 address during launch.

To assign an IPv6 address to an instance during launch

1. Open the Amazon EC2 console at https://console.aws.amazon.com/ec2/.

2. Select your AMI and an IPv6-compatible instance type, and choose **Next: Configure Instance Details**.

3. On the **Configure Instance Details** page, select a VPC for **Network** and a subnet for **Subnet**. For **Auto-assign IPv6 IP**, select **Enable**.

4. Follow the remaining steps in the wizard to launch your instance.

Step 7: (Optional) Configure IPv6 on Your Instances

If you launched your instance using Amazon Linux 2016.09.0 or later, or Windows Server 2008 R2 or later, your instance is configured for IPv6 and no additional steps are required.

If you launched your instance from a different AMI, it may not be configured for DHCPv6, which means that any IPv6 address that you assign to the instance is not automatically recognized on the primary network interface. To verify if the IPv6 address is configured on your network interface, use the `ifconfig` command on Linux, or the `ipconfig` command on Windows.

You can configure your instance using the following steps. You'll need to connect to your instance using its public IPv4 address. For more information, see Connect to Your Linux Instance in the *Amazon EC2 User Guide for Linux Instances* and Connecting to Your Windows Instance in the *Amazon EC2 User Guide for Windows Instances.*

Topics

- Amazon Linux
- Ubuntu
- RHEL/CentOS
- Windows

Amazon Linux

To configure DHCPv6 on Amazon Linux

1. Connect to your instance using the instance's public IPv4 address.

2. Get the latest software packages for your instance:

```
1 sudo yum update -y
```

3. Using a text editor of your choice, open **/etc/sysconfig/network-scripts/ifcfg-eth0** and locate the following line:

```
1 IPV6INIT=no
```

Replace that line with the following:

```
1 IPV6INIT=yes
```

Add the following two lines, and save your changes:

```
1 DHCPV6C=yes
2 DHCPV6C_OPTIONS=-nw
```

4. Open **/etc/sysconfig/network**, remove the following lines, and save your changes:

```
1 NETWORKING_IPV6=no
2 IPV6INIT=no
3 IPV6_ROUTER=no
4 IPV6_AUTOCONF=no
5 IPV6FORWARDING=no
6 IPV6TO4INIT=no
7 IPV6_CONTROL_RADVD=no
```

5. Open **/etc/hosts**, replace the contents with the following, and save your changes:

```
1 127.0.0.1    localhost localhost.localdomain localhost4 localhost4.localdomain4
2 ::1          localhost6 localhost6.localdomain6
```

6. Reboot your instance. Reconnect to your instance and use the `ifconfig` command to verify that the IPv6 address is recognized on the primary network interface.

Ubuntu

You can configure your Ubuntu instance to dynamically recognize any IPv6 address assigned to the network interface. If your instance does not have an IPv6 address, this configuration may cause the boot time of your instance to be extended by up to 5 minutes.

These steps must be performed as the root user.

Topics

- Ubuntu Server 16
- Ubuntu Server 14
- Starting the DHCPv6 Client

Ubuntu Server 16

To configure IPv6 on a running Ubuntu Server 16 instance

1. Connect to your instance using the instance's public IPv4 address.

2. View the contents of the /etc/network/interfaces.d/50-cloud-init.cfg file:

```
1 cat /etc/network/interfaces.d/50-cloud-init.cfg
```

```
1 # This file is generated from information provided by
2 # the datasource.  Changes to it will not persist across an instance.
3 # To disable cloud-init's network configuration capabilities, write a file
4 # /etc/cloud/cloud.cfg.d/99-disable-network-config.cfg with the following:
5 # network: {config: disabled}
6 auto lo
7 iface lo inet loopback
8
9 auto eth0
10 iface eth0 inet dhcp
```

Verify that the loopback network device (`lo`) is configured, and take note of the name of the network interface. In this example, the network interface name is `eth0`; the name may be different depending on the instance type.

3. Create the file /etc/network/interfaces.d/60-default-with-ipv6.cfg and add the following line. If required, replace `eth0` with the name of the network interface that you retrieved in the step above.

```
1 iface eth0 inet6 dhcp
```

4. Reboot your instance, or restart the network interface by running the following command. If required, replace `eth0` with the name of your network interface.

```
1 sudo ifdown eth0 ; sudo ifup eth0
```

5. Reconnect to your instance and use the `ifconfig` command to verify that the IPv6 address is configured on the network interface.

To configure IPv6 using user data

- You can launch a new Ubuntu instance and ensure that any IPv6 address assigned to the instance is automatically configured on the network interface by specifying the following user data during launch:

```
1 #!/bin/bash
2 echo "iface eth0 inet6 dhcp" >> /etc/network/interfaces.d/60-default-with-ipv6.cfg
3 dhclient -6
```

In this case, you do not have to connect to the instance to configure the IPv6 address.

For more information, see Running Commands on Your Linux Instance at Launch in the *Amazon EC2 User Guide for Linux Instances*.

Ubuntu Server 14

If you're using Ubuntu Server 14, you must include a workaround for a known issue that occurs when restarting a dual-stack network interface (the restart results in an extended timeout during which your instance is unreachable).

These steps must be performed as the root user.

To configure IPv6 on a running Ubuntu Server 14 instance

1. Connect to your instance using the instance's public IPv4 address.

2. Edit the /etc/network/interfaces.d/eth0.cfg file so that it contains the following:

```
1 auto lo
2 iface lo inet loopback
3 auto eth0
4 iface eth0 inet dhcp
5     up dhclient -6 $IFACE
```

3. Reboot your instance:

```
1 sudo reboot
```

4. Reconnect to your instance and use the ifconfig command to verify that the IPv6 address is configured on the network interface.

Starting the DHCPv6 Client

Alternatively, to bring up the IPv6 address for the network interface immediately without performing any additional configuration, you can start the DHCPv6 client for the instance. However, the IPv6 address does not persist on the network interface after reboot.

To start the DHCPv6 client on Ubuntu

1. Connect to your instance using the instance's public IPv4 address.

2. Start the DHCPv6 client:

```
1 sudo dhclient -6
```

3. Use the ifconfig command to verify that the IPv6 address is recognized on the primary network interface.

RHEL/CentOS

RHEL 7.4 and CentOS 7 and later use cloud-init to configure your network interface and generate the /etc/sysconfig/network-scripts/ifcfg-eth0 file. You can create a custom cloud-init configuration file to enable DHCPv6, which generates an ifcfg-eth0 file with settings that enable DHCPv6 after each reboot.

Note
Due to a known issue, if you're using RHEL/CentOS 7.4 with the latest version of cloud-init-0.7.9, these steps

might result in you losing connectivity to your instance after reboot. As a workaround, you can manually edit the `/etc/sysconfig/network-scripts/ifcfg-eth0` file.

To configure DHCPv6 on RHEL 7.4 or CentOS 7

1. Connect to your instance using the instance's public IPv4 address.

2. Using a text editor of your choice, create a custom file, for example:

```
/etc/cloud/cloud.cfg.d/99-custom-networking.cfg
```

3. Add the following lines to your file, and save your changes:

```
network:
  version: 1
  config:
  - type: physical
    name: eth0
    subnets:
      - type: dhcp
      - type: dhcp6
```

4. Reboot your instance.

5. Reconnect to your instance and use the `ifconfig` command to verify that the IPv6 address is configured on the network interface.

For RHEL versions 7.3 and earlier, you can use the following procedure to modify the `/etc/sysconfig/network-scripts/ifcfg-eth0` file directly.

To configure DHCPv6 on RHEL 7.3 and earlier

1. Connect to your instance using the instance's public IPv4 address.

2. Using a text editor of your choice, open `/etc/sysconfig/network-scripts/ifcfg-eth0` and locate the following line:

```
IPV6INIT="no"
```

Replace that line with the following:

```
IPV6INIT="yes"
```

Add the following two lines, and save your changes:

```
DHCPV6C=yes
NM_CONTROLLED=no
```

3. Open `/etc/sysconfig/network`, add or amend the following line as follows, and save your changes:

```
NETWORKING_IPV6=yes
```

4. Restart networking on your instance by running the following command:

```
sudo service network restart
```

You can use the `ifconfig` command to verify that the IPv6 address is recognized on the primary network interface.

To configure DHCPv6 on RHEL 6 or CentOS 6

1. Connect to your instance using the instance's public IPv4 address.

2. Follow steps 2 - 4 in the procedure above for configuring RHEL 7/CentOS 7.

3. If you restart networking and you get an error that an IPv6 address cannot be obtained, open /etc/sysconfig/network-scripts/ifup-eth and locate the following line (by default, it's line 327):

```
1 if /sbin/dhclient "$DHCLIENTARGS"; then
```

Remove the quotes that surround $DHCLIENTARGS and save your changes. Restart networking on your instance:

```
1 sudo service network restart
```

Windows

Use the following procedures to configure IPv6 on Windows Server 2003 and Windows Server 2008 SP2.

To ensure that IPv6 is preferred over IPv4, download the fix named **Prefer IPv6 over IPv4 in prefix policies** from the following Microsoft support page: https://support.microsoft.com/en-us/help/929852/how-to-disable-ipv6-or-its-components-in-windows.

To enable and configure IPv6 on Windows Server 2003

1. Get the IPv6 address of your instance by using the describe-instances AWS CLI command, or by checking the **IPv6 IPs** field for the instance in the Amazon EC2 console.

2. Connect to your instance using the instance's public IPv4 address.

3. From within your instance, choose **Start**, **Control Panel**, **Network Connections**, **Local Area Connection**.

4. Choose **Properties**, and then choose **Install**.

5. Choose **Protocol**, and choose **Add**. In the **Network Protocol** list, choose **Microsoft TCP/IP version 6**, and then choose **OK**.

6. Open the command prompt and open the network shell.

```
1 netsh
```

7. Switch to the interface IPv6 context.

```
1 interface ipv6
```

8. Add the IPv6 address to the local area connection using the following command. Replace the value for the IPv6 address with the IPv6 address for your instance.

```
1 add address "Local Area Connection" "ipv6-address"
```

For example:

```
1 add address "Local Area Connection" "2001:db8:1234:1a00:1a01:2b:12:d08b"
```

9. Exit the network shell.

```
1 exit
```

10. Use the `ipconfig` command to verify that the IPv6 address is recognized for the Local Area Connection.

To enable and configure IPv6 on Windows Server 2008 SP2

1. Get the IPv6 address of your instance by using the describe-instances AWS CLI command, or by checking the **IPv6 IPs** field for the instance in the Amazon EC2 console.

2. Connect to your Windows instance using the instance's public IPv4 address.

3. Choose **Start, Control Panel**.

4. Open the **Network and Sharing Center**, then open **Network Connections**.

5. Right-click **Local Area Network** (for the network interface) and choose **Properties**.

6. Choose the **Internet Protocol Version 6 (TCP/IPv6)** check box, and choose **OK**.

7. Open the properties dialog box for Local Area Network again. Choose **Internet Protocol Version 6 (TCP/IPv6)** and choose **Properties**.

8. Choose **Use the following IPv6 address** and do the following:

   - For **IPv6 Address**, enter the IPv6 address you obtained in step 1.
   - For **Subnet prefix length**, enter **64**.

9. Choose **OK** and close the properties dialog box.

10. Open the command prompt. Use the `ipconfig` command to verify that the IPv6 address is recognized for the Local Area Connection.

Security

Amazon VPC provides features that you can use to increase and monitor the security for your VPC:

- Security groups — Act as a firewall for associated Amazon EC2 instances, controlling both inbound and outbound traffic at the instance level
- Network access control lists (ACLs) — Act as a firewall for associated subnets, controlling both inbound and outbound traffic at the subnet level
- Flow logs — Capture information about the IP traffic going to and from network interfaces in your VPC

When you launch an instance in a VPC, you can associate one or more security groups that you've created. Each instance in your VPC could belong to a different set of security groups. If you don't specify a security group when you launch an instance, the instance automatically belongs to the default security group for the VPC. For more information about security groups, see Security Groups for Your VPC

You can secure your VPC instances using only security groups; however, you can add network ACLs as a second layer of defense. For more information about network ACLs, see Network ACLs.

You can monitor the accepted and rejected IP traffic going to and from your instances by creating a flow log for a VPC, subnet, or individual network interface. Flow log data is published to CloudWatch Logs, and can help you diagnose overly restrictive or overly permissive security group and network ACL rules. For more information, see VPC Flow Logs.

You can use AWS Identity and Access Management to control who in your organization has permission to create and manage security groups, network ACLs and flow logs. For example, you can give only your network administrators that permission, but not personnel who only need to launch instances. For more information, see Controlling Access to Amazon VPC Resources.

Amazon security groups and network ACLs don't filter traffic to or from link-local addresses (169.254.0.0/16) or AWS-reserved IPv4 addresses—these are the first four IPv4 addresses of the subnet (including the Amazon DNS server address for the VPC). Similarly, flow logs do not capture IP traffic to or from these addresses. These addresses support the services: Domain Name Services (DNS), Dynamic Host Configuration Protocol (DHCP), Amazon EC2 instance metadata, Key Management Server (KMS—license management for Windows instances), and routing in the subnet. You can implement additional firewall solutions in your instances to block network communication with link-local addresses.

Comparison of Security Groups and Network ACLs

The following table summarizes the basic differences between security groups and network ACLs.

Security Group	Network ACL
Operates at the instance level (first layer of defense)	Operates at the subnet level (second layer of defense)
Supports allow rules only	Supports allow rules and deny rules
Is stateful: Return traffic is automatically allowed, regardless of any rules	Is stateless: Return traffic must be explicitly allowed by rules
We evaluate all rules before deciding whether to allow traffic	We process rules in number order when deciding whether to allow traffic
Applies to an instance only if someone specifies the security group when launching the instance, or associates the security group with the instance later on	Automatically applies to all instances in the subnets it's associated with (backup layer of defense, so you don't have to rely on someone specifying the security group)

The following diagram illustrates the layers of security provided by security groups and network ACLs. For example, traffic from an Internet gateway is routed to the appropriate subnet using the routes in the routing table. The rules of the network ACL associated with the subnet control which traffic is allowed to the subnet. The rules of the security group associated with an instance control which traffic is allowed to the instance.

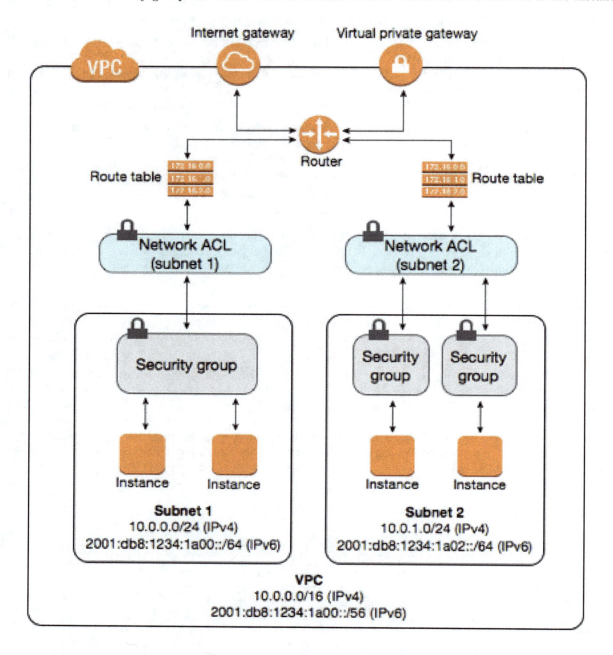

Security Groups for Your VPC

A *security group* acts as a virtual firewall for your instance to control inbound and outbound traffic. When you launch an instance in a VPC, you can assign up to five security groups to the instance. Security groups act at the instance level, not the subnet level. Therefore, each instance in a subnet in your VPC could be assigned to a different set of security groups. If you don't specify a particular group at launch time, the instance is automatically assigned to the default security group for the VPC.

For each security group, you add *rules* that control the inbound traffic to instances, and a separate set of rules that control the outbound traffic. This section describes the basic things you need to know about security groups for your VPC and their rules.

You might set up network ACLs with rules similar to your security groups in order to add an additional layer of security to your VPC. For more information about the differences between security groups and network ACLs, see Comparison of Security Groups and Network ACLs.

Topics

- Security Group Basics
- Default Security Group for Your VPC
- Security Group Rules
- Differences Between Security Groups for EC2-Classic and EC2-VPC
- Working with Security Groups

Security Group Basics

The following are the basic characteristics of security groups for your VPC:

- You have limits on the number of security groups that you can create per VPC, the number of rules that you can add to each security group, and the number of security groups you can associate with a network interface. For more information, see Amazon VPC Limits.
- You can specify allow rules, but not deny rules.
- You can specify separate rules for inbound and outbound traffic.
- When you create a security group, it has no inbound rules. Therefore, no inbound traffic originating from another host to your instance is allowed until you add inbound rules to the security group.
- By default, a security group includes an outbound rule that allows all outbound traffic. You can remove the rule and add outbound rules that allow specific outbound traffic only. If your security group has no outbound rules, no outbound traffic originating from your instance is allowed.
- Security groups are stateful — if you send a request from your instance, the response traffic for that request is allowed to flow in regardless of inbound security group rules. Responses to allowed inbound traffic are allowed to flow out, regardless of outbound rules. **Note**
  Some types of traffic are tracked differently to others. For more information, see Connection Tracking in the *Amazon EC2 User Guide for Linux Instances*.
- Instances associated with a security group can't talk to each other unless you add rules allowing it (exception: the default security group has these rules by default).
- Security groups are associated with network interfaces. After you launch an instance, you can change the security groups associated with the instance, which changes the security groups associated with the primary network interface (eth0). You can also change the security groups associated with any other network interface. For more information about network interfaces, see Elastic Network Interfaces.
- When you create a security group, you must provide it with a name and a description. The following rules apply:
  - Names and descriptions can be up to 255 characters in length.
  - Names and descriptions are limited to the following characters: a-z, A-Z, 0-9, spaces, and ._-:/()#,@[]+=&;{}!$*.
  - A security group name cannot start with **sg-**.

137

- A security group name must be unique within the VPC.

Default Security Group for Your VPC

Your VPC automatically comes with a default security group. Each EC2 instance that you launch in your VPC is automatically associated with the default security group if you don't specify a different security group when you launch the instance.

The following table describes the default rules for a default security group.

Inbound
Source
The security group ID (sg-*xxxxxxxx*)
Outbound
Destination
0.0.0.0/0
::/0

You can change the rules for the default security group.

You can't delete a default security group. If you try to delete the default security group, you'll get the following error: `Client.CannotDelete: the specified group: "sg-51530134" name: "default" cannot be deleted by a user`.

Note
If you've modified the outbound rules for your security group, we do not automatically add an outbound rule for IPv6 traffic when you associate an IPv6 block with your VPC.

Security Group Rules

You can add or remove rules for a security group (also referred to as *authorizing* or *revoking* inbound or outbound access). A rule applies either to inbound traffic (ingress) or outbound traffic (egress). You can grant access to a specific CIDR range, or to another security group in your VPC or in a peer VPC (requires a VPC peering connection).

The following are the basic parts of a security group rule in a VPC:

- (Inbound rules only) The source of the traffic and the destination port or port range. The source can be another security group, an IPv4 or IPv6 CIDR block, or a single IPv4 or IPv6 address.
- (Outbound rules only) The destination for the traffic and the destination port or port range. The destination can be another security group, an IPv4 or IPv6 CIDR block, or a single IPv4 or IPv6 address.
- Any protocol that has a standard protocol number (for a list, see Protocol Numbers). If you specify ICMP as the protocol, you can specify any or all of the ICMP types and codes.
- An optional description for the security group rule to help you identify it later. A description can be up to 255 characters in length. Allowed characters are a-z, A-Z, 0-9, spaces, and ._-:/()#,@[]+=;{}!$*.

When you specify a security group as the source for a rule, this allows instances associated with the source security group to access instances in the security group. This does not add rules from the source security group to this security group. Incoming traffic is allowed based on the private IP addresses of the instances that are associated with the source security group (and not the public IP or Elastic IP addresses).

If you specify a single IPv4 address, specify the address using the /32 prefix length. If you specify a single IPv6 address, specify it using the /128 prefix length.

Some systems for setting up firewalls let you filter on source ports. Security groups let you filter only on destination ports.

When you add or remove rules, they are automatically applied to all instances associated with the security group.

The kind of rules you add may depend on the purpose of the instance. The following table describes example rules for a security group for web servers. The web servers can receive HTTP and HTTPS traffic from all IPv4 and IPv6 addresses, and send SQL or MySQL traffic to a database server.

Inbound	
Source	
0.0.0.0/0	
::/0	
0.0.0.0/0	
::/0	
Your network's public IPv4 address range	
Your network's public IPv4 address range	
Outbound	
Destination	
The ID of the security group for your database servers	
The ID of the security group for your MySQL database servers	

A database server would need a different set of rules; for example, instead of inbound HTTP and HTTPS traffic, you can add a rule that allows inbound MySQL or Microsoft SQL Server access. For an example of security group rules for web servers and database servers, see Security.

For examples of security group rules for specific kinds of access, see Security Group Rules Reference in the *Amazon EC2 User Guide for Linux Instances*.

Stale Security Group Rules

If your VPC has a VPC peering connection with another VPC, a security group rule can reference another security group in the peer VPC. This allows instances associated with the referenced security group to communicate with instances associated with the referencing security group.

If the owner of the peer VPC deletes the referenced security group, or if you or the owner of the peer VPC deletes the VPC peering connection, the security group rule is marked as `stale`. You can delete stale security group rules as you would any other security group rule.

For more information, see Working With Stale Security Groups in the *Amazon VPC Peering Guide*.

Differences Between Security Groups for EC2-Classic and EC2-VPC

If you're already an Amazon EC2 user, you're probably familiar with security groups. However, you can't use the security groups that you've created for use with EC2-Classic with instances in your VPC. You must create security groups specifically for use with instances in your VPC. The rules you create for use with a security group for a VPC can't reference a security group for EC2-Classic, and vice versa.

The following table summarizes the differences between security groups for use with EC2-Classic and those for use with EC2-VPC.

EC2-Classic	EC2-VPC
You can create up to 500 security groups per region.	You can create up to 500 security groups per VPC.
You can add up to 100 rules to a security group.	You can add up to 50 rules to a security group.

EC2-Classic	EC2-VPC
You can add rules for inbound traffic only.	You can add rules for inbound and outbound traffic.
You can assign up to 500 security groups to an instance.	You can assign up to 5 security groups to a network interface.
You can reference security groups from other AWS accounts.	You can reference security groups from your VPC or from a peer VPC in a VPC peering connection only. The peer VPC can be in a different account.
After you launch an instance, you can't change the security groups assigned to it.	You can change the security groups assigned to an instance after it's launched.
When you add a rule to a security group, you don't have to specify a protocol, and only TCP, UDP, or ICMP are available.	When you add a rule to a security group, you must specify a protocol, and it can be any protocol with a standard protocol number, or all protocols (see Protocol Numbers).
When you add a rule to a security group, you must specify port numbers (for TCP or UDP).	When you add a rule to a security group, you can specify port numbers only if the rule is for TCP or UDP, and you can specify all port numbers.
Security groups that are referenced in another security group's rules cannot be deleted.	Security groups that are referenced in another security group's rules can be deleted if the security groups are in different VPCs. If the referenced security group is deleted, the rule is marked as stale. You can use the describe-stale-security-groups AWS CLI command to identify stale rules.
You cannot specify an IPv6 CIDR block or an IPv6 address as the source or destination in a security group rule.	You can specify an IPv6 CIDR block or an IPv6 address as the source or destination in a security group rule.

Working with Security Groups

This section shows you how to work with security groups using the Amazon VPC console.

Topics

- Modifying the Default Security Group
- Creating a Security Group
- Adding, Removing, and Updating Rules
- Changing an Instance's Security Groups
- Deleting a Security Group
- Deleting the 2009-07-15-default Security Group

Modifying the Default Security Group

Your VPC includes a default security group whose initial rules are to deny all inbound traffic, allow all outbound traffic, and allow all traffic between instances in the group. You can't delete this group; however, you can change the group's rules. The procedure is the same as modifying any other security group. For more information, see Adding, Removing, and Updating Rules.

Creating a Security Group

Although you can use the default security group for your instances, you might want to create your own groups to reflect the different roles that instances play in your system.

To create a security group using the console

1. Open the Amazon VPC console at https://console.aws.amazon.com/vpc/.

2. In the navigation pane, choose **Security Groups**.

3. Choose **Create Security Group**.

4. Enter a name of the security group (for example, `my-security-group`) and provide a description. Select the ID of your VPC from the **VPC** menu and choose **Yes, Create**.

To create a security group using the command line

- create-security-group (AWS CLI)
- New-EC2SecurityGroup (AWS Tools for Windows PowerShell)

Describe one or more security groups using the command line

- describe-security-groups (AWS CLI)
- Get-EC2SecurityGroup (AWS Tools for Windows PowerShell)

By default, new security groups start with only an outbound rule that allows all traffic to leave the instances. You must add rules to enable any inbound traffic or to restrict the outbound traffic.

Adding, Removing, and Updating Rules

When you add or remove a rule, any instances already assigned to the security group are subject to the change.

If you have a VPC peering connection, you can reference security groups from the peer VPC as the source or destination in your security group rules. For more information, see Updating Your Security Groups to Reference Peered VPC Security Groups in the *Amazon VPC Peering Guide*.

To add a rule using the console

1. Open the Amazon VPC console at https://console.aws.amazon.com/vpc/.

2. In the navigation pane, choose **Security Groups**.

3. Select the security group to update. The details pane displays the details for the security group, plus tabs for working with its inbound rules and outbound rules.

4. On the **Inbound Rules** tab, choose **Edit**. Select an option for a rule for inbound traffic for **Type**, and then fill in the required information. For example, for a public web server, choose **HTTP** or **HTTPS** and specify a value for **Source** as 0.0.0.0/0. **Note**
If you use 0.0.0.0/0, you enable all IPv4 addresses to access your instance using HTTP or HTTPS. To restrict access, enter a specific IP address or range of addresses.

5. Optionally provide a description for the rule, and choose **Save**.

6. You can also allow communication between all instances associated with this security group. On the **Inbound Rules** tab, choose **All Traffic** from the **Type** list. Start typing the ID of the security group for **Source**; this provides you with a list of security groups. Select the security group from the list and choose **Save**.

7. If you need to, you can use the **Outbound Rules** tab to add rules for outbound traffic.

To delete a rule using the console

1. Open the Amazon VPC console at https://console.aws.amazon.com/vpc/.

2. In the navigation pane, choose **Security Groups**.

3. Select the security group to update. The details pane displays the details for the security group, plus tabs for working with its inbound rules and outbound rules.

4. Choose **Edit**, select the role to delete, and then choose **Remove**, **Save**.

When you modify the protocol, port range, or source or destination of an existing security group rule using the console, the console deletes the existing rule and adds a new one for you.

To update a rule using the console

1. Open the Amazon VPC console at https://console.aws.amazon.com/vpc/.

2. In the navigation pane, choose **Security Groups**.

3. Select the security group to update, and choose **Inbound Rules** to update a rule for inbound traffic or **Outbound Rules** to update a rule for outbound traffic.

4. Choose **Edit**. Modify the rule entry as required and choose **Save**.

To update the protocol, port range, or source or destination of an existing rule using the Amazon EC2 API or a command line tool, you cannot modify the rule; instead, you must delete the existing rule and add a new rule. To update the rule description only, you can use the update-security-group-rule-descriptions-ingress and update-security-group-rule-descriptions-egress commands.

To add a rule to a security group using the command line

- authorize-security-group-ingress and authorize-security-group-egress (AWS CLI)
- Grant-EC2SecurityGroupIngress and Grant-EC2SecurityGroupEgress (AWS Tools for Windows PowerShell)

To delete a rule from a security group using the command line

- revoke-security-group-ingress and revoke-security-group-egress(AWS CLI)
- Revoke-EC2SecurityGroupIngress and Revoke-EC2SecurityGroupEgress (AWS Tools for Windows Power-Shell)

To update the description for a security group rule using the command line

- update-security-group-rule-descriptions-ingress and update-security-group-rule-descriptions-egress (AWS CLI)
- Update-EC2SecurityGroupRuleIngressDescription and Update-EC2SecurityGroupRuleEgressDescription (AWS Tools for Windows PowerShell)

Changing an Instance's Security Groups

After you launch an instance into a VPC, you can change the security groups that are associated with the instance. You can change the security groups for an instance when the instance is in the running or stopped state.

Note

This procedure changes the security groups that are associated with the primary network interface (eth0) of the instance. To change the security groups for other network interfaces, see Changing the Security Group of a Network Interface.

To change the security groups for an instance using the console

1. Open the Amazon EC2 console at https://console.aws.amazon.com/ec2/.

2. In the navigation pane, choose **Instances**.

3. Open the context (right-click) menu for the instance and choose **Networking**, **Change Security Groups**.

4. In the **Change Security Groups** dialog box, select one or more security groups from the list and choose **Assign Security Groups**.

To change the security groups for an instance using the command line

- modify-instance-attribute (AWS CLI)
- Edit-EC2InstanceAttribute (AWS Tools for Windows PowerShell)

Deleting a Security Group

You can delete a security group only if there are no instances assigned to it (either running or stopped). You can assign the instances to another security group before you delete the security group (see Changing an Instance's Security Groups). You can't delete a default security group.

If you're using the console, you can delete more than one security group at a time. If you're using the command line or the API, you can only delete one security group at a time.

To delete a security group using the console

1. Open the Amazon VPC console at https://console.aws.amazon.com/vpc/.

2. In the navigation pane, choose **Security Groups**.

3. Select one or more security groups and choose **Security Group Actions, Delete Security Group**.

4. In the **Delete Security Group** dialog box, choose **Yes, Delete**.

To delete a security group using the command line

- delete-security-group (AWS CLI)
- Remove-EC2SecurityGroup (AWS Tools for Windows PowerShell)

Deleting the 2009-07-15-default Security Group

Any VPC created using an API version older than 2011-01-01 has the 2009-07-15-default security group. This security group exists in addition to the regular default security group that comes with every VPC. You can't attach an Internet gateway to a VPC that has the 2009-07-15-default security group. Therefore, you must delete this security group before you can attach an Internet gateway to the VPC.

Note
If you assigned this security group to any instances, you must assign these instances a different security group before you can delete the security group.

To delete the 2009-07-15-default security group

1. Ensure that this security group is not assigned to any instances.

    1. Open the Amazon EC2 console at https://console.aws.amazon.com/ec2/.

    2. In the navigation pane, choose **Network Interfaces**.

    3. Select the network interface for the instance from the list, and choose **Change Security Groups, Actions**.

    4. In the **Change Security Groups** dialog box, select a new security group from the list, and choose **Save. Note**
    When changing an instance's security group, you can select multiple groups from the list. The security groups that you select replace the current security groups for the instance.

    5. Repeat the preceding steps for each instance.

2. Open the Amazon VPC console at https://console.aws.amazon.com/vpc/.

3. In the navigation pane, choose **Security Groups**.

4. Choose the `2009-07-15-default` security group, then choose **Security Group Actions**, **Delete Security Group**.

5. In the **Delete Security Group** dialog box, choose **Yes, Delete**.

Network ACLs

A *network access control list (ACL)* is an optional layer of security for your VPC that acts as a firewall for controlling traffic in and out of one or more subnets. You might set up network ACLs with rules similar to your security groups in order to add an additional layer of security to your VPC. For more information about the differences between security groups and network ACLs, see Comparison of Security Groups and Network ACLs.

Topics

- Network ACL Basics
- Network ACL Rules
- Default Network ACL
- Custom Network ACL
- Ephemeral Ports
- Working with Network ACLs
- Example: Controlling Access to Instances in a Subnet
- API and Command Overview

Network ACL Basics

The following are the basic things that you need to know about network ACLs:

- Your VPC automatically comes with a modifiable default network ACL. By default, it allows all inbound and outbound IPv4 traffic and, if applicable, IPv6 traffic.
- You can create a custom network ACL and associate it with a subnet. By default, each custom network ACL denies all inbound and outbound traffic until you add rules.
- Each subnet in your VPC must be associated with a network ACL. If you don't explicitly associate a subnet with a network ACL, the subnet is automatically associated with the default network ACL.
- You can associate a network ACL with multiple subnets; however, a subnet can be associated with only one network ACL at a time. When you associate a network ACL with a subnet, the previous association is removed.
- A network ACL contains a numbered list of rules that we evaluate in order, starting with the lowest numbered rule, to determine whether traffic is allowed in or out of any subnet associated with the network ACL. The highest number that you can use for a rule is 32766. We recommend that you start by creating rules in increments (for example, increments of 10 or 100) so that you can insert new rules where you need to later on.
- A network ACL has separate inbound and outbound rules, and each rule can either allow or deny traffic.
- Network ACLs are stateless; responses to allowed inbound traffic are subject to the rules for outbound traffic (and vice versa).

For more information about the number of network ACLs you can create, see Amazon VPC Limits.

Network ACL Rules

You can add or remove rules from the default network ACL, or create additional network ACLs for your VPC. When you add or remove rules from a network ACL, the changes are automatically applied to the subnets it's associated with.

The following are the parts of a network ACL rule:

- Rule number. Rules are evaluated starting with the lowest numbered rule. As soon as a rule matches traffic, it's applied regardless of any higher-numbered rule that may contradict it.
- Protocol. You can specify any protocol that has a standard protocol number. For more information, see Protocol Numbers. If you specify ICMP as the protocol, you can specify any or all of the ICMP types and codes.

- [Inbound rules only] The source of the traffic (CIDR range) and the destination (listening) port or port range.
- [Outbound rules only] The destination for the traffic (CIDR range) and the destination port or port range.
- Choice of ALLOW or DENY for the specified traffic.

Default Network ACL

The default network ACL is configured to allow all traffic to flow in and out of the subnets to which it is associated. Each network ACL also includes a rule whose rule number is an asterisk. This rule ensures that if a packet doesn't match any of the other numbered rules, it's denied. You can't modify or remove this rule.

The following is an example default network ACL for a VPC that supports IPv4 only.

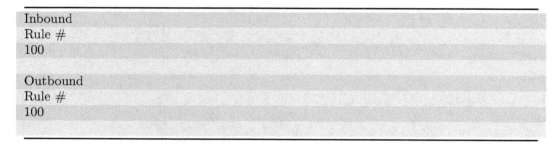

If you create a VPC with an IPv6 CIDR block or if you associate an IPv6 CIDR block with your existing VPC, we automatically add rules that allow all IPv6 traffic to flow in and out of your subnet. We also add rules whose rule numbers are an asterisk that ensures that a packet is denied if it doesn't match any of the other numbered rules. You can't modify or remove these rules. The following is an example default network ACL for a VPC that supports IPv4 and IPv6.

Note
If you've modified your default network ACL's inbound rules, we do not automatically add an ALLOW rule for inbound IPv6 traffic when you associate an IPv6 block with your VPC. Similarly, if you've modified the outbound rules, we do not automatically add an ALLOW rule for outbound IPv6 traffic.

Custom Network ACL

The following table shows an example of a custom network ACL for a VPC that supports IPv4 only. It includes rules that allow HTTP and HTTPS traffic in (inbound rules 100 and 110). There's a corresponding outbound rule that enables responses to that inbound traffic (outbound rule 120, which covers ephemeral ports 32768-65535). For more information about how to select the appropriate ephemeral port range, see Ephemeral Ports.

The network ACL also includes inbound rules that allow SSH and RDP traffic into the subnet. The outbound rule 120 enables responses to egress the subnet.

The network ACL has outbound rules (100 and 110) that allow outbound HTTP and HTTPS traffic out of the subnet. There's a corresponding inbound rule that enables responses to that outbound traffic (inbound rule 140, which covers ephemeral ports 32768-65535).

Note
Each network ACL includes a default rule whose rule number is an asterisk. This rule ensures that if a packet doesn't match any of the other rules, it's denied. You can't modify or remove this rule.

Inbound
Rule #
100
110
120
130
140
Outbound
Rule #
100
110
120

As a packet comes to the subnet, we evaluate it against the ingress rules of the ACL the subnet is associated with (starting at the top of the list of rules, and moving to the bottom). Here's how the evaluation goes if the packet is destined for the SSL port (443). The packet doesn't match the first rule evaluated (rule 100). It does match the second rule (110), which allows the packet into the subnet. If the packet had been destined for port 139 (NetBIOS), it doesn't match any of the rules, and the * rule ultimately denies the packet.

You might want to add a DENY rule in a situation where you legitimately need to open a wide range of ports, but there are certain ports within that range you want to deny. Just make sure to place the DENY rule earlier in the table than the rule that allows the wide range of port traffic.

Important
With Elastic Load Balancing, if the subnet for your back-end instances has a network ACL in which you've added a DENY rule for all traffic with a source of 0.0.0.0/0 or the subnet's CIDR, then your load balancer can't carry out health checks on the instances. For more information about the recommended network ACL rules for your load balancers and back-end instances, see Network ACLs for Load Balancers in a VPC in the *User Guide for Classic Load Balancers*.

The following table shows the same example of a custom network ACL for a VPC that has an associated IPv6 CIDR block. This network ACL includes rules for all IPv6 HTTP and HTTPS traffic. In this case, new rules were inserted between the existing rules for IPv4 traffic; however, you can also add the rules as higher number rules after the IPv4 rules. IPv4 and IPv6 traffic are separate; therefore, none of the rules for the IPv4 traffic apply to the IPv6 traffic.

Inbound
Rule #
100
105
110
115
120

130			
140			
145			
Outbound			
Rule #			
100			
105			
110			
115			
120			
125			

Ephemeral Ports

The example network ACL in the preceding section uses an ephemeral port range of 32768-65535. However, you might want to use a different range for your network ACLs depending on the type of client that you're using or with which you're communicating.

The client that initiates the request chooses the ephemeral port range. The range varies depending on the client's operating system. Many Linux kernels (including the Amazon Linux kernel) use ports 32768-61000. Requests originating from Elastic Load Balancing use ports 1024-65535. Windows operating systems through Windows Server 2003 use ports 1025-5000. Windows Server 2008 and later versions use ports 49152-65535. A NAT gateway uses ports 1024-65535. For example, if a request comes into a web server in your VPC from a Windows XP client on the Internet, your network ACL must have an outbound rule to enable traffic destined for ports 1025-5000.

If an instance in your VPC is the client initiating a request, your network ACL must have an inbound rule to enable traffic destined for the ephemeral ports specific to the type of instance (Amazon Linux, Windows Server 2008, and so on).

In practice, to cover the different types of clients that might initiate traffic to public-facing instances in your VPC, you can open ephemeral ports 1024-65535. However, you can also add rules to the ACL to deny traffic on any malicious ports within that range. Ensure that you place the DENY rules earlier in the table than the ALLOW rules that open the wide range of ephemeral ports.

Working with Network ACLs

This section shows you how to work with network ACLs using the Amazon VPC console.

Topics

- Determining Network ACL Associations
- Creating a Network ACL
- Adding and Deleting Rules
- Associating a Subnet with a Network ACL
- Disassociating a Network ACL from a Subnet
- Changing a Subnet's Network ACL
- Deleting a Network ACL

Determining Network ACL Associations

You can use the Amazon VPC console to determine the network ACL that's associated with a subnet. Network ACLs can be associated with more than one subnet, so you can also determine the subnets that are associated with a network ACL.

To determine which network ACL is associated with a subnet

1. Open the Amazon VPC console at https://console.aws.amazon.com/vpc/.

2. In the navigation pane, choose **Subnets**, and then select the subnet.

   The network ACL associated with the subnet is included in the **Network ACL** tab, along with the network ACL's rules.

To determine which subnets are associated with a network ACL

1. Open the Amazon VPC console at https://console.aws.amazon.com/vpc/.

2. In the navigation pane, choose **Network ACLs**. The **Associated With** column indicates the number of associated subnets for each network ACL.

3. Select a network ACL.

4. In the details pane, choose **Subnet Associations** to display the subnets associated with the network ACL.

Creating a Network ACL

You can create a custom network ACL for your VPC. By default, a network ACL that you create blocks all inbound and outbound traffic until you add rules, and is not associated with a subnet until you explicitly associate it with one.

To create a network ACL

1. Open the Amazon VPC console at https://console.aws.amazon.com/vpc/.

2. In the navigation pane, choose **Network ACLs**.

3. Choose **Create Network ACL**.

4. In the **Create Network ACL** dialog box, optionally name your network ACL, and then select the ID of your VPC from the **VPC** list, and choose **Yes, Create**.

Adding and Deleting Rules

When you add or delete a rule from an ACL, any subnets associated with the ACL are subject to the change. You don't have to terminate and relaunch the instances in the subnet; the changes take effect after a short period.

If you're using the Amazon EC2 API or a command line tool, you can't modify rules; you can only add and delete rules. If you're using the Amazon VPC console, you can modify the entries for existing rules (the console removes the rule and adds a new rule for you). If you need to change the order of a rule in the ACL, you must add a new rule with the new rule number, and then delete the original rule.

To add rules to a network ACL

1. Open the Amazon VPC console at https://console.aws.amazon.com/vpc/.

2. In the navigation pane, choose **Network ACLs**.

3. In the details pane, choose either the **Inbound Rules** or **Outbound Rules** tab, depending on the type of rule that you need to add, and then choose **Edit**.

4. In **Rule #**, enter a rule number (for example, 100). The rule number must not already be used in the network ACL. We process the rules in order, starting with the lowest number. **Tip**
We recommend that you leave gaps between the rule numbers (such as 100, 200, 300), rather than using sequential numbers (101, 102, 103). This makes it easier add a new rule without having to renumber the existing rules.

5. Select a rule from the **Type** list. For example, to add a rule for HTTP, choose **HTTP**. To add a rule to allow all TCP traffic, choose **All TCP**. For some of these options (for example, HTTP), we fill in the port for you. To use a protocol that's not listed, choose **Custom Protocol Rule**.

6. (Optional) If you're creating a custom protocol rule, select the protocol's number and name from the **Protocol** list. For more information, see IANA List of Protocol Numbers.

7. (Optional) If the protocol you've selected requires a port number, enter the port number or port range separated by a hyphen (for example, 49152-65535).

8. In the **Source** or **Destination** field (depending on whether this is an inbound or outbound rule), enter the CIDR range that the rule applies to.

9. From the **Allow/Deny** list, select **ALLOW** to allow the specified traffic or **DENY** to deny the specified traffic.

10. (Optional) To add another rule, choose **Add another rule**, and repeat steps 4 to 9 as required.

11. When you are done, choose **Save**.

To delete a rule from a network ACL

1. Open the Amazon VPC console at https://console.aws.amazon.com/vpc/.

2. In the navigation pane, choose **Network ACLs**, and then select the network ACL.

3. In the details pane, select either the **Inbound Rules** or **Outbound Rules** tab, and then choose **Edit**. Choose **Remove** for the rule you want to delete, and then choose **Save**.

Associating a Subnet with a Network ACL

To apply the rules of a network ACL to a particular subnet, you must associate the subnet with the network ACL. You can associate a network ACL with multiple subnets; however, a subnet can be associated with only one network ACL. Any subnet not associated with a particular ACL is associated with the default network ACL by default.

To associate a subnet with a network ACL

1. Open the Amazon VPC console at https://console.aws.amazon.com/vpc/.

2. In the navigation pane, choose **Network ACLs**, and then select the network ACL.

3. In the details pane, on the **Subnet Associations** tab, choose **Edit**. Select the **Associate** check box for the subnet to associate with the network ACL, and then choose **Save**.

Disassociating a Network ACL from a Subnet

You can disassociate a custom network ACL from a subnet — by doing so, the subnet is then automatically associated with the default network ACL.

To disassociate a subnet from a network ACL

1. Open the Amazon VPC console at https://console.aws.amazon.com/vpc/.

2. In the navigation pane, choose **Network ACLs**, and then select the network ACL.

3. In the details pane, choose the **Subnet Associations** tab.

4. Choose **Edit**, and then deselect the **Associate** check box for the subnet. Choose **Save**.

Changing a Subnet's Network ACL

You can change the network ACL that's associated with a subnet. For example, when you create a subnet, it is initially associated with the default network ACL. You might want to instead associate it with a custom network ACL that you've created.

After changing a subnet's network ACL, you don't have to terminate and relaunch the instances in the subnet; the changes take effect after a short period.

To change a subnet's network ACL association

1. Open the Amazon VPC console at https://console.aws.amazon.com/vpc/.

2. In the navigation pane, choose **Subnets**, and then select the subnet.

3. Choose the **Network ACL** tab, and then choose **Edit**.

4. Select the network ACL to associate the subnet with from the **Change to** list, and then choose **Save**.

Deleting a Network ACL

You can delete a network ACL only if there are no subnets associated with it. You can't delete the default network ACL.

To delete a network ACL

1. Open the Amazon VPC console at https://console.aws.amazon.com/vpc/.

2. In the navigation pane, choose **Network ACLs**.

3. Select the network ACL, and then choose **Delete**.

4. In the confirmation dialog box, choose **Yes, Delete**.

Example: Controlling Access to Instances in a Subnet

In this example, instances in your subnet can communicate with each other, and are accessible from a trusted remote computer. The remote computer may be a computer in your local network or an instance in a different subnet or VPC that you use to connect to your instances to perform administrative tasks. Your security group rules and network ACL rules allow access from the IP address of your remote computer (172.31.1.2/32). All other traffic from the Internet or other networks is denied.

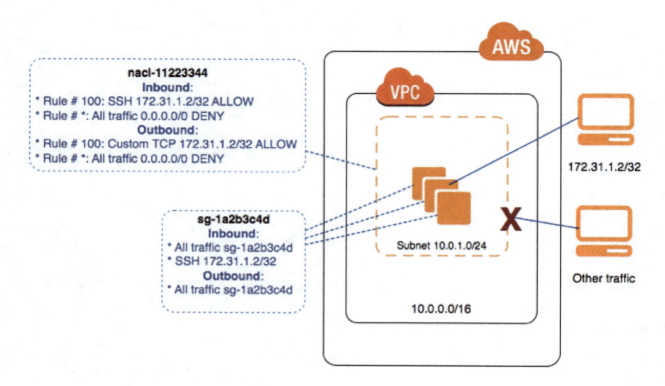

All instances use the same security group (sg-1a2b3c4d), with the following rules.

Inbound Rules		
Protocol Type		
All traffic		
TCP		
Outbound Rules		
Protocol Type		
All traffic		

The subnet is associated with a network ACL that has the following rules.

Inbound Rules	
Rule #	
100	
Outbound Rules	
Rule #	
100	

This scenario gives you the flexibility to change the security groups or security group rules for your instances, and have the network ACL as the backup layer of defense. The network ACL rules apply to all instances in the subnet, so if you accidentally make your security group rules too permissive, the network ACL rules continue to permit access only from the single IP address. For example, the following rules are more permissive than the earlier rules — they allow inbound SSH access from any IP address.

Inbound Rules

Type
All traffic
SSH
Outbound Rules
Type
All traffic

However, only other instances within the subnet and your remote computer are able to access this instance. The network ACL rules still prevent all inbound traffic to the subnet except from your remote computer.

API and Command Overview

You can perform the tasks described on this page using the command line or an API. For more information about the command line interfaces and a list of available APIs, see Accessing Amazon VPC.

Create a network ACL for your VPC

- create-network-acl (AWS CLI)
- New-EC2NetworkAcl (AWS Tools for Windows PowerShell)

Describe one or more of your network ACLs

- describe-network-acls (AWS CLI)
- Get-EC2NetworkAcl (AWS Tools for Windows PowerShell)

Add a rule to a network ACL

- create-network-acl-entry (AWS CLI)
- New-EC2NetworkAclEntry (AWS Tools for Windows PowerShell)

Delete a rule from a network ACL

- delete-network-acl-entry (AWS CLI)
- Remove-EC2NetworkAclEntry (AWS Tools for Windows PowerShell)

Replace an existing rule in a network ACL

- replace-network-acl-entry (AWS CLI)
- Set-EC2NetworkAclEntry (AWS Tools for Windows PowerShell)

Replace a network ACL association

- replace-network-acl-association (AWS CLI)
- Set-EC2NetworkAclAssociation (AWS Tools for Windows PowerShell)

Delete a network ACL

- delete-network-acl (AWS CLI)
- Remove-EC2NetworkAcl (AWS Tools for Windows PowerShell)

Recommended Network ACL Rules for Your VPC

The VPC wizard helps you implement common scenarios for Amazon VPC. If you implement these scenarios as described in the documentation, you'll use the default network access control list (ACL), which allows all inbound and outbound traffic. If you need an additional layer of security, you can create a network ACL and add rules. We recommend the following rules for each scenario.

Topics

- Recommended Rules for Scenario 1
- Recommended Rules for Scenario 2
- Recommended Rules for Scenario 3
- Recommended Rules for Scenario 4

For more information about network ACLs and how to use them, see Network ACLs.

Important

We use the ephemeral port range 32768-65535 as an example, or 1024-65535 for a NAT gateway. You must select a range that is appropriate for your configuration. For more information, see Ephemeral Ports. If the maximum transmission unit (MTU) between hosts in your subnets is different, you must add the following inbound and outbound network ACL rules to ensure that Path MTU Discovery can function correctly and prevent packet loss: **Custom ICMP Rule** type and **Destination Unreachable: fragmentation required, and DF flag set** port range (Type 3, Code 4). For more information, see Network Maximum Transmission Unit (MTU) for Your EC2 Instance in the *Amazon EC2 User Guide for Linux Instances*.

Recommended Rules for Scenario 1

Scenario 1 is a single subnet with instances that can receive and send Internet traffic. For more information, see Scenario 1: VPC with a Single Public Subnet.

The following table shows the rules we recommended. They block all traffic except that which is explicitly required.

Inbound
Rule #
100
110
120
130
140

Outbound
Rule #
100
110
120

Recommended Rules for IPv6

If you implemented scenario 1 with IPv6 support and created a VPC and subnet with associated IPv6 CIDR blocks, you must add separate rules to your network ACL to control inbound and outbound IPv6 traffic.

The following are the IPv6-specific rules for your network ACL (which are in addition to the rules listed above).

Inbound
Rule #
150
160
170
180
190

Outbound
Rule #
130
140
150

Recommended Rules for Scenario 2

Scenario 2 is a public subnet with instances that can receive and send Internet traffic, and a private subnet that can't receive traffic directly from the Internet. However, it can initiate traffic to the Internet (and receive responses) through a NAT gateway or NAT instance in the public subnet. For more information, see Scenario 2: VPC with Public and Private Subnets (NAT).

For this scenario you have a network ACL for the public subnet, and a separate one for the private subnet. The following table shows the rules we recommend for each ACL. They block all traffic except that which is explicitly required. They mostly mimic the security group rules for the scenario.

ACL Rules for the Public Subnet

Inbound
Rule #
100
110
120
130
140

Outbound
Rule #
100
110
120
140
150

ACL Rules for the Private Subnet

Inbound
Rule #
100
120
130

140

Outbound Rule #
100
110
120

Recommended Rules for IPv6

If you implemented scenario 2 with IPv6 support and created a VPC and subnets with associated IPv6 CIDR blocks, you must add separate rules to your network ACLs to control inbound and outbound IPv6 traffic.

The following are the IPv6-specific rules for your network ACLs (which are in addition to the rules listed above).

ACL Rules for the Public Subnet

Inbound Rule #
150
160
170
180
190

Outbound Rule #
160
170
180
200
210

ACL Rules for the Private Subnet

Inbound Rule #
150
170
180
190

Outbound Rule #
130
140
150

Recommended Rules for Scenario 3

Scenario 3 is a public subnet with instances that can receive and send Internet traffic, and a VPN-only subnet with instances that can communicate only with your home network over the VPN connection. For more information, see Scenario 3: VPC with Public and Private Subnets and AWS Managed VPN Access.

For this scenario you have a network ACL for the public subnet, and a separate one for the VPN-only subnet. The following table shows the rules we recommend for each ACL. They block all traffic except that which is explicitly required.

ACL Rules for the Public Subnet

Inbound
Rule #
100
110
120
130
140
Outbound
Rule #
100
110
120
140

ACL Settings for the VPN-Only Subnet

Inbound
Rule #
100
120
130
140
Outbound
Rule #
100
110
120

Recommended Rules for IPv6

If you implemented scenario 3 with IPv6 support and created a VPC and subnets with associated IPv6 CIDR blocks, you must add separate rules to your network ACLs to control inbound and outbound IPv6 traffic.

The following are the IPv6-specific rules for your network ACLs (which are in addition to the rules listed above).

ACL Rules for the Public Subnet

Inbound

Rule #
150
160
170
180
190
Outbound
Rule #
150
160
170
190

ACL Rules for the VPN-only Subnet

Inbound
Rule #
150
Outbound
Rule #
130

Recommended Rules for Scenario 4

Scenario 4 is a single subnet with instances that can communicate only with your home network over a VPN connection. For a more information, see Scenario 4: VPC with a Private Subnet Only and AWS Managed VPN Access.

The following table shows the rules we recommended. They block all traffic except that which is explicitly required.

Inbound
Rule #
100
110
120
Outbound
Rule #
100
120

Recommended Rules for IPv6

If you implemented scenario 4 with IPv6 support and created a VPC and subnet with associated IPv6 CIDR blocks, you must add separate rules to your network ACL to control inbound and outbound IPv6 traffic.

In this scenario, the database servers cannot be reached over the VPN communication via IPv6, therefore no additional network ACL rules are required. The following are the default rules that deny IPv6 traffic to and from the subnet.

ACL Rules for the VPN-only Subnet

Inbound Rule #	
Outbound Rule #	

Controlling Access to Amazon VPC Resources

Your security credentials identify you to services in AWS and grant you unlimited use of your AWS resources, such as your Amazon VPC resources. You can use AWS Identity and Access Management (IAM) to allow other users, services, and applications to use your Amazon VPC resources without sharing your security credentials. You can choose to allow full use or limited use of your resources by granting users permission to use specific Amazon EC2 API actions. Some API actions support resource-level permissions, which allow you to control the specific resources that users can create or modify.

Important
Currently, not all Amazon EC2 API actions support resource-level permissions. If an Amazon EC2 API action does not support resource-level permissions, you can grant users permission to use the action, but you have to specify a * for the resource element of your policy statement. For an example of how to do this, see the following example policy: 1. Managing a VPC We'll add support for additional API actions and ARNs for additional Amazon EC2 resources later. For information about which ARNs you can use with which Amazon EC2 API actions, as well as supported condition keys for each ARN, see Supported Resources and Conditions for Amazon EC2 API Actions in the *Amazon EC2 User Guide for Linux Instances*.

For more information about creating IAM policies for Amazon EC2, supported resources for EC2 API actions, as well as example policies for Amazon EC2, see IAM Policies for Amazon EC2 in the *Amazon EC2 User Guide for Linux Instances*.

Topics

- Example Policies for the AWS CLI or SDK
- Example Policies for the Console

Example Policies for the AWS CLI or SDK

The following examples show policy statements that you can use to control the permissions that IAM users have to Amazon VPC. These examples are designed for users that use the AWS CLI or an AWS SDK.

Topics

- 1. Managing a VPC
- 2. Read-Only Policy for Amazon VPC
- 3. Custom Policy for Amazon VPC
- 4. Launching instances into a specific subnet
- 5. Launching instances into a specific VPC
- 6. Managing security groups in a VPC
- 7. Creating and managing VPC peering connections
- 8. Creating and managing VPC endpoints

For example policies for working with ClassicLink, see Example Policies for CLI or SDK in the *Amazon EC2 User Guide for Linux Instances*.

1. Managing a VPC

The following policy grants users permission to create and manage your VPC. You might attach this policy to a group of network administrators. The `Action` element specifies the API actions related to VPCs, subnets, Internet gateways, customer gateways, virtual private gateways, VPN connections, route tables, Elastic IP addresses, security groups, network ACLs, and DHCP options sets. The policy also allows the group to run, stop, start, and terminate instances. It also allows the group to list Amazon EC2 resources.

The policy uses wildcards to specify all actions for each type of object (for example, `*SecurityGroup*`). Alternatively, you could list each action explicitly. If you use the wildcards, be aware that if we add new actions whose names include any of the wildcarded strings in the policy, the policy would automatically grant the group access to those new actions.

The `Resource` element uses a wildcard to indicate that users can specify all resources with these API actions. The * wildcard is also necessary in cases where the API action does not support resource-level permissions.

```
1  {
2      "Version": "2012-10-17",
3      "Statement":[{
4      "Effect":"Allow",
5      "Action":["ec2:*Vpc*",
6                "ec2:*Subnet*",
7                "ec2:*Gateway*",
8                "ec2:*Vpn*",
9                "ec2:*Route*",
10               "ec2:*Address*",
11               "ec2:*SecurityGroup*",
12               "ec2:*NetworkAcl*",
13               "ec2:*DhcpOptions*",
14               "ec2:RunInstances",
15               "ec2:StopInstances",
16               "ec2:StartInstances",
17               "ec2:TerminateInstances",
18               "ec2:Describe*"],
19      "Resource":"*"
20      }
21  ]
22  }
```

2. Read-Only Policy for Amazon VPC

The following policy grants users permission to list your VPCs and their components. They can't create, update, or delete them.

```
1  {
2      "Version": "2012-10-17",
3      "Statement":[{
4      "Effect":"Allow",
5      "Action":["ec2:DescribeVpcs",
6                "ec2:DescribeSubnets",
7                "ec2:DescribeInternetGateways",
8                "ec2:DescribeEgressOnlyInternetGateways",
9                "ec2:DescribeVpcEndpoints",
10               "ec2:DescribeNatGateways",
11               "ec2:DescribeCustomerGateways",
12               "ec2:DescribeVpnGateways",
13               "ec2:DescribeVpnConnections",
14               "ec2:DescribeRouteTables",
15               "ec2:DescribeAddresses",
16               "ec2:DescribeSecurityGroups",
17               "ec2:DescribeNetworkAcls",
18               "ec2:DescribeDhcpOptions",
19               "ec2:DescribeTags",
20               "ec2:DescribeInstances"],
21      "Resource":"*"
```

```
22      }
23    ]
24 }
```

3. Custom Policy for Amazon VPC

The following policy grants users permission to launch instances, stop instances, start instances, terminate instances, and describe the available resources for Amazon EC2 and Amazon VPC.

The second statement in the policy protects against any other policy that might grant the user access to a wider range of API actions by explicitly denying permissions.

```
1  {
2    "Version": "2012-10-17",
3    "Statement":[{
4      "Effect":"Allow",
5      "Action":["ec2:RunInstances",
6                "ec2:StopInstances",
7                "ec2:StartInstances",
8                "ec2:TerminateInstances",
9                "ec2:Describe*"],
10     "Resource":"*"
11     },
12     {
13     "Effect":"Deny",
14     "NotAction":["ec2:RunInstances",
15                  "ec2:StopInstances",
16                  "ec2:StartInstances",
17                  "ec2:TerminateInstances",
18                  "ec2:Describe*"],
19     "Resource":"*"
20     }
21   ]
22 }
```

4. Launching instances into a specific subnet

The following policy grants users permission to launch instances into a specific subnet, and to use a specific security group in the request. The policy does this by specifying the ARN for subnet-1a2b3c4d, and the ARN for sg-123abc123. If users attempt to launch an instance into a different subnet or using a different security group, the request will fail (unless another policy or statement grants users permission to do so).

The policy also grants permission to use the network interface resource. When launching into a subnet, the RunInstances request creates a primary network interface by default, so the user needs permission to create this resource when launching the instance.

```
1  {
2    "Version": "2012-10-17",
3    "Statement": [{
4      "Effect": "Allow",
5      "Action": "ec2:RunInstances",
6      "Resource": [
7        "arn:aws:ec2:region::image/ami-*",
8        "arn:aws:ec2:region:account:instance/*",
```

```
 9          "arn:aws:ec2:region:account:subnet/subnet-1a2b3c4d",
10          "arn:aws:ec2:region:account:network-interface/*",
11          "arn:aws:ec2:region:account:volume/*",
12          "arn:aws:ec2:region:account:key-pair/*",
13          "arn:aws:ec2:region:account:security-group/sg-123abc123"
14       ]
15     }
16   ]
17 }
```

5. Launching instances into a specific VPC

The following policy grants users permission to launch instances into any subnet within a specific VPC. The policy does this by applying a condition key (`ec2:Vpc`) to the subnet resource.

The policy also grants users permission to launch instances using only AMIs that have the tag "department=dev".

```
 1 {
 2   "Version": "2012-10-17",
 3   "Statement": [{
 4     "Effect": "Allow",
 5     "Action": "ec2:RunInstances",
 6     "Resource": "arn:aws:ec2:region:account:subnet/*",
 7       "Condition": {
 8       "StringEquals": {
 9           "ec2:Vpc": "arn:aws:ec2:region:account:vpc/vpc-1a2b3c4d"
10          }
11     }
12   },
13   {
14     "Effect": "Allow",
15     "Action": "ec2:RunInstances",
16     "Resource": "arn:aws:ec2:region::image/ami-*",
17     "Condition": {
18       "StringEquals": {
19           "ec2:ResourceTag/department": "dev"
20          }
21     }
22   },
23   {
24     "Effect": "Allow",
25     "Action": "ec2:RunInstances",
26     "Resource": [
27       "arn:aws:ec2:region:account:instance/*",
28       "arn:aws:ec2:region:account:volume/*",
29       "arn:aws:ec2:region:account:network-interface/*",
30       "arn:aws:ec2:region:account:key-pair/*",
31       "arn:aws:ec2:region:account:security-group/*"
32       ]
33   }
34   ]
35 }
```

6. Managing security groups in a VPC

The following policy grants users permission to create and delete inbound and outbound rules for any security group within a specific VPC. The policy does this by applying a condition key (`ec2:Vpc`) to the security group resource for the `Authorize` and `Revoke` actions.

The second statement grants users permission to describe all security groups. This is necessary in order for users to be able to modify security group rules using the CLI.

```
1  {
2  "Version": "2012-10-17",
3    "Statement":[{
4      "Effect":"Allow",
5      "Action": [
6        "ec2:AuthorizeSecurityGroupIngress",
7        "ec2:AuthorizeSecurityGroupEgress",
8        "ec2:RevokeSecurityGroupIngress",
9        "ec2:RevokeSecurityGroupEgress"],
10       "Resource": "arn:aws:ec2:region:account:security-group/*",
11       "Condition": {
12         "StringEquals": {
13           "ec2:Vpc": "arn:aws:ec2:region:account:vpc/vpc-1a2b3c4d"
14         }
15       }
16    },
17    {
18      "Effect": "Allow",
19      "Action": "ec2:DescribeSecurityGroups",
20      "Resource": "*"
21    }
22  ]
23 }
```

7. Creating and managing VPC peering connections

The following are examples of policies you can use to manage the creation and modification of VPC peering connections.

a. Create a VPC peering connection

The following policy allows users to create VPC peering connection requests using only VPCs that are tagged with `Purpose=Peering`. The first statement applies a condition key (`ec2:ResourceTag`) to the VPC resource. Note that the VPC resource for the `CreateVpcPeeringConnection` action is always the requester VPC.

The second statement grants users permissions to create the VPC peering connection resource, and therefore uses the * wildcard in place of a specific resource ID.

```
1  {
2  "Version": "2012-10-17",
3  "Statement":[{
4  "Effect":"Allow",
5  "Action": "ec2:CreateVpcPeeringConnection",
6  "Resource": "arn:aws:ec2:region:account:vpc/*",
7    "Condition": {
8      "StringEquals": {
9        "ec2:ResourceTag/Purpose": "Peering"
```

```
10        }
11      }
12    },
13    {
14      "Effect": "Allow",
15      "Action": "ec2:CreateVpcPeeringConnection",
16      "Resource": "arn:aws:ec2:region:account:vpc-peering-connection/*"
17    }
18  ]
19 }
```

The following policy allows users in AWS account 333333333333 to create VPC peering connections using any VPC in the us-east-1 region, but only if the VPC that will be accepting the peering connection is a specific VPC (vpc-aaa111bb) in a specific account (777788889999).

```
1  {
2  "Version": "2012-10-17",
3  "Statement": [{
4  "Effect":"Allow",
5  "Action": "ec2:CreateVpcPeeringConnection",
6  "Resource": "arn:aws:ec2:us-east-1:333333333333:vpc/*"
7  },
8  {
9    "Effect": "Allow",
10   "Action": "ec2:CreateVpcPeeringConnection",
11   "Resource": "arn:aws:ec2:region:333333333333:vpc-peering-connection/*",
12     "Condition": {
13     "ArnEquals": {
14       "ec2:AccepterVpc": "arn:aws:ec2:region:777788889999:vpc/vpc-aaa111bb"
15     }
16   }
17   }
18  ]
19 }
```

b. Accept a VPC peering connection

The following policy allows users to accept VPC peering connection requests from AWS account 444455556666 only. This helps to prevent users from accepting VPC peering connection requests from unknown accounts. The first statement uses the ec2:RequesterVpc condition key to enforce this.

The policy also grants users permissions to accept VPC peering requests only when your VPC has the tag Purpose=Peering.

```
1  {
2  "Version": "2012-10-17",
3  "Statement":[{
4  "Effect":"Allow",
5  "Action": "ec2:AcceptVpcPeeringConnection",
6  "Resource": "arn:aws:ec2:region:account:vpc-peering-connection/*",
7    "Condition": {
8    "ArnEquals": {
9      "ec2:RequesterVpc": "arn:aws:ec2:region:444455556666:vpc/*"
10   }
11  }
12  },
13  {
```

```
14  "Effect": "Allow",
15  "Action": "ec2:AcceptVpcPeeringConnection",
16  "Resource": "arn:aws:ec2:region:account:vpc/*",
17    "Condition": {
18     "StringEquals": {
19       "ec2:ResourceTag/Purpose": "Peering"
20      }
21     }
22    }
23   ]
24  }
```

c. Deleting a VPC peering connection

The following policy allows users in account 444455556666 to delete any VPC peering connection, except those that use the specified VPC vpc-1a2b3c4d, which is in the same account. The policy specifies both the ec2:AccepterVpc and ec2:RequesterVpc condition keys, as the VPC may have been the requester VPC or the peer VPC in the original VPC peering connection request.

```
1  {
2  "Version": "2012-10-17",
3  "Statement": [{
4    "Effect":"Allow",
5    "Action": "ec2:DeleteVpcPeeringConnection",
6    "Resource": "arn:aws:ec2:region:444455556666:vpc-peering-connection/*",
7     "Condition": {
8      "ArnNotEquals": {
9        "ec2:AccepterVpc": "arn:aws:ec2:region:444455556666:vpc/vpc-1a2b3c4d",
10       "ec2:RequesterVpc": "arn:aws:ec2:region:444455556666:vpc/vpc-1a2b3c4d"
11      }
12     }
13    }
14   ]
15  }
```

d. Working within a specific account

The following policy allows users to work with VPC peering connections entirely within a specific account. Users can view, create, accept, reject, and delete VPC peering connections, provided they are all within AWS account 333333333333.

The first statement allows users to view all VPC peering connections. The Resource element requires a * wildcard in this case, as this API action (DescribeVpcPeeringConnections) currently does not support resource-level permissions.

The second statement allows users to create VPC peering connections, and allows access to all VPCs in account 333333333333 in order to do so.

The third statement uses a * wildcard as part of the Action element to allow all VPC peering connection actions. The condition keys ensure that the actions can only be performed on VPC peering connections with VPCs that are part of account 333333333333. For example, a user is not allowed to delete a VPC peering connection if either the accepter or requester VPC is in a different account. A user cannot create a VPC peering connection with a VPC in a different account.

```
1  {
2  "Version": "2012-10-17",
3  "Statement": [{
4    "Effect": "Allow",
```

```
 5  "Action": "ec2:DescribeVpcPeeringConnections",
 6  "Resource": "*"
 7  },
 8  {
 9  "Effect": "Allow",
10  "Action": ["ec2:CreateVpcPeeringConnection","ec2:AcceptVpcPeeringConnection"],
11  "Resource": "arn:aws:ec2:*:333333333333:vpc/*"
12  },
13  {
14  "Effect": "Allow",
15  "Action": "ec2:*VpcPeeringConnection",
16  "Resource": "arn:aws:ec2:*:333333333333:vpc-peering-connection/*",
17  "Condition": {
18   "ArnEquals": {
19    "ec2:AccepterVpc": "arn:aws:ec2:*:333333333333:vpc/*",
20    "ec2:RequesterVpc": "arn:aws:ec2:*:333333333333:vpc/*"
21   }
22  }
23  }
24 ]
25 }
```

8. Creating and managing VPC endpoints

The following policy grants users permission to create, modify, view, and delete VPC endpoints, VPC endpoint services, and VPC endpoint connection notifications. Users can also accept and reject VPC endpoint connection requests. None of the `ec2:*VpcEndpoint*` actions support resource-level permissions, so you have to use the * wildcard for the `Resource` element to allow users to work with all resources.

```
1 {
2     "Version": "2012-10-17",
3     "Statement":[{
4     "Effect":"Allow",
5     "Action":"ec2:*VpcEndpoint*",
6     "Resource":"*"
7     }
8   ]
9 }
```

Example Policies for the Console

You can use IAM policies to grant users permissions to view and work with specific resources in the Amazon VPC console. You can use the example policies in the previous section; however, they are designed for requests that are made with the AWS CLI or an AWS SDK. The console uses additional API actions for its features, so these policies may not work as expected.

This section demonstrates policies that enable users to work with specific parts of the VPC console.

Topics

- 1. Using the VPC wizard
- 2. Managing a VPC
- 3. Managing security groups
- 4. Creating a VPC peering connection

1. Using the VPC wizard

You can use the VPC wizard in the Amazon VPC console to create and set up and configure a VPC for you, so that it's ready for you to use. The wizard provides different configuration options, depending on your requirements. For more information about using the VPC wizard to create a VPC, see Scenarios and Examples.

To enable users to use the VPC wizard, you must grant them permission to create and modify the resources that form part of the selected configuration. The following example policies show the actions that are required for each of the wizard configuration options.

Note

If the VPC wizard fails at any point, it attempts to detach and delete the resources that it's created. If you do not grant users permissions to use these actions, then those resources remain in your account.

Option 1: VPC with a single public subnet

The first VPC wizard configuration option creates a VPC with a single subnet. In your IAM policy, you must grant users permission to use the following actions so they can successfully use this wizard option:

- `ec2:CreateVpc`, `ec2:CreateSubnet`, `ec2:CreateRouteTable`, and `ec2:CreateInternetGateway`: To create a VPC, a subnet, a custom route table, and an Internet gateway.
- `ec2:DescribeAvailabilityZones`: To display the section of the wizard with the **Availability Zone** list and the CIDR block field for the subnet. Even if users intend to leave the default settings, they will not be able to create a VPC unless those options are displayed.
- `ec2:DescribeVpcEndpointServices`: To display the VPC endpoint section of the wizard.
- `ec2:AttachInternetGateway`: To attach the Internet gateway to the VPC.
- `ec2:CreateRoute`: To create a route in the custom route table. The route points traffic to the Internet gateway.
- `ec2:AssociateRouteTable`: To associate the custom route table to the subnet.
- `ec2:ModifyVpcAttribute`: To modify the VPC's attribute to enable DNS hostnames, so that each instance launched into this VPC receives a DNS hostname.

None of the API actions in this policy support resource-level permissions, so you cannot control which specific resources users can use.

```
 1 {
 2     "Version": "2012-10-17",
 3     "Statement": [{
 4         "Effect": "Allow",
 5         "Action": [
 6             "ec2:CreateVpc", "ec2:CreateSubnet", "ec2:DescribeAvailabilityZones", "ec2:
                 DescribeVpcEndpointServices",
 7             "ec2:CreateRouteTable", "ec2:CreateRoute", "ec2:CreateInternetGateway",
 8             "ec2:AttachInternetGateway", "ec2:AssociateRouteTable", "ec2:ModifyVpcAttribute"
 9         ],
10         "Resource": "*"
11     }
12     ]
13 }
```

Option 2: VPC with a public and private subnet

The second VPC wizard configuration option creates a VPC with a public and private subnet, and provides the option to launch a NAT gateway or a NAT instance. The following policy has the same actions as the previous example (option 1), plus actions that allow users to run and configure either a NAT gateway or a NAT instance.

The following actions are required regardless if you're launching a NAT instance or a NAT gateway:

- `ec2:DescribeKeyPairs`: To display a list of existing key pairs and load the NAT section of the wizard.

The following actions are required to create a NAT gateway (these actions are not required for launching a NAT instance):

- `ec2:CreateNatGateway`: To create the NAT gateway.
- `ec2:DescribeNatGateways`: To check NAT gateway status until it's in the available state.
- `ec2:DescribeAddresses`: To list the available Elastic IP addresses in your account to associate with the NAT gateway.

The following actions are required to launch a NAT instance (these actions are not required for creating a NAT gateway):

- `ec2:DescribeImages`: To locate an AMI that's been configured to run as a NAT instance.
- `ec2:RunInstances`: To launch the NAT instance.
- `ec2:AllocateAddress` and `ec2:AssociateAddress`: To allocate an Elastic IP address to your account, and then associate it with the NAT instance.
- `ec2:ModifyInstanceAttribute`: To disable source/destination checking for the NAT instance.
- `ec2:DescribeInstances`: To check the status of the instance until it's in the running state.
- `ec2:DescribeRouteTables`, `ec2:DescribeVpnGateways`, and `ec2:DescribeVpcs`: To gather information about the routes that must be added to the main route table.

The following policy allows users to create either a NAT instance or a NAT gateway.

```
1  {
2    "Version": "2012-10-17",
3    "Statement": [
4      {
5        "Effect": "Allow",
6        "Action": [
7          "ec2:CreateVpc", "ec2:CreateSubnet", "ec2:DescribeAvailabilityZones", "ec2:
              DescribeVpcEndpointServices",
8          "ec2:CreateRouteTable", "ec2:CreateRoute", "ec2:CreateInternetGateway", "ec2:
              CreateNatGateway",
9          "ec2:AttachInternetGateway", "ec2:AssociateRouteTable", "ec2:ModifyVpcAttribute", "ec2
              :DescribeKeyPairs",
10         "ec2:DescribeImages", "ec2:RunInstances", "ec2:AllocateAddress", "ec2:AssociateAddress
              ",
11         "ec2:DescribeAddresses", "ec2:DescribeInstances", "ec2:ModifyInstanceAttribute", "ec2:
              DescribeRouteTables",
12         "ec2:DescribeVpnGateways", "ec2:DescribeVpcs", "ec2:DescribeSubnets", "ec2:
              DescribeNatGateways"
13       ],
14       "Resource": "*"
15     }
16   ]
17 }
```

You can use resource-level permissions on the `ec2:RunInstances` action to control users' ability to launch instances. For example, you can specify the ID of a NAT-enabled AMI so that users can only launch instances from this AMI. To find out which AMI the wizard uses to launch a NAT instance, log in to the Amazon VPC console as a user with full permissions, then carry out the second option of the VPC wizard. Switch to the Amazon EC2 console, select the **Instances** page, select the NAT instance, and note the AMI ID that was used to launch it.

The following policy allows users to launch instances using only `ami-1a2b3c4d`. If users try to launch an instance using any other AMI, the launch fails.

```
1  {
2    "Version": "2012-10-17",
```

```
 3     "Statement": [{
 4       "Effect": "Allow",
 5       "Action": [
 6         "ec2:CreateVpc", "ec2:CreateSubnet", "ec2:DescribeAvailabilityZones", "ec2:
              DescribeVpcEndpointServices",
 7         "ec2:CreateRouteTable", "ec2:CreateRoute", "ec2:CreateInternetGateway",
 8         "ec2:AttachInternetGateway", "ec2:AssociateRouteTable", "ec2:ModifyVpcAttribute",
 9         "ec2:DescribeKeyPairs", "ec2:DescribeImages", "ec2:AllocateAddress", "ec2:
              AssociateAddress",
10         "ec2:DescribeInstances", "ec2:ModifyInstanceAttribute", "ec2:DescribeRouteTables",
11         "ec2:DescribeVpnGateways", "ec2:DescribeVpcs"
12       ],
13       "Resource": "*"
14     },
15            {
16       "Effect": "Allow",
17       "Action": "ec2:RunInstances",
18       "Resource": [
19         "arn:aws:ec2:region::image/ami-1a2b3c4d",
20         "arn:aws:ec2:region:account:instance/*",
21         "arn:aws:ec2:region:account:subnet/*",
22         "arn:aws:ec2:region:account:network-interface/*",
23         "arn:aws:ec2:region:account:volume/*",
24         "arn:aws:ec2:region:account:key-pair/*",
25         "arn:aws:ec2:region:account:security-group/*"
26       ]
27     }
28   ]
29 }
```

Option 3: VPC with public and private subnets and AWS managed VPN access

The third VPC wizard configuration option creates a VPC with a public and private subnet, and creates a VPN connection between your VPC and your own network. In your IAM policy, you must grant users permission to use the same actions as option 1. This allows them to create a VPC and two subnets, and to configure the routing for the public subnet. To create a VPN connection, users must also have permission to use the following actions:

- ec2:CreateCustomerGateway: To create a customer gateway.
- ec2:CreateVpnGateway and ec2:AttachVpnGateway: To create a virtual private gateway, and attach it to the VPC.
- ec2:EnableVgwRoutePropagation: To enable route propagation so that routes are automatically propagated to your route table.
- ec2:CreateVpnConnection: To create a VPN connection.
- ec2:DescribeVpnConnections, ec2:DescribeVpnGateways, and ec2:DescribeCustomerGateways: To display the options on the second configuration page of the wizard.
- ec2:DescribeVpcs and ec2:DescribeRouteTables: To gather information about the routes that must be added to the main route table.

None of the API actions in this policy support resource-level permissions, so you cannot control which specific resources users can use.

```
 1 {
 2   "Version": "2012-10-17",
 3   "Statement": [{
 4     "Effect": "Allow",
 5     "Action": [
```

```
 6      "ec2:CreateVpc", "ec2:CreateSubnet", "ec2:DescribeAvailabilityZones", "ec2:
          DescribeVpcEndpointServices",
 7      "ec2:CreateRouteTable", "ec2:CreateRoute", "ec2:CreateInternetGateway",
 8      "ec2:AttachInternetGateway", "ec2:AssociateRouteTable", "ec2:ModifyVpcAttribute",
 9      "ec2:CreateCustomerGateway", "ec2:CreateVpnGateway", "ec2:AttachVpnGateway",
10      "ec2:EnableVgwRoutePropagation", "ec2:CreateVpnConnection", "ec2:DescribeVpnGateways",
11      "ec2:DescribeCustomerGateways", "ec2:DescribeVpnConnections", "ec2:DescribeRouteTables",
12      "ec2:DescribeNetworkAcls", "ec2:DescribeInternetGateways", "ec2:DescribeVpcs"
13    ],
14    "Resource": "*"
15  }
16  ]
17 }
```

Option 4: VPC with a private subnet only and AWS managed VPN access

The fourth VPC configuration option creates a VPC with a private subnet, and creates a VPN connection between the VPC and your own network. Unlike the other three options, users do not need permission to create or attach an Internet gateway to the VPC, and they do not need permission to create a route table and associate it with the subnet. They will require the same permissions as listed in the previous example (option 3) to establish the VPN connection.

None of the API actions in this policy support resource-level permissions, so you cannot control which specific resources users can use.

```
 1 {
 2    "Version": "2012-10-17",
 3    "Statement": [{
 4      "Effect": "Allow",
 5      "Action": [
 6        "ec2:CreateVpc", "ec2:CreateSubnet", "ec2:DescribeAvailabilityZones", "ec2:
            DescribeVpcEndpointServices",
 7        "ec2:ModifyVpcAttribute", "ec2:CreateCustomerGateway", "ec2:CreateVpnGateway",
 8        "ec2:AttachVpnGateway", "ec2:EnableVgwRoutePropagation", "ec2:CreateVpnConnection",
 9        "ec2:DescribeVpnGateways", "ec2:DescribeCustomerGateways", "ec2:DescribeVpnConnections",
10        "ec2:DescribeRouteTables", "ec2:DescribeNetworkAcls", "ec2:DescribeInternetGateways", "ec2
            :DescribeVpcs"
11      ],
12      "Resource": "*"
13  }
14  ]
15 }
```

2. Managing a VPC

On the **Your VPCs** page in the VPC console, you can create or delete a VPC. To view VPCs, users must have permission to use the `ec2:DescribeVPCs` action. To create a VPC using the **Create VPC** dialog box, users must have permission to use the `ec2:CreateVpc` action.

Note

By default, the VPC console creates a tag with a key of `Name` and a value that the user specifies. If users do not have permission to the use the `ec2:CreateTags` action, then they will see an error in the **Create VPC** dialog box when they try to create a VPC. However, the VPC may have been successfully created.

When you set up a VPC, you typically create a number of dependent objects, such as subnets and an Internet gateway. You cannot delete a VPC until you've disassociated and deleted these dependent objects. When you delete a VPC using the console, it performs these actions for you (except terminating your instances; you have to do this yourself).

The following example allows users to view and create VPCs on the **Your VPCs** page, and to delete VPCs that have been created with the first option in the VPC wizard - a VPC with a single public subnet. This VPC has one subnet that's associated with a custom route table, and an Internet gateway that's attached to it. To delete the VPC and its components using the console, you must grant users permission to use a number of `ec2:Describe*` actions, so that the console can check if there are any other resources that are dependent on this VPC. You must also grant users permission to disassociate the route table from the subnet, detach the Internet gateway from the VPC, and permission to delete both these resources.

```
1  {
2      "Version": "2012-10-17",
3      "Statement": [{
4          "Effect": "Allow",
5          "Action": [
6              "ec2:DescribeVpcs", "ec2:DescribeRouteTables", "ec2:DescribeVpnGateways", "ec2:
                   DescribeInternetGateways",
7              "ec2:DescribeSubnets", "ec2:DescribeDhcpOptions", "ec2:DescribeInstances", "ec2:
                   DescribeVpcAttribute",
8              "ec2:DescribeNetworkAcls", "ec2:DescribeNetworkInterfaces", "ec2:DescribeAddresses",
9              "ec2:DescribeVpcPeeringConnections", "ec2:DescribeSecurityGroups",
10             "ec2:CreateVpc", "ec2:DeleteVpc", "ec2:DetachInternetGateway", "ec2:
                   DeleteInternetGateway",
11             "ec2:DisassociateRouteTable", "ec2:DeleteSubnet", "ec2:DeleteRouteTable"
12         ],
13         "Resource": "*"
14     }
15     ]
16  }
```

You can't apply resource-level permissions to any of the `ec2:Describe*` API actions, but you can apply resource-level permissions to some of the `ec2:Delete*` actions to control which resources users can delete.

For example, the following policy allows users to delete only route tables and Internet gateways that have the tag **Purpose=Test**. Users cannot delete individual route tables or Internet gateways that do not have this tag, and similarly, users cannot use the VPC console to delete a VPC that's associated with a different route table or Internet gateway.

```
1  {
2      "Version": "2012-10-17",
3      "Statement": [{
4          "Effect": "Allow",
5          "Action": [
6              "ec2:DescribeVpcs", "ec2:DescribeRouteTables", "ec2:DescribeVpnGateways", "ec2:
                   DescribeInternetGateways",
7              "ec2:DescribeSubnets", "ec2:DescribeDhcpOptions", "ec2:DescribeInstances", "ec2:
                   DescribeVpcAttribute",
8              "ec2:DescribeNetworkAcls", "ec2:DescribeNetworkInterfaces", "ec2:DescribeAddresses",
9              "ec2:DescribeVpcPeeringConnections", "ec2:DescribeSecurityGroups",
10             "ec2:CreateVpc", "ec2:DeleteVpc", "ec2:DetachInternetGateway",
11             "ec2:DisassociateRouteTable", "ec2:DeleteSubnet"
12         ],
13         "Resource": "*"
14     },
15     {
16         "Effect": "Allow",
```

```
17      "Action":  "ec2:DeleteInternetGateway",
18      "Resource": "arn:aws:ec2:region:account:internet-gateway/*",
19      "Condition": {
20        "StringEquals": {
21          "ec2:ResourceTag/Purpose": "Test"
22        }
23      }
24    },
25    {
26      "Effect": "Allow",
27      "Action": "ec2:DeleteRouteTable",
28      "Resource": "arn:aws:ec2:region:account:route-table/*",
29      "Condition": {
30        "StringEquals": {
31          "ec2:ResourceTag/Purpose": "Test"
32        }
33      }
34    }
35  ]
36 }
```

3. Managing security groups

To view security groups on the **Security Groups** page in the Amazon VPC console, users must have permission to use the ec2:DescribeSecurityGroups action. To use the **Create Security Group** dialog box to create a security group, users must have permission to use the ec2:DescribeVpcs and ec2:CreateSecurityGroup actions. If users do not have permission to use the ec2:DescribeSecurityGroups action, they can still create a security group using the dialog box, but they may encounter an error that indicates that the group was not created.

In the **Create Security Group** dialog box, users must add the security group name and description, but they will not be able to enter a value for the **Name tag** field unless they've been granted permission to use the ec2:CreateTags action. However, they do not need this action to successfully create a security group.

The following policy allows users to view and create security groups, and add and remove inbound and outbound rules to any security group that's associated with **vpc-1a2b3c4d**.

```
1 {
2    "Version": "2012-10-17",
3    "Statement": [{
4      "Effect": "Allow",
5      "Action": [
6        "ec2:DescribeSecurityGroups", "ec2:DescribeVpcs", "ec2:CreateSecurityGroup"
7      ],
8      "Resource": "*"
9    },
10   {
11     "Effect": "Allow",
12     "Action": [
13       "ec2:DeleteSecurityGroup", "ec2:AuthorizeSecurityGroupIngress", "ec2:
            AuthorizeSecurityGroupEgress",
14       "ec2:RevokeSecurityGroupIngress", "ec2:RevokeSecurityGroupEgress"
15     ],
16     "Resource": "arn:aws:ec2:*:*:security-group/*",
17     "Condition":{
```

```
18        "ArnEquals": {
19            "ec2:Vpc": "arn:aws:ec2:*:*:vpc/vpc-1a2b3c4d"
20        }
21    }
22  }
23  ]
24 }
```

4. Creating a VPC peering connection

To view VPC peering connections in the Amazon VPC console, users must have permission to use the `ec2:DescribePeeringConnections` action. To use the **Create VPC Peering Connection** dialog box, users must have permission to use the `ec2:DescribeVpcs` action. This allows them to view and select a VPC; without this action, the dialog box cannot load. You can apply resource-level permissions to all the `ec2:*PeeringConnection` actions, except `ec2:DescribeVpcPeeringConnections`.

The following policy allows users to view VPC peering connections, and to use the **Create VPC Peering Connection** dialog box to create a VPC peering connection using a specific requester VPC (`vpc-1a2b3c4d`) only. If users try to create a VPC peering connection with a different requester VPC, the request fails.

```
1 {
2   "Version": "2012-10-17",
3   "Statement":[{
4   "Effect":"Allow",
5   "Action": [
6    "ec2:DescribeVpcPeeringConnections", "ec2:DescribeVpcs"
7   ],
8   "Resource": "*"
9  },
10  {
11   "Effect":"Allow",
12   "Action": "ec2:CreateVpcPeeringConnection",
13   "Resource": [
14    "arn:aws:ec2:*:*:vpc/vpc-1a2b3c4d",
15    "arn:aws:ec2:*:*:vpc-peering-connection/*"
16   ]
17  }
18  ]
19 }
```

For more examples of writing IAM policies for working with VPC peering connections, see 7. Creating and managing VPC peering connections.

VPC Flow Logs

VPC Flow Logs is a feature that enables you to capture information about the IP traffic going to and from network interfaces in your VPC. Flow log data is stored using Amazon CloudWatch Logs. After you've created a flow log, you can view and retrieve its data in Amazon CloudWatch Logs.

Flow logs can help you with a number of tasks; for example, to troubleshoot why specific traffic is not reaching an instance, which in turn helps you diagnose overly restrictive security group rules. You can also use flow logs as a security tool to monitor the traffic that is reaching your instance.

There is no additional charge for using flow logs; however, standard CloudWatch Logs charges apply. For more information, see Amazon CloudWatch Pricing.

Topics

- Flow Logs Basics
- Flow Log Limitations
- Flow Log Records
- IAM Roles for Flow Logs
- Controlling the Use of Flow Logs
- Working With Flow Logs
- Troubleshooting
- API and CLI Overview
- Examples: Flow Log Records
- Example: Creating a CloudWatch Metric Filter and Alarm for a Flow Log

Flow Logs Basics

You can create a flow log for a VPC, a subnet, or a network interface. If you create a flow log for a subnet or VPC, each network interface in the VPC or subnet is monitored. Flow log data is published to a log group in CloudWatch Logs, and each network interface has a unique log stream. Log streams contain *flow log records*, which are log events consisting of fields that describe the traffic for that network interface. For more information, see Flow Log Records.

To create a flow log, you specify the resource for which to create the flow log, the type of traffic to capture (accepted traffic, rejected traffic, or all traffic), the name of a log group in CloudWatch Logs to which the flow log is published, and the ARN of an IAM role that has sufficient permissions to publish the flow log to the CloudWatch Logs log group. If you specify the name of a log group that does not exist, we attempt to create the log group for you. After you've created a flow log, it can take several minutes to begin collecting data and publishing to CloudWatch Logs. Flow logs do not capture real-time log streams for your network interfaces.

You can create multiple flow logs that publish data to the same log group in CloudWatch Logs. If the same network interface is present in one or more flow logs in the same log group, it has one combined log stream. If you've specified that one flow log should capture rejected traffic, and the other flow log should capture accepted traffic, then the combined log stream captures all traffic.

If you launch more instances into your subnet after you've created a flow log for your subnet or VPC, then a new log stream is created for each new network interface as soon as any network traffic is recorded for that network interface.

You can create flow logs for network interfaces that are created by other AWS services; for example, Elastic Load Balancing, Amazon RDS, Amazon ElastiCache, Amazon Redshift, and Amazon WorkSpaces. However, you cannot use these services' consoles or APIs to create the flow logs; you must use the Amazon EC2 console or the Amazon EC2 API. Similarly, you cannot use the CloudWatch Logs console or API to create log streams for your network interfaces.

If you no longer require a flow log, you can delete it. Deleting a flow log disables the flow log service for the resource, and no new flow log records or log streams are created. It does not delete any existing flow log records or log streams for a network interface. To delete an existing log stream, you can use the CloudWatch Logs console. After you've deleted a flow log, it can take several minutes to stop collecting data.

Flow Log Limitations

To use flow logs, you need to be aware of the following limitations:

- You cannot enable flow logs for network interfaces that are in the EC2-Classic platform. This includes EC2-Classic instances that have been linked to a VPC through ClassicLink.
- You cannot enable flow logs for VPCs that are peered with your VPC unless the peer VPC is in your account.
- You cannot tag a flow log.
- After you've created a flow log, you cannot change its configuration; for example, you can't associate a different IAM role with the flow log. Instead, you can delete the flow log and create a new one with the required configuration.
- None of the flow log API actions (`ec2:*FlowLogs`) support resource-level permissions. To create an IAM policy to control the use of the flow log API actions, you must grant users permissions to use all resources for the action by using the * wildcard for the resource element in your statement. For more information, see Controlling Access to Amazon VPC Resources.
- If your network interface has multiple IPv4 addresses and traffic is sent to a secondary private IPv4 address, the flow log displays the primary private IPv4 address in the destination IP address field.

Flow logs do not capture all IP traffic. The following types of traffic are not logged:

- Traffic generated by instances when they contact the Amazon DNS server. If you use your own DNS server, then all traffic to that DNS server is logged.
- Traffic generated by a Windows instance for Amazon Windows license activation.
- Traffic to and from `169.254.169.254` for instance metadata.
- Traffic to and from `169.254.169.123` for the Amazon Time Sync Service.
- DHCP traffic.
- Traffic to the reserved IP address for the default VPC router. For more information, see VPC and Subnet Sizing.
- Traffic between an endpoint network interface and a Network Load Balancer network interface. For more information, see VPC Endpoint Services (AWS PrivateLink).

Flow Log Records

A flow log record represents a network flow in your flow log. Each record captures the network flow for a specific 5-tuple, for a specific capture window. A 5-tuple is a set of five different values that specify the source, destination, and protocol for an internet protocol (IP) flow. The capture window is a duration of time during which the flow logs service aggregates data before publishing flow log records. The capture window is approximately 10 minutes, but can take up to 15 minutes. A flow log record is a space-separated string that has the following format:

version account-id interface-id srcaddr dstaddr srcport dstport protocol packets bytes start end action log-status

Field	Description
version	The VPC Flow Logs version.
account-id	The AWS account ID for the flow log.
interface-id	The ID of the network interface for which the log stream applies.
srcaddr	The source IPv4 or IPv6 address. The IPv4 address of the network interface is always its private IPv4 address.

Field	Description
dstaddr	The destination IPv4 or IPv6 address. The IPv4 address of the network interface is always its private IPv4 address.
srcport	The source port of the traffic.
dstport	The destination port of the traffic.
protocol	The IANA protocol number of the traffic. For more information, go to Assigned Internet Protocol Numbers.
packets	The number of packets transferred during the capture window.
bytes	The number of bytes transferred during the capture window.
start	The time, in Unix seconds, of the start of the capture window.
end	The time, in Unix seconds, of the end of the capture window.
action	The action associated with the traffic:[See the AWS documentation website for more details]
log-status	The logging status of the flow log:[See the AWS documentation website for more details]

If a field is not applicable for a specific record, the record displays a '-' symbol for that entry.

For examples of flow log records, see Examples: Flow Log Records.

You can work with flow log records as you would with any other log events collected by CloudWatch Logs. For more information about monitoring log data and metric filters, see Searching and Filtering Log Data in the *Amazon CloudWatch User Guide*. For an example of setting up a metric filter and alarm for a flow log, see Example: Creating a CloudWatch Metric Filter and Alarm for a Flow Log.

You can export log data to Amazon S3 and use Amazon Athena, an interactive query service, to analyze the data. For more information, see Querying Amazon VPC Flow Logs in the *Amazon Athena User Guide*.

IAM Roles for Flow Logs

The IAM role that's associated with your flow log must have sufficient permissions to publish flow logs to the specified log group in CloudWatch Logs. The IAM policy that's attached to your IAM role must include at least the following permissions:

```
1  {
2    "Version": "2012-10-17",
3    "Statement": [
4      {
5        "Action": [
6          "logs:CreateLogGroup",
7          "logs:CreateLogStream",
8          "logs:PutLogEvents",
9          "logs:DescribeLogGroups",
10         "logs:DescribeLogStreams"
11       ],
12       "Effect": "Allow",
13       "Resource": "*"
14     }
```

```
15     ]
16 }
```

You must also ensure that your role has a trust relationship that allows the flow logs service to assume the role (in the IAM console, choose your role, and then choose **Edit trust relationship** to view the trust relationship):

```
1  {
2    "Version": "2012-10-17",
3    "Statement": [
4      {
5        "Sid": "",
6        "Effect": "Allow",
7        "Principal": {
8          "Service": "vpc-flow-logs.amazonaws.com"
9        },
10       "Action": "sts:AssumeRole"
11     }
12   ]
13 }
```

Alternatively, you can follow the procedures below to create a new role for use with flow logs.

Creating a Flow Logs Role

To create an IAM role for flow logs

1. Open the IAM console at https://console.aws.amazon.com/iam/.

2. In the navigation pane, choose **Roles**, **Create role**.

3. Choose **EC2** and then the **EC2** use case. Choose **Next: Permissions**.

4. On the **Attach permissions policy** page, choose **Next: Review**.

5. Enter a name for your role; for example, `Flow-Logs-Role`, and optionally provide a description. Choose **Create role**.

6. Select the name of your role. Under **Permissions**, choose **Add inline policy**.

7. Choose the **JSON** tab.

8. In the section IAM Roles for Flow Logs above, copy the first policy and paste it in the window. Choose **Review policy**.

9. Enter a name for your policy, and then choose **Create policy**.

10. In the section IAM Roles for Flow Logs above, copy the second policy (the trust relationship), and then choose **Trust relationships**, **Edit trust relationship**. Delete the existing policy document, and paste in the new one. When you are done, choose **Update Trust Policy**.

11. On the **Summary** page, take note of the ARN for your role. You need this ARN when you create your flow log.

Controlling the Use of Flow Logs

By default, IAM users do not have permission to work with flow logs. You can create an IAM user policy that grants users the permissions to create, describe, and delete flow logs. To create a flow log, users must have permissions to use the `iam:PassRole` action for the IAM role that's associated with the flow log.

The following is an example policy that grants users full permissions to create, describe, and delete flow logs, and view flow log records in CloudWatch Logs.

```
1  {
2      "Version": "2012-10-17",
3      "Statement": [
4          {
5              "Effect": "Allow",
6              "Action": [
7                  "ec2:DeleteFlowLogs",
8                  "ec2:CreateFlowLogs",
9                  "ec2:DescribeFlowLogs",
10                 "logs:GetLogEvents"
11             ],
12             "Resource": "*"
13         },
14         {
15             "Effect": "Allow",
16             "Action": [
17                 "iam:PassRole"
18             ],
19             "Resource": "arn:aws:iam::account:role/flow-log-role-name"
20         }
21     ]
22 }
```

For more information about permissions, see Granting IAM Users Required Permissions for Amazon EC2 Resources in the *Amazon EC2 API Reference*.

Working With Flow Logs

You can work with flow logs using the Amazon EC2, Amazon VPC, and CloudWatch consoles.

Topics

- Creating a Flow Log
- Viewing Flow Logs
- Deleting a Flow Log

Creating a Flow Log

You can create a flow log from the VPC page and the Subnet page in the Amazon VPC console, or from the Network Interfaces page in the Amazon EC2 console.

To create a flow log for a network interface

1. Open the Amazon EC2 console at https://console.aws.amazon.com/ec2/.

2. In the navigation pane, choose **Network Interfaces**.

3. Select a network interface, choose the **Flow Logs** tab, and then **Create Flow Log**.

4. In the dialog box, complete following information. When you are done, choose **Create Flow Log**:

    - **Filter**: Select whether the flow log should capture rejected traffic, accepted traffic, or all traffic.
    - **Role**: Specify the name of an IAM role that has permissions to publish logs to CloudWatch Logs.

- **Destination Log Group**: Enter the name of a log group in CloudWatch Logs to which the flow logs are to be published. You can use an existing log group, or you can enter a name for a new log group, which we create for you.

To create a flow log for a VPC or a subnet

1. Open the Amazon VPC console at https://console.aws.amazon.com/vpc/.

2. In the navigation pane, choose **Your VPCs**, or choose **Subnets**.

3. Select your VPC or subnet, choose the **Flow Logs** tab, and then **Create Flow Log**. **Note**
   To create flow logs for multiple VPCs, choose the VPCs, and then select **Create Flow Log** from the **Actions** menu. To create flow logs for multiple subnets, choose the subnets, and then select **Create Flow Log** from the **Subnet Actions** menu.

4. In the dialog box, complete following information. When you are done, choose **Create Flow Log**:
   - **Filter**: Select whether the flow log should capture rejected traffic, accepted traffic, or all traffic.
   - **Role**: Specify the name of an IAM role that has permission to publish logs to CloudWatch Logs.
   - **Destination Log Group**: Enter the name of a log group in CloudWatch Logs to which the flow logs will be published. You can use an existing log group, or you can enter a name for a new log group, which we'll create for you.

Viewing Flow Logs

You can view information about your flow logs in the Amazon EC2 and Amazon VPC consoles by viewing the **Flow Logs** tab for a specific resource. When you select the resource, all the flow logs for that resource are listed. The information displayed includes the ID of the flow log, the flow log configuration, and information about the status of the flow log.

To view information about your flow logs for your network interfaces

1. Open the Amazon EC2 console at https://console.aws.amazon.com/ec2/.

2. In the navigation pane, choose **Network Interfaces**.

3. Select a network interface, and choose the **Flow Logs** tab. Information about the flow logs is displayed on the tab.

To view information about your flow logs for your VPCs or subnets

1. Open the Amazon VPC console at https://console.aws.amazon.com/vpc/.

2. In the navigation pane, choose **Your VPCs**, or choose **Subnets**.

3. Select your VPC or subnet, and then choose the **Flow Logs** tab. Information about the flow logs is displayed on the tab.

You can view your flow log records using the CloudWatch Logs console. It may take a few minutes after you've created your flow log for it to be visible in the console.

To view your flow log records for a flow log

1. Open the CloudWatch console at https://console.aws.amazon.com/cloudwatch/.

2. In the navigation pane, choose **Logs**.

3. Choose the name of the log group that contains your flow log.

4. A list of log streams for each network interface is displayed. Choose the name of the log stream that contains the ID of the network interface for which you want to view the flow log records. For more information about flow log records, see Flow Log Records.

Deleting a Flow Log

You can delete a flow log using the Amazon EC2 and Amazon VPC consoles.

Note
These procedures disable the flow log service for a resource. To delete the log streams for your network interfaces, use the CloudWatch Logs console.

To delete a flow log for a network interface

1. Open the Amazon EC2 console at https://console.aws.amazon.com/ec2/.

2. In the navigation pane, choose **Network Interfaces**, and then select the network interface.

3. Choose the **Flow Logs** tab, and then choose the delete button (a cross) for the flow log to delete.

4. In the confirmation dialog box, choose **Yes, Delete**.

To delete a flow log for a VPC or subnet

1. Open the Amazon VPC console at https://console.aws.amazon.com/vpc/.

2. In the navigation pane, choose **Your VPCs**, or choose your **Subnets**, and then select the resource.

3. Choose the **Flow Logs** tab, and then choose the delete button (a cross) for the flow log to delete.

4. In the confirmation dialog box, choose **Yes, Delete**.

Troubleshooting

Incomplete Flow Log Records

If your flow log records are incomplete, or are no longer being published, there may be a problem delivering the flow logs to the CloudWatch Logs log group. In either the Amazon EC2 console or the Amazon VPC console, go to the **Flow Logs** tab for the relevant resource. For more information, see Viewing Flow Logs. The flow logs table displays any errors in the **Status** column. Alternatively, use the describe-flow-logs command, and check the value that's returned in the `DeliverLogsErrorMessage` field. One of the following errors may be displayed:

- `Rate limited`: This error can occur if CloudWatch logs throttling has been applied — when the number of flow log records for a network interface is higher than the maximum number of records that can be published within a specific timeframe. This error can also occur if you've reached the limit on the number of CloudWatch Logs log groups that you can create. For more information, see CloudWatch Limits in the *Amazon CloudWatch User Guide*.
- `Access error`: The IAM role for your flow log does not have sufficient permissions to publish flow log records to the CloudWatch log group. For more information, see IAM Roles for Flow Logs.
- `Unknown error`: An internal error has occurred in the flow logs service.

Flow Log is Active, But No Flow Log Records or Log Group

You've created a flow log, and the Amazon VPC or Amazon EC2 console displays the flow log as `Active`. However, you cannot see any log streams in CloudWatch Logs, or your CloudWatch Logs log group has not been created. The cause may be one of the following:

- The flow log is still in the process of being created. In some cases, it can take tens of minutes after you've created the flow log for the log group to be created, and for data to be displayed.
- There has been no traffic recorded for your network interfaces yet. The log group in CloudWatch Logs is only created when traffic is recorded.

API and CLI Overview

You can perform the tasks described on this page using the command line or API. For more information about the command line interfaces and a list of available API actions, see Accessing Amazon VPC.

Create a flow log

- create-flow-logs (AWS CLI)
- New-EC2FlowLogs (AWS Tools for Windows PowerShell)
- CreateFlowLogs (Amazon EC2 Query API)

Describe your flow logs

- describe-flow-logs (AWS CLI)
- Get-EC2FlowLogs (AWS Tools for Windows PowerShell)
- DescribeFlowLogs (Amazon EC2 Query API)

View your flow log records (log events)

- get-log-events (AWS CLI)
- Get-CWLLogEvents (AWS Tools for Windows PowerShell)
- GetLogEvents (CloudWatch API)

Delete a flow log

- delete-flow-logs (AWS CLI)
- Remove-EC2FlowLogs (AWS Tools for Windows PowerShell)
- DeleteFlowLogs (Amazon EC2 Query API)

Examples: Flow Log Records

Flow Log Records for Accepted and Rejected Traffic

The following is an example of a flow log record in which SSH traffic (destination port 22, TCP protocol) to network interface `eni-abc123de` in account 123456789010 was allowed.

```
2 123456789010 eni-abc123de 172.31.16.139 172.31.16.21 20641 22 6 20 4249 1418530010 1418530070
    ACCEPT OK
```

The following is an example of a flow log record in which RDP traffic (destination port 3389, TCP protocol) to network interface `eni-abc123de` in account 123456789010 was rejected.

```
2 123456789010 eni-abc123de 172.31.9.69 172.31.9.12 49761 3389 6 20 4249 1418530010 1418530070
    REJECT OK
```

Flow Log Records for No Data and Skipped Records

The following is an example of a flow log record in which no data was recorded during the capture window.

```
2 123456789010 eni-1a2b3c4d - - - - - - - 1431280876 1431280934 - NODATA
```

The following is an example of a flow log record in which records were skipped during the capture window.

```
2 123456789010 eni-4b118871 - - - - - - - 1431280876 1431280934 - SKIPDATA
```

Security Group and Network ACL Rules

If you're using flow logs to diagnose overly restrictive or permissive security group rules or network ACL rules, then be aware of the statefulness of these resources. Security groups are stateful — this means that responses to allowed traffic are also allowed, even if the rules in your security group do not permit it. Conversely, network ACLs are stateless, therefore responses to allowed traffic are subject to network ACL rules.

For example, you use the `ping` command from your home computer (IP address is `203.0.113.12`) to your instance (the network interface's private IP address is `172.31.16.139`). Your security group's inbound rules allow ICMP traffic and the outbound rules do not allow ICMP traffic; however, because security groups are stateful, the response ping from your instance is allowed. Your network ACL permits inbound ICMP traffic but does not permit outbound ICMP traffic. Because network ACLs are stateless, the response ping is dropped and will not reach your home computer. In a flow log, this is displayed as 2 flow log records:

- An `ACCEPT` record for the originating ping that was allowed by both the network ACL and the security group, and therefore was allowed to reach your instance.
- A `REJECT` record for the response ping that the network ACL denied.

```
1 2 123456789010 eni-1235b8ca 203.0.113.12 172.31.16.139 0 0 1 4 336 1432917027 1432917142 ACCEPT
    OK
```

```
1 2 123456789010 eni-1235b8ca 172.31.16.139 203.0.113.12 0 0 1 4 336 1432917094 1432917142 REJECT
    OK
```

If your network ACL permits outbound ICMP traffic, the flow log displays two `ACCEPT` records (one for the originating ping and one for the response ping). If your security group denies inbound ICMP traffic, the flow log displays a single `REJECT` record, because the traffic was not permitted to reach your instance.

Flow Log Record for IPv6 Traffic

The following is an example of a flow log record in which SSH traffic (port 22) from IPv6 address `2001:db8 :1234:a100:8d6e:3477:df66:f105` to network interface `eni-f41c42bf` in account `123456789010` was allowed.

```
1 2 123456789010 eni-f41c42bf 2001:db8:1234:a100:8d6e:3477:df66:f105 2001:db8:1234:a102
    :3304:8879:34cf:4071 34892 22 6 54 8855 1477913708 1477913820 ACCEPT OK
```

Example: Creating a CloudWatch Metric Filter and Alarm for a Flow Log

In this example, you have a flow log for `eni-1a2b3c4d`. You want to create an alarm that alerts you if there have been 10 or more rejected attempts to connect to your instance over TCP port 22 (SSH) within a 1 hour time period. First, you must create a metric filter that matches the pattern of the traffic for which you want to create the alarm. Then, you can create an alarm for the metric filter.

To create a metric filter for rejected SSH traffic and create an alarm for the filter

1. Open the CloudWatch console at https://console.aws.amazon.com/cloudwatch/.

2. In the navigation pane, choose **Logs**, select the flow log group for your flow log, and then choose **Create Metric Filter**.

3. In the **Filter Pattern** field, enter the following:

```
1 [version, account, eni, source, destination, srcport, destport="22", protocol="6", packets,
    bytes, windowstart, windowend, action="REJECT", flowlogstatus]
```

4. In the **Select Log Data to Test** list, select the log stream for your network interface. You can optionally choose **Test Pattern** to view the lines of log data that match the filter pattern. When you're ready, choose **Assign Metric**.

5. Provide a metric namespace, a metric name, and ensure that the metric value is set to **1**. When you're done, choose **Create Filter**.

6. In the navigation pane, choose **Alarms**, and then choose **Create Alarm**.

7. In the **Custom Metrics** section, choose the namespace for the metric filter that you created. **Note** It can take a few minutes for a new metric to display in the console.

8. Select the metric name that you created, and then choose **Next**.

9. Enter a name and description for the alarm. In the **is** fields, choose $>=$ and enter **10**. In the **for** field, leave the default **1** for the consecutive periods.

10. Choose **1 Hour** from the **Period** list, and **Sum** from the **Statistic** list. The `Sum` statistic ensures that you are capturing the total number of data points for the specified time period.

11. In the **Actions** section, you can choose to send a notification to an existing list, or you can create a new list and enter the email addresses that should receive a notification when the alarm is triggered. When you are done, choose **Create Alarm**.

VPC Networking Components

You can use the following components to configure networking in your VPC:

- Network Interfaces
- Route Tables
- Internet Gateways
- Egress-Only Internet Gateways
- DHCP Options Sets
- DNS
- Elastic IP Addresses
- VPC Endpoints
- NAT
- VPC Peering
- ClassicLink

Elastic Network Interfaces

An elastic network interface (referred to as a *network interface* in this documentation) is a virtual network interface that can include the following attributes:

- a primary private IPv4 address
- one or more secondary private IPv4 addresses
- one Elastic IP address per private IPv4 address
- one public IPv4 address, which can be auto-assigned to the network interface for eth0 when you launch an instance
- one or more IPv6 addresses
- one or more security groups
- a MAC address
- a source/destination check flag
- a description

You can create a network interface, attach it to an instance, detach it from an instance, and attach it to another instance. A network interface's attributes follow it as it is attached or detached from an instance and reattached to another instance. When you move a network interface from one instance to another, network traffic is redirected to the new instance.

Each instance in your VPC has a default network interface (the primary network interface) that is assigned a private IPv4 address from the IPv4 address range of your VPC. You cannot detach a primary network interface from an instance. You can create and attach an additional network interface to any instance in your VPC. The number of network interfaces you can attach varies by instance type. For more information, see IP Addresses Per Network Interface Per Instance Type in the *Amazon EC2 User Guide for Linux Instances*.

Attaching multiple network interfaces to an instance is useful when you want to:

- Create a management network.
- Use network and security appliances in your VPC.
- Create dual-homed instances with workloads/roles on distinct subnets.
- Create a low-budget, high-availability solution.

For more information about network interfaces and instructions for working with them using the Amazon EC2 console, see Elastic Network Interfaces in the *Amazon EC2 User Guide for Linux Instances*.

Route Tables

A *route table* contains a set of rules, called *routes*, that are used to determine where network traffic is directed.

Each subnet in your VPC must be associated with a route table; the table controls the routing for the subnet. A subnet can only be associated with one route table at a time, but you can associate multiple subnets with the same route table.

Topics

- Route Table Basics
- Route Priority
- Routing Options
- Working with Route Tables
- API and Command Overview

Route Table Basics

The following are the basic things that you need to know about route tables:

- Your VPC has an implicit router.
- Your VPC automatically comes with a main route table that you can modify.
- You can create additional custom route tables for your VPC.
- Each subnet must be associated with a route table, which controls the routing for the subnet. If you don't explicitly associate a subnet with a particular route table, the subnet is implicitly associated with the main route table.
- You cannot delete the main route table, but you can replace the main route table with a custom table that you've created (so that this table is the default table each new subnet is associated with).
- Each route in a table specifies a destination CIDR and a target (for example, traffic destined for the external corporate network 172.16.0.0/12 is targeted for the virtual private gateway). We use the most specific route that matches the traffic to determine how to route the traffic.
    - CIDR blocks for IPv4 and IPv6 are treated separately. For example, a route with a destination CIDR of 0.0.0.0/0 (all IPv4 addresses) does not automatically include all IPv6 addresses. You must create a route with a destination CIDR of ::/0 for all IPv6 addresses.
- Every route table contains a local route for communication within the VPC over IPv4. If your VPC has more than one IPv4 CIDR block, your route tables contain a local route for each IPv4 CIDR block. If you've associated an IPv6 CIDR block with your VPC, your route tables contain a local route for the IPv6 CIDR block. You cannot modify or delete these routes.
- When you add an Internet gateway, an egress-only Internet gateway, a virtual private gateway, a NAT device, a peering connection, or a VPC endpoint in your VPC, you must update the route table for any subnet that uses these gateways or connections.
- There is a limit on the number of route tables you can create per VPC, and the number of routes you can add per route table. For more information, see Amazon VPC Limits.

Main Route Tables

When you create a VPC, it automatically has a main route table. On the **Route Tables** page in the Amazon VPC console, you can view the main route table for a VPC by looking for **Yes** in the **Main** column. The main route table controls the routing for all subnets that are not explicitly associated with any other route table. You can add, remove, and modify routes in the main route table.

You can explicitly associate a subnet with the main route table, even if it's already implicitly associated. You might do that if you change which table is the main route table, which changes the default for additional new subnets, or any subnets that are not explicitly associated with any other route table. For more information, see Replacing the Main Route Table.

Custom Route Tables

Your VPC can have route tables other than the default table. One way to protect your VPC is to leave the main route table in its original default state (with only the local route), and explicitly associate each new subnet you create with one of the custom route tables you've created. This ensures that you explicitly control how each subnet routes outbound traffic.

The following diagram shows the routing for a VPC with both an Internet gateway and a virtual private gateway, plus a public subnet and a VPN-only subnet. The main route table came with the VPC, and it also has a route for the VPN-only subnet. A custom route table is associated with the public subnet. The custom route table has a route over the Internet gateway (the destination is 0.0.0.0/0, and the target is the Internet gateway).

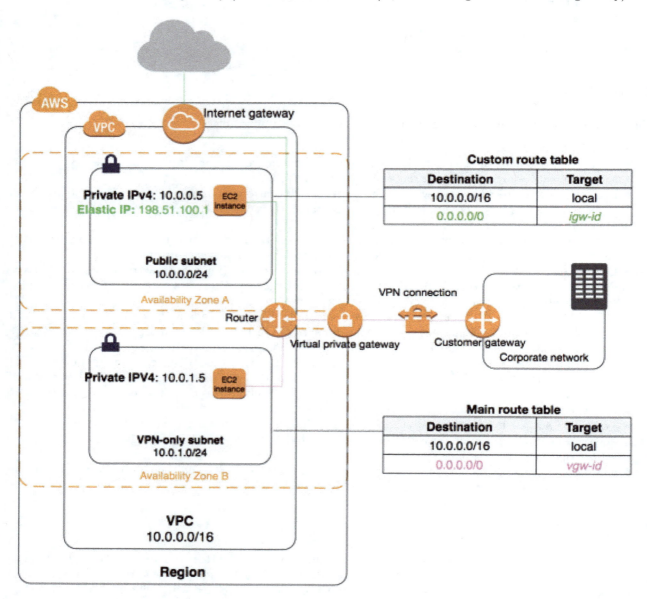

If you create a new subnet in this VPC, it's automatically associated with the main route table, which routes its traffic to the virtual private gateway. If you were to set up the reverse configuration (the main route table with the route to the Internet gateway, and the custom route table with the route to the virtual private gateway), then a new subnet automatically has a route to the Internet gateway.

Route Table Association

The VPC console shows the number of subnets explicitly associated with each route table, and provides information about subnets that are implicitly associated with the main route table. For more information, see Determining Which Subnets Are Explicitly Associated with a Table).

Subnets can be implicitly or explicitly associated with the main route table. Subnets typically won't have an explicit association to the main route table, although it might happen temporarily if you're replacing the main route table.

You might want to make changes to the main route table, but to avoid any disruption to your traffic, you can first test the route changes using a custom route table. After you're satisfied with the testing, you then replace the main route table with the new custom table.

The following diagram shows a VPC with two subnets that are implicitly associated with the main route table (Route Table A), and a custom route table (Route Table B) that isn't associated with any subnets.

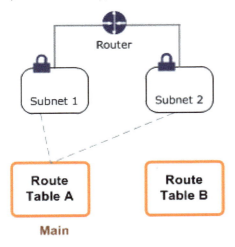

You can create an explicit association between Subnet 2 and Route Table B.

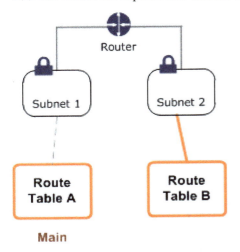

After you've tested Route Table B, you can make it the main route table. Note that Subnet 2 still has an explicit association with Route Table B, and Subnet 1 has an implicit association with Route Table B because it is the new main route table. Route Table A is no longer in use.

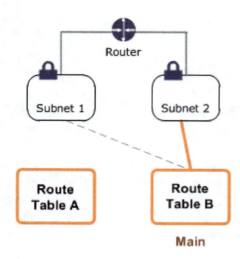

If you disassociate Subnet 2 from Route Table B, there's still an implicit association between Subnet 2 and Route Table B. If you no longer need Route Table A, you can delete it.

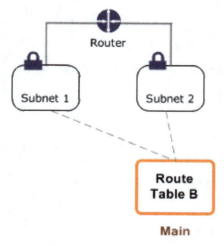

Route Priority

We use the most specific route in your route table that matches the traffic to determine how to route the traffic (longest prefix match).

Routes to IPv4 and IPv6 addresses or CIDR blocks are independent of each other; we use the most specific route that matches either IPv4 traffic or IPv6 traffic to determine how to route the traffic.

For example, the following route table has a route for IPv4 Internet traffic (0.0.0.0/0) that points to an Internet gateway, and a route for 172.31.0.0/16 IPv4 traffic that points to a peering connection (pcx-1a2b3c4d). Any traffic from the subnet that's destined for the 172.31.0.0/16 IP address range uses the peering connection, because this route is more specific than the route for Internet gateway. Any traffic destined for a target within the VPC (10.0.0.0/16) is covered by the Local route, and therefore routed within the VPC. All other traffic from the subnet uses the Internet gateway.

Destination	Target
10.0.0.0/16	Local
172.31.0.0/16	pcx-1a2b3c4d

Destination	Target
0.0.0.0/0	igw-11aa22bb

If you've attached a virtual private gateway to your VPC and enabled route propagation on your route table, routes representing your VPN connection automatically appear as propagated routes in your route table. For more information, see Route Tables and VPN Route Priority.

In this example, an IPv6 CIDR block is associated with your VPC. In your route table, IPv6 traffic destined for within the VPC (2001:db8:1234:1a00::/56) is covered by the Local route, and is routed within the VPC. The route table also has a route for 172.31.0.0/16 IPv4 traffic that points to a peering connection (pcx-1a2b3c4d), a route for all IPv4 traffic (0.0.0.0/0) that points to an Internet gateway, and a route for all IPv6 traffic (::/0) that points to an egress-only Internet gateway. IPv4 and IPv6 traffic are treated separately; therefore, all IPv6 traffic (except for traffic within the VPC) is routed to the egress-only Internet gateway.

Destination	Target
10.0.0.0/16	Local
2001:db81a00::/56	Local
172.31.0.0/16	pcx-1a2b3c4d
0.0.0.0/0	igw-11aa22bb
::/0	eigw-aabb1122

Routing Options

The following topics explain routing for specific gateways or connections in your VPC.

Topics

- Route Tables for an Internet Gateway
- Route Tables for a NAT Device
- Route Tables for a Virtual Private Gateway
- Route Tables for a VPC Peering Connection
- Route Tables for ClassicLink
- Route Tables for a VPC Endpoint
- Route Tables for an Egress-Only Internet Gateway

Route Tables for an Internet Gateway

You can make a subnet a public subnet by adding a route to an Internet gateway. To do this, create and attach an Internet gateway to your VPC, and then add a route with a destination of 0.0.0.0/0 for IPv4 traffic or ::/0 for IPv6 traffic, and a target of the Internet gateway ID (igw-xxxxxxxx). For more information, see Internet Gateways.

Route Tables for a NAT Device

To enable instances in a private subnet to connect to the Internet, you can create a NAT gateway or launch a NAT instance in a public subnet, and then add a route for the private subnet that routes IPv4 Internet traffic (0.0.0.0/0) to the NAT device. For more information, see NAT Gateways and NAT Instances. NAT devices cannot be used for IPv6 traffic.

Route Tables for a Virtual Private Gateway

You can use an AWS managed VPN connection to enable instances in your VPC to communicate with your own network. To do this, create and attach a virtual private gateway to your VPC, and then add a route with the destination of your network and a target of the virtual private gateway (vgw-xxxxxxxx). You can then create and configure your VPN connection. For more information, see AWS Managed VPN Connections.

We currently do not support IPv6 traffic over a VPN connection. However, we support IPv6 traffic routed through a virtual private gateway to an AWS Direct Connect connection. For more information, see the AWS Direct Connect User Guide.

Route Tables for a VPC Peering Connection

A VPC peering connection is a networking connection between two VPCs that allows you to route traffic between them using private IPv4 addresses. Instances in either VPC can communicate with each other as if they are part of the same network.

To enable the routing of traffic between VPCs in a VPC peering connection, you must add a route to one or more of your VPC route tables that points to the VPC peering connection to access all or part of the CIDR block of the other VPC in the peering connection. Similarly, the owner of the other VPC must add a route to their VPC route table to route traffic back to your VPC.

For example, you have a VPC peering connection (pcx-1a2b1a2b) between two VPCs, with the following information:

- VPC A: vpc-1111aaaa, CIDR block is 10.0.0.0/16
- VPC B: vpc-2222bbbb, CIDR block is 172.31.0.0/16

To enable traffic between the VPCs and allow access to the entire IPv4 CIDR block of either VPC, the VPC A route table is configured as follows.

Destination	Target
10.0.0.0/16	Local
172.31.0.0/16	pcx-1a2b1a2b

The VPC B route table is configured as follows.

Destination	Target
172.31.0.0/16	Local
10.0.0.0/16	pcx-1a2b1a2b

Your VPC peering connection can also support IPv6 communication between instances in the VPCs, provided the VPCs and instances are enabled for IPv6 communication. For more information, see VPCs and Subnets. To enable the routing of IPv6 traffic between VPCs, you must add a route to your route table that points to the VPC peering connection to access all or part of the IPv6 CIDR block of the peer VPC.

For example, using the same VPC peering connection (pcx-1a2b1a2b) above, assume the VPCs have the following information:

- VPC A: IPv6 CIDR block is 2001:db8:1234:1a00::/56
- VPC B: IPv6 CIDR block is 2001:db8:5678:2b00::/56

To enable IPv6 communication over the VPC peering connection, add the following route to the route table for VPC A:

Destination	Target
10.0.0.0/16	Local
172.31.0.0/16	pcx-1a2b1a2b
2001:db8:5678:2b00::/56	pcx-1a2b1a2b

Add the following route to the route table for VPC B:

Destination	Target
172.31.0.0/16	Local
10.0.0.0/16	pcx-1a2b1a2b
2001:db81a00::/56	pcx-1a2b1a2b

For more information about VPC peering connections, see the Amazon VPC Peering Guide.

Route Tables for ClassicLink

ClassicLink is a feature that enables you to link an EC2-Classic instance to a VPC, allowing communication between the EC2-Classic instance and instances in the VPC using private IPv4 addresses. For more information about ClassicLink, see ClassicLink.

When you enable a VPC for ClassicLink, a route is added to all of the VPC route tables with a destination of 10.0.0.0/8 and a target of `local`. This allows communication between instances in the VPC and any EC2-Classic instances that are then linked to the VPC. If you add another route table to a ClassicLink-enabled VPC, it automatically receives a route with a destination of 10.0.0.0/8 and a target of `local`. If you disable ClassicLink for a VPC, this route is automatically deleted in all the VPC route tables.

If any of your VPC route tables have existing routes for address ranges within the 10.0.0.0/8 CIDR, then you cannot enable your VPC for ClassicLink. This does not include local routes for VPCs with 10.0.0.0/16 and 10.1.0.0/16 IP address ranges.

If you've already enabled a VPC for ClassicLink, you may not be able to add any more specific routes to your route tables for the 10.0.0.0/8 IP address range.

If you modify a VPC peering connection to enable communication between instances in your VPC and an EC2-Classic instance that's linked to the peer VPC, a static route is automatically added to your route tables with a destination of 10.0.0.0/8 and a target of `local`. If you modify a VPC peering connection to enable communication between a local EC2-Classic instance linked to your VPC and instances in a peer VPC, you must manually add a route to your main route table with a destination of the peer VPC CIDR block, and a target of the VPC peering connection. The EC2-Classic instance relies on the main route table for routing to the peer VPC. For more information, see Configurations With ClassicLink in the *Amazon VPC Peering Guide*.

Route Tables for a VPC Endpoint

A VPC endpoint enables you to create a private connection between your VPC and another AWS service. When you create an endpoint, you specify the route tables in your VPC that are used by the endpoint. A route is automatically added to each of the route tables with a destination that specifies the prefix list ID of the service (`pl-xxxxxxxx`), and a target with the endpoint ID (`vpce-xxxxxxxx`). You cannot explicitly delete or modify the endpoint route, but you can change the route tables that are used by the endpoint.

For more information about routing for endpoints, and the implications for routes to AWS services, see Routing for Gateway Endpoints.

Route Tables for an Egress-Only Internet Gateway

You can create an egress-only Internet gateway for your VPC to enable instances in a private subnet to initiate outbound communication to the Internet, but prevent the Internet from initiating connections with the instances. An egress-only Internet gateway is used for IPv6 traffic only. To configure routing for an egress-only Internet gateway, add a route for the private subnet that routes IPv6 Internet traffic (::/0) to the egress-only Internet gateway. For more information, see Egress-Only Internet Gateways.

Working with Route Tables

This section shows you how to work with route tables.

Note
When you use the wizard in the console to create a VPC with a gateway, the wizard automatically updates the route tables to use the gateway. If you're using the command line tools or API to set up your VPC, you must update the route tables yourself.

Topics

- Determining Which Route Table a Subnet Is Associated With
- Determining Which Subnets Are Explicitly Associated with a Table
- Creating a Custom Route Table
- Adding and Removing Routes from a Route Table
- Enabling and Disabling Route Propagation
- Associating a Subnet with a Route Table
- Changing a Subnet Route Table
- Disassociating a Subnet from a Route Table
- Replacing the Main Route Table
- Deleting a Route Table

Determining Which Route Table a Subnet Is Associated With

You can determine which route table a subnet is associated with by looking at the subnet details in the Amazon VPC console.

To determine which route table a subnet is associated with

1. Open the Amazon VPC console at https://console.aws.amazon.com/vpc/.

2. In the navigation pane, choose **Subnets**.

3. The subnet details are displayed in the **Summary** tab. Choose the **Route Table** tab to view the route table ID and its routes. If it's the main route table, the console doesn't indicate whether the association is implicit or explicit. To determine if the association to the main route table is explicit, see Determining Which Subnets Are Explicitly Associated with a Table.

Determining Which Subnets Are Explicitly Associated with a Table

You can determine how many and which subnets are explicitly associated with a route table.

The main route table can have explicit and implicit associations. Custom route tables have only explicit associations.

Subnets that aren't explicitly associated with any route table have an implicit association with the main route table. You can explicitly associate a subnet with the main route table (for an example of why you might do that, see Replacing the Main Route Table).

To determine which subnets are explicitly associated

1. Open the Amazon VPC console at https://console.aws.amazon.com/vpc/.

2. In the navigation pane, choose **Route Tables**.

3. View the **Explicitly Associated With** column to determine the number of explicitly associated subnets.

4. Select the required route table.

5. Choose the **Subnet Associations** tab in the details pane. The subnets explicitly associated with the table are listed on the tab. Any subnets not associated with any route table (and thus implicitly associated with the main route table) are also listed.

Creating a Custom Route Table

You can create a custom route table for your VPC using the Amazon VPC console.

To create a custom route table

1. Open the Amazon VPC console at https://console.aws.amazon.com/vpc/.

2. In the navigation pane, choose **Route Tables**.

3. Choose **Create Route Table**.

4. In the **Create Route Table** dialog box, you can optionally name your route table for **Name tag**. Doing so creates a tag with a key of Name and a value that you specify. Select your VPC for **VPC**, and then choose **Yes, Create**.

Adding and Removing Routes from a Route Table

You can add, delete, and modify routes in your route tables. You can only modify routes that you've added.

To modify or add a route to a route table

1. Open the Amazon VPC console at https://console.aws.amazon.com/vpc/.

2. In the navigation pane, choose **Route Tables**, and then select the route table.

3. In the **Routes** tab, choose **Edit**.

4. To modify an existing route, replace the destination CIDR block or a single IP address for **Destination**, and then select a target for **Target**. Choose **Add another route, Save**.

To delete a route from a route table

1. Open the Amazon VPC console at https://console.aws.amazon.com/vpc/.

2. In the navigation pane, choose **Route Tables**, and then select the route table.

3. In the **Routes** tab, choose **Edit**, and then choose **Remove** for the route to delete.

4. Choose **Save** when you're done.

Enabling and Disabling Route Propagation

Route propagation allows a virtual private gateway to automatically propagate routes to the route tables so that you don't need to manually enter VPN routes to your route tables. You can enable or disable route propagation.

For more information about VPN routing options, see VPN Routing Options.

To enable route propagation

1. Open the Amazon VPC console at https://console.aws.amazon.com/vpc/.

2. In the navigation pane, choose **Route Tables**, and then select the route table.

3. On the **Route Propagation** tab, choose **Edit**.

4. Select the **Propagate** check box next to the virtual private gateway, and then choose **Save**.

To disable route propagation

1. Open the Amazon VPC console at https://console.aws.amazon.com/vpc/.

2. In the navigation pane, choose **Route Tables**, and then select the route table.

3. On the **Route Propagation** tab, choose **Edit**.

4. Clear the **Propagate** check box, and then choose **Save**.

Associating a Subnet with a Route Table

To apply route table routes to a particular subnet, you must associate the route table with the subnet. A route table can be associated with multiple subnets; however, a subnet can only be associated with one route table at a time. Any subnet not explicitly associated with a table is implicitly associated with the main route table by default.

To associate a route table with a subnet

1. Open the Amazon VPC console at https://console.aws.amazon.com/vpc/.

2. In the navigation pane, choose **Route Tables**, and then select the route table.

3. On the **Subnet Associations** tab, choose **Edit**.

4. Select the **Associate** check box for the subnet to associate with the route table, and then choose **Save**.

Changing a Subnet Route Table

You can change which route table a subnet is associated with.

To change a subnet route table association

1. Open the Amazon VPC console at https://console.aws.amazon.com/vpc/.

2. In the navigation pane, choose **Subnets**, and then select the subnet.

3. In the **Route Table** tab, choose **Edit**.

4. Select the new route table with which to associate the subnet from the **Change to** list, and then choose **Save**.

Disassociating a Subnet from a Route Table

You can disassociate a subnet from a route table. Until you associate the subnet with another route table, it's implicitly associated with the main route table.

To disassociate a subnet from a route table

1. Open the Amazon VPC console at https://console.aws.amazon.com/vpc/.

2. In the navigation pane, choose **Route Tables**, and then select the route table.

3. In the **Subnet Associations** tab, choose **Edit**.

4. Clear the **Associate** check box for the subnet, and then choose **Save**.

Replacing the Main Route Table

You can change which route table is the main route table in your VPC.

To replace the main route table

1. Open the Amazon VPC console at https://console.aws.amazon.com/vpc/.

2. In the navigation pane, choose **Route Tables**.

3. Select the route table that should be the new main route table, and then choose **Set as Main Table**.

4. In the confirmation dialog box, choose **Yes, Set**.

The following procedure describes how to remove an explicit association between a subnet and the main route table. The result is an implicit association between the subnet and the main route table. The process is the same as disassociating any subnet from any route table.

To remove an explicit association with the main route table

1. Open the Amazon VPC console at https://console.aws.amazon.com/vpc/.

2. In the navigation pane, choose **Route Tables**, and then select the route table.

3. In the **Subnet Associations** tab, choose **Edit**.

4. Clear the **Associate** check box for the subnet, and then choose **Save**.

Deleting a Route Table

You can delete a route table only if there are no subnets associated with it. You can't delete the main route table.

To delete a route table

1. Open the Amazon VPC console at https://console.aws.amazon.com/vpc/.

2. In the navigation pane, choose **Route Tables**.

3. Select the route table, and then choose **Delete Route Table**.

4. In the confirmation dialog box, choose **Yes, Delete**.

API and Command Overview

You can perform the tasks described on this page using the command line or API. For more information about the command line interface and a list of available API operations, see Accessing Amazon VPC.

Create a custom route table

- create-route-table (AWS CLI)
- New-EC2RouteTable (AWS Tools for Windows PowerShell)

Add a route to a route table

- create-route (AWS CLI)
- New-EC2Route (AWS Tools for Windows PowerShell)

Associate a subnet with a route table

- associate-route-table (AWS CLI)
- Register-EC2RouteTable (AWS Tools for Windows PowerShell)

Describe one or more route tables

- describe-route-tables (AWS CLI)
- Get-EC2RouteTable (AWS Tools for Windows PowerShell)

Delete a route from a route table

- delete-route (AWS CLI)
- Remove-EC2Route (AWS Tools for Windows PowerShell)

Replace an existing route in a route table

- replace-route (AWS CLI)
- Set-EC2Route (AWS Tools for Windows PowerShell)

Disassociate a subnet from a route table

- disassociate-route-table (AWS CLI)
- Unregister-EC2RouteTable (AWS Tools for Windows PowerShell)

Change the route table associated with a subnet

- replace-route-table-association (AWS CLI)
- Set-EC2RouteTableAssociation (AWS Tools for Windows PowerShell)

Create a static route associated with a VPN connection

- create-vpn-connection-route (AWS CLI)
- New-EC2VpnConnectionRoute (AWS Tools for Windows PowerShell)

Delete a static route associated with a VPN connection

- delete-vpn-connection-route (AWS CLI)
- Remove-EC2VpnConnectionRoute (AWS Tools for Windows PowerShell)

Enable a virtual private gateway (VGW) to propagate routes to the routing tables of a VPC

- enable-vgw-route-propagation (AWS CLI)
- Enable-EC2VgwRoutePropagation (AWS Tools for Windows PowerShell)

Disable a VGW from propagating routes to the routing tables of a VPC

- disable-vgw-route-propagation (AWS CLI)
- Disable-EC2VgwRoutePropagation (AWS Tools for Windows PowerShell)

Delete a route table

- delete-route-table (AWS CLI)
- Remove-EC2RouteTable (AWS Tools for Windows PowerShell)

Internet Gateways

An internet gateway is a horizontally scaled, redundant, and highly available VPC component that allows communication between instances in your VPC and the internet. It therefore imposes no availability risks or bandwidth constraints on your network traffic.

An internet gateway serves two purposes: to provide a target in your VPC route tables for internet-routable traffic, and to perform network address translation (NAT) for instances that have been assigned public IPv4 addresses.

An internet gateway supports IPv4 and IPv6 traffic.

Enabling Internet Access

To enable access to or from the internet for instances in a VPC subnet, you must do the following:

- Attach an internet gateway to your VPC.
- Ensure that your subnet's route table points to the internet gateway.
- Ensure that instances in your subnet have a globally unique IP address (public IPv4 address, Elastic IP address, or IPv6 address).
- Ensure that your network access control and security group rules allow the relevant traffic to flow to and from your instance.

To use an internet gateway, your subnet's route table must contain a route that directs internet-bound traffic to the internet gateway. You can scope the route to all destinations not explicitly known to the route table (0.0.0.0/0 for IPv4 or ::/0 for IPv6), or you can scope the route to a narrower range of IP addresses; for example, the public IPv4 addresses of your company's public endpoints outside of AWS, or the Elastic IP addresses of other Amazon EC2 instances outside your VPC. If your subnet is associated with a route table that has a route to an internet gateway, it's known as a *public subnet*.

To enable communication over the internet for IPv4, your instance must have a public IPv4 address or an Elastic IP address that's associated with a private IPv4 address on your instance. Your instance is only aware of the private (internal) IP address space defined within the VPC and subnet. The internet gateway logically provides the one-to-one NAT on behalf of your instance, so that when traffic leaves your VPC subnet and goes to the internet, the reply address field is set to the public IPv4 address or Elastic IP address of your instance, and not its private IP address. Conversely, traffic that's destined for the public IPv4 address or Elastic IP address of your instance has its destination address translated into the instance's private IPv4 address before the traffic is delivered to the VPC.

To enable communication over the internet for IPv6, your VPC and subnet must have an associated IPv6 CIDR block, and your instance must be assigned an IPv6 address from the range of the subnet. IPv6 addresses are globally unique, and therefore public by default.

In the following diagram, Subnet 1 in the VPC is associated with a custom route table that points all internet-bound IPv4 traffic to an internet gateway. The instance has an Elastic IP address, which enables communication with the internet.

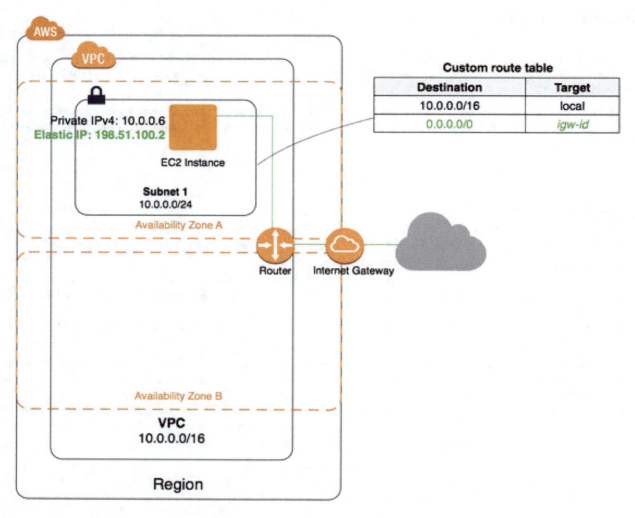

Custom route table

Destination	Target
10.0.0.0/16	local
0.0.0.0/0	igw-id

Internet Access for Default and Nondefault VPCs

The following table provides an overview of whether your VPC automatically comes with the components required for internet access over IPv4 or IPv6.

	Default VPC	Nondefault VPC
Internet gateway	Yes	Yes, if you created the VPC using the first or second option in the VPC wizard. Otherwise, you must manually create and attach the internet gateway.
Route table with route to internet gateway for IPv4 traffic (0.0.0.0/0)	Yes	Yes, if you created the VPC using the first or second option in the VPC wizard. Otherwise, you must manually create the route table and add the route.

	Default VPC	Nondefault VPC
Route table with route to internet gateway for IPv6 traffic (::/0)	No	Yes, if you created the VPC using the first or second option in the VPC wizard, and if you specified the option to associate an IPv6 CIDR block with the VPC. Otherwise, you must manually create the route table and add the route.
Public IPv4 address automatically assigned to instance launched into subnet	Yes (default subnet)	No (nondefault subnet)
IPv6 address automatically assigned to instance launched into subnet	No (default subnet)	No (nondefault subnet)

For more information about default VPCs, see Default VPC and Default Subnets. For more information about using the VPC wizard to create a VPC with an internet gateway, see Scenario 1: VPC with a Single Public Subnet or Scenario 2: VPC with Public and Private Subnets (NAT).

For more information about IP addressing in your VPC, and controlling how instances are assigned public IPv4 or IPv6 addresses, see IP Addressing in Your VPC.

When you add a new subnet to your VPC, you must set up the routing and security that you want for the subnet.

Creating a VPC with an Internet Gateway

The following sections describe how to manually create a public subnet to support internet access.

Topics

- Creating a Subnet
- Creating and Attaching an Internet Gateway
- Creating a Custom Route Table
- Updating the Security Group Rules
- Adding Elastic IP Addresses
- Detaching an Internet Gateway from Your VPC
- Deleting an Internet Gateway
- API and Command Overview

Creating a Subnet

To add a subnet to your VPC

1. Open the Amazon VPC console at https://console.aws.amazon.com/vpc/.

2. In the navigation pane, choose **Subnets**, and then choose **Create Subnet**.

3. In the **Create Subnet** dialog box, select the VPC, select the Availability Zone, and specify the IPv4 CIDR block for the subnet.

4. (Optional, IPv6 only) For **IPv6 CIDR block**, choose **Specify a custom IPv6 CIDR**.

5. Choose **Yes, Create**.

For more information about subnets, see VPCs and Subnets.

Creating and Attaching an Internet Gateway

To create an internet gateway and attach it to your VPC

1. Open the Amazon VPC console at https://console.aws.amazon.com/vpc/.

2. In the navigation pane, choose **Internet Gateways**, and then choose **Create internet gateway**.

3. Optionally name your internet gateway, and then choose **Create**.

4. Select the internet gateway that you just created, and then choose **Actions, Attach to VPC**.

5. Select your VPC from the list, and then choose **Attach**.

Creating a Custom Route Table

When you create a subnet, we automatically associate it with the main route table for the VPC. By default, the main route table doesn't contain a route to an internet gateway. The following procedure creates a custom route table with a route that sends traffic destined outside the VPC to the internet gateway, and then associates it with your subnet.

To create a custom route table

1. Open the Amazon VPC console at https://console.aws.amazon.com/vpc/.

2. In the navigation pane, choose **Route Tables**, and then choose **Create Route Table**.

3. In the **Create Route Table** dialog box, optionally name your route table, then select your VPC, and then choose **Yes, Create**.

4. Select the custom route table that you just created. The details pane displays tabs for working with its routes, associations, and route propagation.

5. On the **Routes** tab, choose **Edit, Add another route**, and add the following routes as necessary. Choose **Save** when you're done.

    - For IPv4 traffic specify 0.0.0.0/0 in the **Destination** box, and select the internet gateway ID in the **Target** list.
    - For IPv6 traffic, specify ::/0 in the **Destination** box, and select the internet gateway ID in the **Target** list.

6. On the **Subnet Associations** tab, choose **Edit**, select the **Associate** check box for the subnet, and then choose **Save**.

For more information about route tables, see Route Tables.

Updating the Security Group Rules

Your VPC comes with a default security group. Each instance that you launch into a VPC is automatically associated with its default security group. The default settings for a default security group allow no inbound traffic from the internet and allow all outbound traffic to the internet. Therefore, to enable your instances to communicate with the internet, create a new security group that allows public instances to access the internet.

To create a new security group and associate it with your instances

1. Open the Amazon VPC console at https://console.aws.amazon.com/vpc/.

2. In the navigation pane, choose **Security Groups**, and then choose **Create Security Group**.

3. In the **Create Security Group** dialog box, specify a name for the security group and a description. Select the ID of your VPC from the **VPC** list, and then choose **Yes, Create**.

4. Select the security group. The details pane displays the details for the security group, plus tabs for working with its inbound rules and outbound rules.

5. On the **Inbound Rules** tab, choose **Edit**. Choose **Add Rule**, and complete the required information. For example, select **HTTP** or **HTTPS** from the **Type** list, and enter the **Source** as 0.0.0.0/0 for IPv4 traffic, or ::/0 for IPv6 traffic. Choose **Save** when you're done.

6. Open the Amazon EC2 console at https;//console.aws.amazon.com/ec2/.

7. In the navigation pane, choose **Instances** .

8. Select the instance, choose **Actions**, then **Networking**, and then select **Change Security Groups**.

9. In the **Change Security Groups** dialog box, clear the check box for the currently selected security group, and select the new one. Choose **Assign Security Groups**.

For more information about security groups, see Security Groups for Your VPC.

Adding Elastic IP Addresses

After you've launched an instance into the subnet, you must assign it an Elastic IP address if you want it to be reachable from the internet over IPv4.

Note
If you assigned a public IPv4 address to your instance during launch, then your instance is reachable from the internet, and you do not need to assign it an Elastic IP address. For more information about IP addressing for your instance, see IP Addressing in Your VPC.

To allocate an Elastic IP address and assign it to an instance using the console

1. Open the Amazon VPC console at https://console.aws.amazon.com/vpc/.

2. In the navigation pane, choose **Elastic IPs**.

3. Choose **Allocate new address**.

4. Choose **Allocate. Note**
   If your account supports EC2-Classic, first choose **VPC**.

5. Select the Elastic IP address from the list, choose **Actions**, and then choose **Associate address**.

6. Choose **Instance** or **Network interface**, and then select either the instance or network interface ID. Select the private IP address with which to associate the Elastic IP address, and then choose **Associate**.

For more information about Elastic IP addresses, see Elastic IP Addresses.

Detaching an Internet Gateway from Your VPC

If you no longer need internet access for instances that you launch into a nondefault VPC, you can detach an internet gateway from a VPC. You can't detach an internet gateway if the VPC has resources with associated public IP addresses or Elastic IP addresses.

To detach an internet gateway

1. Open the Amazon VPC console at https://console.aws.amazon.com/vpc/.

2. In the navigation pane, choose **Elastic IPs** and select the Elastic IP address.

3. Choose **Actions, Disassociate address**. Choose **Disassociate address**.

4. In the navigation pane, choose **Internet Gateways** .

5. Select the internet gateway and choose **Actions, Detach from VPC**.

6. In the **Detach from VPC** dialog box, choose **Detach**.

Deleting an Internet Gateway

If you no longer need an internet gateway, you can delete it. You can't delete an internet gateway if it's still attached to a VPC.

To delete an internet gateway

1. Open the Amazon VPC console at https://console.aws.amazon.com/vpc/.

2. In the navigation pane, choose **Internet Gateways**.

3. Select the internet gateway and choose **Actions**, **Delete internet gateway**.

4. In the **Delete internet gateway** dialog box, choose **Delete**.

API and Command Overview

You can perform the tasks described on this page using the command line or an API. For more information about the command line interfaces and a list of available API actions, see Accessing Amazon VPC.

Create an internet gateway

- create-internet-gateway (AWS CLI)
- New-EC2InternetGateway (AWS Tools for Windows PowerShell)

Attach an internet gateway to a VPC

- attach-internet-gateway (AWS CLI)
- Add-EC2InternetGateway (AWS Tools for Windows PowerShell)

Describe an internet gateway

- describe-internet-gateways (AWS CLI)
- Get-EC2InternetGateway (AWS Tools for Windows PowerShell)

Detach an internet gateway from a VPC

- detach-internet-gateway (AWS CLI)
- Dismount-EC2InternetGateway (AWS Tools for Windows PowerShell)

Delete an internet gateway

- delete-internet-gateway (AWS CLI)
- Remove-EC2InternetGateway (AWS Tools for Windows PowerShell)

Egress-Only Internet Gateways

An egress-only Internet gateway is a horizontally scaled, redundant, and highly available VPC component that allows outbound communication over IPv6 from instances in your VPC to the Internet, and prevents the Internet from initiating an IPv6 connection with your instances.

Note
An egress-only Internet gateway is for use with IPv6 traffic only. To enable outbound-only Internet communication over IPv4, use a NAT gateway instead. For more information, see NAT Gateways.

Topics

- Egress-Only Internet Gateway Basics
- Working with Egress-Only Internet Gateways
- API and CLI Overview

Egress-Only Internet Gateway Basics

An instance in your public subnet can connect to the Internet through the Internet gateway if it has a public IPv4 address or an IPv6 address. Similarly, resources on the Internet can initiate a connection to your instance using its public IPv4 address or its IPv6 address; for example, when you connect to your instance using your local computer.

IPv6 addresses are globally unique, and are therefore public by default. If you want your instance to be able to access the Internet, but you want to prevent resources on the Internet from initiating communication with your instance, you can use an egress-only Internet gateway. To do this, create an egress-only Internet gateway in your VPC, and then add a route to your route table that points all IPv6 traffic (::/0) or a specific range of IPv6 address to the egress-only Internet gateway. IPv6 traffic in the subnet that's associated with the route table is routed to the egress-only Internet gateway.

An egress-only Internet gateway is stateful: it forwards traffic from the instances in the subnet to the Internet or other AWS services, and then sends the response back to the instances.

An egress-only Internet gateway has the following characteristics:

- You cannot associate a security group with an egress-only Internet gateway. You can use security groups for your instances in the private subnet to control the traffic to and from those instances.
- You can use a network ACL to control the traffic to and from the subnet for which the egress-only Internet gateway routes traffic.

In the following diagram, a VPC has an IPv6 CIDR block, and a subnet in the VPC has an IPv6 CIDR block. A custom route table is associated with Subnet 1 and points all Internet-bound IPv6 traffic (::/0) to an egress-only Internet gateway in the VPC.

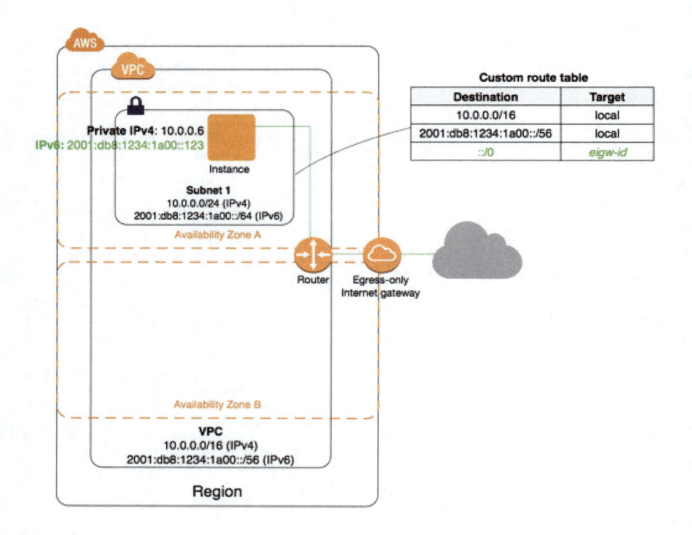

Custom route table	
Destination	**Target**
10.0.0.0/16	local
2001:db8:1234:1a00::/56	local
::/0	eigw-id

Working with Egress-Only Internet Gateways

The following sections describe how to create an egress-only Internet gateway for your private subnet, and configure routing for the subnet.

Creating an Egress-Only Internet Gateway

You can create an egress-only Internet gateway for your VPC using the Amazon VPC console.

To create an egress-only Internet Gateway

1. Open the Amazon VPC console at https://console.aws.amazon.com/vpc/.

2. In the navigation pane, choose **Egress Only Internet Gateways**.

3. Choose **Create Egress Only Internet Gateway**.

4. Select the VPC in which to create the egress-only Internet gateway. Choose **Create**.

Viewing Your Egress-Only Internet Gateway

You can view information about your egress-only Internet gateway in the Amazon VPC console.

To view information about an egress-only Internet gateway

1. Open the Amazon VPC console at https://console.aws.amazon.com/vpc/.

2. In the navigation pane, choose **Egress Only Internet Gateways**.

3. Select the egress-only Internet gateway to view its information in the details pane.

Creating a Custom Route Table

To send traffic destined outside the VPC to the egress-only Internet gateway, you must create a custom route table, add a route that sends traffic to the gateway, and then associate it with your subnet.

To create a custom route table and add a route to the egress-only Internet gateway

1. Open the Amazon VPC console at https://console.aws.amazon.com/vpc/.

2. In the navigation pane, choose **Route Tables**, **Create Route Table**.

3. In the **Create Route Table** dialog box, optionally name your route table, then select your VPC, and then choose **Yes, Create**.

4. Select the custom route table that you just created. The details pane displays tabs for working with its routes, associations, and route propagation.

5. On the **Routes** tab, choose **Edit**, specify ::/0 in the **Destination** box, select the egress-only Internet gateway ID in the **Target** list, and then choose **Save**.

6. On the **Subnet Associations** tab, choose **Edit** and select the **Associate** check box for the subnet. Choose **Save**.

Alternatively, you can add a route to an existing route table that's associated with your subnet. Select your existing route table, and follow steps 5 and 6 above to add a route for the egress-only Internet gateway.

For more information about route tables, see Route Tables.

Deleting an Egress-Only Internet Gateway

If you no longer need an egress-only Internet gateway, you can delete it. Any route in a route table that points to the deleted egress-only Internet gateway remains in a `blackhole` status until you manually delete or update the route.

To delete an egress-only Internet gateway

1. Open the Amazon VPC console at https://console.aws.amazon.com/vpc/.

2. In the navigation pane, choose **Egress Only Internet Gateways** and select the egress-only Internet gateway.

3. Choose **Delete**.

4. Choose **Delete Egress Only Internet Gateway** in the confirmation dialog box.

API and CLI Overview

You can perform the tasks described on this page using the command line or an API. For more information about the command line interfaces and a list of available API actions, see Accessing Amazon VPC.

Create an egress-only Internet gateway

- create-egress-only-internet-gateway (AWS CLI)
- New-EC2EgressOnlyInternetGateway (AWS Tools for Windows PowerShell)

Describe an egress-only Internet gateway

- describe-egress-only-internet-gateways (AWS CLI)
- Get-EC2EgressOnlyInternetGatewayList (AWS Tools for Windows PowerShell)

Delete an egress-only Internet gateway

- delete-egress-only-internet-gateway (AWS CLI)
- Remove-EC2EgressOnlyInternetGateway (AWS Tools for Windows PowerShell)

NAT

You can use a NAT device to enable instances in a private subnet to connect to the Internet (for example, for software updates) or other AWS services, but prevent the Internet from initiating connections with the instances. A NAT device forwards traffic from the instances in the private subnet to the Internet or other AWS services, and then sends the response back to the instances. When traffic goes to the Internet, the source IPv4 address is replaced with the NAT device's address and similarly, when the response traffic goes to those instances, the NAT device translates the address back to those instances' private IPv4 addresses.

NAT devices are not supported for IPv6 traffic—use an egress-only Internet gateway instead. For more information, see Egress-Only Internet Gateways.

Note
We use the term *NAT* in this documentation to follow common IT practice, though the actual role of a NAT device is both address translation and port address translation (PAT).

AWS offers two kinds of NAT devices—a *NAT gateway* or a *NAT instance*. We recommend NAT gateways, as they provide better availability and bandwidth over NAT instances. The NAT Gateway service is also a managed service that does not require your administration efforts. A NAT instance is launched from a NAT AMI. You can choose to use a NAT instance for special purposes.

- NAT Gateways
- NAT Instances
- Comparison of NAT Instances and NAT Gateways

NAT Gateways

You can use a network address translation (NAT) gateway to enable instances in a private subnet to connect to the internet or other AWS services, but prevent the internet from initiating a connection with those instances. For more information about NAT, see NAT.

You are charged for creating and using a NAT gateway in your account. NAT gateway hourly usage and data processing rates apply. Amazon EC2 charges for data transfer also apply. For more information, see Amazon VPC Pricing.

NAT gateways are not supported for IPv6 traffic—use an egress-only internet gateway instead. For more information, see Egress-Only Internet Gateways.

Topics

- NAT Gateway Basics
- Working with NAT Gateways
- Troubleshooting NAT Gateways
- Controlling the Use of NAT Gateways
- Tagging a NAT Gateway
- API and CLI Overview
- Monitoring Your NAT Gateway with Amazon CloudWatch

NAT Gateway Basics

To create a NAT gateway, you must specify the public subnet in which the NAT gateway should reside. For more information about public and private subnets, see Subnet Routing. You must also specify an Elastic IP address to associate with the NAT gateway when you create it. After you've created a NAT gateway, you must update the route table associated with one or more of your private subnets to point Internet-bound traffic to the NAT gateway. This enables instances in your private subnets to communicate with the internet.

Each NAT gateway is created in a specific Availability Zone and implemented with redundancy in that zone. You have a limit on the number of NAT gateways you can create in an Availability Zone. For more information, see Amazon VPC Limits.

Note

If you have resources in multiple Availability Zones and they share one NAT gateway, in the event that the NAT gateway's Availability Zone is down, resources in the other Availability Zones lose internet access. To create an Availability Zone-independent architecture, create a NAT gateway in each Availability Zone and configure your routing to ensure that resources use the NAT gateway in the same Availability Zone.

If you no longer need a NAT gateway, you can delete it. Deleting a NAT gateway disassociates its Elastic IP address, but does not release the address from your account.

The following diagram illustrates the architecture of a VPC with a NAT gateway. The main route table sends internet traffic from the instances in the private subnet to the NAT gateway. The NAT gateway sends the traffic to the internet gateway using the NAT gateway's Elastic IP address as the source IP address.

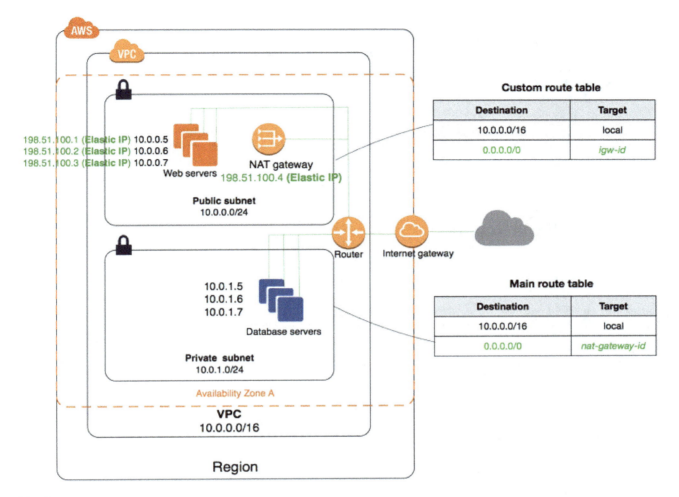

Custom route table	
Destination	**Target**
10.0.0.0/16	local
0.0.0.0/0	*igw-id*

Main route table	
Destination	**Target**
10.0.0.0/16	local
0.0.0.0/0	*nat-gateway-id*

Topics

- NAT Gateway Rules and Limitations
- Migrating from a NAT Instance
- Using a NAT Gateway with VPC Endpoints, VPN, AWS Direct Connect, or VPC Peering

NAT Gateway Rules and Limitations

A NAT gateway has the following characteristics and limitations:

- A NAT gateway supports 5 Gbps of bandwidth and automatically scales up to 45 Gbps. If you require more, you can distribute the workload by splitting your resources into multiple subnets, and creating a NAT gateway in each subnet.
- You can associate exactly one Elastic IP address with a NAT gateway. You cannot disassociate an Elastic IP address from a NAT gateway after it's created. To use a different Elastic IP address for your NAT gateway, you must create a new NAT gateway with the required address, update your route tables, and then delete the existing NAT gateway if it's no longer required.
- A NAT gateway supports the following protocols: TCP, UDP, and ICMP.
- You cannot associate a security group with a NAT gateway. You can use security groups for your instances in the private subnets to control the traffic to and from those instances.
- You can use a network ACL to control the traffic to and from the subnet in which the NAT gateway is located. The network ACL applies to the NAT gateway's traffic. A NAT gateway uses ports 1024–65535. For more information, see Network ACLs.

- When a NAT gateway is created, it receives a network interface that's automatically assigned a private IP address from the IP address range of your subnet. You can view the NAT gateway's network interface in the Amazon EC2 console. For more information, see Viewing Details about a Network Interface. You cannot modify the attributes of this network interface.
- A NAT gateway cannot be accessed by a ClassicLink connection associated with your VPC.
- A NAT gateway can support up to 55,000 simultaneous connections to each unique destination. This limit also applies if you create approximately 900 connections per second to a single destination (about 55,000 connections per minute). If the destination IP address, the destination port, or the protocol (TCP/UDP/ICMP) changes, you can create an additional 55,000 connections. For more than 55,000 connections, there is an increased chance of connection errors due to port allocation errors. These errors can be monitored by viewing the `ErrorPortAllocation` CloudWatch metric for your NAT gateway. For more information, see Monitoring Your NAT Gateway with Amazon CloudWatch.

Migrating from a NAT Instance

If you're already using a NAT instance, you can replace it with a NAT gateway. To do this, you can create a NAT gateway in the same subnet as your NAT instance, and then replace the existing route in your route table that points to the NAT instance with a route that points to the NAT gateway. To use the same Elastic IP address for the NAT gateway that you currently use for your NAT instance, you must first also disassociate the Elastic IP address for your NAT instance and associate it with your NAT gateway when you create the gateway.

Note
If you change your routing from a NAT instance to a NAT gateway, or if you disassociate the Elastic IP address from your NAT instance, any current connections are dropped and have to be re-established. Ensure that you do not have any critical tasks (or any other tasks that operate through the NAT instance) running.

Using a NAT Gateway with VPC Endpoints, VPN, AWS Direct Connect, or VPC Peering

A NAT gateway cannot send traffic over VPC endpoints, VPN connections, AWS Direct Connect, or VPC peering connections. If your instances in the private subnet must access resources over a VPC endpoint, a VPN connection, or AWS Direct Connect, use the private subnet's route table to route the traffic directly to these devices.

For example, your private subnet's route table has the following routes: internet-bound traffic (0.0.0.0/0) is routed to a NAT gateway, Amazon S3 traffic (pl-xxxxxxxx; a specific IP address range for Amazon S3) is routed to a VPC endpoint, and 10.25.0.0/16 traffic is routed to a VPC peering connection. The pl-xxxxxxxx and 10.25.0.0/16 IP address ranges are more specific than 0.0.0.0/0; when your instances send traffic to Amazon S3 or the peered VPC, the traffic is sent to the VPC endpoint or the VPC peering connection. When your instances send traffic to the internet (other than the Amazon S3 IP addresses), the traffic is sent to the NAT gateway.

You cannot route traffic to a NAT gateway through a VPC peering connection, a VPN connection, or AWS Direct Connect. A NAT gateway cannot be used by resources on the other side of these connections.

Working with NAT Gateways

You can use the Amazon VPC console to create, view, and delete a NAT gateway. You can also use the Amazon VPC wizard to create a VPC with a public subnet, a private subnet, and a NAT gateway. For more information, see Scenario 2: VPC with Public and Private Subnets (NAT).

Topics
- Creating a NAT Gateway
- Updating Your Route Table
- Deleting a NAT Gateway
- Testing a NAT Gateway

Creating a NAT Gateway

To create a NAT gateway, you must specify a subnet and an Elastic IP address. Ensure that the Elastic IP address is currently not associated with an instance or a network interface. If you are migrating from a NAT instance to a NAT gateway and you want to reuse the NAT instance's Elastic IP address, you must first disassociate the address from your NAT instance.

To create a NAT gateway

1. Open the Amazon VPC console at https://console.aws.amazon.com/vpc/.

2. In the navigation pane, choose **NAT Gateways, Create NAT Gateway**.

3. Specify the subnet in which to create the NAT gateway, and select the allocation ID of an Elastic IP address to associate with the NAT gateway. When you're done, choose **Create a NAT Gateway**.

4. The NAT gateway displays in the console. After a few moments, its status changes to `Available`, after which it's ready for you to use.

If the NAT gateway goes to a status of `Failed`, there was an error during creation. For more information, see NAT Gateway Goes to a Status of Failed.

Updating Your Route Table

After you've created your NAT gateway, you must update your route tables for your private subnets to point internet traffic to the NAT gateway. We use the most specific route that matches the traffic to determine how to route the traffic (longest prefix match). For more information, see Route Priority.

To create a route for a NAT gateway

1. Open the Amazon VPC console at https://console.aws.amazon.com/vpc/.

2. In the navigation pane, choose **Route Tables**.

3. Select the route table associated with your private subnet and choose **Routes, Edit**.

4. Choose **Add another route**. For **Destination**, type 0.0.0.0/0. For **Target**, select the ID of your NAT gateway. **Note**
If you're migrating from using a NAT instance, you can replace the current route that points to the NAT instance with a route to the NAT gateway.

5. Choose **Save**.

To ensure that your NAT gateway can access the internet, the route table associated with the subnet in which your NAT gateway resides must include a route that points internet traffic to an internet gateway. For more information, see Creating a Custom Route Table. If you delete a NAT gateway, the NAT gateway routes remain in a `blackhole` status until you delete or update the routes. For more information, see Adding and Removing Routes from a Route Table.

Deleting a NAT Gateway

You can delete a NAT gateway using the Amazon VPC console. After you've deleted a NAT gateway, its entry remains visible in the Amazon VPC console for a short while (usually an hour), after which it's automatically removed. You cannot remove this entry yourself.

To delete a NAT gateway

1. Open the Amazon VPC console at https://console.aws.amazon.com/vpc/.

2. In the navigation pane, choose **NAT Gateways**.

3. Select the NAT gateway, and choose **Actions, Delete NAT Gateway**.

4. In the confirmation dialog box, choose **Delete NAT Gateway**.

Testing a NAT Gateway

After you've created your NAT gateway and updated your route tables, you can ping the internet from an instance in your private subnet to test that it can connect to the internet. For an example of how to do this, see Testing the internet Connection.

If you're able to connect to the internet, you can also perform the following tests to determine if the internet traffic is being routed through the NAT gateway:

- You can trace the route of traffic from an instance in your private subnet. To do this, run the `traceroute` command from a Linux instance in your private subnet. In the output, you should see the private IP address of the NAT gateway in one of the hops (it's usually the first hop).
- Use a third-party website or tool that displays the source IP address when you connect to it from an instance in your private subnet. The source IP address should be the Elastic IP address of your NAT gateway. You can get the Elastic IP address and private IP address of your NAT gateway by viewing its information on the **NAT Gateways** page in the Amazon VPC console.

If the preceding tests fail, see Troubleshooting NAT Gateways.

Testing the internet Connection

The following example demonstrates how to test if your instance in a private subnet can connect to the internet.

1. Launch an instance in your public subnet (you use this as a bastion host). For more information, see Launching an Instance into Your Subnet. In the launch wizard, ensure that you select an Amazon Linux AMI, and assign a public IP address to your instance. Ensure that your security group rules allow inbound SSH traffic from the range of IP addresses for your local network (you can also use 0.0.0.0/0 for this test), and outbound SSH traffic to the IP address range of your private subnet.

2. Launch an instance in your private subnet. In the launch wizard, ensure that you select an Amazon Linux AMI. Do not assign a public IP address to your instance. Ensure that your security group rules allow inbound SSH traffic from the private IP address of your instance that you launched in the public subnet, and all outbound ICMP traffic. You must choose the same key pair that you used to launch your instance in the public subnet.

3. Configure SSH agent forwarding on your local computer, and connect to your bastion host in the public subnet. For more information, see To configure SSH agent forwarding for Linux or macOS or To configure SSH agent forwarding for Windows (PuTTY).

4. From your bastion host, connect to your instance in the private subnet, and then test the internet connection from your instance in the private subnet. For more information, see To test the internet connection.

To configure SSH agent forwarding for Linux or macOS

1. From your local machine, add your private key to the authentication agent.

   For Linux, use the following command:

```
1 ssh-add -c mykeypair.pem
```

   For macOS, use the following command:

```
1 ssh-add -K mykeypair.pem
```

2. Connect to your instance in the public subnet using the `-A` option to enable SSH agent forwarding, and use the instance's public address; for example:

```
1 ssh -A ec2-user@54.0.0.123
2 ```<a name="ssh-forwarding-windows"></a>
```

To configure SSH agent forwarding for Windows (PuTTY)

1. Download and install Pageant from the PuTTY download page, if not already installed.

2. Convert your private key to .ppk format. For more information, see Converting Your Private Key Using PuTTYgen in the *Amazon EC2 User Guide for Linux Instances*.

3. Start Pageant, right-click the Pageant icon on the taskbar (it may be hidden), and choose **Add Key**. Select the .ppk file that you created, type the passphrase if necessary, and choose **Open**.

4. Start a PuTTY session and connect to your instance in the public subnet using its public IP address. For more information, see Starting a PuTTY Session. In the **Auth** category, ensure that you select the **Allow agent forwarding** option, and leave the **Private key file for authentication** box blank.

To test the internet connection

1. From your instance in the public subnet, connect to your instance in your private subnet by using its private IP address, for example:

```
1 ssh ec2-user@10.0.1.123
```

2. From your private instance, test that you can connect to the internet by running the **ping** command for a website that has ICMP enabled, for example:

```
1 ping ietf.org
```

```
1 PING ietf.org (4.31.198.44) 56(84) bytes of data.
2 64 bytes from mail.ietf.org (4.31.198.44): icmp_seq=1 ttl=47 time=86.0 ms
3 64 bytes from mail.ietf.org (4.31.198.44): icmp_seq=2 ttl=47 time=75.6 ms
4 ...
```

Press **Ctrl+C** on your keyboard to cancel the **ping** command. If the **ping** command fails, see Instances in Private Subnet Cannot Access internet.

3. (Optional) If you no longer require your instances, terminate them. For more information, see Terminate Your Instance in the *Amazon EC2 User Guide for Linux Instances*.

Troubleshooting NAT Gateways

The following topics help you to troubleshoot common problems you may encounter when creating or using a NAT gateway.

Topics

- NAT Gateway Goes to a Status of Failed
- You've Reached Your Elastic IP Address or NAT Gateway Limit
- The Availability Zone Is Unsupported (`NotAvailableInZone`)
- You Created a NAT Gateway and It's No Longer Visible
- NAT Gateway Doesn't Respond to a Ping Command
- Instances in Private Subnet Cannot Access internet
- TCP Connection to a Specific Endpoint Fails
- Traceroute Output Does Not Display NAT Gateway Private IP Address
- Internet Connection Drops After 5 Minutes
- IPsec Connection Cannot Be Established
- Cannot Initiate More Connections to a Destination

NAT Gateway Goes to a Status of Failed

If you create a NAT gateway and it goes to a status of `Failed`, there was an error when it was created. To view the error message, go to the Amazon VPC console, choose **NAT Gateways**, select your NAT gateway, and then view the error message in the **Status** box in the details pane.

Note
A failed NAT gateway is automatically deleted after a short period; usually about an hour.

The following table lists the possible causes of the failure as indicated in the Amazon VPC console. After you've applied any of the remedial steps indicated, you can try to create a NAT gateway again.

Displayed error	Reason	Remedial steps
Subnet has insufficient free addresses to create this NAT gateway	The subnet you specified does not have any free private IP addresses. The NAT gateway requires a network interface with a private IP address allocated from the subnet's range.	You can check how many IP addresses are available in your subnet by going to the Subnets page in the Amazon VPC console, and viewing the Available IPs box in the details pane for your subnet. To create free IP addresses in your subnet, you can delete unused network interfaces, or terminate instances that you do not require.
Network vpc-xxxxxxxx has no Internet gateway attached	A NAT gateway must be created in a VPC with an internet gateway.	Create and attach an internet gateway to your VPC. For more information, see Creating and Attaching an Internet Gateway.
Elastic IP address eipalloc-xxxxxxxx could not be associated with this NAT gateway	The Elastic IP address that you specified does not exist or could not be found.	Check the allocation ID of the Elastic IP address to ensure that you entered it correctly. Ensure that you have specified an Elastic IP address that's in the same region in which you're creating the NAT gateway.
Elastic IP address eipalloc-xxxxxxxx is already associated	The Elastic IP address that you specified is already associated with another resource, and cannot be associated with the NAT gateway.	You can check which resource is associated with the Elastic IP address by going to the Elastic IPs page in the Amazon VPC console, and viewing the values specified for the instance ID or network interface ID. If you do not require the Elastic IP address for that resource, you can disassociate it. Alternatively, allocate a new Elastic IP address to your account. For more information, see Working with Elastic IP Addresses.

Displayed error	Reason	Remedial steps
Network interface eni-xxxxxxxx, created and used internally by this NAT gateway is in an invalid state. Please try again.	There was a problem creating or using the network interface for the NAT gateway.	You cannot fix this error. Try creating a NAT gateway again.

You've Reached Your Elastic IP Address or NAT Gateway Limit

If you've reached your Elastic IP address limit, you can disassociate an Elastic IP address from another resource, or you can request a limit increase using the Amazon VPC Limits form.

If you've reached your NAT gateway limit, you can do one of the following:

- Request a limit increase using the Amazon VPC Limits form. The NAT gateway limit is enforced per Availability Zone.
- Check the status of your NAT gateway. A status of `Pending`, `Available`, or `Deleting` counts against your limit. If you've recently deleted a NAT gateway, wait a few minutes for the status to go from `Deleting` to `Deleted`, then try creating a new NAT gateway.
- If you do not need your NAT gateway in a specific Availability Zone, try creating a NAT gateway in an Availability Zone where you haven't reached your limit.

For more information about limits, see Amazon VPC Limits.

The Availability Zone Is Unsupported (`NotAvailableInZone`)

In some cases, you may be trying to create the NAT gateway in a constrained Availability Zone — a zone in which our ability to expand is constrained. We cannot support NAT gateways in these zones. You can create a NAT gateway in another Availability Zone and use it for private subnets in the constrained zone. You can also move your resources to an unconstrained Availability Zone so that your resources and your NAT gateway are in the same Availability Zone.

You Created a NAT Gateway and It's No Longer Visible

There may have been an error when your NAT gateway was being created, and it failed. A NAT gateway with a status of `failed` is visible in the Amazon VPC console for a short while (usually an hour), after which it's automatically deleted. Review the information in NAT Gateway Goes to a Status of Failed, and try creating a new NAT gateway.

NAT Gateway Doesn't Respond to a Ping Command

If you try to ping a NAT gateway's Elastic IP address or private IP address from the internet (for example, from your home computer) or from any instance in your VPC, you do not get a response. A NAT gateway only passes traffic from an instance in a private subnet to the internet.

To test that your NAT gateway is working, see Testing a NAT Gateway.

Instances in Private Subnet Cannot Access internet

If you followed the preceding steps to test your NAT gateway and the `ping` command fails, or your instances cannot access the internet, check the following information:

- Check that the NAT gateway is in the `Available` state. In the Amazon VPC console, go to the **NAT Gateways** page and view the status information in the details pane. If the NAT gateway is in a failed state, there may have been an error when it was created. For more information, see NAT Gateway Goes to a Status of Failed.
- Check that you've configured your route tables correctly:
  - The NAT gateway must be in a public subnet with a route table that routes internet traffic to an internet gateway. For more information, see Creating a Custom Route Table.
  - Your instance must be in a private subnet with a route table that routes internet traffic to the NAT gateway. For more information, see Updating Your Route Table.
  - Check that there are no other route table entries that route all or part of the internet traffic to another device instead of the NAT gateway.
- Ensure that your security group rules for your private instance allow outbound internet traffic. For the `ping` command to work, the rules must also allow outbound ICMP traffic. **Note**
  The NAT gateway itself allows all outbound traffic and traffic received in response to an outbound request (it is therefore stateful).
- Ensure that the network ACLs that are associated with the private subnet and public subnets do not have rules that block inbound or outbound internet traffic. For the `ping` command to work, the rules must also allow inbound and outbound ICMP traffic. **Note**
  You can enable flow logs to help you diagnose dropped connections because of network ACL or security group rules. For more information, see VPC Flow Logs.
- If you are using the `ping` command, ensure that you are pinging a website that has ICMP enabled. If not, you will not receive reply packets. To test this, perform the same `ping` command from the command line terminal on your own computer.
- Check that your instance is able to ping other resources, for example, other instances in the private subnet (assuming that security group rules allow this).
- Ensure that your connection is using a TCP, UDP, or ICMP protocol only.

TCP Connection to a Specific Endpoint Fails

If a TCP connection to a specific endpoint or host is failing even though TCP connections to other endpoints are working normally, verify whether the endpoint to which you are trying to connect is responding with fragmented TCP packets. A NAT gateway currently does not support IP fragmentation for TCP. For more information, see Comparison of NAT Instances and NAT Gateways.

To check if the endpoint is sending fragmented TCP packets, use an instance in a public subnet with a public IP address to do the following:

- Trigger a response large enough to cause fragmentation from the specific endpoint.
- Use the `tcpdump` utility to verify that the endpoint is sending fragmented packets.

Important
You must use an instance in a public subnet to perform these checks; you cannot use the instance from which the original connection was failing, or an instance in a private subnet behind a NAT gateway or a NAT instance.

If the endpoint is sending fragmented TCP packets, you can use a NAT instance instead of a NAT gateway.

Note
A NAT gateway also doesn't support IP fragmentation for the ICMP protocol. Diagnostic tools that send or receive large ICMP packets will report packet loss. For example, the command `ping -s 10000 example.com` does not work behind a NAT gateway.

Traceroute Output Does Not Display NAT Gateway Private IP Address

Your instance can access the internet, but when you perform the `traceroute` command, the output does not display the private IP address of the NAT gateway. In this case, your instance is accessing the internet using a different device, such as an internet gateway. In the route table of the subnet in which your instance is located, check the following information:

- Ensure that there is a route that sends internet traffic to the NAT gateway.
- Ensure that there isn't a more specific route that's sending internet traffic to other devices, such as a virtual private gateway or an internet gateway.

Internet Connection Drops After 5 Minutes

If a connection that's using a NAT gateway is idle for 5 minutes or more, the connection times out. You can initiate more traffic over the connection or use a TCP keepalive to prevent the connection from being dropped.

IPsec Connection Cannot Be Established

NAT gateways currently do not support the IPsec protocol; however, you can use NAT-Traversal (NAT-T) to encapsulate IPsec traffic in UDP, which is a supported protocol for NAT gateways. Ensure that you test your NAT-T and IPsec configuration to verify that your IPsec traffic is not dropped.

Cannot Initiate More Connections to a Destination

You may have reached the limit for simultaneous connections. For more information, see NAT Gateway Rules and Limitations. If your instances in the private subnet create a large number of connections, you may reach this limit. You can do one of the following:

- Create a NAT gateway per Availability Zone and spread your clients across those zones.
- Create additional NAT gateways in the public subnet and split your clients into multiple private subnets, each with a route to a different NAT gateway.
- Limit the number of connections your clients can create to the destination.
- To release the capacity, close idle connections.

Controlling the Use of NAT Gateways

By default, IAM users do not have permission to work with NAT gateways. You can create an IAM user policy that grants users permissions to create, describe, and delete NAT gateways. We currently do not support resource-level permissions for any of the `ec2:*NatGateway*` API operations. For more information about IAM policies for Amazon VPC, see Controlling Access to Amazon VPC Resources.

Tagging a NAT Gateway

You can tag your NAT gateway to help you identify it or categorize it according to your organization's needs. For information about working with tags, see Tagging Your Amazon EC2 Resources in the *Amazon EC2 User Guide for Linux Instances.*

Cost allocation tags are supported for NAT gateways, therefore you can also use tags to organize your AWS bill and reflect your own cost structure. For more information, see Using Cost Allocation Tags in the *AWS Billing and Cost Management User Guide.* For more information about setting up a cost allocation report with tags, see Monthly Cost Allocation Report in *About AWS Account Billing.*

API and CLI Overview

You can perform the tasks described on this page using the command line or API. For more information about the command line interfaces and a list of available API operations, see Accessing Amazon VPC.

Create a NAT gateway

- create-nat-gateway (AWS CLI)
- New-EC2NatGateway (AWS Tools for Windows PowerShell)
- CreateNatGateway (Amazon EC2 Query API)

Tag a NAT gateway

- create-tags (AWS CLI)
- New-EC2Tag (AWS Tools for Windows PowerShell)
- CreateTags (Amazon EC2 Query API)

Describe a NAT gateway

- describe-nat-gateways (AWS CLI)
- Get-EC2NatGateway (AWS Tools for Windows PowerShell)
- DescribeNatGateways (Amazon EC2 Query API)

Delete a NAT gateway

- delete-nat-gateway (AWS CLI)
- Remove-EC2NatGateway (AWS Tools for Windows PowerShell)
- DeleteNatGateway (Amazon EC2 Query API)

Monitoring Your NAT Gateway with Amazon CloudWatch

You can monitor your NAT gateway using CloudWatch, which collects information from your NAT gateway and creates readable, near real-time metrics. You can use this information to monitor and troubleshoot your NAT gateway. NAT gateway metric data is provided at 1-minute frequency, and statistics are recorded for a period of 15 months.

For more information about Amazon CloudWatch, see the Amazon CloudWatch User Guide. For more information about pricing, see Amazon CloudWatch Pricing.

Topics

- NAT Gateway Metrics and Dimensions
- Creating CloudWatch Alarms to Monitor a NAT Gateway

NAT Gateway Metrics and Dimensions

NAT gateway metrics are sent to CloudWatch at 1-minute intervals. You can use the following procedures to view the metrics for your NAT gateway.

Currently, you can view NAT gateway metrics using the CloudWatch console or a command line tool only.

To view metrics using the CloudWatch console

Metrics are grouped first by the service namespace, and then by the various dimension combinations within each namespace.

1. Open the CloudWatch console at https://console.aws.amazon.com/cloudwatch/.

2. In the navigation pane, choose **Metrics**.

3. Under **All metrics**, choose the **NAT gateway** metric namespace.

4. To view the metrics, select the metric dimension .

To view metrics using the AWS CLI

- At a command prompt, use the following command to list the metrics that are available for the NAT gateway service:

```
1 aws cloudwatch list-metrics --namespace "AWS/NATGateway"
```

The following metrics are available from the NAT gateway service.

Metric	Description
PacketsOutToDestination	The number of packets sent out through the NAT gateway to the destination. A value greater than zero indicates that there is traffic going to the internet from clients that are behind the NAT gateway. If the value for `PacketsOutToDestination` is less than the value for `PacketsInFromSource`, there may be data loss during NAT gateway processing. Unit: Count

Metric	Description
PacketsOutToSource	The number of packets sent through the NAT gateway to the clients in your VPC. A value greater than zero indicates that there is traffic coming from the internet to clients that are behind the NAT gateway. If the value for `PacketsOutToSource` is less than the value for `PacketsInFromDestination`, there may be data loss during NAT gateway processing, or traffic being actively blocked by the NAT gateway. Unit: Count
PacketsInFromSource	The number of packets received by the NAT gateway from clients in your VPC. If the value for `PacketsOutToDestination` is less than the value for `PacketsInFromSource`, there may be data loss during NAT gateway processing. Unit: Count
PacketsInFromDestination	The number of packets received by the NAT gateway from the destination. If the value for `PacketsOutToSource` is less than the value for `PacketsInFromDestination`, there may be data loss during NAT gateway processing, or traffic being actively blocked by the NAT gateway. Unit: Count
BytesOutToDestination	The number of bytes sent out through the NAT gateway to the destination. A value greater than zero indicates that there is traffic going to the internet from clients that are behind the NAT gateway. If the value for `BytesOutToDestination` is less than the value for `BytesInFromSource`, there may be data loss during NAT gateway processing. Unit: Bytes
BytesOutToSource	The number of bytes sent through the NAT gateway to the clients in your VPC. A value greater than zero indicates that there is traffic coming from the internet to clients that are behind the NAT gateway. If the value for `BytesOutToSource` is less than the value for `BytesInFromDestination`, there may be data loss during NAT gateway processing, or traffic being actively blocked by the NAT gateway. Units: Bytes
BytesInFromSource	The number of bytes received by the NAT gateway from clients in your VPC. If the value for `BytesOutToDestination` is less than the value for `BytesInFromSource`, there may be data loss during NAT gateway processing. Units: Bytes

Metric	Description
BytesInFromDestination	The number of bytes received by the NAT gateway from the destination. If the value for `BytesOutToSource` is less than the value for `BytesInFromDestination`, there may be data loss during NAT gateway processing, or traffic being actively blocked by the NAT gateway. Units: Bytes
ErrorPortAllocation	The number of times the NAT gateway could not allocate a source port. A value greater than zero indicates that too many concurrent connections are open through the NAT gateway. Units: Count
ActiveConnectionCount	The total number of concurrent active TCP connections through the NAT gateway. A value of zero indicates that there are no active connections through the NAT gateway. Units: Count
ConnectionAttemptCount	The number of connection attempts made through the NAT gateway. If the value for `ConnectionEstablishedCount` is less than the value for `ConnectionAttemptCount`, this indicates that clients behind the NAT gateway attempted to establish new connections for which there was no response. Unit: Count
ConnectionEstablishedCount	The number of connections established through the NAT gateway. If the value for `ConnectionEstablishedCount` is less than the value for `ConnectionAttemptCount`, this indicates that clients behind the NAT gateway attempted to establish new connections for which there was no response. Unit: Count
IdleTimeoutCount	The number of connections that transitioned from the active state to the idle state. An active connection transitions to idle if it was not closed gracefully and there was no activity for the last 350 seconds. A value greater than zero indicates that there are connections that have been moved to an idle state. If the value for `IdleTimeoutCount` increases, it may indicate that clients behind the NAT gateway are re-using stale connections. Unit: Count
PacketsDropCount	The number of packets dropped by the NAT gateway. A value greater than zero may indicate an ongoing transient issue with the NAT gateway. If this value is high, see the AWS service health dashboard. Units: Count

You can filter the NAT gateway data using the following dimensions.

Dimension	Description

Dimension	Description
NatGatewayId	This dimension filters data by the NAT gateway ID.

Creating CloudWatch Alarms to Monitor a NAT Gateway

You can create a CloudWatch alarm that sends an Amazon SNS message when the alarm changes state. An alarm watches a single metric over a time period that you specify. It sends a notification to an Amazon SNS topic based on the value of the metric relative to a given threshold over a number of time periods.

For example, you can create an alarm that monitors the amount of traffic coming in or leaving the NAT gateway. The following alarm monitors the amount of outbound traffic from clients in your VPC through the NAT gateway to the internet. It sends a notification when the number of bytes reaches a threshold of 5,000,000 during a 15-minute period.

To create an alarm for outbound traffic through the NAT gateway

1. Open the CloudWatch console at https://console.aws.amazon.com/cloudwatch/.

2. In the navigation pane, choose **Alarms**, **Create Alarm**.

3. Choose **NAT gateway**.

4. Select the NAT gateway and the **BytesOutToDestination** metric and choose **Next**.

5. Configure the alarm as follows, and choose **Create Alarm** when you are done:

   - Under **Alarm Threshold**, enter a name and description for your alarm. For **Whenever**, choose >= and enter 5000000. Enter **1** for the consecutive periods.
   - Under **Actions**, select an existing notification list or choose **New list** to create a new one.
   - Under **Alarm Preview**, select a period of 15 minutes and specify a statistic of **Sum**.

You can create an alarm that monitors the `ErrorPortAllocation` metric and sends a notification when the value is greater than zero (0) for three consecutive 5-minute periods.

To create an alarm to monitor port allocation errors

1. Open the CloudWatch console at https://console.aws.amazon.com/cloudwatch/.

2. In the navigation pane, choose **Alarms**, **Create Alarm**.

3. Choose **NAT Gateway**.

4. Select the NAT gateway and the **ErrorPortAllocation** metric and choose **Next**.

5. Configure the alarm as follows, and choose **Create Alarm** when you are done:

   - Under **Alarm Threshold**, enter a name and description for your alarm. For **Whenever**, choose > and enter 0. Enter **3** for the consecutive periods.
   - Under **Actions**, select an existing notification list or choose **New list** to create a new one.
   - Under **Alarm Preview**, select a period of 5 minutes and specify a statistic of **Maximum**.

For more examples of creating alarms, see Creating Amazon CloudWatch Alarms in the *Amazon CloudWatch User Guide*.

NAT Instances

You can use a network address translation (NAT) instance in a public subnet in your VPC to enable instances in the private subnet to initiate outbound IPv4 traffic to the Internet or other AWS services, but prevent the instances from receiving inbound traffic initiated by someone on the Internet.

For more information about public and private subnets, see Subnet Routing. For more information about NAT, see NAT.

NAT is not supported for IPv6 traffic—use an egress-only Internet gateway instead. For more information, see Egress-Only Internet Gateways.

Note
You can also use a NAT gateway, which is a managed NAT service that provides better availability, higher bandwidth, and requires less administrative effort. For common use cases, we recommend that you use a NAT gateway rather than a NAT instance. For more information, see NAT Gateways and Comparison of NAT Instances and NAT Gateways.

Topics

- NAT Instance Basics
- Setting up the NAT Instance
- Creating the NATSG Security Group
- Disabling Source/Destination Checks
- Updating the Main Route Table
- Testing Your NAT Instance Configuration

NAT Instance Basics

The following figure illustrates the NAT instance basics. The main route table is associated with the private subnet and sends the traffic from the instances in the private subnet to the NAT instance in the public subnet. The NAT instance sends the traffic to the Internet gateway for the VPC. The traffic is attributed to the Elastic IP address of the NAT instance. The NAT instance specifies a high port number for the response; if a response comes back, the NAT instance sends it to an instance in the private subnet based on the port number for the response.

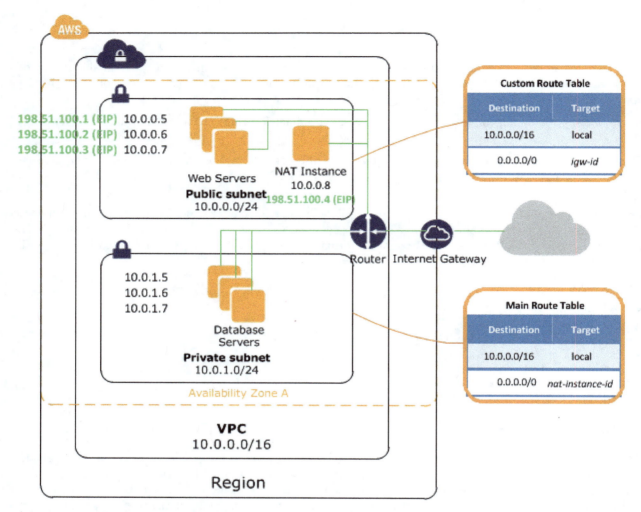

Amazon provides Amazon Linux AMIs that are configured to run as NAT instances. These AMIs include the string `amzn-ami-vpc-nat` in their names, so you can search for them in the Amazon EC2 console.

When you launch an instance from a NAT AMI, the following configuration occurs on the instance:

- IPv4 forwarding is enabled and ICMP redirects are disabled in `/etc/sysctl.d/10-nat-settings.conf`
- A script located at `/usr/sbin/configure-pat.sh` runs at startup and configures iptables IP masquerading.

Note
We recommend that you always use the latest version of the NAT AMI to take advantage of configuration updates.
If you add and remove secondary IPv4 CIDR blocks on your VPC, ensure that you use AMI version `amzn-ami-vpc-nat-hvm-2017.03.1.20170623-x86_64-ebs` or later.

Your NAT instance limit depends on your instance type limit for the region. For more information, see the EC2 FAQs. For a list of available NAT AMIs, see the Amazon Linux AMI matrix.

Setting up the NAT Instance

You can use the VPC wizard to set up a VPC with a NAT instance; for more information, see Scenario 2: VPC with Public and Private Subnets (NAT). The wizard performs many of the configuration steps for you, including launching a NAT instance, and setting up the routing. However, if you prefer, you can create and configure a VPC and a NAT instance manually using the steps below.

1. Create a VPC with two subnets. **Note**
   The steps below are for manually creating and configuring a VPC; not for creating a VPC using the VPC wizard.

   1. Create a VPC (see Creating a VPC)

   2. Create two subnets (see Creating a Subnet)

   3. Attach an Internet gateway to the VPC (see Creating and Attaching an Internet Gateway)

   4. Create a custom route table that sends traffic destined outside the VPC to the Internet gateway, and then associate it with one subnet, making it a public subnet (see Creating a Custom Route Table)

2. Create the NATSG security group (see Creating the NATSG Security Group). You'll specify this security group when you launch the NAT instance.

3. Launch an instance into your public subnet from an AMI that's been configured to run as a NAT instance. Amazon provides Amazon Linux AMIs that are configured to run as NAT instances. These AMIs include the string `amzn-ami-vpc-nat` in their names, so you can search for them in the Amazon EC2 console.

   1. Open the Amazon EC2 console.

   2. On the dashboard, choose the **Launch Instance** button, and complete the wizard as follows:

      1. On the **Choose an Amazon Machine Image (AMI)** page, select the **Community AMIs** category, and search for `amzn-ami-vpc-nat`. In the results list, each AMI's name includes the version to enable you to select the most recent AMI, for example, 2013.09. Choose **Select**.

      2. On the **Choose an Instance Type** page, select the instance type, then choose **Next: Configure Instance Details**.

      3. On the **Configure Instance Details** page, select the VPC you created from the **Network** list, and select your public subnet from the **Subnet** list.

      4. (Optional) Select the **Public IP** check box to request that your NAT instance receives a public IP address. If you choose not to assign a public IP address now, you can allocate an Elastic IP address and assign it to your instance after it's launched. For more information about assigning a public IP at launch, see Assigning a Public IPv4 Address During Instance Launch. Choose **Next: Add Storage**.

      5. You can choose to add storage to your instance, and on the next page, you can add tags. Choose **Next: Configure Security Group** when you are done.

      6. On the **Configure Security Group** page, select the **Select an existing security group** option, and select the NATSG security group that you created. Choose **Review and Launch**.

      7. Review the settings that you've chosen. Make any changes that you need, and then choose **Launch** to choose a key pair and launch your instance.

4. (Optional) Connect to the NAT instance, make any modifications that you need, and then create your own AMI that's configured to run as a NAT instance. You can use this AMI the next time that you need to launch a NAT instance. For more information about creating an AMI, see Creating Amazon EBS-Backed AMIs in the *Amazon EC2 User Guide for Linux Instances*.

5. Disable the `SrcDestCheck` attribute for the NAT instance (see Disabling Source/Destination Checks)

6. If you did not assign a public IP address to your NAT instance during launch (step 3), you need to associate an Elastic IP address with it.

   1. Open the Amazon VPC console at https://console.aws.amazon.com/vpc/.

   2. In the navigation pane, choose **Elastic IPs**, and then choose **Allocate new address**.

   3. Choose **Allocate**.

4. Select the Elastic IP address from the list, and then choose **Actions, Associate address**.

5. Select the network interface resource, then select the network interface for the NAT instance. Select the address to associate the Elastic IP with from the **Private IP** list, and then choose **Associate**.

7. Update the main route table to send traffic to the NAT instance. For more information, see Updating the Main Route Table.

Launching a NAT Instance Using the Command Line

To launch a NAT instance into your subnet, use one of the following commands. For more information about these command line interfaces, see Accessing Amazon VPC.

- run-instances (AWS CLI)
- New-EC2Instance (AWS Tools for Windows PowerShell)

To get the ID of an AMI that's configured to run as a NAT instance, use a command to describe images, and use filters to return results only for AMIs that are owned by Amazon, and that have the `amzn-ami-vpc-nat` string in their names. The following example uses the AWS CLI:

```
1 aws ec2 describe-images --filter Name="owner-alias",Values="amazon" --filter Name="name",Values
    ="amzn-ami-vpc-nat*"
```

Creating the NATSG Security Group

Define the NATSG security group as described in the following table to enable your NAT instance to receive Internet-bound traffic from instances in a private subnet, as well as SSH traffic from your network. The NAT instance can also send traffic to the Internet, which enables the instances in the private subnet to get software updates.

NATSG: Recommended Rules

Inbound
Source
10.0.1.0/24
10.0.1.0/24
Public IP address range of your home network
Outbound
Destination
0.0.0.0/0
0.0.0.0/0

To create the NATSG security group

1. Open the Amazon VPC console at https://console.aws.amazon.com/vpc/.

2. In the navigation pane, choose **Security Groups**, and then choose **Create Security Group**.

3. In the **Create Security Group** dialog box, specify `NATSG` as the name of the security group, and provide a description. Select the ID of your VPC from the **VPC** list, and then choose **Yes, Create**.

4. Select the NATSG security group that you just created. The details pane displays the details for the security group, plus tabs for working with its inbound and outbound rules.

5. Add rules for inbound traffic using the **Inbound Rules** tab as follows:

   1. Choose **Edit**.

2. Choose **Add another rule**, and select **HTTP** from the **Type** list. In the **Source** field, specify the IP address range of your private subnet.

3. Choose **Add another rule**, and select **HTTPS** from the **Type** list. In the **Source** field, specify the IP address range of your private subnet.

4. Choose **Add another rule**, and select **SSH** from the **Type** list. In the **Source** field, specify the public IP address range of your network.

5. Choose **Save**.

6. Add rules for outbound traffic using the **Outbound Rules** tab as follows:

   1. Choose **Edit**.

   2. Choose **Add another rule**, and select **HTTP** from the **Type** list. In the **Destination** field, specify `0.0.0.0/0`

   3. Choose **Add another rule**, and select **HTTPS** from the **Type** list. In the **Destination** field, specify `0.0.0.0/0`

   4. Choose **Save**.

For more information about security groups, see Security Groups for Your VPC.

Disabling Source/Destination Checks

Each EC2 instance performs source/destination checks by default. This means that the instance must be the source or destination of any traffic it sends or receives. However, a NAT instance must be able to send and receive traffic when the source or destination is not itself. Therefore, you must disable source/destination checks on the NAT instance.

You can disable the `SrcDestCheck` attribute for a NAT instance that's either running or stopped using the console or the command line.

To disable source/destination checking using the console

1. Open the Amazon EC2 console at https://console.aws.amazon.com/ec2/.

2. In the navigation pane, choose **Instances**.

3. Select the NAT instance, choose **Actions**, select **Networking**, and then select **Change Source/Dest. Check**.

4. For the NAT instance, verify that this attribute is disabled. Otherwise, choose **Yes, Disable**.

To disable source/destination checking using the command line

You can use one of the following commands. For more information about these command line interfaces, see Accessing Amazon VPC.

- modify-instance-attribute (AWS CLI)
- Edit-EC2InstanceAttribute (AWS Tools for Windows PowerShell)

Updating the Main Route Table

The private subnet in your VPC is not associated with a custom route table, therefore it uses the main route table. By default, the main route table enables the instances in your VPC to communicate with each other. You must add route that sends all other subnet traffic to the NAT instance.

To update the main route table

1. Open the Amazon VPC console at https://console.aws.amazon.com/vpc/.

2. In the navigation pane, choose **Route Tables**.

3. Select the main route table for your VPC (the **Main** column displays **Yes**) . The details pane displays tabs for working with its routes, associations, and route propagation.

4. On the **Routes** tab, choose **Edit**, specify 0.0.0.0/0 in the **Destination** box, select the instance ID of the NAT instance from the **Target** list, and then choose **Save**.

5. On the **Subnet Associations** tab, choose **Edit**, and then select the **Associate** check box for the subnet. Choose **Save**.

For more information about route tables, see Route Tables.

Testing Your NAT Instance Configuration

After you have launched a NAT instance and completed the configuration steps above, you can perform a test to check if an instance in your private subnet can access the Internet through the NAT instance by using the NAT instance as a bastion server. To do this, update your NAT instance's security group rules to allow inbound and outbound ICMP traffic and allow outbound SSH traffic, launch an instance into your private subnet, configure SSH agent forwarding to access instances in your private subnet, connect to your instance, and then test the Internet connectivity.

To update your NAT instance's security group

1. Open the Amazon EC2 console at https://console.aws.amazon.com/ec2/.

2. In the navigation pane, choose **Security Groups**.

3. Find the security group associated with your NAT instance, and choose **Edit** in the **Inbound** tab.

4. Choose **Add Rule**, select **All ICMP - IPv4** from the **Type** list, and select **Custom** from the **Source** list. Enter the IP address range of your private subnet, for example, **10.0.1.0/24**. Choose **Save**.

5. In the **Outbound** tab, choose **Edit**.

6. Choose **Add Rule**, select **SSH** from the **Type** list, and select **Custom** from the **Destination** list. Enter the IP address range of your private subnet, for example, **10.0.1.0/24**. Choose **Save**.

7. Choose **Add Rule**, select **All ICMP - IPv4** from the **Type** list, and select **Custom** from the **Destination** list. Enter 0.0.0.0/0, and then choose **Save**.

To launch an instance into your private subnet

1. Open the Amazon EC2 console at https://console.aws.amazon.com/ec2/.

2. In the navigation pane, choose **Instances**.

3. Launch an instance into your private subnet. For more information, see Launching an Instance into Your Subnet. Ensure that you configure the following options in the launch wizard, and then choose **Launch**:

   - On the **Choose an Amazon Machine Image (AMI)** page, select an Amazon Linux AMI from the **Quick Start** category.
   - On the **Configure Instance Details** page, select your private subnet from the **Subnet** list, and do not assign a public IP address to your instance.
   - On the **Configure Security Group** page, ensure that your security group includes an inbound rule that allows SSH access from your NAT instance's private IP address, or from the IP address range of your public subnet, and ensure that you have an outbound rule that allows outbound ICMP traffic.
   - In the **Select an existing key pair or create a new key pair** dialog box, select the same key pair you used to launch the NAT instance.

To configure SSH agent forwarding for Linux or OS X

1. From your local machine, add your private key to the authentication agent.

   For Linux, use the following command:

```
1 ssh-add -c mykeypair.pem
```

   For OS X, use the following command:

```
1 ssh-add -K mykeypair.pem
```

2. Connect to your NAT instance using the -A option to enable SSH agent forwarding, for example:

```
1 ssh -A ec2-user@54.0.0.123
```

To configure SSH agent forwarding for Windows (PuTTY)

1. Download and install Pageant from the PuTTY download page, if not already installed.

2. Convert your private key to .ppk format. For more information, see Converting Your Private Key Using PuTTYgen.

3. Start Pageant, right-click the Pageant icon on the taskbar (it may be hidden), and choose **Add Key**. Select the .ppk file you created, enter the passphrase if required, and choose **Open**.

4. Start a PuTTY session to connect to your NAT instance. In the **Auth** category, ensure that you select the **Allow agent forwarding** option, and leave the **Private key file for authentication** field blank.

To test the Internet connection

1. Test that your NAT instance can communicate with the Internet by running the **ping** command for a website that has ICMP enabled; for example:

```
1 ping ietf.org
```

```
1 PING ietf.org (4.31.198.44) 56(84) bytes of data.
2 64 bytes from mail.ietf.org (4.31.198.44): icmp_seq=1 ttl=48 time=74.9 ms
3 64 bytes from mail.ietf.org (4.31.198.44): icmp_seq=2 ttl=48 time=75.1 ms
4 ...
```

   Press **Ctrl+C** on your keyboard to cancel the **ping** command.

2. From your NAT instance, connect to your instance in your private subnet by using its private IP address, for example:

```
1 ssh ec2-user@10.0.1.123
```

3. From your private instance, test that you can connect to the Internet by running the **ping** command:

```
1 ping ietf.org
```

```
1 PING ietf.org (4.31.198.44) 56(84) bytes of data.
2 64 bytes from mail.ietf.org (4.31.198.44): icmp_seq=1 ttl=47 time=86.0 ms
3 64 bytes from mail.ietf.org (4.31.198.44): icmp_seq=2 ttl=47 time=75.6 ms
4 ...
```

   Press **Ctrl+C** on your keyboard to cancel the **ping** command.

   If the **ping** command fails, check the following information:

   - Check that your NAT instance's security group rules allow inbound ICMP traffic from your private subnet. If not, your NAT instance cannot receive the **ping** command from your private instance.
   - Check that you've configured your route tables correctly. For more information, see Updating the Main Route Table.

- Ensure that you've disabled source/destination checking for your NAT instance. For more information, see Disabling Source/Destination Checks.
- Ensure that you are pinging a website that has ICMP enabled. If not, you will not receive reply packets. To test this, perform the same `ping` command from the command line terminal on your own computer.

4. (Optional) Terminate your private instance if you no longer require it. For more information, see Terminate Your Instance in the *Amazon EC2 User Guide for Linux Instances*.

Comparison of NAT Instances and NAT Gateways

The following is a high-level summary of the differences between NAT instances and NAT gateways.

Attribute	NAT gateway	NAT instance
Availability	Highly available. NAT gateways in each Availability Zone are implemented with redundancy. Create a NAT gateway in each Availability Zone to ensure zone-independent architecture.	Use a script to manage failover between instances.
Bandwidth	Can scale up to 45 Gbps.	Depends on the bandwidth of the instance type.
Maintenance	Managed by AWS.You do not need to perform any maintenance.	Managed by you, for example, by installing software updates or operating system patches on the instance.
Performance	Software is optimized for handling NAT traffic.	A generic Amazon Linux AMI that's configured to perform NAT.
Cost	Charged depending on the number of NAT gateways you use, duration of usage, and amount of data that you send through the NAT gateways.	Charged depending on the number of NAT instances that you use, duration of usage, and instance type and size.
Type and size	Uniform offering; you don't need to decide on the type or size.	Choose a suitable instance type and size, according to your predicted workload.
Public IP addresses	Choose the Elastic IP address to associate with a NAT gateway at creation.	Use an Elastic IP address or a public IP address with a NAT instance. You can change the public IP address at any time by associating a new Elastic IP address with the instance.
Private IP addresses	Automatically selected from the subnet's IP address range when you create the gateway.	Assign a specific private IP address from the subnet's IP address range when you launch the instance.
Security groups	Cannot be associated with a NAT gateway. You can associate security groups with your resources behind the NAT gateway to control inbound and outbound traffic.	Associate with your NAT instance and the resources behind your NAT instance to control inbound and outbound traffic.
Network ACLs	Use a network ACL to control the traffic to and from the subnet in which your NAT gateway resides.	Use a network ACL to control the traffic to and from the subnet in which your NAT instance resides.
Flow logs	Use flow logs to capture the traffic.	Use flow logs to capture the traffic.
Port forwarding	Not supported.	Manually customize the configuration to support port forwarding.

Attribute	NAT gateway	NAT instance
Bastion servers	Not supported.	Use as a bastion server.
Traffic metrics	View CloudWatch metrics for the NAT gateway.	View CloudWatch metrics for the instance.
Timeout behavior	When a connection times out, a NAT gateway returns an RST packet to any resources behind the NAT gateway that attempt to continue the connection (it does not send a FIN packet).	When a connection times out, a NAT instance sends a FIN packet to resources behind the NAT instance to close the connection.
IP fragmentation	Supports forwarding of IP fragmented packets for the UDP protocol. Does not support fragmentation for the TCP and ICMP protocols. Fragmented packets for these protocols will get dropped.	Supports reassembly of IP fragmented packets for the UDP, TCP, and ICMP protocols.

DHCP Options Sets

This topic describes DHCP options sets and how to specify the DHCP options for your VPC.

Topics

- Overview of DHCP Options Sets
- Amazon DNS Server
- Changing DHCP Options
- Working with DHCP Options Sets
- API and Command Overview

Overview of DHCP Options Sets

The Dynamic Host Configuration Protocol (DHCP) provides a standard for passing configuration information to hosts on a TCP/IP network. The `options` field of a DHCP message contains the configuration parameters. Some of those parameters are the domain name, domain name server, and the netbios-node-type.

DHCP options sets are associated with your AWS account so that you can use them across all of your virtual private clouds (VPC).

The Amazon EC2 instances you launch into a nondefault VPC are private by default; they're not assigned a public IPv4 address unless you specifically assign one during launch, or you modify the subnet's public IPv4 address attribute. By default, all instances in a nondefault VPC receive an unresolvable host name that AWS assigns (for example, ip-10-0-0-202). You can assign your own domain name to your instances, and use up to four of your own DNS servers. To do that, you must specify a special set of DHCP options to use with the VPC.

The following table lists all the supported options for a DHCP options set. You can specify only the options you need in your DHCP options set. For more information about the options, see RFC 2132.

DHCP Option Name	Description
domain-name-servers	The IP addresses of up to four domain name servers, or AmazonProvidedDNS. The default DHCP option set specifies AmazonProvidedDNS. If specifying more than one domain name server, separate them with commas. Although you can specify up to four domain name servers, note that some operating systems may impose lower limits. If you want your instance to receive a custom DNS hostname as specified in `domain-name`, you must set `domain-name-servers` to a custom DNS server.

DHCP Option Name	Description
domain-name	If you're using AmazonProvidedDNS in us-east-1, specify `ec2.internal`. If you're using AmazonProvidedDNS in another region, specify *region*.compute.internal (for example, `ap-northeast-1.compute.internal`). Otherwise, specify a domain name (for example, `example.com`). This value is used to complete unqualified DNS hostnames. For more information about DNS hostnames and DNS support in your VPC, see Using DNS with Your VPC. Some Linux operating systems accept multiple domain names separated by spaces. However, other Linux operating systems and Windows treat the value as a single domain, which results in unexpected behavior. If your DHCP options set is associated with a VPC that has instances with multiple operating systems, specify only one domain name.
ntp-servers	The IP addresses of up to four Network Time Protocol (NTP) servers. For more information, see section 8.3 of RFC 2132.
netbios-name-servers	The IP addresses of up to four NetBIOS name servers.
netbios-node-type	The NetBIOS node type (1, 2, 4, or 8). We recommend that you specify 2 (point-to-point, or P-node). Broadcast and multicast are not currently supported. For more information about these node types, see section 8.7 of RFC 2132 and section 10 of RFC1001.

Amazon DNS Server

When you create a VPC, we automatically create a set of DHCP options and associate them with the VPC. This set includes two options: `domain-name-servers=AmazonProvidedDNS`, and `domain-name=`*domain-name-for-your-region*. AmazonProvidedDNS is an Amazon DNS server, and this option enables DNS for instances that need to communicate over the VPC's Internet gateway. The string `AmazonProvidedDNS` maps to a DNS server running on a reserved IP address at the base of the VPC IPv4 network range, plus two. For example, the DNS Server on a 10.0.0.0/16 network is located at 10.0.0.2. For VPCs with multiple IPv4 CIDR blocks, the DNS server IP address is located in the primary CIDR block.

When you launch an instance into a VPC, we provide the instance with a private DNS hostname, and a public DNS hostname if the instance receives a public IPv4 address. If `domain-name-servers` in your DHCP options is set to AmazonProvidedDNS, the public DNS hostname takes the form `ec2-public-ipv4-address.compute-1.amazonaws.com` for the us-east-1 region, and `ec2-public-ipv4-address.region.compute.amazonaws.com` for other regions. The private hostname takes the form `ip-private-ipv4-address.ec2.internal` for the us-east-1 region, and `ip-private-ipv4-address.region.compute.internal` for other regions. To change these to custom DNS hostnames, you must set `domain-name-servers` to a custom DNS server.

The Amazon DNS server in your VPC is used to resolve the DNS domain names that you specify in a private hosted zone in Route 53. For more information about private hosted zones, see Working with Private Hosted Zones in the *Amazon Route 53 Developer Guide.*

Services that use the Hadoop framework, such as Amazon EMR, require instances to resolve their own fully qualified domain names (FQDN). In such cases, DNS resolution can fail if the `domain-name-servers` option is set to a custom value. To ensure proper DNS resolution, consider adding a conditional forwarder on your DNS server to forward queries for the domain `region-name.compute.internal` to the Amazon DNS server. For more information about launching an Amazon EMR cluster into a VPC, see Setting Up a VPC to Host Clusters in the *Amazon EMR Developer Guide.*

Note
You can use the Amazon DNS server IP address 169.254.169.253, though some servers don't allow its use. Windows Server 2008, for example, disallows the use of a DNS server located in the 169.254.x.x network range.

Changing DHCP Options

After you create a set of DHCP options, you can't modify them. If you want your VPC to use a different set of DHCP options, you must create a new set and associate them with your VPC. You can also set up your VPC to use no DHCP options at all.

You can have multiple sets of DHCP options, but you can associate only one set of DHCP options with a VPC at a time. If you delete a VPC, the DHCP options set associated with the VPC are also deleted.

After you associate a new set of DHCP options with a VPC, any existing instances and all new instances that you launch in the VPC use these options. You don't need to restart or relaunch the instances. They automatically pick up the changes within a few hours, depending on how frequently the instance renews its DHCP lease. If you want, you can explicitly renew the lease using the operating system on the instance.

Working with DHCP Options Sets

This section shows you how to work with DHCP options sets.

Topics
- Creating a DHCP Options Set
- Changing the Set of DHCP Options a VPC Uses
- Changing a VPC to use No DHCP Options
- Deleting a DHCP Options Set

Creating a DHCP Options Set

You can create as many additional DHCP options sets as you want. However, you can only associate a VPC with one set of DHCP options at a time. After you create a set of DHCP options, you must configure your VPC to use it. For more information, see Changing the Set of DHCP Options a VPC Uses.

To create a DHCP options set

1. Open the Amazon VPC console at https://console.aws.amazon.com/vpc/.

2. In the navigation pane, choose **DHCP Options Sets**, and then choose **Create DHCP options set**.

3. In the dialog box, enter values for the options that you want to use, and then choose **Yes, Create**.
   Important
   If your VPC has an Internet gateway, make sure to specify your own DNS server or Amazon's DNS server (AmazonProvidedDNS) for the **Domain name servers** value. Otherwise, the instances that need to communicate with the Internet won't have access to DNS.

   The new set of DHCP options appears in your list of DHCP options.

4. Make a note of the ID of the new set of DHCP options (dopt-*xxxxxxx*). You will need it to associate the new set of options with your VPC.

Although you've created a set of DHCP options, you must associate it with your VPC for the options to take effect. You can create multiple sets of DHCP options, but you can associate only one set of DHCP options with your VPC at a time.

Changing the Set of DHCP Options a VPC Uses

You can change which set of DHCP options your VPC uses. If you want the VPC to use no DHCP options, see Changing a VPC to use No DHCP Options.

Note

The following procedure assumes that you've already created the DHCP options set you want to change to. If you haven't, create the options set now. For more information, see Creating a DHCP Options Set.

To change the DHCP options set associated with a VPC

1. Open the Amazon VPC console at https://console.aws.amazon.com/vpc/.

2. In the navigation pane, choose **Your VPCs**.

3. Select the VPC, and select **Edit DHCP Options Set** from the **Actions** list.

4. In the **DHCP Options Set** list, select a set of options from the list, and then choose **Save**.

After you associate a new set of DHCP options with the VPC, any existing instances and all new instances that you launch in that VPC use the options. You don't need to restart or relaunch the instances. They automatically pick up the changes within a few hours, depending on how frequently the instance renews its DHCP lease. If you want, you can explicitly renew the lease using the operating system on the instance.

Changing a VPC to use No DHCP Options

You can set up your VPC to use no set of DHCP options.

1. Open the Amazon VPC console at https://console.aws.amazon.com/vpc/.

2. In the navigation pane, choose **Your VPCs**.

3. Select the VPC, and select **Edit DHCP Options Set** from the **Actions** list.

4. In the **DHCP Options Set** list, select **No DHCP Options Set** from the list, and then choose **Save**.

You don't need to restart or relaunch the instances. They automatically pick up the changes within a few hours, depending on how frequently the instance renews its DHCP lease. If you want, you can explicitly renew the lease using the operating system on the instance.

Deleting a DHCP Options Set

When you no longer need a DHCP options set, use the following procedure to delete it. The VPC must not be using the set of options.

To delete a DHCP options set

1. Open the Amazon VPC console at https://console.aws.amazon.com/vpc/.

2. In the navigation pane, choose **DHCP Options Sets**.

3. Select the set of DHCP options to delete, and then choose **Delete**.

4. In the confirmation dialog box, choose **Yes, Delete**.

API and Command Overview

You can perform the tasks described on this page using the command line or an API. For more information about the command line interfaces and a list of available APIs, see Accessing Amazon VPC.

Create a set of DHCP options for your VPC

- create-dhcp-options (AWS CLI)
- New-EC2DhcpOption (AWS Tools for Windows PowerShell)

Associate a set of DHCP options with the specified VPC, or no DHCP options

- associate-dhcp-options (AWS CLI)
- Register-EC2DhcpOption (AWS Tools for Windows PowerShell)

Describes one or more sets of DHCP options

- describe-dhcp-options (AWS CLI)
- Get-EC2DhcpOption (AWS Tools for Windows PowerShell)

Deletes a set of DHCP options

- delete-dhcp-options (AWS CLI)
- Remove-EC2DhcpOption (AWS Tools for Windows PowerShell)

Using DNS with Your VPC

Domain Name System (DNS) is a standard by which names used on the Internet are resolved to their corresponding IP addresses. A DNS hostname is a name that uniquely and absolutely names a computer; it's composed of a host name and a domain name. DNS servers resolve DNS hostnames to their corresponding IP addresses.

Public IPv4 addresses enable communication over the Internet, while private IPv4 addresses enable communication within the network of the instance (either EC2-Classic or a VPC). For more information, see IP Addressing in Your VPC.

We provide an Amazon DNS server. To use your own DNS server, create a new set of DHCP options for your VPC. For more information, see DHCP Options Sets.

Topics

- DNS Hostnames
- DNS Support in Your VPC
- DNS Limits
- Viewing DNS Hostnames for Your EC2 Instance
- Updating DNS Support for Your VPC
- Using Private Hosted Zones

DNS Hostnames

When you launch an instance into a default VPC, we provide the instance with public and private DNS hostnames that correspond to the public IPv4 and private IPv4 addresses for the instance. When you launch an instance into a nondefault VPC, we provide the instance with a private DNS hostname and we might provide a public DNS hostname, depending on the DNS attributes you specify for the VPC and if your instance has a public IPv4 address.

An Amazon-provided private (internal) DNS hostname resolves to the private IPv4 address of the instance, and takes the form `ip-private-ipv4-address.ec2.internal` for the us-east-1 region, and `ip-private-ipv4-address.region.compute.internal` for other regions (where `private.ipv4.address` is the reverse lookup IP address). You can use the private DNS hostname for communication between instances in the same network, but we can't resolve the DNS hostname outside the network that the instance is in.

A public (external) DNS hostname takes the form `ec2-public-ipv4-address.compute-1.amazonaws.com` for the us-east-1 region, and `ec2-public-ipv4-address.region.amazonaws.com` for other regions. We resolve a public DNS hostname to the public IPv4 address of the instance outside the network of the instance, and to the private IPv4 address of the instance from within the network of the instance.

We do not provide DNS hostnames for IPv6 addresses.

DNS Support in Your VPC

Your VPC has attributes that determine whether your instance receives public DNS hostnames, and whether DNS resolution through the Amazon DNS server is supported.

Attribute	Description
enableDnsHostnames	Indicates whether the instances launched in the VPC get public DNS hostnames. If this attribute is **true**, instances in the VPC get public DNS hostnames, but only if the **enableDnsSupport** attribute is also set to **true**.
enableDnsSupport	Indicates whether the DNS resolution is supported for the VPC. If this attribute is **false**, the Amazon-provided DNS server in the VPC that resolves public DNS hostnames to IP addresses is not enabled. If this attribute is **true**, queries to the Amazon provided DNS server at the 169.254.169.253 IP address, or the reserved IP address at the base of the VPC IPv4 network range plus two will succeed. For more information, see Amazon DNS Server.

If both attributes are set to **true**, the following occurs:

- Your instance receives a public DNS hostname.
- The Amazon-provided DNS server can resolve Amazon-provided private DNS hostnames.

If either or both of the attributes is set to **false**, the following occurs:

- Your instance does not receive a public DNS hostname that can be viewed in the Amazon EC2 console or described by a command line tool or AWS SDK.
- The Amazon-provided DNS server cannot resolve Amazon-provided private DNS hostnames.
- Your instance receives a custom private DNS hostname if you've specified a custom domain name in your DHCP options set. If you are not using the Amazon-provided DNS server, your custom domain name servers must resolve the hostname as appropriate.

By default, both attributes are set to **true** in a default VPC or a VPC created by the VPC wizard. By default, only the **enableDnsSupport** attribute is set to **true** in a VPC created on the **Your VPCs** page of the VPC console or using the AWS CLI, API, or an AWS SDK.

The Amazon DNS server can resolve private DNS hostnames to private IPv4 addresses for all address spaces, including where the IPv4 address range of your VPC falls outside of the private IPv4 addresses ranges specified by RFC 1918.

Important
If you created your VPC before October 2016, the Amazon DNS server does not resolve private DNS hostnames if your VPC's IPv4 address range falls outside of the private IPv4 addresses ranges specified by RFC 1918. If you want to enable the Amazon DNS server to resolve private DNS hostnames for these addresses, contact AWS Support.

If you enable DNS hostnames and DNS support in a VPC that didn't previously support them, an instance that you already launched into that VPC gets a public DNS hostname if it has a public IPv4 address or an Elastic IP address.

DNS Limits

Each Amazon EC2 instance limits the number of packets that can be sent to the Amazon-provided DNS server to a maximum of 1024 packets per second per network interface. This limit cannot be increased. The number of DNS queries per second supported by the Amazon-provided DNS server varies by the type of query, the size of response, and the protocol in use. For more information and recommendations for a scalable DNS architecture, see the Hybrid Cloud DNS Solutions for Amazon VPC whitepaper.

Viewing DNS Hostnames for Your EC2 Instance

You can view the DNS hostnames for a running instance or a network interface using the Amazon EC2 console or the command line.

Instance

To view DNS hostnames for an instance using the console

1. Open the Amazon EC2 console at https://console.aws.amazon.com/ec2/.

2. In the navigation pane, choose **Instances**.

3. Select your instance from the list.

4. In the details pane, the **Public DNS (IPv4)** and **Private DNS** fields display the DNS hostnames, if applicable.

To view DNS hostnames for an instance using the command line

You can use one of the following commands. For more information about these command line interfaces, see Accessing Amazon VPC.

- describe-instances (AWS CLI)
- Get-EC2Instance (AWS Tools for Windows PowerShell)

Network Interface

To view the private DNS hostname for a network interface using the console

1. Open the Amazon EC2 console at https://console.aws.amazon.com/ec2/.

2. In the navigation pane, choose **Network Interfaces**.

3. Select the network interface from the list.

4. In the details pane, the **Private DNS (IPv4)** field displays the private DNS hostname.

To view DNS hostnames for a network interface using the command line

You can use one of the following commands. For more information about these command line interfaces, see Accessing Amazon VPC.

- describe-network-interfaces (AWS CLI)
- Get-EC2NetworkInterface (AWS Tools for Windows PowerShell)

Updating DNS Support for Your VPC

You can view and update the DNS support attributes for your VPC using the Amazon VPC console.

To describe and update DNS support for a VPC using the console

1. Open the Amazon VPC console at https://console.aws.amazon.com/vpc/.

2. In the navigation pane, choose **Your VPCs**.

3. Select the VPC from the list.

4. Review the information in the **Summary** tab. In this example, both settings are enabled.

DNS resolution: yes

DNS hostnames: yes

5. To update these settings, choose **Actions** and either **Edit DNS Resolution** or **Edit DNS Hostnames**. In the dialog box that opens, choose **Yes** or **No**, and **Save**.

To describe DNS support for a VPC using the command line

You can use one of the following commands. For more information about these command line interfaces, see Accessing Amazon VPC.

- describe-vpc-attribute (AWS CLI)
- Get-EC2VpcAttribute (AWS Tools for Windows PowerShell)

To update DNS support for a VPC using the command line

You can use one of the following commands. For more information about these command line interfaces, see Accessing Amazon VPC.

- modify-vpc-attribute (AWS CLI)
- Edit-EC2VpcAttribute (AWS Tools for Windows PowerShell)

Using Private Hosted Zones

If you want to access the resources in your VPC using custom DNS domain names, such as example.com, instead of using private IPv4 addresses or AWS-provided private DNS hostnames, you can create a private hosted zone in Route 53. A private hosted zone is a container that holds information about how you want to route traffic for a domain and its subdomains within one or more VPCs without exposing your resources to the Internet. You can then create Route 53 resource record sets, which determine how Route 53 responds to queries for your domain and subdomains. For example, if you want browser requests for example.com to be routed to a web server in your VPC, you'll create an A record in your private hosted zone and specify the IP address of that web server. For more information about creating a private hosted zone, see Working with Private Hosted Zones in the *Amazon Route 53 Developer Guide.*

To access resources using custom DNS domain names, you must be connected to an instance within your VPC. From your instance, you can test that your resource in your private hosted zone is accessible from its custom DNS name by using the `ping` command; for example, `ping mywebserver.example.com`. (You must ensure that your instance's security group rules allow inbound ICMP traffic for the `ping` command to work.)

You can access a private hosted zone from an EC2-Classic instance that is linked to your VPC via ClassicLink, provided your VPC is enabled for ClassicLink DNS support. For more information, see Enabling ClassicLink DNS Support in the *Amazon EC2 User Guide for Linux Instances.* Otherwise, private hosted zones do not support transitive relationships outside of the VPC; for example, you cannot access your resources using their custom private DNS names from the other side of a VPN connection.

Important

If you are using custom DNS domain names defined in a private hosted zone in Amazon Route 53, you must set the following VPC attributes to `true`: `enableDnsHostnames` and `enableDnsSupport`. For more information, see Updating DNS Support for Your VPC.

VPC Peering

A VPC peering connection is a networking connection between two VPCs that enables you to route traffic between them privately. Instances in either VPC can communicate with each other as if they are within the same network. You can create a VPC peering connection between your own VPCs, with a VPC in another AWS account, or with a VPC in a different AWS Region.

AWS uses the existing infrastructure of a VPC to create a VPC peering connection; it is neither a gateway nor a VPN connection, and does not rely on a separate piece of physical hardware. There is no single point of failure for communication or a bandwidth bottleneck.

For more information about working with VPC peering connections, and examples of scenarios in which you can use a VPC peering connection, see the Amazon VPC Peering Guide.

Elastic IP Addresses

An *Elastic IP address* is a static, public IPv4 address designed for dynamic cloud computing. You can associate an Elastic IP address with any instance or network interface for any VPC in your account. With an Elastic IP address, you can mask the failure of an instance by rapidly remapping the address to another instance in your VPC. Note that the advantage of associating the Elastic IP address with the network interface instead of directly with the instance is that you can move all the attributes of the network interface from one instance to another in a single step.

We currently do not support Elastic IP addresses for IPv6.

Topics

- Elastic IP Address Basics
- Working with Elastic IP Addresses
- API and CLI Overview

Elastic IP Address Basics

The following are the basic things that you need to know about Elastic IP addresses:

- You first allocate an Elastic IP address for use in a VPC, and then associate it with an instance in your VPC (it can be assigned to only one instance at a time).
- An Elastic IP address is a property of network interfaces. You can associate an Elastic IP address with an instance by updating the network interface attached to the instance.
- If you associate an Elastic IP address with the eth0 network interface of your instance, its current public IPv4 address (if it had one) is released to the EC2-VPC public IP address pool. If you disassociate the Elastic IP address, the eth0 network interface is automatically assigned a new public IPv4 address within a few minutes. This doesn't apply if you've attached a second network interface to your instance.
- There are differences between an Elastic IP address that you use in a VPC and one that you use in EC2-Classic. For more information, see Elastic IP Address Differences Between EC2-Classic and Amazon EC2-VPC in the *Amazon EC2 User Guide for Linux Instances*).
- You can move an Elastic IP address from one instance to another. The instance can be in the same VPC or another VPC, but not in EC2-Classic.
- Your Elastic IP addresses remain associated with your AWS account until you explicitly release them.
- To ensure efficient use of Elastic IP addresses, we impose a small hourly charge when they aren't associated with a running instance, or when they are associated with a stopped instance or an unattached network interface. While your instance is running, you aren't charged for one Elastic IP address associated with the instance, but you are charged for any additional Elastic IP addresses associated with the instance. For more information, see Amazon EC2 Pricing.
- You're limited to five Elastic IP addresses; to help conserve them, you can use a NAT device (see NAT).
- An Elastic IP address is accessed through the Internet gateway of a VPC. If you have set up a VPN connection between your VPC and your network, the VPN traffic traverses a virtual private gateway, not an Internet gateway, and therefore cannot access the Elastic IP address.
- You can move an Elastic IP address that you've allocated for use in the EC2-Classic platform to the VPC platform. For more information, see Migrating an Elastic IP Address from EC2-Classic to EC2-VPC in the *Amazon EC2 User Guide.*
- You can tag an Elastic IP address that's allocated for use in a VPC; however, cost allocation tags are not supported. If you recover an Elastic IP address, tags are not recovered.

Working with Elastic IP Addresses

You can allocate an Elastic IP address and then associate it with an instance in a VPC.

To allocate an Elastic IP address for use in a VPC

1. Open the Amazon VPC console at https://console.aws.amazon.com/vpc/.

2. In the navigation pane, choose **Elastic IPs**.

3. Choose **Allocate new address**.

4. Choose **Allocate. Note**
   If your account supports EC2-Classic, first choose **VPC**.

To view your Elastic IP addresses

1. Open the Amazon VPC console at https://console.aws.amazon.com/vpc/.

2. In the navigation pane, choose **Elastic IPs**.

3. To filter the displayed list, start typing part of the Elastic IP address or the ID of the instance to which it's assigned in the search box.

To associate an Elastic IP address with a running instance in a VPC

1. Open the Amazon VPC console at https://console.aws.amazon.com/vpc/.

2. In the navigation pane, choose **Elastic IPs**.

3. Select an Elastic IP address that's allocated for use with a VPC (the **Scope** column has a value of `vpc`), choose **Actions**, and then choose **Associate address**.

4. Choose **Instance** or **Network interface**, and then select either the instance or network interface ID. Select the private IP address with which to associate the Elastic IP address. Choose **Associate. Note**
   A network interface can have several attributes, including an Elastic IP address. You can create a network interface and attach and detach it from instances in your VPC. The advantage of making the Elastic IP address an attribute of the network interface instead of associating it directly with the instance is that you can move all the attributes of the network interface from one instance to another in a single step. For more information, see Elastic Network Interfaces.

After you associate the Elastic IP address with your instance, it receives a DNS hostname if DNS hostnames are enabled. For more information, see Using DNS with Your VPC.

You can apply tags to your Elastic IP address to help you identify it or categorize it according to your organization's needs.

To tag an Elastic IP address

1. Open the Amazon VPC console at https://console.aws.amazon.com/vpc/.

2. In the navigation pane, choose **Elastic IPs**.

3. Select the Elastic IP address and choose **Tags**.

4. Choose **Add/Edit Tags**, enter the tag keys and values as required, and choose **Save**.

To change which instance an Elastic IP address is associated with, disassociate it from the currently associated instance, and then associate it with the new instance in the VPC.

To disassociate an Elastic IP address

1. Open the Amazon VPC console at https://console.aws.amazon.com/vpc/.

2. In the navigation pane, choose **Elastic IPs**.

3. Select the Elastic IP address, choose **Actions**, and then choose **Disassociate address**.

4. When prompted, choose **Disassociate address**.

If you no longer need an Elastic IP address, we recommend that you release it (the address must not be associated with an instance). You incur charges for any Elastic IP address that's allocated for use with a VPC but not associated with an instance.

To release an Elastic IP address

1. Open the Amazon VPC console at https://console.aws.amazon.com/vpc/.

2. In the navigation pane, choose **Elastic IPs**.

3. Select the Elastic IP address, choose **Actions**, and then choose **Release addresses**.

4. When prompted, choose **Release**.

If you release your Elastic IP address, you might be able to recover it. You cannot recover the Elastic IP address if it has been allocated to another AWS account, or if it results in you exceeding your Elastic IP address limit.

Currently, you can recover an Elastic IP address using the Amazon EC2 API or a command line tool only.

To recover an Elastic IP address using the AWS CLI

- Use the allocate-address command and specify the IP address using the --address parameter.

```
1 aws ec2 allocate-address --domain vpc --address 203.0.113.3
```

API and CLI Overview

You can perform the tasks described on this page using the command line or an API. For more information about the command line interfaces and a list of available APIs, see Accessing Amazon VPC.

Acquire an Elastic IP address

- allocate-address (AWS CLI)
- New-EC2Address (AWS Tools for Windows PowerShell)

Associate an Elastic IP address with an instance or network interface

- associate-address (AWS CLI)
- Register-EC2Address (AWS Tools for Windows PowerShell)

Describe one or more Elastic IP addresses

- describe-addresses (AWS CLI)
- Get-EC2Address (AWS Tools for Windows PowerShell)

Tag an Elastic IP address

- create-tags (AWS CLI)
- New-EC2Tag (AWS Tools for Windows PowerShell)

Disassociate an Elastic IP address

- disassociate-address (AWS CLI)
- Unregister-EC2Address (AWS Tools for Windows PowerShell)

Release an Elastic IP address

- release-address (AWS CLI)
- Remove-EC2Address (AWS Tools for Windows PowerShell)

VPC Endpoints

A VPC endpoint enables you to privately connect your VPC to supported AWS services and VPC endpoint services powered by PrivateLink without requiring an internet gateway, NAT device, VPN connection, or AWS Direct Connect connection. Instances in your VPC do not require public IP addresses to communicate with resources in the service. Traffic between your VPC and the other service does not leave the Amazon network.

Endpoints are virtual devices. They are horizontally scaled, redundant, and highly available VPC components that allow communication between instances in your VPC and services without imposing availability risks or bandwidth constraints on your network traffic.

There are two types of VPC endpoints: *interface* and *gateway*.

Interface Endpoints (Powered by AWS PrivateLink)
An interface endpoint is an elastic network interface with a private IP address that serves as an entry point for traffic destined to a supported service. The following services are supported:

- Amazon CloudWatch Logs
- Amazon EC2 API
- Amazon Kinesis Data Streams
- Amazon SNS
- AWS KMS
- AWS Service Catalog
- AWS Systems Manager
- Elastic Load Balancing API
- Endpoint services hosted by other AWS accounts
- Supported AWS Marketplace partner services

Gateway Endpoints
A gateway endpoint is a gateway that is a target for a specified route in your route table, used for traffic destined to a supported AWS service. The following AWS services are supported:

- Amazon S3
- DynamoDB

Controlling the Use of VPC Endpoints
By default, IAM users do not have permission to work with endpoints. You can create an IAM user policy that grants users the permissions to create, modify, describe, and delete endpoints. We currently do not support resource-level permissions for any of the `ec2:*VpcEndpoint*` API actions, or for the `ec2:DescribePrefixLists` action. You cannot create an IAM policy that grants users the permissions to use a specific endpoint or prefix list. For more information, see the following example: 8. Creating and managing VPC endpoints.

Interface VPC Endpoints (AWS PrivateLink)

An interface VPC endpoint (interface endpoint) enables you to connect to services powered by AWS PrivateLink. These services include some AWS services, services hosted by other AWS customers and partners in their own VPCs (referred to as *endpoint services*), and supported AWS Marketplace partner services. The owner of the service is the *service provider*, and you, as the principal creating the interface endpoint, are the *service consumer*.

The following are the general steps for setting up an interface endpoint:

1. Choose the VPC in which to create the interface endpoint, and provide the name of the AWS service, endpoint service, or AWS Marketplace service to which you're connecting.

2. Choose a subnet in your VPC to use the interface endpoint. We create an *endpoint network interface* in the subnet. You can specify more than one subnet in different Availability Zones (as supported by the service) to help ensure that your interface endpoint is resilient to Availability Zone failures. In that case, we create an endpoint network interface in each subnet that you specify. **Note**
An endpoint network interface is a requester-managed network interface. You can view it in your account, but you cannot manage it yourself. For more information, see Elastic Network Interfaces.

3. Specify the security groups to associate with the endpoint network interface. The security group rules control the traffic to the endpoint network interface from resources in your VPC. If you do not specify a security group, we associate the default security group for the VPC.

4. (Optional; AWS services and AWS Marketplace partner services only) Enable private DNS for the endpoint to enable you to make requests to the service using its default DNS hostname.

5. After you create the interface endpoint, it's available to use when it's accepted by the service provider. The service provider must configure the service to accept requests automatically or manually. AWS services and AWS Marketplace services generally accept all endpoint requests automatically. For more information about the lifecycle of an endpoint, see Interface Endpoint Lifecycle.

Services cannot initiate requests to resources in your VPC through the endpoint. An endpoint only returns responses to traffic initiated from resources in your VPC.

For more information about supported services, see VPC Endpoints.

Topics

- Private DNS
- Interface Endpoint Properties and Limitations
- Interface Endpoint Lifecycle
- Pricing for Interface Endpoints
- Creating an Interface Endpoint
- Viewing Your Interface Endpoint
- Creating and Managing a Notification for an Interface Endpoint
- Accessing a Service Through an Interface Endpoint
- Modifying an Interface Endpoint

Private DNS

When you create an interface endpoint, we generate endpoint-specific DNS hostnames that you can use to communicate with the service. For AWS services and AWS Marketplace partner services, you can optionally enable private DNS for the endpoint. This option associates a private hosted zone with your VPC. The hosted zone contains a record set for the default DNS name for the service (for example, `ec2.us-east-1.amazonaws.com`) that resolves to the private IP addresses of the endpoint network interfaces in your VPC. This enables you to make requests to the service using its default DNS hostname instead of the endpoint-specific DNS hostnames. For example, if your existing applications make requests to an AWS service, they can continue to make requests through the interface endpoint without requiring any configuration changes.

In the following diagram, you have created an interface endpoint for Amazon Kinesis Data Streams and an endpoint network interface in subnet 2. You have not enabled private DNS for the interface endpoint. Instances in either subnet can communicate with Amazon Kinesis Data Streams through the interface endpoint using an endpoint-specific DNS hostname (DNS name B). Instance in subnet 1 can communicate with Amazon Kinesis Data Streams over public IP address space in the AWS Region using the default DNS name for the service (DNS name A).

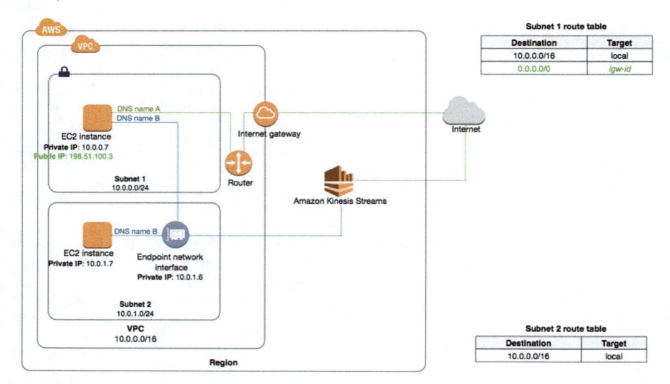

DNS name A: kinesis.us-east-1.amazonaws.com (default DNS hostname)

DNS name B: vpce-123-ab.kinesis.us-east-1.vpce.amazonaws.com (endpoint-specific hostname)

In the next diagram, you have enabled private DNS for the endpoint. Instances in either subnet can communicate with Amazon Kinesis Data Streams through the interface endpoint using an endpoint-specific DNS hostname (DNS name B) or the default DNS name for the service (DNS name A).

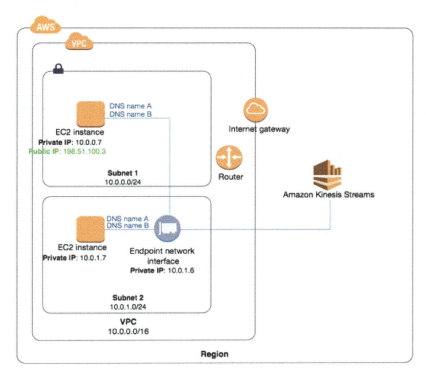

Subnet 1 route table	
Destination	**Target**
10.0.0.0/16	local
0.0.0.0/0	*igw-id*

Subnet 2 route table	
Destination	**Target**
10.0.0.0/16	local

DNS name A: kinesis.us-east-1.amazonaws.com (default DNS hostname)

DNS name B: vpce-123-ab.kinesis.us-east-1.vpce.amazonaws.com (endpoint-specific hostname)

Important

To use private DNS, you must set the following VPC attributes to `true`: `enableDnsHostnames` and `enableDnsSupport`. For more information, see Updating DNS Support for Your VPC. IAM users must have permission to work with hosted zones. For more information, see Authentication and Access Control for Route 53.

Interface Endpoint Properties and Limitations

To use interface endpoints, you need to be aware of their properties and current limitations:

- An interface endpoint can be accessed through an AWS Direct Connect connection. It can also be accessed through an intra-region VPC peering connection from C5 and M5 instance types only. You cannot access an interface endpoint through an AWS VPN connection, an inter-region VPC peering connection, or an intra-region VPC peering connection from an instance type other than C5 or M5.
- For each interface endpoint, you can choose only one subnet per Availability Zone.
- Interface endpoints do not support the use of endpoint policies. Full access to the service through the interface endpoint is allowed.
- Services may not be available in all Availability Zones through an interface endpoint. To find out which Availability Zones are supported, use the describe-vpc-endpoint-services command or use the Amazon VPC console. For more information, see Creating an Interface Endpoint.
- Availability Zones in your account might not map to the same locations as Availability Zones in another account; for example, your Availability Zone `us-east-1a` might not be the same location as `us-east-1a` for another account. For more information, see Region and Availability Zone Concepts. When you create an interface endpoint, it's created in the Availability Zone for your account.
- Each interface endpoint can support a bandwidth of up to 10 Gbps per Availability Zone by default. Additional capacity may be added automatically based on your usage.
- If the network ACL for your subnet restricts traffic, you may not be able to send traffic through the endpoint network interface. Ensure that you add appropriate rules that allow traffic to and from the CIDR block of the subnet.

251

- An interface endpoint supports TCP traffic only.
- Endpoints are supported within the same region only. You cannot create an endpoint between a VPC and a service in a different region.
- You cannot tag an endpoint.
- Endpoints support IPv4 traffic only.
- You cannot transfer an endpoint from one VPC to another, or from one service to another.
- You have a limit on the number of endpoints you can create per VPC. For more information, see VPC Endpoints.

Interface Endpoint Lifecycle

An interface endpoint goes through various stages starting from when you create it (the endpoint connection request). At each stage, there may be actions that the service consumer and service provider can take.

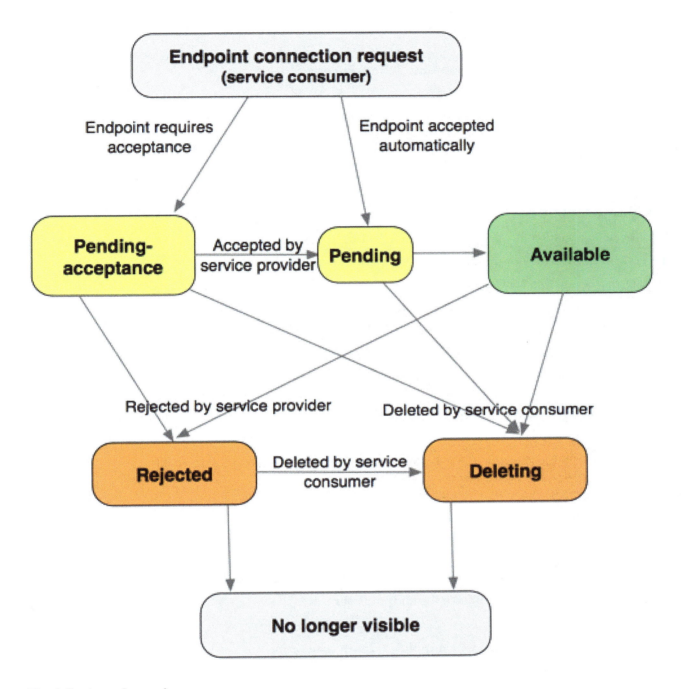

The following rules apply:

- A service provider can configure their service to accept interface endpoint requests automatically or manually. AWS services and AWS Marketplace services generally accept all endpoint requests automatically.
- A service provider cannot delete an interface endpoint to their service. Only the service consumer that requested the interface endpoint connection can delete the interface endpoint.
- A service provider can reject the interface endpoint after it has been accepted (either manually or automatically) and is in the `available` state.

Pricing for Interface Endpoints

You are charged for creating and using an interface endpoint to a service. Hourly usage rates and data processing rates apply. For more information, see Amazon VPC Pricing.

Creating an Interface Endpoint

To create an interface endpoint, you must specify the VPC in which to create the interface endpoint, and the service to which to establish the connection.

If you're connecting to an AWS service or AWS Marketplace partner service, you can enable private DNS for the interface endpoint. This enables you to make requests to the service using its default DNS name instead of the endpoint-specific DNS hostnames that we generate when you create the interface endpoint.

For specific information for AWS services, see VPC Endpoints.

To create an interface endpoint to an AWS service using the console

1. Open the Amazon VPC console at https://console.aws.amazon.com/vpc/.

2. In the navigation pane, choose **Endpoints**, **Create Endpoint**.

3. For **Service category**, ensure that **AWS services** is selected.

4. For **Service Name**, choose the service to which to connect. For **Type**, ensure that it indicates **Interface**.

5. Complete the following information and then choose **Create endpoint**.

   - For **VPC**, select a VPC in which to create the endpoint.
   - For **Subnets**, select the subnets (Availability Zones) in which to create the endpoint network interfaces. **Note**
     Not all Availability Zones may be supported for all AWS services.
   - For **Enable Private DNS Name**, optionally select the check box to enable private DNS for the interface endpoint. **Note**
     To use the private DNS option, the following attributes of your VPC must be set to `true`: `enableDnsHostnames` and `enableDnsSupport`. For more information, see Updating DNS Support for Your VPC.
   - For **Security group**, select the security groups to associate with the endpoint network interfaces.

To create an interface endpoint to an endpoint service, you must have the name of the service to which to connect. The service provider can provide you with the name.

To create an interface endpoint to an endpoint service

1. Open the Amazon VPC console at https://console.aws.amazon.com/vpc/.

2. In the navigation pane, choose **Endpoints**, **Create Endpoint**.

3. For **Service category**, choose **Find service by name**.

4. For **Service Name**, enter the name of the service (for example, `com.amazonaws.vpce.us-east-1.vpce-svc-0e123abc123198abc`) and choose **Verify**.

5. Complete the following information and then choose **Create endpoint**.

   - For **VPC**, select a VPC in which to create the endpoint.
   - For **Subnets**, select the subnets (Availability Zones) in which to create the endpoint network interfaces. **Note**
     Not all Availability Zones may be supported for the service.
   - For **Security group**, select the security groups to associate with the endpoint network interfaces.

To create an interface endpoint to an AWS Marketplace partner service

1. Go to the PrivateLink page on AWS Marketplace and subscribe to a service from a software as a service (SaaS) provider. Services that support interface endpoints include an option to connect via an endpoint.

2. Open the Amazon VPC console at https://console.aws.amazon.com/vpc/.

3. In the navigation pane, choose **Endpoints**, **Create Endpoint**.

4. For **Service category**, choose **Your AWS Marketplace services**.

5. Choose the AWS Marketplace service to which you've subscribed.

6. Complete the following information and then choose **Create endpoint**.

   - For **VPC**, select a VPC in which to create the endpoint.
   - For **Subnets**, select the subnets (Availability Zones) in which to create the endpoint network interfaces.
     Note
     Not all Availability Zones may be supported for the service.
   - For **Security group**, select the security groups to associate with the endpoint network interfaces.

To create an interface endpoint using the AWS CLI

1. Use the describe-vpc-endpoint-services command to get a list of available services. In the output that's returned, take note of the name of the service to which to connect. The `ServiceType` field indicates whether you connect to the service via an interface or gateway endpoint. The `ServiceName` field provides the name of the service.

```
aws ec2 describe-vpc-endpoint-services
```

```
{
    "ServiceDetails": [
        ...
        {
            "ServiceType": [
                {
                    "ServiceType": "Interface"
                }
            ],
            "PrivateDnsName": "elasticloadbalancing.us-east-1.amazonaws.com",
            "ServiceName": "com.amazonaws.us-east-1.elasticloadbalancing",
            "VpcEndpointPolicySupported": false,
            "Owner": "amazon",
            "AvailabilityZones": [
                "us-east-1a",
                "us-east-1b",
                "us-east-1c",
                "us-east-1d",
                "us-east-1e",
                "us-east-1f"
            ],
            "AcceptanceRequired": false,
            "BaseEndpointDnsNames": [
                "elasticloadbalancing.us-east-1.vpce.amazonaws.com"
            ]
        },
        ...
}
```

2. To create an interface endpoint, use the create-vpc-endpoint command and specify the VPC ID, type of VPC endpoint (interface), service name, subnets that will use the endpoint, and security groups to associate with the endpoint network interfaces.

The following example creates an interface endpoint to the Elastic Load Balancing service.

```
1 aws ec2 create-vpc-endpoint --vpc-id vpc-ec43eb89 --vpc-endpoint-type Interface --service-
    name com.amazonaws.us-east-1.elasticloadbalancing --subnet-id subnet-abababab --
    security-group-id sg-1a2b3c4d
```

```
1  {
2      "VpcEndpoint": {
3          "PolicyDocument": "{\n  \"Statement\": [\n    {\n      \"Action\": \"*\", \n
               \"Effect\": \"Allow\", \n      \"Principal\": \"*\", \n      \"Resource\":
               \"*\"\n    }\n  ]\n}",
4          "VpcId": "vpc-ec43eb89",
5          "NetworkInterfaceIds": [
6              "eni-bf8aa46b"
7          ],
8          "SubnetIds": [
9              "subnet-abababab"
10         ],
11         "PrivateDnsEnabled": true,
12         "State": "pending",
13         "ServiceName": "com.amazonaws.us-east-1.elasticloadbalancing",
14         "RouteTableIds": [],
15         "Groups": [
16             {
17                 "GroupName": "default",
18                 "GroupId": "sg-1a2b3c4d"
19             }
20         ],
21         "VpcEndpointId": "vpce-088d25a4bbf4a7abc",
22         "VpcEndpointType": "Interface",
23         "CreationTimestamp": "2017-09-05T20:14:41.240Z",
24         "DnsEntries": [
25             {
26                 "HostedZoneId": "Z7HUB22UULQXV",
27                 "DnsName": "vpce-088d25a4bbf4a7abc-ks83awe7.elasticloadbalancing.us-east-1.
                     vpce.amazonaws.com"
28             },
29             {
30                 "HostedZoneId": "Z7HUB22UULQXV",
31                 "DnsName": "vpce-088d25a4bbf4a7abc-ks83awe7-us-east-1a.elasticloadbalancing
                     .us-east-1.vpce.amazonaws.com"
32             },
33             {
34                 "HostedZoneId": "Z1K56Z6FNPJRR",
35                 "DnsName": "elasticloadbalancing.us-east-1.amazonaws.com"
36             }
37         ]
38     }
39 }
```

Alternatively, the following example creates an interface endpoint to an endpoint service in another AWS account (the service provider provides you with the name of the endpoint service).

```
1 aws ec2 create-vpc-endpoint --vpc-id vpc-ec43eb89 --vpc-endpoint-type Interface --service-
    name com.amazonaws.vpce.us-east-1.vpce-svc-0e123abc123198abc --subnet-id subnet-
    abababab --security-group-id sg-1a2b3c4d
```

In the output that's returned, take note of the `DnsName` fields. You can use these DNS names to access the AWS service.

To describe available services using the AWS Tools for Windows PowerShell or API

- Get-EC2VpcEndpointService (AWS Tools for Windows PowerShell)
- DescribeVpcEndpointServices (Amazon EC2 Query API)

To create a VPC endpoint using the AWS Tools for Windows PowerShell or API

- New-EC2VpcEndpoint (AWS Tools for Windows PowerShell)
- CreateVpcEndpoint (Amazon EC2 Query API)

Viewing Your Interface Endpoint

After you've created an interface endpoint, you can view information about it.

To view information about an interface endpoint using the console

1. Open the Amazon VPC console at https://console.aws.amazon.com/vpc/.

2. In the navigation pane, choose **Endpoints** and select your interface endpoint.

3. To view information about the interface endpoint, choose **Details**. The **DNS Names** field displays the DNS names to use to access the service.

4. To view the subnets in which the interface endpoint has been created, and the ID of the endpoint network interface in each subnet, choose **Subnets**.

5. To view the security groups that are associated with the endpoint network interface, choose **Security Groups**.

To describe your interface endpoint using the AWS CLI

- You can describe your endpoint using the describe-vpc-endpoints command.

```
1 aws ec2 describe-vpc-endpoints --vpc-endpoint-ids vpce-088d25a4bbf4a7abc
```

To describe your VPC endpoints using the AWS Tools for Windows PowerShell or API

- Get-EC2VpcEndpoint (AWS Tools for Windows PowerShell)
- DescribeVpcEndpoints (Amazon EC2 Query API)

Creating and Managing a Notification for an Interface Endpoint

You can create a notification to receive alerts for specific events that occur on your interface endpoint. For example, you can receive an email when the interface endpoint is accepted by the service provider. To create a notification, you must associate an Amazon SNS topic with the notification. You can subscribe to the SNS topic to receive an email notification when an endpoint event occurs.

The Amazon SNS topic that you use for notifications must have a topic policy that allows Amazon's VPC endpoint service to publish notifications on your behalf. Ensure that you include the following statement in your topic policy. For more information, see Managing Access to Your Amazon SNS Topics in the *Amazon Simple Notification Service Developer Guide*.

```
1 {
2   "Version": "2012-10-17",
3   "Statement": [
4     {
5       "Effect": "Allow",
6       "Principal": {
```

```
 7        "Service": "vpce.amazonaws.com"
 8      },
 9      "Action": "SNS:Publish",
10      "Resource": "arn:aws:sns:region:account:topic-name"
11    }
12  ]
13 }
```

To create a notification for an interface endpoint

1. Open the Amazon VPC console at https://console.aws.amazon.com/vpc/.

2. In the navigation pane, choose **Endpoints** and select your interface endpoint.

3. Choose **Actions, Create notification**.

4. Choose the ARN for the SNS topic to associate with the notification.

5. For **Events**, select the endpoint events for which to receive notifications.

6. Choose **Create Notification**.

After you create a notification, you can change the SNS topic that's associated with the notification, or you can specify different endpoint events for the notification.

To modify a notification for an endpoint service

1. Open the Amazon VPC console at https://console.aws.amazon.com/vpc/.

2. In the navigation pane, choose **Endpoints** and select your interface endpoint.

3. Choose **Actions, Modify Notification**.

4. Specify the ARN for the SNS topic and change the endpoint events as required.

5. Choose **Modify Notification**.

If you no longer need a notification, you can delete it.

To delete a notification

1. Open the Amazon VPC console at https://console.aws.amazon.com/vpc/.

2. In the navigation pane, choose **Endpoints** and select your interface endpoint.

3. Choose **Actions, Delete notification**.

4. Choose **Yes, Delete**.

To create and manage a notification using the AWS CLI

1. To create a notification for an interface endpoint, use the create-vpc-endpoint-connection-notification command and specify the ARN of the SNS topic, the events for which to be notified, and the ID of the endpoint; for example:

```
1 aws ec2 create-vpc-endpoint-connection-notification --connection-notification-arn arn:aws:
    sns:us-east-2:123456789012:EndpointNotification --connection-events Accept Reject --vpc
    -endpoint-id vpce-123abc3420c1931d7
```

2. To view your notifications, use the describe-vpc-endpoint-connection-notifications command:

```
1 aws ec2 describe-vpc-endpoint-connection-notifications
```

3. To change the SNS topic or endpoint events for the notification, use the modify-vpc-endpoint-connection-notification command; for example:

```
1  aws ec2 modify-vpc-endpoint-connection-notification --connection-notification-id vpce-nfn
      -008776de7e03f5abc --connection-events Accept --connection-notification-arn arn:aws:sns
      :us-east-2:123456789012:mytopic
```

4. To delete a notification, use the delete-vpc-endpoint-connection-notifications command:

```
1  aws ec2 delete-vpc-endpoint-connection-notifications --connection-notification-ids vpce-nfn
      -008776de7e03f5abc
```

Accessing a Service Through an Interface Endpoint

After you've created an interface endpoint, you can submit requests to the supported service via an endpoint URL. You can use the following:

- The endpoint-specific regional DNS hostname that we generate for the interface endpoint. The hostname includes a unique endpoint identifier, service identifier, the region, and `vpce.amazonaws.com` in its name; for example, `vpce-0fe5b17a0707d6abc-29p5708s.ec2.us-east-1.vpce.amazonaws.com`.
- The endpoint-specific zonal DNS hostname that we generate for each Availability Zone in which the endpoint is available. The hostname includes the Availability Zone in its name; for example, `vpce-0 fe5b17a0707d6abc-29p5708s-us-east-1a.ec2.us-east-1.vpce.amazonaws.com`. You might use this option if your architecture isolates Availability Zones (for example, for fault containment or to reduce regional data transfer costs). **Note**
  A request to the zonal DNS hostname is destined to the corresponding Availability Zone location in the service provider's account, which might not have the same Availability Zone name as your account. For more information, see Region and Availability Zone Concepts.
- If you have enabled private DNS for the endpoint (a private hosted zone), the default DNS hostname for the AWS service for the region; for example, `ec2.us-east-1.amazonaws.com`.
- The private IP address of the endpoint network interface in the VPC.

For example, in a subnet in which you have an interface endpoint to Elastic Load Balancing and for which you have not enabled the private DNS option, use the following AWS CLI command from an instance to describe your load balancers. The command uses the endpoint-specific regional DNS hostname to make the request via the interface endpoint:

```
1  aws elbv2 describe-load-balancers --endpoint-url https://vpce-0f89a33420c193abc-bluzidnv.
      elasticloadbalancing.us-east-1.vpce.amazonaws.com/
```

If you enable the private DNS option, you do not have to specify the endpoint URL in the request. The AWS CLI uses the default endpoint for the service for the region (`elasticloadbalancing.us-east-1.amazonaws.com`).

Modifying an Interface Endpoint

You can modify an interface endpoint by changing the subnet in which the interface endpoint is located, and changing the security groups that are associated with the endpoint network interface. If you remove a subnet for the interface endpoint, the corresponding endpoint network interface in the subnet is deleted.

To change the subnets for an interface endpoint

1. Open the Amazon VPC console at https://console.aws.amazon.com/vpc/.

2. In the navigation pane, choose **Endpoints** and select the interface endpoint.

3. Choose **Actions, Manage Subnets**.

4. Select or deselect the subnets as required, and choose **Modify Subnets**.

To add or remove the security groups associated with an interface endpoint

1. Open the Amazon VPC console at https://console.aws.amazon.com/vpc/.

2. In the navigation pane, choose **Endpoints** and select the interface endpoint.

3. Choose **Actions**, **Manage security groups**.

4. Select or deselect the security groups as required, and choose **Save**.

To modify a VPC endpoint using the AWS CLI

1. Use the describe-vpc-endpoints command to get the ID of your interface endpoint.

```
1 aws ec2 describe-vpc-endpoints
```

2. The following example uses the modify-vpc-endpoint command to add subnet `subnet-aabb1122` to the interface endpoint.

```
1 aws ec2 modify-vpc-endpoint --vpc-endpoint-id vpce-0fe5b17a0707d6abc --add-subnet-id subnet
    -aabb1122
```

To modify a VPC endpoint using the AWS Tools for Windows PowerShell or an API

- Edit-EC2VpcEndpoint (AWS Tools for Windows PowerShell)
- ModifyVpcEndpoint (Amazon EC2 Query API)

Gateway VPC Endpoints

To create and set up a gateway endpoint, follow these general steps:

1. Specify the VPC in which to create the endpoint, and the service to which you're connecting. A service is identified by a *prefix list*—the name and ID of a service for a region. A prefix list ID uses the form `pl-xxxxxxx` and a prefix list name uses the form `com.amazonaws.<region>.<service>`. Use the prefix list name (service name) to create an endpoint.

2. Attach an *endpoint policy* to your endpoint that allows access to some or all of the service to which you're connecting. For more information, see Using VPC Endpoint Policies.

3. Specify one or more route tables to control the routing of traffic between your VPC and the other service. Subnets that use these route tables have access to the endpoint, and traffic from instances in these subnets to the service is then routed through the endpoint.

In the following diagram, instances in subnet 2 can access Amazon S3 through the gateway endpoint.

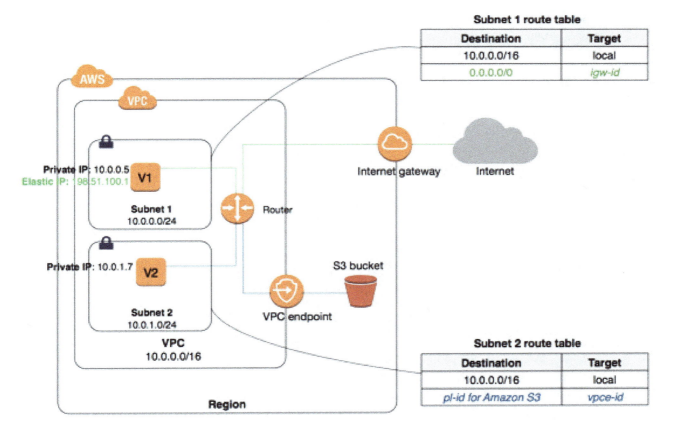

You can create multiple endpoints in a single VPC, for example, to multiple services. You can also create multiple endpoints for a single service, and use different route tables to enforce different access policies from different subnets to the same service.

After you've created an endpoint, you can modify the endpoint policy that's attached to your endpoint, and add or remove the route tables that are used by the endpoint.

There is no additional charge for using gateway endpoints. Standard charges for data transfer and resource usage apply. For more information about pricing, see Amazon EC2 Pricing.

Topics

- Routing for Gateway Endpoints

- Gateway Endpoint Limitations
- Endpoints for Amazon S3
- Endpoints for Amazon DynamoDB
- Creating a Gateway Endpoint
- Modifying Your Security Group
- Modifying a Gateway Endpoint

Routing for Gateway Endpoints

When you create or modify an endpoint, you specify the VPC route tables that are used to access the service via the endpoint. A route is automatically added to each of the route tables with a destination that specifies the prefix list ID of the service (`pl-xxxxxxxx`), and a target with the endpoint ID (`vpce-xxxxxxxx`); for example:

Destination	Target
10.0.0.0/16	Local
pl-1a2b3c4d	vpce-11bb22cc

The prefix list ID logically represents the range of public IP addresses used by the service. All instances in subnets associated with the specified route tables automatically use the endpoint to access the service; subnets that are not associated with the specified route tables do not use the endpoint. This enables you to keep resources in other subnets separate from your endpoint.

To view the current public IP address range for a service, you can use the describe-prefix-lists command.

Note
The range of public IP addresses for a service may change from time to time. Consider the implications before you make routing or other decisions based on the current IP address range for a service.

The following rules apply:

- You can have multiple endpoint routes to different services in a route table, and you can have multiple endpoint routes to the same service in different route tables, but you cannot have multiple endpoints to the same service in a single route table. For example, if you have two endpoints to Amazon S3 in your VPC, you cannot use the same route table for both endpoints.
- You cannot explicitly add, modify, or delete an endpoint route in your route table by using the route table APIs, or by using the Route Tables page in the Amazon VPC console. You can only add an endpoint route by associating a route table with an endpoint. To change the route tables that are associated with your endpoint, you can modify the endpoint.
- An endpoint route is automatically deleted when you remove the route table association from the endpoint (by modifying the endpoint), or when you delete your endpoint.

We use the most specific route that matches the traffic to determine how to route the traffic (longest prefix match). If you have an existing route in your route table for all internet traffic (`0.0.0.0/0`) that points to an internet gateway, the endpoint route takes precedence for all traffic destined for the service, because the IP address range for the service is more specific than `0.0.0.0/0`. All other internet traffic goes to your internet gateway, including traffic that's destined for the service in other regions.

However, if you have existing, more specific routes to IP address ranges that point to an internet gateway or a NAT device, those routes take precedence. If you have existing routes destined for an IP address range that is identical to the IP address range used by the service, then your routes take precedence.

Example: An Endpoint Route in a Route Table

In this scenario, you have an existing route in your route table for all internet traffic (`0.0.0.0/0`) that points to an internet gateway. Any traffic from the subnet that's destined for another AWS service uses the internet gateway.

Destination	Target
10.0.0.0/16	Local
0.0.0.0/0	igw-1a2b3c4d

You create an endpoint to a supported AWS service, and associate your route table with the endpoint. An endpoint route is automatically added to the route table, with a destination of `pl-1a2b3c4d` (assume this represents the service to which you've created the endpoint). Now, any traffic from the subnet that's destined for that AWS service in the same region goes to the endpoint, and does not go to the internet gateway. All other internet traffic goes to your internet gateway, including traffic that's destined for other services, and destined for the AWS service in other regions.

Destination	Target
10.0.0.0/16	Local
0.0.0.0/0	igw-1a2b3c4d
pl-1a2b3c4d	vpce-11bb22cc

Example: Adjusting Your Route Tables for Endpoints

In this scenario, you have configured your route table to enable instances in your subnet to communicate with Amazon S3 buckets through an internet gateway. You've added a route with `54.123.165.0/24` as a destination (assume this is an IP address range currently within Amazon S3), and the internet gateway as the target. You then create an endpoint, and associate this route table with the endpoint. An endpoint route is automatically added to the route table. You then use the describe-prefix-lists command to view the IP address range for Amazon S3. The range is `54.123.160.0/19`, which is less specific than the range that's pointing to your internet gateway. This means that any traffic destined for the `54.123.165.0/24` IP address range continues to use the internet gateway, and does not use the endpoint (for as long as this remains the public IP address range for Amazon S3).

Destination	Target
10.0.0.0/16	Local
54.123.165.0/24	igw-1a2b3c4d
pl-1a2b3c4d	vpce-11bb22cc

To ensure that all traffic destined for Amazon S3 in the same region is routed via the endpoint, you must adjust the routes in your route table. To do this, you can delete the route to the internet gateway. Now, all traffic to Amazon S3 in the same region uses the endpoint, and the subnet that's associated with your route table is a private subnet.

Destination	Target
10.0.0.0/16	Local
pl-1a2b3c4d	vpce-11bb22cc

Gateway Endpoint Limitations

To use gateway endpoints, you need to be aware of the current limitations:

- You cannot use a prefix list ID in an outbound rule in a network ACL to allow or deny outbound traffic to the service specified in an endpoint. If your network ACL rules restrict traffic, you must specify the CIDR block (IP address range) for the service instead. You can, however, use a prefix list ID in an outbound security group rule. For more information, see Security Groups.
- Endpoints are supported within the same region only. You cannot create an endpoint between a VPC and a service in a different region.
- You cannot tag an endpoint.
- Endpoints support IPv4 traffic only.
- You cannot transfer an endpoint from one VPC to another, or from one service to another.
- You have a limit on the number of endpoints you can create per VPC. For more information, see VPC Endpoints.
- Endpoint connections cannot be extended out of a VPC. Resources on the other side of a VPN connection, VPC peering connection, AWS Direct Connect connection, or ClassicLink connection in your VPC cannot use the endpoint to communicate with resources in the endpoint service.
- You must enable DNS resolution in your VPC, or if you're using your own DNS server, ensure that DNS requests to the required service (such as Amazon S3) are resolved correctly to the IP addresses maintained by AWS. For more information, see Using DNS with Your VPC and AWS IP Address Ranges in the *Amazon Web Services General Reference.*

For more information about rules and limitations that are specific to Amazon S3, see Endpoints for Amazon S3.

For more information about rules and limitations that are specific to DynamoDB, see Endpoints for Amazon DynamoDB.

Creating a Gateway Endpoint

To create an endpoint, you must specify the VPC in which you want to create the endpoint, and the service to which you want to establish the connection.

To create a gateway endpoint using the console

1. Open the Amazon VPC console at https://console.aws.amazon.com/vpc/.

2. In the navigation pane, choose **Endpoints, Create Endpoint**.

3. For **Service Name**, choose the service to which to connect. To create a gateway endpoint to DynamoDB or Amazon S3, ensure that the **Type** column indicates **Gateway**.

4. Complete the following information, and choose **Create endpoint**.

   - For **VPC**, select a VPC in which to create the endpoint.
   - For **Configure route tables**, select the route tables to be used by the endpoint. We automatically add a route that points traffic destined for the service to the endpoint to the selected route tables.
   - For **Policy**, choose the type of policy. You can leave the default option, **Full Access**, to allow full access to the service. Alternatively, you can select **Custom**, and then use the AWS Policy Generator to create a custom policy, or type your own policy in the policy window.

After you've created an endpoint, you can view information about it.

To view information about a gateway endpoint using the console

1. Open the Amazon VPC console at https://console.aws.amazon.com/vpc/.

2. In the navigation pane, choose **Endpoints** and select your endpoint.

3. To view information about the endpoint, choose **Summary**. You can get the prefix list name for the service in the **Service** box.

4. To view information about the route tables that are used by the endpoint, choose **Route Tables**.

5. To view the IAM policy that's attached to your endpoint, choose **Policy**. **Note**
The **Policy** tab only displays the endpoint policy. It does not display any information about IAM policies for IAM users that have permission to work with endpoints. It also does not display service-specific policies; for example, S3 bucket policies.

To create and view an endpoint using the AWS CLI

1. Use the describe-vpc-endpoint-services command to get a list of available services. In the output that's returned, take note of the name of the service to which you want to connect. The `serviceType` field indicates whether you connect to the service via an interface endpoint or a gateway endpoint.

```
1 aws ec2 describe-vpc-endpoint-services
```

```
1 {
2     "serviceDetailSet": [
3         {
4             "serviceType": [
5                 {
6                     "serviceType": "Gateway"
7                 }
8     ...
```

2. To create a gateway endpoint (for example, to Amazon S3), use the create-vpc-endpoint command and specify the VPC ID, service name, and route tables that will use the endpoint. You can optionally use the `--policy-document` parameter to specify a custom policy to control access to the service. If the parameter is not used, we attach a default policy that allows full access to the service.

```
1 aws ec2 create-vpc-endpoint --vpc-id vpc-1a2b3c4d --service-name com.amazonaws.us-east-1.s3
    --route-table-ids rtb-11aa22bb
```

3. Describe your endpoint using the describe-vpc-endpoints command.

```
1 aws ec2 describe-vpc-endpoints
```

To describe available services using the AWS Tools for Windows PowerShell or API

- Get-EC2VpcEndpointService (AWS Tools for Windows PowerShell)
- DescribeVpcEndpointServices (Amazon EC2 Query API)

To create a VPC endpoint using the AWS Tools for Windows PowerShell or API

- New-EC2VpcEndpoint (AWS Tools for Windows PowerShell)
- CreateVpcEndpoint (Amazon EC2 Query API)

To describe your VPC endpoints using the AWS Tools for Windows PowerShell or API

- Get-EC2VpcEndpoint (AWS Tools for Windows PowerShell)
- DescribeVpcEndpoints (Amazon EC2 Query API)

Modifying Your Security Group

If the VPC security group associated with your instance restricts outbound traffic, you must add a rule to allow traffic destined for the AWS service to leave your instance.

To add an outbound rule for a gateway endpoint

1. Open the Amazon VPC console at https://console.aws.amazon.com/vpc/.

2. In the navigation pane, choose **Security Groups**.

3. Select your VPC security group, choose the **Outbound Rules** tab, and then choose **Edit**.

4. Select the type of traffic from the **Type** list, and enter the port range, if required. For example, if you use your instance to retrieve objects from Amazon S3, choose **HTTPS** from the **Type** list.

5. The **Destination** list displays the prefix list IDs and names for the available AWS services. Choose the prefix list ID for the AWS service, or type it in.

6. Choose **Save**.

For more information about security groups, see Security Groups for Your VPC.

To get the prefix list name, ID, and IP address range for an AWS service using the command line or API

- describe-prefix-lists (AWS CLI)
- Get-EC2PrefixList (AWS Tools for Windows PowerShell)
- DescribePrefixLists (Amazon EC2 Query API)

Modifying a Gateway Endpoint

You can modify a gateway endpoint by changing or removing its policy, and adding or removing the route tables that are used by the endpoint.

To change the policy associated with a gateway endpoint

1. Open the Amazon VPC console at https://console.aws.amazon.com/vpc/.

2. In the navigation pane, choose **Endpoints** and select your endpoint.

3. Choose **Actions**, **Edit policy**.

4. You can choose **Full Access** to allow full access. Alternatively, choose **Custom**, and then use the AWS Policy Generator to create a custom policy, or type your own policy in the policy window. When you're done, choose **Save**. **Note**
It can take a few minutes for policy changes to take effect.

To add or remove route tables used by a gateway endpoint

1. Open the Amazon VPC console at https://console.aws.amazon.com/vpc/.

2. In the navigation pane, choose **Endpoints** and select your endpoint.

3. Choose **Actions**, **Manage route tables**.

4. Select or deselect the required route tables, and choose **Modify Route Tables**.

To modify a gateway endpoint using the AWS CLI

1. Use the describe-vpc-endpoints command to get the ID of your gateway endpoint.

```
1 aws ec2 describe-vpc-endpoints
```

2. The following example uses the modify-vpc-endpoint command to associate route table `rtb-aaa222bb` with the gateway endpoint, and reset the policy document.

```
1 aws ec2 modify-vpc-endpoint --vpc-endpoint-id vpce-1a2b3c4d --add-route-table-ids rtb-
    aaa222bb --reset-policy
```

To modify a VPC endpoint using the AWS Tools for Windows PowerShell or an API

- Edit-EC2VpcEndpoint (AWS Tools for Windows PowerShell)
- ModifyVpcEndpoint (Amazon EC2 Query API)

Endpoints for Amazon S3

If you've already set up access to your Amazon S3 resources from your VPC, you can continue to use Amazon S3 DNS names to access those resources after you've set up an endpoint. However, take note of the following:

- Your endpoint has a policy that controls the use of the endpoint to access Amazon S3 resources. The default policy allows access by any user or service within the VPC, using credentials from any AWS account, to any Amazon S3 resource; including Amazon S3 resources for an AWS account other than the account with which the VPC is associated. For more information, see Controlling Access to Services with VPC Endpoints.
- The source IPv4 addresses from instances in your affected subnets as received by Amazon S3 change from public IPv4 addresses to the private IPv4 addresses from your VPC. An endpoint switches network routes, and disconnects open TCP connections. Your tasks are interrupted during the changeover, and any previous connections using public IPv4 addresses are not resumed. We recommend that you do not have any critical tasks running when you create or modify an endpoint; or that you test to ensure that your software can automatically reconnect to Amazon S3 after the connection break.
- You cannot use an IAM policy or bucket policy to allow access from a VPC IPv4 CIDR range (the private IPv4 address range). VPC CIDR blocks can be overlapping or identical, which may lead to unexpected results. Therefore, you cannot use the `aws:SourceIp` condition in your IAM policies for requests to Amazon S3 through a VPC endpoint. This applies to IAM policies for users and roles, and any bucket policies. If a statement includes the `aws:SourceIp` condition, the value fails to match any provided IP address or range. Instead, you can do the following:
    - Use your route tables to control which instances can access resources in Amazon S3 via the endpoint.
    - For bucket policies, you can restrict access to a specific endpoint or to a specific VPC. For more information, see Using Amazon S3 Bucket Policies.
- Endpoints currently do not support cross-region requests—ensure that you create your endpoint in the same region as your bucket. You can find the location of your bucket by using the Amazon S3 console, or by using the get-bucket-location command. Use a region-specific Amazon S3 endpoint to access your bucket; for example, `mybucket.s3-us-west-2.amazonaws.com`. For more information about region-specific endpoints for Amazon S3, see Amazon Simple Storage Service (S3) in *Amazon Web Services General Reference*. If you use the AWS CLI to make requests to Amazon S3, set your default region to the same region as your bucket, or use the `--region` parameter in your requests. **Note**
Treat Amazon S3's US Standard region as mapped to the `us-east-1` region.
- Endpoints are currently supported for IPv4 traffic only.

Before you use endpoints with Amazon S3, ensure that you have also read the following general limitations: Gateway Endpoint Limitations.

If you use other AWS services in your VPC, they may use S3 buckets for certain tasks. Ensure that your endpoint policy allows full access to Amazon S3 (the default policy), or that it allows access to the specific buckets that are used by these services. Alternatively, only create an endpoint in a subnet that is not used by any of these services, to allow the services to continue accessing S3 buckets using public IP addresses.

The following table lists AWS services that may be affected by an endpoint, and any specific information for each service.

AWS service	Note
Amazon AppStream 2.0	Your endpoint policy must allow access to the specific buckets that are used by AppStream 2.0 for storing user content. For more information, see Home Folders and VPC Endpoints in the Amazon AppStream 2.0 Developer Guide.

AWS service	Note
AWS CloudFormation	If you have resources in your VPC that must respond to a wait condition or custom resource request, your endpoint policy must allow at least access to the specific buckets that are used by these resources. For more information, see AWS CloudFormation and VPC Endpoints.
AWS CodeDeploy	Your endpoint policy must allow full access to Amazon S3, or allow access to any S3 buckets that you've created for your AWS CodeDeploy deployments.
Elastic Beanstalk	Your endpoint policy must allow at least access to any S3 buckets used for Elastic Beanstalk applications. For more information, see Using Elastic Beanstalk with Amazon S3 in the AWS Elastic Beanstalk Developer Guide.
AWS OpsWorks	Your endpoint policy must allow at least access to specific buckets that are used by AWS OpsWorks. For more information, see Running a Stack in a VPC in the AWS OpsWorks User Guide.
Amazon WorkDocs	If you use an Amazon WorkDocs client in Amazon WorkSpaces or an EC2 instance, your endpoint policy must allow full access to Amazon S3.
Amazon WorkSpaces	Amazon WorkSpaces does not directly depend on Amazon S3. However, if you provide Amazon WorkSpaces users with internet access, then take note that websites, HTML emails, and internet services from other companies may depend on Amazon S3. Ensure that your endpoint policy allows full access to Amazon S3 to allow these services to continue to work correctly.

Traffic between your VPC and S3 buckets does not leave the Amazon network.

Using Endpoint Policies for Amazon S3

The following are example endpoint policies for accessing Amazon S3. For more information, see Using VPC Endpoint Policies.

Important
All types of policies — IAM user policies, endpoint policies, S3 bucket policies, and Amazon S3 ACL policies (if any) — must grant the necessary permissions for access to Amazon S3 to succeed.

Example Example: Restricting Access to a Specific Bucket
You can create a policy that restricts access to specific S3 buckets only. This is useful if you have other AWS services in your VPC that use S3 buckets. The following is an example of a policy that restricts access to `my_secure_bucket` only.

```
1 {
```

```
 2    "Statement": [
 3      {
 4        "Sid": "Access-to-specific-bucket-only",
 5        "Principal": "*",
 6        "Action": [
 7          "s3:GetObject",
 8          "s3:PutObject"
 9        ],
10        "Effect": "Allow",
11        "Resource": ["arn:aws:s3:::my_secure_bucket",
12                     "arn:aws:s3:::my_secure_bucket/*"]
13      }
14    ]
15 }
```

Example Example: Enabling Access to the Amazon Linux AMI Repositories

The Amazon Linux AMI repositories are Amazon S3 buckets in each region. If you want instances in your VPC to access the repositories through an endpoint, create an endpoint policy that enables access to these buckets. The following policy allows access to the Amazon Linux repositories.

```
 1 {
 2    "Statement": [
 3      {
 4        "Sid": "AmazonLinuxAMIRepositoryAccess",
 5        "Principal": "*",
 6        "Action": [
 7          "s3:GetObject"
 8        ],
 9        "Effect": "Allow",
10        "Resource": [
11          "arn:aws:s3:::packages.*.amazonaws.com/*",
12          "arn:aws:s3:::repo.*.amazonaws.com/*"
13        ]
14      }
15    ]
16 }
```

The following policy allows access to the Amazon Linux 2 repositories.

```
 1 {
 2    "Statement": [
 3      {
 4        "Sid": "AmazonLinux2AMIRepositoryAccess",
 5        "Principal": "*",
 6        "Action": [
 7          "s3:GetObject"
 8        ],
 9        "Effect": "Allow",
10        "Resource": [
11          "arn:aws:s3:::amazonlinux.*.amazonaws.com/*"
12        ]
13      }
14    ]
15 }
```

Using Amazon S3 Bucket Policies

You can use bucket policies to control access to buckets from specific endpoints, or specific VPCs.

You cannot use the `aws:SourceIp` condition in your bucket policies for requests to Amazon S3 through a VPC endpoint. The condition fails to match any specified IP address or IP address range, and may have an undesired effect when you make requests to an Amazon S3 bucket. For example:

- You have a bucket policy with a `Deny` effect and a `NotIpAddress` condition that's intended to grant access from a single or limited range of IP addresses only. For requests to the bucket through an endpoint, the `NotIpAddress` condition is always matched, and the statement's effect applies, assuming other constraints in the policy match. Access to the bucket is denied.
- You have a bucket policy with a `Deny` effect and an `IpAddress` condition that's intended to deny access to a single or limited range of IP addresses only. For requests to the bucket through an endpoint, the condition is not matched, and the statement does not apply. Access to the bucket is allowed, assuming there are other statements that allow access without an `IpAddress` condition.

Adjust your bucket policy to limit access to a specific VPC or a specific endpoint instead.

For more information about bucket policies for Amazon S3, see Using Bucket Policies and User Policies in *Amazon Simple Storage Service Developer Guide*.

Example Example: Restricting Access to a Specific Endpoint

The following is an example of an S3 bucket policy that allows access to a specific bucket, `my_secure_bucket`, from endpoint `vpce-1a2b3c4d` only. The policy denies all access to the bucket if the specified endpoint is not being used. The `aws:sourceVpce` condition is used to specify the endpoint. The `aws:sourceVpce` condition does not require an ARN for the VPC endpoint resource, only the endpoint ID.

```
{
  "Version": "2012-10-17",
  "Id": "Policy1415115909152",
  "Statement": [
    {
      "Sid": "Access-to-specific-VPCE-only",
      "Principal": "*",
      "Action": "s3:*",
      "Effect": "Deny",
      "Resource": ["arn:aws:s3:::my_secure_bucket",
                   "arn:aws:s3:::my_secure_bucket/*"],
      "Condition": {
        "StringNotEquals": {
          "aws:sourceVpce": "vpce-1a2b3c4d"
        }
      }
    }
  ]
}
```

Example Example: Restricting Access to a Specific VPC

You can create a bucket policy that restricts access to a specific VPC by using the `aws:sourceVpc` condition. This is useful if you have multiple endpoints configured in the same VPC, and you want to manage access to your S3 buckets for all of your endpoints. The following is an example of a policy that allows VPC `vpc-111bbb22` to access `my_secure_bucket` and its objects. The policy denies all access to the bucket if the specified VPC is not being used. The `aws:sourceVpc` condition does not require an ARN for the VPC resource, only the VPC ID.

```
{
  "Version": "2012-10-17",
  "Id": "Policy1415115909152",
```

```
 4    "Statement": [
 5      {
 6        "Sid": "Access-to-specific-VPC-only",
 7        "Principal": "*",
 8        "Action": "s3:*",
 9        "Effect": "Deny",
10        "Resource": ["arn:aws:s3:::my_secure_bucket",
11                     "arn:aws:s3:::my_secure_bucket/*"],
12        "Condition": {
13          "StringNotEquals": {
14            "aws:sourceVpc": "vpc-111bbb22"
15          }
16        }
17      }
18    ]
19  }
```

Endpoints for Amazon DynamoDB

If you've already set up access to your DynamoDB tables from your VPC, you can continue to access the tables as you normally would after you set up an endpoint. However, take note of the following:

- Your endpoint has a policy that controls the use of the endpoint to access DynamoDB resources. The default policy allows access by any user or service within the VPC, using credentials from any AWS account, to any DynamoDB resource. For more information, see Controlling Access to Services with VPC Endpoints.
- DynamoDB does not support resource-based policies (for example, on tables). Access to DynamoDB is controlled though the endpoint policy and IAM policies for individual IAM users and roles.
- You cannot access Amazon DynamoDB Streams through a VPC endpoint.
- Endpoints currently do not support cross-region requests—ensure that you create your endpoint in the same region as your DynamoDB tables.
- If you use AWS CloudTrail to log DynamoDB operations, the log files contain the private IP address of the EC2 instance in the VPC and the endpoint ID for any actions performed through the endpoint.
- The source IPv4 addresses from instances in your affected subnets change from public IPv4 addresses to the private IPv4 addresses from your VPC. An endpoint switches network routes, and disconnects open TCP connections. Your tasks are interrupted during the changeover, and any previous connections using public IPv4 addresses are not resumed. We recommend that you do not have any critical tasks running when you create or modify an endpoint; or that you test to ensure that your software can automatically reconnect to DynamoDB after the connection break.

Before you use endpoints with DynamoDB, ensure that you have also read the following general limitations: Gateway Endpoint Limitations.

Using Endpoint Policies for DynamoDB

The following are example endpoint policies for accessing DynamoDB.

Important
All types of policies — IAM user policies and endpoint policies — must grant the necessary permissions for access to DynamoDB to succeed.

Example Example: Read-Only Access
You can create a policy that restricts actions to only listing and describing DynamoDB tables through the VPC endpoint.

```
1  {
2    "Statement": [
3      {
4        "Sid": "ReadOnly",
5        "Principal": "*",
6        "Action": [
7          "dynamodb:DescribeTable",
8          "dynamodb:ListTables"
9        ],
10       "Effect": "Allow",
11       "Resource": "*"
12     }
13   ]
14 }
```

Example Example: Restrict Access to a Specific Table
You can create a policy that restricts access to a specific DynamoDB table. In this example, the endpoint policy allows access to `StockTable` only.

```
 1  {
 2    "Statement": [
 3      {
 4        "Sid": "AccessToSpecificTable",
 5        "Principal": "*",
 6        "Action": [
 7          "dynamodb:Batch*",
 8          "dynamodb:Delete*",
 9          "dynamodb:DescribeTable",
10          "dynamodb:GetItem",
11          "dynamodb:PutItem",
12          "dynamodb:Update*"
13        ],
14        "Effect": "Allow",
15        "Resource": "arn:aws:dynamodb:us-east-1:123456789012:table/StockTable"
16      }
17    ]
18  }
```

Using IAM Policies to Control Access to DynamoDB

You can create an IAM policy for your IAM users, groups, or roles to restrict access to DynamoDB tables from a specific VPC endpoint only. To do this, you can use the `aws:sourceVpce` condition key for the table resource in your IAM policy.

For more information about managing access to DynamoDB, see Authentication and Access Control for Amazon DynamoDB in the *Amazon DynamoDB Developer Guide*.

Example Example: Restrict Access from a Specific Endpoint
In this example, users are denied permission to work with DynamoDB tables, except if accessed through endpoint `vpce-11aa22bb`.

```
 1  {
 2    "Version": "2012-10-17",
 3    "Statement": [
 4      {
 5        "Sid": "AccessFromSpecificEndpoint",
 6        "Action": "dynamodb:*",
 7        "Effect": "Deny",
 8        "Resource": "arn:aws:dynamodb:region:account-id:table/*",
 9        "Condition": { "StringNotEquals" : { "aws:sourceVpce": "vpce-11aa22bb" } }
10      }
11    ]
12  }
```

Controlling Access to Services with VPC Endpoints

When you create a gateway endpoint, you can attach an endpoint policy to it that controls access to the service to which you are connecting. Endpoint policies must be written in JSON format.

If you're using an endpoint to Amazon S3, you can also use Amazon S3 bucket policies to control access to buckets from specific endpoints, or specific VPCs. For more information, see Using Amazon S3 Bucket Policies.

Topics

- Using VPC Endpoint Policies
- Security Groups

Using VPC Endpoint Policies

A VPC endpoint policy is an IAM resource policy that you attach to an endpoint when you create or modify the endpoint. If you do not attach a policy when you create an endpoint, we attach a default policy for you that allows full access to the service. An endpoint policy does not override or replace IAM user policies or service-specific policies (such as S3 bucket policies). It is a separate policy for controlling access from the endpoint to the specified service.

Important
Only gateway endpoints support the use of endpoint policies. Use the describe-vpc-endpoint-services command to verify if endpoint policies are supported.

You cannot attach more than one policy to an endpoint; however, you can modify the policy at any time. Note that if you do modify a policy, it can take a few minutes for the changes to take effect. For more information about writing policies, see Overview of IAM Policies in the *IAM User Guide*.

Your endpoint policy can be like any IAM policy; however, take note of the following:

- Only the parts of the policy that relate to the specified service will work. You cannot use an endpoint policy to allow resources in your VPC to perform other actions; for example, if you add EC2 actions to an endpoint policy for an endpoint to Amazon S3, they will have no effect.
- Your policy must contain a Principal element. For an endpoint policy, if you specify the principal in the format `"AWS": "AWS-account-ID"` or `"AWS": "arn:aws:iam::AWS-account-ID:root"`, access is granted to the AWS account root user only, and not all IAM users and roles for the account.
- The size of an endpoint policy cannot exceed 20,480 characters (including whitespace).

For example endpoint policies, see the following topics:

- Using Endpoint Policies for Amazon S3
- Using Endpoint Policies for DynamoDB

Security Groups

By default, Amazon VPC security groups allow all outbound traffic, unless you've specifically restricted outbound access.

When you create an interface endpoint, you can associate security groups with the endpoint network interface that is created in your VPC. If you do not specify a security group, the default security group for your VPC is automatically associated with the endpoint network interface. You must ensure that the rules for the security group allow communication between the endpoint network interface and the resources in your VPC that communicate with the service.

For a gateway endpoint, if your security group's outbound rules are restricted, you must add a rule that allows outbound traffic from your VPC to the service that's specified in your endpoint. To do this, you can use the service's prefix list ID as the destination in the outbound rule. For more information, see Modifying Your Security Group.

Deleting a VPC Endpoint

If you no longer require an endpoint, you can delete it. Deleting a gateway endpoint also deletes the endpoint routes in the route tables that were used by the endpoint, but doesn't affect any security groups associated with the VPC in which the endpoint resides. Deleting an interface endpoint also deletes the endpoint network interfaces.

To delete an endpoint

1. Open the Amazon VPC console at https://console.aws.amazon.com/vpc/.

2. In the navigation pane, choose **Endpoints** and select your endpoint.

3. Choose **Actions**, **Delete Endpoint**.

4. In the confirmation screen, choose **Yes, Delete**.

To delete a VPC endpoint

- delete-vpc-endpoints (AWS CLI)
- Remove-EC2VpcEndpoint (AWS Tools for Windows PowerShell)
- DeleteVpcEndpoints (Amazon EC2 Query API)

VPC Endpoint Services (AWS PrivateLink)

You can create your own application in your VPC and configure it as an AWS PrivateLink-powered service (referred to as an *endpoint service*). Other AWS principals can create a connection from their VPC to your endpoint service using an interface VPC endpoint. You are the *service provider*, and the AWS principals that create connections to your service are *service consumers*.

The following are the general steps to create an endpoint service.

1. Create a Network Load Balancer for your application in your VPC and configure it for each subnet (Availability Zone) in which the service should be available. The load balancer receives requests from service consumers and routes it to your service. For more information, see Getting Started with Network Load Balancers in the *User Guide for Network Load Balancers*. We recommend that you configure your service in all Availability Zones within the region.

2. Create a VPC endpoint service configuration and specify your Network Load Balancer.

The following are the general steps to enable service consumers to connect to your service.

1. Grant permissions to specific service consumers (AWS accounts, IAM users, and IAM roles) to create a connection to your endpoint service.

2. A service consumer that has been granted permissions creates an interface endpoint to your service, optionally in each Availability Zone in which you've configured your service.

3. To activate the connection, accept the interface endpoint connection request. By default, connection requests must be manually accepted. However, you can configure the acceptance settings for your endpoint service so that any connection requests are automatically accepted.

The combination of permissions and acceptance settings can help you control which service consumers (AWS principals) can access to your service. For example, you can grant permissions to selected principals that you trust and automatically accept all connection requests, or you can grant permissions to a wider group of principals and manually accept specific connection requests that you trust.

In the following diagram, the account owner of VPC B is a service provider, and has a service running on instances in subnet B. The owner of VPC B has a service endpoint (vpce-svc-1234) with an associated Network Load Balancer that points to the instances in subnet B as targets. Instances in subnet A of VPC A use an interface endpoint to access the services in subnet B.

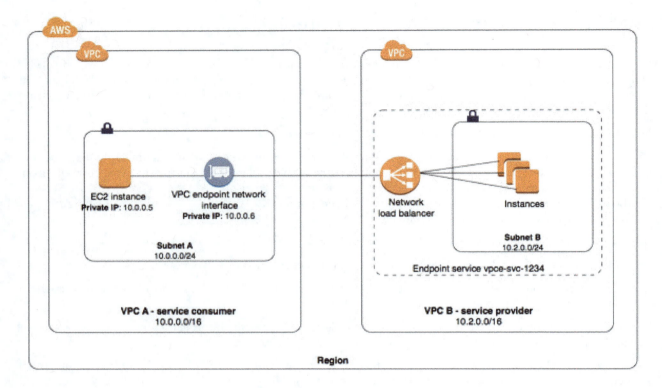

For low latency and fault tolerance, we recommend using a Network Load Balancer with targets in every Availability Zone of the AWS Region. To help achieve high availability for service consumers that use zonal DNS hostnames to access the service, you can enable cross-zone load balancing. Cross-zone load balancing enables the load balancer to distribute traffic across the registered targets in all enabled Availability Zones. For more information, see Cross-Zone Load Balancing in the *User Guide for Network Load Balancers*. Regional data transfer charges may apply to your account when you enable cross-zone load balancing.

In the following diagram, the owner of VPC B is ther service provider, and has configured a Network Load Balancer with targets in two different Availability Zones. The service consumer (VPC A) has created interface endpoints in the same two Availability Zones in their VPC. Requests to the service from instances in VPC A can use either interface endpoint.

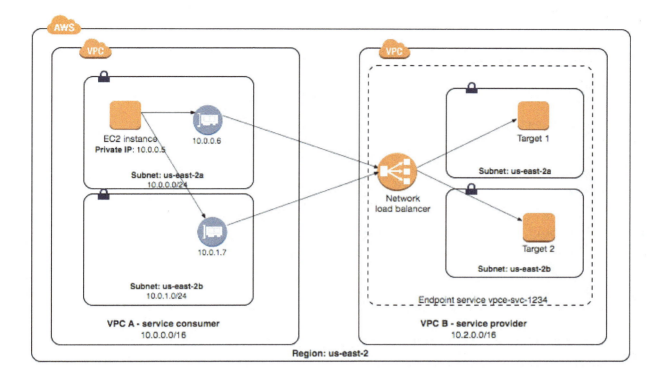

Topics

- Endpoint Service Limitations
- Creating a VPC Endpoint Service Configuration
- Adding and Removing Permissions for Your Endpoint Service
- Changing the Network Load Balancers and Acceptance Settings
- Accepting and Rejecting Interface Endpoint Connection Requests
- Creating and Managing a Notification for an Endpoint Service
- Using Proxy Protocol for Connection Information
- Deleting an Endpoint Service Configuration

Endpoint Service Limitations

To use endpoint services, you need to be aware of the current rules and limitations:

- You cannot tag an endpoint service.
- An endpoint service supports IPv4 traffic over TCP only.
- Service consumers must use the endpoint-specific DNS hostnames to access the endpoint service. Private DNS is not supported. For more information, see Accessing a Service Through an Interface Endpoint.
- Endpoint services are only available in the AWS Region in which they are created.
- If an endpoint service is associated with multiple Network Load Balancers, then for a specific Availability Zone, an interface endpoint will establish a connection with one load balancer only.
- Availability Zones in your account might not map to the same locations as Availability Zones in another account; for example, your Availability Zone us-east-1a might not be the same location as us-east-1a for another account. For more information, see Region and Availability Zone Concepts. When you configure an endpoint service, it's configured in the Availability Zones as mapped to your account.

Creating a VPC Endpoint Service Configuration

You can create an endpoint service configuration using the Amazon VPC console or the command line. Before you begin, ensure that you have created one or more Network Load Balancers in your VPC for your service. For more information, see Getting Started with Network Load Balancers in the *User Guide for Network Load Balancers.*

In your configuration, you can optionally specify that any interface endpoint connection requests to your service must be manually accepted by you. You can create a notification to receive alerts when there are connection requests. If you do not accept a connection, service consumers cannot access your service.

Note
Regardless of the acceptance settings, service consumers must also have permissions to create a connection to your service.

To create an endpoint service using the console

1. Open the Amazon VPC console at https://console.aws.amazon.com/vpc/.

2. In the navigation pane, choose **Endpoint Services**, **Create Endpoint Service**.

3. For **Associate Network Load Balancers**, select the Network Load Balancers to associate with the endpoint service.

4. For **Require acceptance for endpoint**, select the check box to accept connection requests to your service manually. If you do not select this option, endpoint connections are automatically accepted.

5. Choose **Create service**.

After you create an endpoint service configuration, you must add permissions to enable service consumers to create interface endpoints to your service.

To create an endpoint service using the AWS CLI

- Use the create-vpc-endpoint-service-configuration command and specify one or more ARNs for your Network Load Balancers. You can optionally specify if acceptance is required for connecting to your service.

```
1 aws ec2 create-vpc-endpoint-service-configuration --network-load-balancer-arns arn:aws:
      elasticloadbalancing:us-east-1:123456789012:loadbalancer/net/nlb-vpce/e94221227f1ba532
      --acceptance-required
```

```
1  {
2      "ServiceConfiguration": {
3          "ServiceType": [
4              {
5                  "ServiceType": "Interface"
6              }
7          ],
8          "NetworkLoadBalancerArns": [
9              "arn:aws:elasticloadbalancing:us-east-1:123456789012:loadbalancer/net/nlb-vpce/
                  e94221227f1ba532"
10         ],
11         "ServiceName": "com.amazonaws.vpce.us-east-1.vpce-svc-03d5ebb7d9579a2b3",
12         "ServiceState": "Available",
13         "ServiceId": "vpce-svc-03d5ebb7d9579a2b3",
14         "AcceptanceRequired": true,
15         "AvailabilityZones": [
16             "us-east-1d"
17         ],
18         "BaseEndpointDnsNames": [
19             "vpce-svc-03d5ebb7d9579a2b3.us-east-1.vpce.amazonaws.com"
```

```
20        ]
21     }
22 }
```

To create an endpoint service using the AWS Tools for Windows PowerShell or API

- New-EC2VpcEndpointServiceConfiguration (AWS Tools for Windows PowerShell)
- CreateVpcEndpointServiceConfiguration (Amazon EC2 Query API)

Adding and Removing Permissions for Your Endpoint Service

After you've created your endpoint service configuration, you can control which service consumers can create an interface endpoint to connect to your service. Service consumers are IAM principals—IAM users, IAM roles, and AWS accounts. To add or remove permissions for a principal, you need its Amazon Resource Name (ARN).

- For an AWS account (and therefore all principals in the account), the ARN is in the form `arn:aws:iam::aws-account-id:root`.
- For a specific IAM user, the ARN is in the form `arn:aws:iam::aws-account-id:user/user-name`.
- For a specific IAM role, the ARN is in the form `arn:aws:iam::aws-account-id:role/role-name`.

To add or remove permissions using the console

1. Open the Amazon VPC console at https://console.aws.amazon.com/vpc/.

2. In the navigation pane, choose **Endpoint Services** and select your endpoint service.

3. Choose **Actions, Add principals to whitelist**.

4. Specify the ARN for the principal for which to add permissions. To add more principals, choose **Add principal**. To remove a principal, choose the cross icon next to the entry. **Note**
   Specify * to add permissions for all principals. This enables all principals in all AWS accounts to create an interface endpoint to your endpoint service.

5. Choose **Add to Whitelisted principals**.

6. To remove a principal, select it in the list and choose **Delete**.

To add and remove permissions using the AWS CLI

1. To add permissions for your endpoint service, use the modify-vpc-endpoint-service-permissions command and use the `--add-allowed-principals` parameter to add one or more ARNs for the principals.

```
1 aws ec2 modify-vpc-endpoint-service-permissions --service-id vpce-svc-03d5ebb7d9579a2b3 --
    add-allowed-principals '["arn:aws:iam::123456789012:root"]'
```

2. To view the permissions you've added for your endpoint service, use the describe-vpc-endpoint-service-permissions command.

```
1 aws ec2 describe-vpc-endpoint-service-permissions --service-id vpce-svc-03d5ebb7d9579a2b3
```

```
1 {
2     "AllowedPrincipals": [
3         {
4             "PrincipalType": "Account",
5             "Principal": "arn:aws:iam::123456789012:root"
6         }
7     ]
8 }
```

3. To remove permissions for your endpoint service, use the modify-vpc-endpoint-service-permissions command and use the `--remove-allowed-principals` parameter to remove one or more ARNs for the principals.

```
1  aws ec2 modify-vpc-endpoint-service-permissions --service-id vpce-svc-03d5ebb7d9579a2b3 --
      remove-allowed-principals '["arn:aws:iam::123456789012:root"]'
```

To modify endpoint service permissions using the AWS Tools for Windows PowerShell or API

- Edit-EC2EndpointServicePermission (AWS Tools for Windows PowerShell)
- ModifyVpcEndpointServicePermissions (Amazon EC2 Query API)

Changing the Network Load Balancers and Acceptance Settings

You can modify your endpoint service configuration by changing the Network Load Balancers that are associated with the endpoint service, and by changing whether acceptance is required for requests to connect to your endpoint service.

You cannot disassociate a load balancer if there are interface endpoints attached to your endpoint service.

To change the network load balancers for your endpoint service using the console

1. Open the Amazon VPC console at https://console.aws.amazon.com/vpc/.
2. In the navigation pane, choose **Endpoint Services** and select your endpoint service.
3. Choose **Actions, Associate/Disassociate Network Load Balancers**.
4. Select or deselect the load balancers as required, and choose **Save**.

To modify the acceptance setting using the console

1. Open the Amazon VPC console at https://console.aws.amazon.com/vpc/.
2. In the navigation pane, choose **Endpoint Services** and select your endpoint service.
3. Choose **Actions, Modify endpoint acceptance setting**.
4. Select or deselect **Require acceptance for endpoint**, and choose **Modify**.

To modify the load balancers and acceptance settings using the AWS CLI

1. To change the load balancers for your endpoint service, use the modify-vpc-endpoint-service-configuration command and use the `--add-network-load-balancer-arn` or `--remove-network-load-balancer-arn` parameter; for example:

```
1  aws ec2 modify-vpc-endpoint-service-configuration --service-id vpce-svc-09222513e6e77dc86
      --remove-network-load-balancer-arn arn:aws:elasticloadbalancing:us-east-1:123456789012:
      loadbalancer/net/nlb-vpce/e94221227f1ba532
```

2. To change whether acceptance is required, use the modify-vpc-endpoint-service-configuration command and specify `--acceptance-required` or `--no-acceptance-required`; for example:

```
1  aws ec2 modify-vpc-endpoint-service-configuration --service-id vpce-svc-09222513e6e77dc86
      --no-acceptance-required
```

To modify an endpoint service configuration using the AWS Tools for Windows PowerShell or API

- Edit-EC2VpcEndpointServiceConfiguration (AWS Tools for Windows PowerShell)
- ModifyVpcEndpointServiceConfiguration (Amazon EC2 Query API)

Accepting and Rejecting Interface Endpoint Connection Requests

After you've created an endpoint service, service consumers for which you've added permission can create an interface endpoint to connect to your service. For more information about creating an interface endpoint, see Interface VPC Endpoints (AWS PrivateLink).

If you specified that acceptance is required for connection requests, you must manually accept or reject interface endpoint connection requests to your endpoint service. After an interface endpoint is accepted, it becomes `available`.

You can reject an interface endpoint connection after it's in the `available` state.

To accept or reject a connection request using the console

1. Open the Amazon VPC console at https://console.aws.amazon.com/vpc/.

2. In the navigation pane, choose **Endpoint Services** and select your endpoint service.

3. The **Endpoint Connections** tab lists endpoint connections that are currently pending your approval. Select the endpoint, choose **Actions**, and choose **Accept endpoint connection request** to accept the connection or **Reject endpoint connection request** to reject it.

To accept or reject a connection request using the AWS CLI

1. The view the endpoint connections that are pending acceptance, use the describe-vpc-endpoint-connections command and filter by the `pendingAcceptance` state.

```
1 aws ec2 describe-vpc-endpoint-connections --filters Name=vpc-endpoint-state,Values=
    pendingAcceptance
```

```
1  {
2      "VpcEndpointConnections": [
3          {
4              "VpcEndpointId": "vpce-0c1308d7312217abc",
5              "ServiceId": "vpce-svc-03d5ebb7d9579a2b3",
6              "CreationTimestamp": "2017-11-30T10:00:24.350Z",
7              "VpcEndpointState": "pendingAcceptance",
8              "VpcEndpointOwner": "123456789012"
9          }
10     ]
11 }
```

2. To accept an endpoint connection request, use the accept-vpc-endpoint-connections command and specify the endpoint ID and endpoint service ID.

```
1 aws ec2 accept-vpc-endpoint-connections --service-id vpce-svc-03d5ebb7d9579a2b3 --vpc-
    endpoint-ids vpce-0c1308d7312217abc
```

3. To reject an endpoint connection request, use the reject-vpc-endpoint-connections command.

```
1 aws ec2 reject-vpc-endpoint-connections --service-id vpce-svc-03d5ebb7d9579a2b3 --vpc-
    endpoint-ids vpce-0c1308d7312217abc
```

To accept and reject endpoint connections using the AWS Tools for Windows PowerShell or API

- Confirm-EC2EndpointConnection and Deny-EC2EndpointConnection (AWS Tools for Windows PowerShell)
- AcceptVpcEndpointConnections and RejectVpcEndpointConnections (Amazon EC2 Query API)

Creating and Managing a Notification for an Endpoint Service

You can create a notification to receive alerts for specific events that occur on the endpoints that are attached to your endpoint service. For example, you can receive an email when an endpoint request is accepted or rejected for your endpoint service. To create a notification, you must associate an Amazon SNS topic with the notification. You can subscribe to the SNS topic to receive an email notification when an endpoint event occurs. For more information, see the Amazon Simple Notification Service Developer Guide.

The Amazon SNS topic that you use for notifications must have a topic policy that allows the Amazon VPC endpoint service to publish notifications on your behalf. Ensure that you include the following statement in your topic policy. For more information, see Managing Access to Your Amazon SNS Topics in the *Amazon Simple Notification Service Developer Guide.*

```
1  {
2    "Version": "2012-10-17",
3    "Statement": [
4      {
5        "Effect": "Allow",
6        "Principal": {
7          "Service": "vpce.amazonaws.com"
8        },
9        "Action": "SNS:Publish",
10       "Resource": "arn:aws:sns:region:account:topic-name"
11     }
12   ]
13 }
```

To create a notification for an endpoint service

1. Open the Amazon VPC console at https://console.aws.amazon.com/vpc/.

2. In the navigation pane, choose **Endpoint Services** and select your endpoint service.

3. Choose **Notifications, Create Notification.**

4. Choose the ARN for the SNS topic to associate with the notification.

5. For **Events,** select the endpoint events for which to receive notifications.

6. Choose **Create Notification.**

After you create a notification, you can change the SNS topic that's associated with the notification, or you can specify different endpoint events for the notification.

To modify a notification for an endpoint service

1. Open the Amazon VPC console at https://console.aws.amazon.com/vpc/.

2. In the navigation pane, choose **Endpoint Services** and select your endpoint service.

3. Choose **Notifications, Actions, Modify Notification.**

4. Specify the ARN for the SNS topic and select or deselect the endpoint events as required.

5. Choose **Modify Notification.**

If you no longer need a notification, you can delete it.

To delete a notification

1. Open the Amazon VPC console at https://console.aws.amazon.com/vpc/.

2. In the navigation pane, choose **Endpoint Services** and select your endpoint service.

3. Choose **Notifications, Actions, Delete Notification.**

4. Choose **Yes, Delete**.

To create and manage a notification using the AWS CLI

1. To create a notification for an endpoint service, use the create-vpc-endpoint-connection-notification command and specify the ARN of the SNS topic, the events for which to be notified, and the ID of the endpoint service; for example:

```
1 aws ec2 create-vpc-endpoint-connection-notification --connection-notification-arn arn:aws:
    sns:us-east-2:123456789012:VpceNotification --connection-events Connect Accept Delete
    Reject --service-id vpce-svc-1237881c0d25a3abc
```

```
1  {
2      "ConnectionNotification": {
3          "ConnectionNotificationState": "Enabled",
4          "ConnectionNotificationType": "Topic",
5          "ServiceId": "vpce-svc-1237881c0d25a3abc",
6          "ConnectionEvents": [
7              "Reject",
8              "Accept",
9              "Delete",
10             "Connect"
11         ],
12         "ConnectionNotificationId": "vpce-nfn-008776de7e03f5abc",
13         "ConnectionNotificationArn": "arn:aws:sns:us-east-2:123456789012:VpceNotification"
14     }
15 }
```

2. To view your notifications, use the describe-vpc-endpoint-connection-notifications command:

```
1 aws ec2 describe-vpc-endpoint-connection-notifications
```

3. To change the SNS topic or endpoint events for the notification, use the modify-vpc-endpoint-connection-notification command; for example:

```
1 aws ec2 modify-vpc-endpoint-connection-notification --connection-notification-id vpce-nfn
    -008776de7e03f5abc --connection-events Accept Reject --connection-notification-arn arn:
    aws:sns:us-east-2:123456789012:mytopic
```

4. To delete a notification, use the delete-vpc-endpoint-connection-notifications command:

```
1 aws ec2 delete-vpc-endpoint-connection-notifications --connection-notification-ids vpce-nfn
    -008776de7e03f5abc
```

To create and manage a notification using the AWS Tools for Windows PowerShell or API

- New-EC2VpcEndpointConnectionNotification, Get-EC2EndpointConnectionNotification, Edit-EC2VpcEndpointConnectionNotification, and Remove-EC2EndpointConnectionNotification (AWS Tools for Windows PowerShell)
- CreateVpcEndpointConnectionNotification, DescribeVpcEndpointConnectionNotifications, ModifyVpcEndpointConnectionNotification, and DeleteVpcEndpointConnectionNotifications (Amazon EC2 Query API)

Using Proxy Protocol for Connection Information

A Network Load Balancer provides source IP addresses to your application (your service). When service consumers send traffic to your service through an interface endpoint, the source IP addresses provided to your application are the private IP addresses of the Network Load Balancer nodes, and not the IP addresses of the service consumers.

If you need the IP addresses of the service consumers and their corresponding interface endpoint IDs, enable Proxy Protocol on your load balancer and get the client IP addresses from the Proxy Protocol header. For more information, see Proxy Protocol in the *User Guide for Network Load Balancers*.

Deleting an Endpoint Service Configuration

You can delete an endpoint service configuration. Deleting the configuration does not delete the application hosted in your VPC or the associated load balancers.

Before you delete the endpoint service configuration, you must reject any `available` or `pending-acceptance` VPC endpoints that are attached to the service. For more information, see Accepting and Rejecting Interface Endpoint Connection Requests.

To delete an endpoint service configuration using the console

1. Open the Amazon VPC console at https://console.aws.amazon.com/vpc/.

2. In the navigation pane, choose **Endpoint Services** and select the service.

3. Choose **Actions**, **Delete**.

4. Choose **Yes, Delete**.

To delete an endpoint service configuration using the AWS CLI

- Use the delete-vpc-endpoint-service-configurations command and specify the ID of the service.

```
1 aws ec2 delete-vpc-endpoint-service-configurations --service-ids vpce-svc-03d5ebb7d9579a2b3
```

To delete an endpoint service configuration using the AWS Tools for Windows PowerShell or API

- Remove-EC2EndpointServiceConfiguration (AWS Tools for Windows PowerShell)
- DeleteVpcEndpointServiceConfigurations (Amazon EC2 Query API)

ClassicLink

ClassicLink allows you to link an EC2-Classic instance to a VPC in your account, within the same region. This allows you to associate the VPC security groups with the EC2-Classic instance, enabling communication between your EC2-Classic instance and instances in your VPC using private IPv4 addresses. ClassicLink removes the need to make use of public IPv4 addresses or Elastic IP addresses to enable communication between instances in these platforms. For more information about private and public IPv4 addresses, see IP Addressing in Your VPC.

ClassicLink is available to all users with accounts that support the EC2-Classic platform, and can be used with any EC2-Classic instance.

There is no additional charge for using ClassicLink. Standard charges for data transfer and instance hour usage apply.

For more information about ClassicLink and how to use it, see the following topics in the *Amazon EC2 User Guide*:

- ClassicLink Basics
- ClassicLink Limitations
- Working with ClassicLink
- ClassicLink API and CLI Overview

VPN Connections

You can connect your Amazon VPC to remote networks by using a VPN connection. The following are some of the connectivity options available to you.

VPN connectivity option	Description
AWS managed VPN	You can create an IPsec VPN connection between your VPC and your remote network. On the AWS side of the VPN connection, a virtual private gateway provides two VPN endpoints (tunnels) for automatic failover. You configure your customer gateway on the remote side of the VPN connection. For more information, see AWS Managed VPN Connections, and the Amazon VPC Network Administrator Guide.
AWS VPN CloudHub	If you have more than one remote network (for example, multiple branch offices), you can create multiple AWS managed VPN connections via your virtual private gateway to enable communication between these networks. For more information, see Providing Secure Communication Between Sites Using VPN CloudHub.
Third party software VPN appliance	You can create a VPN connection to your remote network by using an Amazon EC2 instance in your VPC that's running a third party software VPN appliance. AWS does not provide or maintain third party software VPN appliances; however, you can choose from a range of products provided by partners and open source communities. Find third party software VPN appliances on the AWS Marketplace.

You can also use AWS Direct Connect to create a dedicated private connection from a remote network to your VPC. You can combine this connection with an AWS managed VPN connection to create an IPsec-encrypted connection. For more information, see What is AWS Direct Connect? in the *AWS Direct Connect User Guide*. For more information about the different VPC and VPN connectivity options, see the Amazon Virtual Private Cloud Connectivity Options whitepaper.

AWS Managed VPN Connections

By default, instances that you launch into an Amazon VPC can't communicate with your own (remote) network. You can enable access to your remote network from your VPC by attaching a virtual private gateway to the VPC, creating a custom route table, updating your security group rules, and creating an AWS managed VPN connection.

Although the term *VPN connection* is a general term, in the Amazon VPC documentation, a VPN connection refers to the connection between your VPC and your own network. AWS supports Internet Protocol security (IPsec) VPN connections.

Your AWS managed VPN connection is either an AWS Classic VPN or an AWS VPN. For more information, see AWS Managed VPN Categories.

Important
We currently do not support IPv6 traffic through a VPN connection.

Topics

- Components of Your VPN
- AWS Managed VPN Categories
- VPN Configuration Examples
- VPN Routing Options
- Configuring the VPN Tunnels for Your VPN Connection
- Using Redundant VPN Connections to Provide Failover

For information about how you're charged for using a VPN connection with your VPC, see the Amazon VPC product page.

Components of Your VPN

A VPN connection consists of the following components. For more information about VPN limits, see Amazon VPC Limits.

Virtual Private Gateway

A *virtual private gateway* is the VPN concentrator on the Amazon side of the VPN connection. You create a virtual private gateway and attach it to the VPC from which you want to create the VPN connection.

When you create a virtual private gateway, you can specify the private Autonomous System Number (ASN) for the Amazon side of the gateway. If you don't specify an ASN, the virtual private gateway is created with the default ASN (64512). You cannot change the ASN after you've created the virtual private gateway. To check the ASN for your virtual private gateway, view its details in the **Virtual Private Gateways** screen in the Amazon VPC console, or use the describe-vpn-gateways AWS CLI command.

Note
If you create your virtual private gateway before 2018-06-30, the default ASN is 17493 in the Asia Pacific (Singapore) region, 10124 in the Asia Pacific (Tokyo) region, 9059 in the EU (Ireland) region, and 7224 in all other regions.

Customer Gateway

A *customer gateway* is a physical device or software application on your side of the VPN connection.

To create a VPN connection, you must create a customer gateway resource in AWS, which provides information to AWS about your customer gateway device. The following table describes the information you'll need to create a customer gateway resource.

Item	Description
Internet-routable IP address (static) of the customer gateway's external interface.	The public IP address value must be static. If your customer gateway is behind a network address translation (NAT) device that's enabled for NAT traversal (NAT-T), use the public IP address of your NAT device, and adjust your firewall rules to unblock UDP port 4500.
The type of routing—static or dynamic.	For more information, see VPN Routing Options.
(Dynamic routing only) Border Gateway Protocol (BGP) Autonomous System Number (ASN) of the customer gateway.	You can use an existing ASN assigned to your network. If you don't have one, you can use a private ASN (in the 64512–65534 range). If you use the VPC wizard in the console to set up your VPC, we automatically use 65000 as the ASN.

To use Amazon VPC with a VPN connection, you or your network administrator must also configure the customer gateway device or application in your remote network. When you create the VPN connection, we provide you with the required configuration information and your network administrator typically performs this configuration. For information about the customer gateway requirements and configuration, see the Your Customer Gateway in the *Amazon VPC Network Administrator Guide*.

The VPN tunnel comes up when traffic is generated from your side of the VPN connection. The virtual private gateway is not the initiator; your customer gateway must initiate the tunnels. If your VPN connection experiences a period of idle time (usually 10 seconds, depending on your configuration), the tunnel may go down. To prevent this, you can use a network monitoring tool to generate keepalive pings; for example, by using IP SLA.

For a list of customer gateways that we have tested with Amazon VPC, see Amazon Virtual Private Cloud FAQs.

AWS Managed VPN Categories

Your AWS managed VPN connection is either an AWS Classic VPN connection or an AWS VPN connection. Any new VPN connection that you create is an AWS VPN connection. The following features are supported on AWS VPN connections only:

- NAT traversal
- 4-byte ASN (in addition to 2-byte ASN)
- CloudWatch metrics
- Reusable IP addresses for your customer gateways
- Additional encryption options; including AES 256-bit encryption, SHA-2 hashing, and additional Diffie-Hellman groups
- Configurable tunnel options
- Custom private ASN for the Amazon side of a BGP session

You can find out the category of your AWS managed VPN connection by using the Amazon VPC console or a command line tool.

To identify the VPN category using the console

1. Open the Amazon VPC console at https://console.aws.amazon.com/vpc/.

2. In the navigation pane, choose **VPN Connections**.

3. Select the VPN connection, and check the value for **Category** in the details pane. A value of VPN indicates an AWS VPN connection. A value of VPN-Classic indicates an AWS Classic VPN connection.

To identify the VPN category using a command line tool

- You can use the describe-vpn-connections AWS CLI command. In the output that's returned, take note of the Category value. A value of VPN indicates an AWS VPN connection. A value of VPN-Classic indicates an AWS Classic VPN connection.

  In the following example, the VPN connection is an AWS VPN connection.

```
1 aws ec2 describe-vpn-connections --vpn-connection-ids vpn-1a2b3c4d
```

```
1  {
2      "VpnConnections": [
3          {
4              "VpnConnectionId": "vpn-1a2b3c4d",
5
6              ...
7
8              "State": "available",
9              "VpnGatewayId": "vgw-11aa22bb",
10             "CustomerGatewayId": "cgw-ab12cd34",
11             "Type": "ipsec.1",
12             "Category": "VPN"
13         }
14     ]
15 }
```

Alternatively, use one of the following commands:

- DescribeVpnConnections (Amazon EC2 Query API)
- Get-EC2VpnConnection (Tools for Windows PowerShell)

Migrating to AWS VPN

If your existing VPN connection is an AWS Classic VPN connection, you can migrate to an AWS VPN connection by creating a new virtual private gateway and VPN connection, detaching the old virtual private gateway from your VPC, and attaching the new virtual private gateway to your VPC.

If your existing virtual private gateway is associated with multiple VPN connections, you must recreate each VPN connection for the new virtual private gateway. If there are multiple AWS Direct Connect private virtual interfaces attached to your virtual private gateway, you must recreate each private virtual interface for the new virtual private gateway. For more information, see Creating a Virtual Interface in the *AWS Direct Connect User Guide*.

If your existing AWS managed VPN connection is an AWS VPN connection, you cannot migrate to an AWS Classic VPN connection.

Note
During this procedure, connectivity over the current VPC connection is interrupted when you disable route propagation and detach the old virtual private gateway from your VPC. Connectivity is restored when the new virtual private gateway is attached to your VPC and the new VPN connection is active. Ensure that you plan for the expected downtime.

To migrate to an AWS VPN connection

1. Open the Amazon VPC console at https://console.aws.amazon.com/vpc/.

2. In the navigation pane, choose **Virtual Private Gateways, Create Virtual Private Gateway** and create a virtual private gateway.

3. In the navigation pane, choose **VPN Connections, Create VPN Connection**. Specify the following information, and choose **Yes, Create**.

   - **Virtual Private Gateway**: Select the virtual private gateway that you created in the previous step.
   - **Customer Gateway**: Choose **Existing**, and select the existing customer gateway for your current AWS Classic VPN connection.
   - Specify the routing options as required.

4. Select the new VPN connection and choose **Download Configuration**. Download the appropriate configuration file for your customer gateway device.

5. Use the configuration file to configure VPN tunnels on your customer gateway device. For examples, see the *Amazon VPC Network Administrator Guide*. Do not enable the tunnels yet. Contact your vendor if you need guidance on keeping the newly configured tunnels disabled.

6. (Optional) Create test VPC and attach the virtual private gateway to the test VPC. Change the encryption domain/source destination addresses as required, and test connectivity from a host in your local network to a test instance in the test VPC.

7. If you are using route propagation for your route table, choose **Route Tables** in the navigation pane. Select the route table for your VPC, and choose **Route Propagation, Edit**. Clear the check box for the old virtual private gateway and choose **Save. Note**
   From this step onwards, connectivity is interrupted until the new virtual private gateway is attached and the new VPN connection is active.

8. In the navigation pane, choose **Virtual Private Gateways**. Select the old virtual private gateway and choose **Actions, Detach from VPC, Yes, Detach**. Select the new virtual private gateway, and choose **Actions, Attach to VPC**. Specify the VPC for your VPN connection, and choose **Yes, Attach**.

9. In the navigation pane, choose **Route Tables**. Select the route table for your VPC and do one of the following:

   - If you are using route propagation, choose **Route Propagation, Edit**. Select the new virtual private gateway that's attached to the VPC and choose **Save**.
   - If you are using static routes, choose **Routes, Edit**. Modify the route to point to the new virtual private gateway, and choose **Save**.

10. Enable the new tunnels on your customer gateway device and disable the old tunnels. To bring the tunnel up, you must initiate the connection from your local network.

    If applicable, check your route table to ensure that the routes are being propagated. The routes propagate to the route table when the status of the VPN tunnel is UP. **Note**
    If you need to revert to your previous configuration, detach the new virtual private gateway and follow steps 8 and 9 to re-attach the old virtual private gateway and update your routes.

11. If you no longer need your AWS Classic VPN connection and do not want to continue incurring charges for it, remove the previous tunnel configurations from your customer gateway device, and delete the VPN connection. To do this, go to **VPN Connections**, select the VPN connection, and choose **Delete**.
    Important
    After you've deleted the AWS Classic VPN connection, you cannot revert or migrate your new AWS VPN connection back to an AWS Classic VPN connection.

VPN Configuration Examples

The following diagrams illustrate single and multiple VPN connections. The VPC has an attached virtual private gateway, and your remote network includes a customer gateway, which you must configure to enable the VPN connection. You set up the routing so that any traffic from the VPC bound for your network is routed to the virtual private gateway.

When you create multiple VPN connections to a single VPC, you can configure a second customer gateway to create a redundant connection to the same external location. You can also use it to create VPN connections to multiple geographic locations.

Single VPN Connection

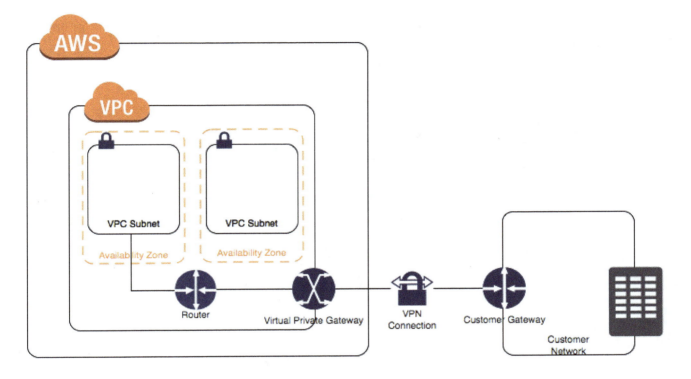

Multiple VPN connections

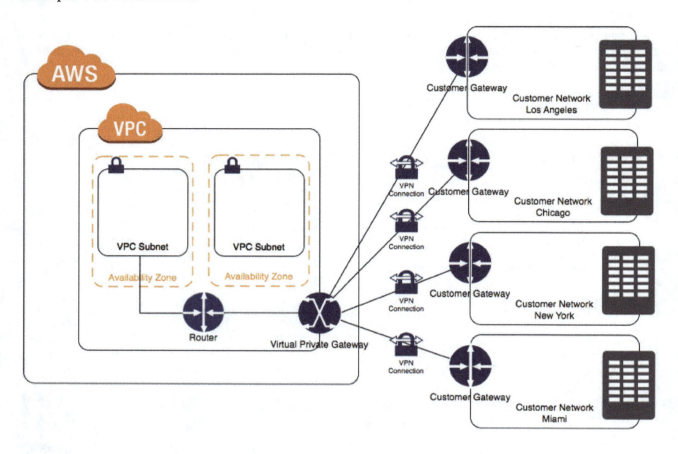

VPN Routing Options

When you create a VPN connection, you must do the following:

- Specify the type of routing that you plan to use (static or dynamic)
- Update the route table for your subnet

There are limits on the number of routes that you can add to a route table. For more information, see the Route Tables section in Amazon VPC Limits.

Static and Dynamic Routing

The type of routing that you select can depend on the make and model of your VPN devices. If your VPN device supports Border Gateway Protocol (BGP), specify dynamic routing when you configure your VPN connection. If your device does not support BGP, specify static routing. For a list of static and dynamic routing devices that have been tested with Amazon VPC, see the Amazon Virtual Private Cloud FAQs.

When you use a BGP device, you don't need to specify static routes to the VPN connection because the device uses BGP to advertise its routes to the virtual private gateway. If you use a device that doesn't support BGP, you must select static routing and enter the routes (IP prefixes) for your network that should be communicated to the virtual private gateway.

We recommend that you use BGP-capable devices, when available, because the BGP protocol offers robust liveness detection checks that can assist failover to the second VPN tunnel if the first tunnel goes down. Devices that don't support BGP may also perform health checks to assist failover to the second tunnel when needed.

Route Tables and VPN Route Priority

Route tables determine where network traffic is directed. In your route table, you must add a route for your remote network and specify the virtual private gateway as the target. This enables traffic from your VPC that's destined for your remote network to route via the virtual private gateway and over one of the VPN tunnels. You can enable route propagation for your route table to automatically propagate your network routes to the table for you.

Only IP prefixes that are known to the virtual private gateway, whether through BGP advertisements or static route entry, can receive traffic from your VPC. The virtual private gateway does not route any other traffic destined outside of received BGP advertisements, static route entries, or its attached VPC CIDR.

When a virtual private gateway receives routing information, it uses path selection to determine how to route traffic to your remote network. Longest prefix match applies; otherwise, the following rules apply:

- If any propagated routes from a VPN connection or AWS Direct Connect connection overlap with the local route for your VPC, the local route is most preferred even if the propagated routes are more specific.
- If any propagated routes from a VPN connection or AWS Direct Connect connection have the same destination CIDR block as other existing static routes (longest prefix match cannot be applied), we prioritize the static routes whose targets are an Internet gateway, a virtual private gateway, a network interface, an instance ID, a VPC peering connection, a NAT gateway, or a VPC endpoint.

If you have overlapping routes within a VPN connection and longest prefix match cannot be applied, then we prioritize the routes as follows in the VPN connection, from most preferred to least preferred:

- BGP propagated routes from an AWS Direct Connect connection
- Manually added static routes for a VPN connection
- BGP propagated routes from a VPN connection

In this example, your route table has a static route to an internet gateway (that you added manually), and a propagated route to a virtual private gateway. Both routes have a destination of 172.31.0.0/24. In this case, all traffic destined for 172.31.0.0/24 is routed to the internet gateway — it is a static route and therefore takes priority over the propagated route.

Destination	Target
10.0.0.0/16	Local
172.31.0.0/24	vgw-1a2b3c4d (propagated)
172.31.0.0/24	igw-11aa22bb

Configuring the VPN Tunnels for Your VPN Connection

You use a VPN connection to connect your remote network to a VPC. Each VPN connection has two tunnels, with each tunnel using a unique virtual private gateway public IP address. It is important to configure both tunnels for redundancy. When one tunnel becomes unavailable (for example, down for maintenance), network traffic is automatically routed to the available tunnel for that specific VPN connection.

The following diagram shows the two tunnels of the VPN connection.

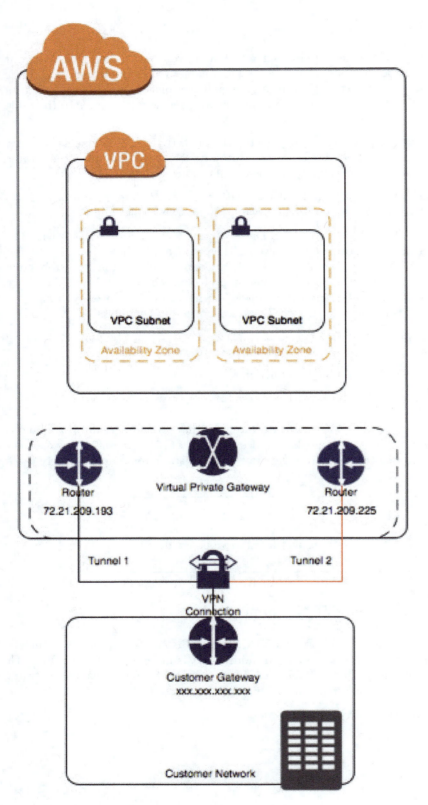

When you create a VPN connection, you download a configuration file specific to your customer gateway device that contains information for configuring the device, including information for configuring each tunnel. You can optionally specify some of the tunnel options yourself when you create the VPN connection. Otherwise, AWS provides default values.

The following table describes the tunnel options that you can configure.

Item	Description	AWS-provided default value
Inside tunnel CIDR	The range of inside IP addresses for the VPN tunnel. You can specify a size /30 CIDR block from the 169.254.0.0/16 range. The CIDR block must be unique across all VPN connections that use the same virtual private gateway. The following CIDR blocks are reserved and cannot be used: [See the AWS documentation website for more details]	A size /30 CIDR block from the 169.254.0.0/16 range.
Pre-shared key (PSK)	The pre-shared key (PSK) to establish the initial IKE Security Association between the virtual private gateway and customer gateway. The PSK must be between 8 and 64 characters in length and cannot start with zero (0). Allowed characters are alphanumeric characters, periods (.), and underscores (_).	A 32-character alphanumeric string.

You cannot modify tunnel options after you create the VPN connection. To change the inside tunnel IP addresses or the PSKs for an existing connection, you must delete the VPN connection and create a new one. You cannot configure tunnel options for an AWS Classic VPN connection.

Using Redundant VPN Connections to Provide Failover

As described earlier, a VPN connection has two tunnels to help ensure connectivity in case one of the VPN connections becomes unavailable. To protect against a loss of connectivity in case your customer gateway becomes unavailable, you can set up a second VPN connection to your VPC and virtual private gateway by using a second customer gateway. By using redundant VPN connections and customer gateways, you can perform maintenance on one of your customer gateways while traffic continues to flow over the second customer gateway's VPN connection. To establish redundant VPN connections and customer gateways on your remote network, you need to set up a second VPN connection. The customer gateway IP address for the second VPN connection must be publicly accessible.

The following diagram shows the two tunnels of each VPN connection and two customer gateways.

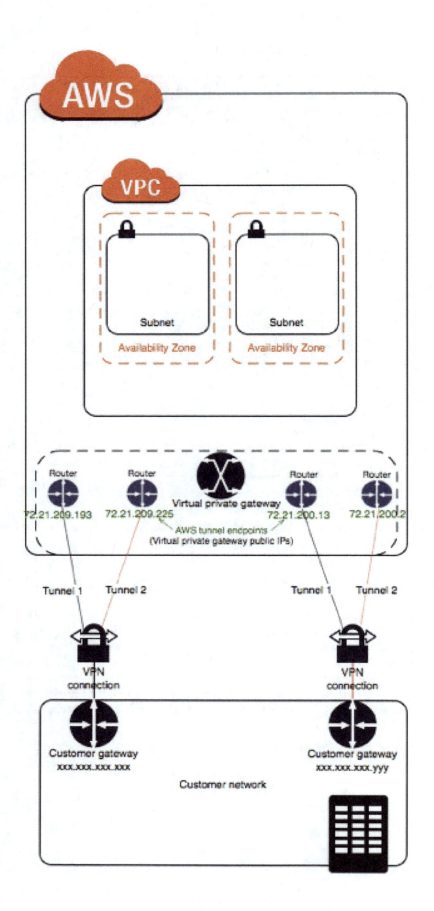

Dynamically routed VPN connections use the Border Gateway Protocol (BGP) to exchange routing information between your customer gateways and the virtual private gateways. Statically routed VPN connections require you to enter static routes for the remote network on your side of the customer gateway. BGP-advertised and statically entered route information allow gateways on both sides to determine which tunnels are available and reroute traffic if a failure occurs. We recommend that you configure your network to use the routing information provided by BGP (if available) to select an available path. The exact configuration depends on the architecture of your network.

Setting Up an AWS VPN Connection

Use the following procedures to manually set up the VPN connection. Alternatively, you can let the VPC creation wizard take care of many of these steps for you. For more information about using the VPC creation wizard to set up the virtual private gateway, see Scenario 3: VPC with Public and Private Subnets and AWS Managed VPN Access or Scenario 4: VPC with a Private Subnet Only and AWS Managed VPN Access.

To set up a VPN connection, you need to complete the following steps:

- Step 1: Create a Customer Gateway
- Step 2: Create a Virtual Private Gateway
- Step 3: Enable Route Propagation in Your Route Table
- Step 4: Update Your Security Group
- Step 5: Create a VPN Connection and Configure the Customer Gateway

These procedures assume that you have a VPC with one or more subnets.

Create a Customer Gateway

A customer gateway provides information to AWS about your customer gateway device or software application. For more information, see Customer Gateway.

To create a customer gateway using the console

1. Open the Amazon VPC console at https://console.aws.amazon.com/vpc/.

2. In the navigation pane, choose **Customer Gateways**, and then **Create Customer Gateway**.

3. Complete the following and then choose **Create Customer Gateway**:

   - (Optional) For **Name**, type a name for your customer gateway. Doing so creates a tag with a key of Name and the value that you specify.
   - For **Routing**, select the routing type.
   - For dynamic routing, for **BGP ASN**, type the Border Gateway Protocol (BGP) Autonomous System Number (ASN).
   - For **IP Address**, type the static, internet-routable IP address for your customer gateway device. If your customer gateway is behind a NAT device that's enabled for NAT-T, use the public IP address of the NAT device.

To create a customer gateway using the command line or API

- CreateCustomerGateway (Amazon EC2 Query API)
- create-customer-gateway (AWS CLI)
- New-EC2CustomerGateway (AWS Tools for Windows PowerShell)

Create a Virtual Private Gateway

When you create a virtual private gateway, you can optionally specify the private Autonomous System Number (ASN) for the Amazon side of the gateway. The ASN must be different from the BGP ASN specified for the customer gateway.

After you create a virtual private gateway, you must attach it to your VPC.

To create a virtual private gateway and attach it to your VPC

1. In the navigation pane, choose **Virtual Private Gateways**, **Create Virtual Private Gateway**.

2. (Optional) Type a name for your virtual private gateway. Doing so creates a tag with a key of Name and the value that you specify.

3. For **ASN**, leave the default selection to use the default Amazon ASN. Otherwise, choose **Custom ASN** and type a value. For a 16-bit ASN, the value must be in the 64512 to 65534 range. For a 32-bit ASN, the value must be in the 4200000000 to 4294967294 range.

4. Choose **Create Virtual Private Gateway**.

5. Select the virtual private gateway that you created, and then choose **Actions, Attach to VPC**.

6. Select your VPC from the list and choose **Yes, Attach**.

To create a virtual private gateway using the command line or API

- CreateVpnGateway (Amazon EC2 Query API)
- create-vpn-gateway (AWS CLI)
- New-EC2VpnGateway (AWS Tools for Windows PowerShell)

To attach a virtual private gateway to a VPC using the command line or API

- AttachVpnGateway (Amazon EC2 Query API)
- attach-vpn-gateway (AWS CLI)
- Add-EC2VpnGateway (AWS Tools for Windows PowerShell)

Enable Route Propagation in Your Route Table

To enable instances in your VPC to reach your customer gateway, you must configure your route table to include the routes used by your VPN connection and point them to your virtual private gateway. You can enable route propagation for your route table to automatically propagate those routes to the table for you.

For static routing, the static IP prefixes that you specify for your VPN configuration are propagated to the route table when the status of the VPN connection is UP. Similarly, for dynamic routing, the BGP-advertised routes from your customer gateway are propagated to the route table when the status of the VPN connection is UP.

Note
If your connection is interrupted, any propagated routes in your route table are not automatically removed. You may have to disable route propagation to remove the propagated routes; for example, if you want traffic to fail over to a static route.

To enable route propagation using the console

1. In the navigation pane, choose **Route Tables**, and then select the route table that's associated with the subnet; by default, this is the main route table for the VPC.

2. On the **Route Propagation** tab in the details pane, choose **Edit**, select the virtual private gateway that you created in the previous procedure, and then choose **Save**.

Note
For static routing, if you do not enable route propagation, you must manually enter the static routes used by your VPN connection. To do this, select your route table, choose **Routes, Edit**. For **Destination**, add the static route used by your VPN connection . For **Target**, select the virtual private gateway ID, and choose **Save**.

To disable route propagation using the console

1. In the navigation pane, choose **Route Tables**, and then select the route table that's associated with the subnet.

2. Choose **Route Propagation, Edit**. Clear the **Propagate** check box for the virtual private gateway, and choose **Save**.

To enable route propagation using the command line or API

- EnableVgwRoutePropagation (Amazon EC2 Query API)
- enable-vgw-route-propagation (AWS CLI)
- Enable-EC2VgwRoutePropagation (AWS Tools for Windows PowerShell)

To disable route propagation using the command line or API

- DisableVgwRoutePropagation (Amazon EC2 Query API)
- disable-vgw-route-propagation (AWS CLI)
- Disable-EC2VgwRoutePropagation (AWS Tools for Windows PowerShell)

Update Your Security Group

To allow access to instances in your VPC from your network, you must update your security group rules to enable inbound SSH, RDP, and ICMP access.

To add rules to your security group to enable inbound SSH, RDP and ICMP access

1. In the navigation pane, choose **Security Groups**, and then select the default security group for the VPC.

2. On the **Inbound** tab in the details pane, add rules that allow inbound SSH, RDP, and ICMP access from your network, and then choose **Save**. For more information about adding inbound rules, see Adding, Removing, and Updating Rules.

For more information about working with security groups using the AWS CLI, see Security Groups for Your VPC.

Create a VPN Connection and Configure the Customer Gateway

After you create the VPN connection, download the configuration information and use it to configure the customer gateway device or software application.

To create a VPN connection and configure the customer gateway

1. In the navigation pane, choose **VPN Connections, Create VPN Connection**.

2. Complete the following information, and then choose **Create VPN Connection**:

   - (Optional) For **Name tag**, type a name for your VPN connection. Doing so creates a tag with a key of `Name` and the value that you specify.

   - Select the virtual private gateway that you created earlier.

   - Select the customer gateway that you created earlier.

   - Select one of the routing options based on whether your VPN router supports Border Gateway Protocol (BGP):

     - If your VPN router supports BGP, choose **Dynamic (requires BGP)**.
     - If your VPN router does not support BGP, choose **Static**. For **Static IP Prefixes**, specify each IP prefix for the private network of your VPN connection.

   - Under **Tunnel Options**, you can optionally specify the following information for each tunnel:

     - A size /30 CIDR block from the `169.254.0.0/16` range for the inside tunnel IP addresses.
     - The IKE pre-shared key (PSK).

     For more information about these options, see Configuring the VPN Tunnels for Your VPN Connection.

   It may take a few minutes to create the VPN connection. When it's ready, select the connection and choose **Download Configuration**.

3. In the **Download Configuration** dialog box, select the vendor, platform, and software that corresponds to your customer gateway device or software, and then choose **Yes, Download**.

4. Give the configuration file to your network administrator, along with this guide: Amazon VPC Network Administrator Guide. After the network administrator configures the customer gateway, the VPN connection is operational.

To create a VPN connection using the command line or API

- CreateVpnConnection (Amazon EC2 Query API)
- create-vpn-connection (AWS CLI)
- New-EC2VpnConnection (AWS Tools for Windows PowerShell)

Editing Static Routes for a VPN Connection

For static routing, you can add, modify, or remove the static routes for your VPN configuration.

To add, modify, or remove a static route

1. Open the Amazon VPC console at https://console.aws.amazon.com/vpc/.

2. In the navigation pane, choose **VPN Connections**.

3. Choose **Static Routes**, **Edit**.

4. Modify your existing static IP prefixes, or choose **Remove** to delete them. Choose **Add Another Rule** to add a new IP prefix to your configuration. When you are done, choose **Save**.

Note
If you have not enabled route propagation for your route table, you must manually update the routes in your route table to reflect the updated static IP prefixes in your VPN connection. For more information, see Enable Route Propagation in Your Route Table.

To add a static route using the command line or API

- CreateVpnConnectionRoute (Amazon EC2 Query API)
- create-vpn-connection-route (AWS CLI)
- New-EC2VpnConnectionRoute (AWS Tools for Windows PowerShell)

To delete a static route using the command line or API

- DeleteVpnConnectionRoute (Amazon EC2 Query API)
- delete-vpn-connection-route (AWS CLI)
- Remove-EC2VpnConnectionRoute (AWS Tools for Windows PowerShell)

Replacing Compromised Credentials

If you believe that the tunnel credentials for your VPN connection have been compromised, you can change the IKE pre-shared key. To do so, delete the VPN connection, create a new one using the same virtual private gateway, and configure the new keys on your customer gateway. You can specify your own pre-shared keys when you create the VPN connection. You also need to confirm that the tunnel's inside and outside addresses match, because these might change when you recreate the VPN connection. While you perform the procedure, communication with your instances in the VPC stops, but the instances continue to run uninterrupted. After the network administrator implements the new configuration information, your VPN connection uses the new credentials, and the network connection to your instances in the VPC resumes.

Important
This procedure requires assistance from your network administrator group.

To change the IKE pre-shared key

1. Delete the VPN connection. For more information, see Deleting a VPN Connection. You don't need to delete the VPC or the virtual private gateway.

2. Create a new VPN connection and specify your own pre-shared keys for the tunnels or let AWS generate new pre-shared keys for you. For more information, see Create a VPN Connection and Configure the Customer Gateway.

3. Download the new configuration file.

Testing the VPN Connection

After you create theVPN connection and configure the customer gateway, you can launch an instance and test the connection by pinging the instance. You need to use an AMI that responds to ping requests, and you need to ensure that your instance's security group is configured to enable inbound ICMP. We recommend you use one of the Amazon Linux AMIs. If you are using instances running Windows Server, you'll need to log in to the instance and enable inbound ICMPv4 on the Windows firewall in order to ping the instance.

Important
You must configure any security group or network ACL in your VPC that filters traffic to the instance to allow inbound and outbound ICMP traffic.

To test end-to-end connectivity

1. Open the Amazon EC2 console at https://console.aws.amazon.com/ec2/.

2. On the dashboard, choose **Launch Instance**.

3. On the **Choose an Amazon Machine Image (AMI)** page, choose an AMI, and then choose **Select**.

4. Choose an instance type, and then choose **Next: Configure Instance Details**.

5. On the **Configure Instance Details** page, for **Network**, select your VPC. For **Subnet**, select your subnet. Choose **Next** until you reach the **Configure Security Group** page.

6. Select the **Select an existing security group** option, and then select the default group that you modified earlier. Choose **Review and Launch**.

7. Review the settings that you've chosen. Make any changes that you need, and then choose **Launch** to select a key pair and launch the instance.

8. After the instance is running, get its private IP address (for example, `10.0.0.4`). The Amazon EC2 console displays the address as part of the instance's details.

9. From a computer in your network that is behind the customer gateway, use the `ping` command with the instance's private IP address. A successful response is similar to the following:

```
1 ping 10.0.0.4
```

```
 1 Pinging 10.0.0.4 with 32 bytes of data:
 2
 3 Reply from 10.0.0.4: bytes=32 time<1ms TTL=128
 4 Reply from 10.0.0.4: bytes=32 time<1ms TTL=128
 5 Reply from 10.0.0.4: bytes=32 time<1ms TTL=128
 6
 7 Ping statistics for 10.0.0.4:
 8 Packets: Sent = 3, Received = 3, Lost = 0 (0% loss),
 9
10 Approximate round trip times in milliseconds:
11 Minimum = 0ms, Maximum = 0ms, Average = 0ms
```

You can now use SSH or RDP to connect to your instance in the VPC. For more information about how to connect to a Linux instance, see Connect to Your Linux Instance in the *Amazon EC2 User Guide for Linux Instances*. For more information about how to connect to a Windows instance, see Connect to Your Windows Instance in the *Amazon EC2 User Guide for Windows Instances*.

Deleting a VPN Connection

If you no longer need a VPN connection, you can delete it.

Important
If you delete your VPN connection and then create a new one, you have to download new configuration information and have your network administrator reconfigure the customer gateway.

To delete a VPN connection using the console

1. Open the Amazon VPC console at https://console.aws.amazon.com/vpc/.

2. In the navigation pane, choose **VPN Connections**.

3. Select the VPN connection and choose **Actions, Delete**.

4. Choose **Delete**.

If you no longer require a customer gateway, you can delete it. You can't delete a customer gateway that's being used in a VPN connection.

To delete a customer gateway using the console

1. In the navigation pane, choose **Customer Gateways**.

2. Select the customer gateway to delete and choose **Actions, Delete Customer Gateway**.

3. Choose **Yes, Delete**.

If you no longer require a virtual private gateway for your VPC, you can detach it.

To detach a virtual private gateway using the console

1. In the navigation pane, choose **Virtual Private Gateways**.

2. Select the virtual private gateway and choose **Actions, Detach from VPC**.

3. Choose **Yes, Detach**.

If you no longer require a detached virtual private gateway, you can delete it. You can't delete a virtual private gateway that's still attached to a VPC.

To delete a virtual private gateway using the console

1. In the navigation pane, choose **Virtual Private Gateways**.

2. Select the virtual private gateway to delete and choose **Actions, Delete Virtual Private Gateway**.

3. Choose **Yes, Delete**.

To delete a VPN connection using the command line or API

- DeleteVpnConnection (Amazon EC2 Query API)
- delete-vpn-connection (AWS CLI)
- Remove-EC2VpnConnection (AWS Tools for Windows PowerShell)

To delete a customer gateway using the command line or API

- DeleteCustomerGateway (Amazon EC2 Query API)
- delete-customer-gateway (AWS CLI)
- Remove-EC2CustomerGateway (AWS Tools for Windows PowerShell)

To detach a virtual private gateway using the command line or API

- DetachVpnGateway (Amazon EC2 Query API)
- detach-vpn-gateway (AWS CLI)
- Dismount-EC2VpnGateway (AWS Tools for Windows PowerShell)

To delete a virtual private gateway using the command line or API

- DeleteVpnGateway (Amazon EC2 Query API)
- delete-vpn-gateway (AWS CLI)
- Remove-EC2VpnGateway (AWS Tools for Windows PowerShell)

Providing Secure Communication Between Sites Using VPN Cloud-Hub

If you have multiple VPN connections, you can provide secure communication between sites using the AWS VPN CloudHub. This enables your remote sites to communicate with each other, and not just with the VPC. The VPN CloudHub operates on a simple hub-and-spoke model that you can use with or without a VPC. This design is suitable for customers with multiple branch offices and existing internet connections who'd like to implement a convenient, potentially low-cost hub-and-spoke model for primary or backup connectivity between these remote offices.

The following diagram shows the VPN CloudHub architecture, with blue dashed lines indicating network traffic between remote sites being routed over their VPN connections.

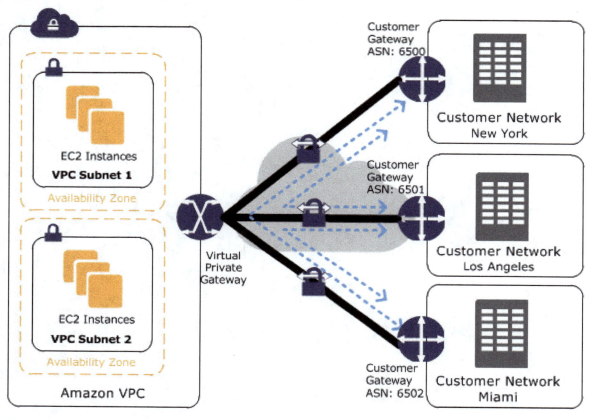

To use the AWS VPN CloudHub, you must create a virtual private gateway with multiple customer gateways. You must use a unique Border Gateway Protocol (BGP) Autonomous System Number (ASN) for each customer gateway. Customer gateways advertise the appropriate routes (BGP prefixes) over their VPN connections. These routing advertisements are received and re-advertised to each BGP peer, enabling each site to send data to and receive data from the other sites. The sites must not have overlapping IP ranges. Each site can also send and receive data from the VPC as if they were using a standard VPN connection.

Sites that use AWS Direct Connect connections to the virtual private gateway can also be part of the AWS VPN CloudHub. For example, your corporate headquarters in New York can have an AWS Direct Connect connection to the VPC and your branch offices can use VPN connections to the VPC. The branch offices in Los Angeles and Miami can send and receive data with each other and with your corporate headquarters, all using the AWS VPN CloudHub.

To configure the AWS VPN CloudHub, you use the AWS Management Console to create multiple customer gateways, each with the public IP address of the gateway and the ASN. Next, you create a VPN connection from each customer gateway to a common virtual private gateway. Each VPN connection must advertise its specific BGP routes. This is done using the network statements in the VPN configuration files for the VPN connection. The network statements differ slightly depending on the type of router you use.

When using an AWS VPN CloudHub, you pay typical Amazon VPC VPN connection rates. You are billed the connection rate for each hour that each VPN is connected to the virtual private gateway. When you send data from one site to another using the AWS VPN CloudHub, there is no cost to send data from your site to the virtual private gateway. You only pay standard AWS data transfer rates for data that is relayed from the virtual private gateway to your endpoint. For example, if you have a site in Los Angeles and a second site in New York and both sites have a VPN connection to the virtual private gateway, you pay $.05 per hour for each VPN connection (for a total of $.10 per hour). You also pay the standard AWS data transfer rates for all data that you send from Los Angeles to New York (and vice versa) that traverses each VPN connection; network traffic sent over the VPN connection to the virtual private gateway is free but network traffic sent over the VPN connection from the virtual private gateway to the endpoint is billed at the standard AWS data transfer rate. For more information, see VPN Connection Pricing.

Monitoring Your VPN Connection

Monitoring is an important part of maintaining the reliability, availability, and performance of your VPN connection. You should collect monitoring data from all of the parts of your AWS solution so that you can more easily debug a multi-point failure if one occurs. Before you start monitoring your VPN connection; however, you should create a monitoring plan that includes answers to the following questions:

- What are your monitoring goals?
- What resources will you monitor?
- How often will you monitor these resources?
- What monitoring tools will you use?
- Who will perform the monitoring tasks?
- Who should be notified when something goes wrong?

The next step is to establish a baseline for normal VPN performance in your environment, by measuring performance at various times and under different load conditions. As you monitor your VPN, store historical monitoring data so that you can compare it with current performance data, identify normal performance patterns and performance anomalies, and devise methods to address issues.

To establish a baseline, you should monitor the following items:

- The state of your VPN tunnels
- Data into the tunnel
- Data out of the tunnel

Topics

- Monitoring Tools
- Monitoring with Amazon CloudWatch

Monitoring Tools

AWS provides various tools that you can use to monitor a VPN connection. You can configure some of these tools to do the monitoring for you, while some of the tools require manual intervention. We recommend that you automate monitoring tasks as much as possible.

Automated Monitoring Tools

You can use the following automated monitoring tools to watch a VPN connection and report when something is wrong:

- **Amazon CloudWatch Alarms** – Watch a single metric over a time period that you specify, and perform one or more actions based on the value of the metric relative to a given threshold over a number of time periods. The action is a notification sent to an Amazon SNS topic. CloudWatch alarms do not invoke actions simply because they are in a particular state; the state must have changed and been maintained for a specified number of periods. For more information, see Monitoring with Amazon CloudWatch.
- **AWS CloudTrail Log Monitoring** – Share log files between accounts, monitor CloudTrail log files in real time by sending them to CloudWatch Logs, write log processing applications in Java, and validate that your log files have not changed after delivery by CloudTrail. For more information, see Logging API Calls Using AWS CloudTrail in the *Amazon EC2 API Reference* and Working with CloudTrail Log Files in the *AWS CloudTrail User Guide*

Manual Monitoring Tools

Another important part of monitoring a VPN connection involves manually monitoring those items that the CloudWatch alarms don't cover. The Amazon VPC and CloudWatch console dashboards provide an at-a-glance view of the state of your AWS environment.

- The Amazon VPC dashboard shows:
  - Service health by region
  - VPN connections
  - VPN tunnel status (In the navigation pane, choose **VPN Connections**, select a VPN connection, and then choose **Tunnel Details**)
- The CloudWatch home page shows:
  - Current alarms and status
  - Graphs of alarms and resources
  - Service health status

  In addition, you can use CloudWatch to do the following:

  - Create customized dashboards to monitor the services you care about
  - Graph metric data to troubleshoot issues and discover trends
  - Search and browse all your AWS resource metrics
  - Create and edit alarms to be notified of problems

Monitoring with Amazon CloudWatch

You can monitor VPN tunnels using CloudWatch, which collects and processes raw data from the VPN service into readable, near real-time metrics. These statistics are recorded for a period of 15 months, so that you can access historical information and gain a better perspective on how your web application or service is performing. VPN metric data is automatically sent to CloudWatch as it becomes available.

Important
CloudWatch metrics are not supported for AWS Classic VPN connections. For more information, see AWS Managed VPN Categories.

For more information, see the Amazon CloudWatch User Guide.

Topics

- VPN Metrics and Dimensions
- Creating CloudWatch Alarms to Monitor VPN Tunnels

VPN Metrics and Dimensions

When you create a new VPN connection, the VPN service sends the following metrics about your VPN tunnels to CloudWatch as it becomes available. You can use the following procedures to view the metrics for VPN tunnels.

To view metrics using the CloudWatch console

Metrics are grouped first by the service namespace, and then by the various dimension combinations within each namespace.

1. Open the CloudWatch console at https://console.aws.amazon.com/cloudwatch/.

2. In the navigation pane, choose **Metrics**.

3. Under **All metrics**, choose the **VPN** metric namespace.

4. Select the metric dimension to view the metrics (for example, for the VPN connection).

To view metrics using the AWS CLI

- At a command prompt, use the following command:

```
1. aws cloudwatch list-metrics --namespace "AWS/VPN"
```

The following metrics are available from Amazon VPC VPN.

Metric	Description
TunnelState	The state of the tunnel. 0 indicates DOWN and 1 indicates UP. Units: Boolean
TunnelDataIn	The bytes received through the VPN tunnel. Each metric data point represents the number of bytes received after the previous data point. Use the Sum statistic to show the total number of bytes received during the period. This metric counts the data after decryption. Units: Bytes

Metric	Description
TunnelDataOut	The bytes sent through the VPN tunnel. Each metric data point represents the number of bytes sent after the previous data point. Use the Sum statistic to show the total number of bytes sent during the period. This metric counts the data before encryption. Units: Bytes

You can filter the Amazon VPC VPN data using the following dimensions.

Dimension	Description
VpnId	This dimension filters the data by the VPN connection.
TunnelIpAddress	This dimension filters the data by the IP address of the tunnel for the virtual private gateway.

Creating CloudWatch Alarms to Monitor VPN Tunnels

You can create a CloudWatch alarm that sends an Amazon SNS message when the alarm changes state. An alarm watches a single metric over a time period you specify, and sends a notification to an Amazon SNS topic based on the value of the metric relative to a given threshold over a number of time periods.

For example, you can create an alarm that monitors the state of a VPN tunnel and sends a notification when the tunnel state is DOWN for 3 consecutive 5-minute periods.

To create an alarm for tunnel state

1. Open the CloudWatch console at https://console.aws.amazon.com/cloudwatch/.

2. In the navigation pane, choose **Alarms**, **Create Alarm**.

3. Choose **VPN Tunnel Metrics**.

4. Choose the IP address of the VPN tunnel and the **TunnelState** metric. Choose **Next**.

5. Configure the alarm as follows, and choose **Create Alarm** when you are done:

   - Under **Alarm Threshold**, enter a name and description for your alarm. For **Whenever**, choose <= and enter 0. Enter **3** for the consecutive periods.
   - Under **Actions**, select an existing notification list or choose **New list** to create a new one.
   - Under **Alarm Preview**, select a period of 5 minutes and specify a statistic of **Maximum**.

You can create an alarm that monitors the state of the VPN connection. For example, the following alarm sends a notification when the status of both tunnels is DOWN for 1 consecutive 5-minute period.

To create an alarm for VPN connection state

1. Open the CloudWatch console at https://console.aws.amazon.com/cloudwatch/.

2. In the navigation pane, choose **Alarms**, **Create Alarm**.

3. Choose **VPN Connection Metrics**.

4. Select your VPN connection and the **TunnelState** metric. Choose **Next**.

5. Configure the alarm as follows, and choose **Create Alarm** when you are done:

313

- Under **Alarm Threshold**, enter a name and description for your alarm. For **Whenever**, choose <= and enter 0. Enter **1** for the consecutive periods.

- Under **Actions**, select an existing notification list or choose **New list** to create a new one.

- Under **Alarm Preview**, select a period of 5 minutes and specify a statistic of **Maximum**.

  Alternatively, if you've configured your VPN connection so that both tunnels are up, you can specify a statistic of **Minimum** to send a notification when at least one tunnel is down.

You can also create alarms that monitor the amount of traffic coming in or leaving the VPN tunnel. For example, the following alarm monitors the amount of traffic coming into the VPN tunnel from your network, and sends a notification when the number of bytes reaches a threshold of 5,000,000 during a 15 minute period.

To create an alarm for incoming network traffic

1. Open the CloudWatch console at https://console.aws.amazon.com/cloudwatch/.

2. In the navigation pane, choose **Alarms**, **Create Alarm**.

3. Choose **VPN Tunnel Metrics**.

4. Select the IP address of the VPN tunnel and the **TunnelDataIn** metric. Choose **Next**.

5. Configure the alarm as follows, and choose **Create Alarm** when you are done:

   - Under **Alarm Threshold**, enter a name and description for your alarm. For **Whenever**, choose >= and enter 5000000. Enter **1** for the consecutive periods.
   - Under **Actions**, select an existing notification list or choose **New list** to create a new one.
   - Under **Alarm Preview**, select a period of 15 minutes and specify a statistic of **Sum**.

The following alarm monitors the amount of traffic leaving the VPN tunnel to your network, and sends a notification when the number of bytes is less than 1,000,000 during a 15 minute period.

To create an alarm for outgoing network traffic

1. Open the CloudWatch console at https://console.aws.amazon.com/cloudwatch/.

2. In the navigation pane, choose **Alarms**, **Create Alarm**.

3. Choose **VPN Tunnel Metrics**.

4. Select the IP address of the VPN tunnel and the **TunnelDataOut** metric. Choose **Next**.

5. Configure the alarm as follows, and choose **Create Alarm** when you are done:

   - Under **Alarm Threshold**, enter a name and description for your alarm. For **Whenever**, choose <= and enter 1000000. Enter **1** for the consecutive periods.
   - Under **Actions**, select an existing notification list or choose **New list** to create a new one.
   - Under **Alarm Preview**, select a period of 15 minutes and specify a statistic of **Sum**.

For more examples of creating alarms, see Creating Amazon CloudWatch Alarms in the *Amazon CloudWatch User Guide*.

Amazon VPC Limits

The following tables list the limits for Amazon VPC resources per region for your AWS account. Unless indicated otherwise, you can request an increase for these limits using the AWS Support Center.

To request a limit increase

1. Open the AWS Support Center page, sign in if necessary, and choose **Create Case**.

2. For **Regarding**, choose **Service Limit Increase**.

3. For **Limit Type**, choose **VPC**. Choose the region and the applicable limit.

4. Complete the rest of the form and choose **Submit**.

If you want to increase a limit that applies per resource, we increase the limit for all resources in the region; for example, the limit for security groups per VPC applies to all VPCs in the region.

Topics

- VPC and Subnets
- DNS
- Elastic IP Addresses (IPv4)
- Flow Logs
- Gateways
- Network ACLs
- Network Interfaces
- Route Tables
- Security Groups
- VPC Peering Connections
- VPC Endpoints
- VPN Connections

VPC and Subnets

Resource	Default limit	Comments
VPCs per region	5	The limit for internet gateways per region is directly correlated to this one. Increasing this limit increases the limit on internet gateways per region by the same amount. The number of VPCs in the region multiplied by the number of security groups per VPC cannot exceed 5000.
Subnets per VPC	200	-
IPv4 CIDR blocks per VPC	5	This limit is made up of your primary CIDR block plus 4 secondary CIDR blocks.
IPv6 CIDR blocks per VPC	1	This limit cannot be increased.

DNS

For more information, see DNS Limits.

Elastic IP Addresses (IPv4)

Resource	Default limit	Comments
Elastic IP addresses per region	5	This is the limit for the number of Elastic IP addresses for use in EC2-VPC. For Elastic IP addresses for use in EC2-Classic, see Amazon EC2 Limits in the *Amazon Web Services General Reference*.

Flow Logs

Resource	Default limit	Comments
Flow logs per single network interface, single subnet, or single VPC in a region	2	This limit cannot be increased. You can effectively have 6 flow logs per network interface if you create 2 flow logs for the subnet, and 2 flow logs for the VPC in which your network interface resides.

Gateways

Resource	Default limit	Comments
Customer gateways per region	50	To increase this limit, contact AWS Support.
Egress-only internet gateways per region	5	This limit is directly correlated with the limit on VPCs per region. To increase this limit, increase the limit on VPCs per region. Only one egress-only internet gateway can be attached to a VPC at a time.
Internet gateways per region	5	This limit is directly correlated with the limit on VPCs per region. To increase this limit, increase the limit on VPCs per region. Only one internet gateway can be attached to a VPC at a time.
NAT gateways per Availability Zone	5	A NAT gateway in the pending, active, or deleting state counts against your limit.
Virtual private gateways per region	5	Only one virtual private gateway can be attached to a VPC at a time.

Network ACLs

Resource	Default limit	Comments
Network ACLs per VPC	200	You can associate one network ACL to one or more subnets in a VPC. This limit is not the same as the number of rules per network ACL.
Rules per network ACL	20	This is the one-way limit for a single network ACL, where the limit for ingress rules is 20, and the limit for egress rules is 20. This limit includes both IPv4 and IPv6 rules, and includes the default deny rules (rule number 32767 for IPv4 and 32768 for IPv6, or an asterisk * in the Amazon VPC console). This limit can be increased up to a maximum of 40; however, network performance may be impacted due to the increased workload to process the additional rules.

Network Interfaces

Resource	Default limit	Comments
Network interfaces per instance	-	This limit varies by instance type. For more information, see IP Addresses Per ENI Per Instance Type.
Network interfaces per region	350	This limit is the greater of either the default limit (350) or your On-Demand Instance limit multiplied by 5. The default limit for On-Demand Instances is 20. If your On-Demand Instance limit is below 70, the default limit of 350 applies. To increase this limit, submit a request or increase your On-Demand Instance limit.

Route Tables

Resource	Default limit	Comments
Route tables per VPC	200	This limit includes the main route table.
Routes per route table (non-propagated routes)	50	You can increase this limit up to a maximum of 100; however, network performance may be impacted. This limit is enforced separately for IPv4 routes and IPv6 routes (you can have 50 each, and a maximum of 100 each).
BGP advertised routes per route table (propagated routes)	100	This limit cannot be increased. If you require more than 100 prefixes, advertise a default route.

Security Groups

Resource	Default limit	Comments
Security groups per VPC (per region)	500	The number of VPCs in the region multiplied by the number of security groups per VPC cannot exceed 5000.
Inbound or outbound rules per security group	50	You can have 50 inbound and 50 outbound rules per security group (giving a total of 100 combined inbound and outbound rules). To change this limit, create a case in the AWS Support Center — a limit change applies to both inbound and outbound rules. However, the limit for inbound or outbound rules per security group multiplied by the limit for security groups per network interface cannot exceed 250. For example, if you want to increase the limit to 100, we decrease your number of security groups per network interface to 2. This limit is enforced separately for IPv4 rules and IPv6 rules; for example, your security group can have 50 inbound rules for IPv4 traffic and 50 inbound rules for IPv6 traffic. A rule that references a security group counts as one rule for IPv4 and one rule for IPv6.

Resource	Default limit	Comments
Security groups per network interface	5	To increase or decrease this limit, you can contact AWS Support. The maximum is 16. The limit for security groups per network interface multiplied by the limit for rules per security group cannot exceed 250. For example, if you increase the limit to 10, we decrease your number of rules per security group to 25.

VPC Peering Connections

Resource	Default limit	Comments
Active VPC peering connections per VPC	50	The maximum limit is 125 peering connections per VPC. The number of entries per route table should be increased accordingly; however, network performance may be impacted.
Outstanding VPC peering connection requests	25	This is the limit for the number of outstanding VPC peering connection requests that you've requested from your account. To increase this limit, contact AWS Support.
Expiry time for an unaccepted VPC peering connection request	1 week (168 hours)	To increase this limit, contact AWS Support.

VPC Endpoints

Resource	Default limit	Comments
Gateway VPC endpoints per region	20	To increase this limit, contact AWS Support. The maximum limit is 255 endpoints per VPC, regardless of your endpoint limit per region.
Interface VPC endpoints per VPC	20	-

VPN Connections

Resource	Default limit	Comments
VPN connections per region	50	-
VPN connections per VPC (per virtual private gateway)	10	-

Document History

The following table describes the important changes in each release of the *Amazon VPC User Guide*, *Amazon VPC Peering Guide*, and *Amazon VPC Network Administrator Guide*.

Feature	API Version	Description	Release Date
Inter-region peering	2016-11-15	You can create a VPC peering connection between VPCs in different regions. For more information, see the Amazon VPC Peering Guide.	29 November 2017
VPC endpoint services	2016-11-15	You can create your own PrivateLink service in a VPC and enable other AWS accounts and users to connect to your service through an interface VPC endpoint. For more information, see VPC Endpoint Services (AWS PrivateLink).	28 November 2017
Create default subnet	2016-11-15	You can create a default subnet in an Availability Zone that does not have one. For more information, see Creating a Default Subnet.	9 November 2017
Interface VPC endpoints for AWS services	2016-11-15	You can create an interface endpoint to privately connect to some AWS services. An interface endpoint is a network interface with a private IP address that serves as an entry point for traffic to the service. For more information, see VPC Endpoints.	8 November 2017

Feature	API Version	Description	Release Date
Custom ASN	2016-11-15	When you create a virtual private gateway, you can specify the private Autonomous System Number (ASN) for the Amazon side of the gateway. For more information, see Virtual Private Gateway.	10 October 2017
VPN tunnel options	2016-11-15	You can specify inside tunnel CIDR blocks and custom pre-shared keys for your VPN tunnels. For more information, see Configuring the VPN Tunnels for Your VPN Connection, and Overview of Setting Up a VPN Connection in the Amazon VPC Network Administrator Guide.	3 October 2017
VPN categories	2016-11-15	You can view the category of your VPN connection. For more information, see AWS Managed VPN Categories.	3 October 2017
Tagging support for NAT gateways	2016-11-15	You can tag your NAT gateway. For more information, see Tagging a NAT Gateway.	7 September 2017
Amazon CloudWatch metrics for NAT gateways	2016-11-15	You can view CloudWatch metrics for your NAT gateway. For more information, see Monitoring Your NAT Gateway with Amazon CloudWatch.	7 September 2017
Security group rule descriptions	2016-11-15	You can add descriptions to your security group rules. For more information, see Security Group Rules.	31 August 2017
Secondary IPv4 CIDR blocks for your VPC	2016-11-15	You can add multiple IPv4 CIDR blocks to your VPC. For more information, see Adding IPv4 CIDR Blocks to a VPC.	29 August 2017

Feature	API Version	Description	Release Date
VPC endpoints for DynamoDB	2016-11-15	You can access Amazon DynamoDB from your VPC using VPC endpoints. For more information, see Endpoints for Amazon DynamoDB.	16 August 2017
Recover Elastic IP addresses	2016-11-15	If you release an Elastic IP address, you might be able to recover it. For more information, see Working with Elastic IP Addresses.	11 August 2017
Create default VPC	2016-11-15	You can create a new default VPC if you delete your existing default VPC. For more information, see Creating a Default VPC.	27 July 2017
VPN metrics	2016-11-15	You can view CloudWatch metrics for your VPN connections. For more information, see Monitoring Your VPN Connection.	15 May 2017
IPv6 support	2016-11-15	You can associate an IPv6 CIDR block with your VPC and assign IPv6 addresses to resources in your VPC. For more information, see IP Addressing in Your VPC.	1 December 2016
DNS resolution support for non-RFC 1918 IP address ranges		The Amazon DNS server can now resolve private DNS hostnames to private IP addresses for all address spaces. For more information, see Using DNS with Your VPC.	24 October 2016

Feature	API Version	Description	Release Date
DNS resolution support for VPC peering	2016-04-01	You can enable a local VPC to resolve public DNS hostnames to private IP addresses when queried from instances in the peer VPC. For more information, see Modifying Your VPC Peering Connection in the Amazon VPC Peering Guide.	28 July 2016
Stale security group rules	2015-10-01	You can identify if your security group is being referenced in the rules of a security group in a peer VPC, and you can identify stale security group rules. For more information, see Working With Stale Security Groups in the Amazon VPC Peering Guide.	12 May 2016
Using ClassicLink over a VPC peering connection	2015-10-01	You can modify your VPC peering connection to enable local linked EC2-Classic instances to communicate with instances in a peer VPC, or vice versa. For more information, see Configurations With ClassicLink in the Amazon VPC Peering Guide.	26 April 2016
NAT gateways	2015-10-01	You can create a NAT gateway in a public subnet and enable instances in a private subnet to initiate outbound traffic to the Internet or other AWS services. For more information, see NAT Gateways.	17 December 2015

Feature	API Version	Description	Release Date
VPN enhancements	2015-04-15	A VPN connection now supports the AES 256-bit encryption function, SHA-256 hashing function, NAT traversal, and additional Diffie-Hellman groups during Phase 1 and Phase 2 of a connection. In addition, you can now use the same customer gateway IP address for each VPN connection that uses the same customer gateway device.	28 October 2015
VPC flow logs	2015-04-15	You can create a flow log to capture information about the IP traffic going to and from network interfaces in your VPC. For more information, see VPC Flow Logs.	10 June 2015
VPC endpoints	2015-03-01	An endpoint enables you to create a private connection between your VPC and another AWS service without requiring access over the Internet, through a VPN connection, through a NAT instance, or through AWS Direct Connect. For more information, see VPC Endpoints.	11 May 2015

Feature	API Version	Description	Release Date
ClassicLink	2014-10-01	ClassicLink allows you to link your EC2-Classic instance to a VPC in your account. You can associate VPC security groups with the EC2-Classic instance, enabling communication between your EC2-Classic instance and instances in your VPC using private IP addresses. For more information, see ClassicLink.	7 January 2015
Use private hosted zones	2014-09-01	You can access resources in your VPC using custom DNS domain names that you define in a private hosted zone in Route 53. For more information, see Using Private Hosted Zones.	5 November 2014
Modify a subnet's public IP addressing attribute	2014-06-15	You can modify the public IP addressing attribute of your subnet to indicate whether instances launched into that subnet should receive a public IP address. For more information, see Modifying the Public IPv4 Addressing Attribute for Your Subnet.	21 June 2014
VPC peering	2014-02-01	You can create a VPC peering connection between two VPCs, which allows instances in either VPC to communicate with each other using private IP addresses - as if they are within the same VPC. For more information, see VPC Peering.	24 March 2014

Feature	API Version	Description	Release Date
New EC2 launch wizard	2013-10-01	Added information about the redesigned EC2 launch wizard. For more information, see Step 3: Launch an Instance into Your VPC.	10 October 2013
Assigning a public IP address	2013-07-15	Added information about a new public IP addressing feature for instances launched in a VPC. For more information, see Assigning a Public IPv4 Address During Instance Launch.	20 August 2013
Enabling DNS hostnames and disabling DNS resolution	2013-02-01	By default, DNS resolution is enabled. You can now disable DNS resolution using the Amazon VPC console, the Amazon EC2 command line interface, or the Amazon EC2 API actions. By default, DNS hostnames are disabled for non-default VPCs. You can now enable DNS hostnames using the Amazon VPC console, the Amazon EC2 command line interface, or the Amazon EC2 API actions. For more information, see Using DNS with Your VPC.	11 March 2013

Feature	API Version	Description	Release Date
VPN connections using static routing configuration	2012-08-15	You can create IPsec VPN connections to Amazon VPC using static routing configurations. Previously, VPN connections required the use of the Border Gateway Protocol (BGP). We now support both types of connections and you can now establish connectivity from devices that do not support BGP, including Cisco ASA and Microsoft Windows Server 2008 R2.	13 September 2012
Automatic route propagation	2012-08-15	You can now configure automatic propagation of routes from your VPN and Direct Connect links to your VPC routing tables. This feature simplifies the effort to create and maintain connectivity to Amazon VPC.	13 September 2012
AWS VPN CloudHub and redundant VPN connections		You can securely communicate from one site to another with or without a VPC. You can use redundant VPN connections to provide a fault-tolerant connection to your VPC.	29 September 2011
VPC Everywhere	2011-07-15	Support in five AWS regions, VPCs in multiple Availability Zones, multiple VPCs per AWS account, multiple VPN connections per VPC, Microsoft Windows Server 2008 R2 and Microsoft SQL Server Reserved Instances.	03 August 2011

Feature	API Version	Description	Release Date
Dedicated Instances	2011-02-28	Dedicated Instances are Amazon EC2 instances launched within your VPC that run hardware dedicated to a single customer. Dedicated Instances let you take full advantage of the benefits of Amazon VPC and AWS elastic provisioning, pay only for what you use, and a private, isolated virtual network—all while isolating your instances at the hardware level.	27 March 2011

AWS Glossary

Blank

placeholder
This page redirects to the AWS Glossary in the *AWS General Reference.*